Power Query for Excel Users

A practical guide to cleaning, transforming, and automating Excel data with Power Query

Oscar Martínez Valero

<packt>

Power Query for Excel Users

Portfolio Director: Pavan Ramchandani
Relationship Lead: Tejashwini R
Program Manager: Divij Kotian
Content Engineer: Akanksha Gupta
Technical Editor: Vidhisha Patidar
Indexer: Tejal Soni
Production Designer: Salma Patel
Growth Lead: Nivedita Singh

First published: July 2026

Production reference: 1280726

Published by Packt Publishing Ltd.
Grosvenor House
11 St Paul's Square
Birmingham
B3 1RB, UK.

ISBN 978-1-80742-773-3
www.packtpub.com

To Kathrin, my partner in crime, and to Alex and David, our children: the three of you give meaning to all that I do.

– Oscar Martínez Valero

Contributors

About the author

Oscar Martínez Valero is a data professional focused on Microsoft technologies with over 15 years of experience bridging finance, technology, and analytics. From Mexico and living in Switzerland, he specializes in BI, AI, and automation solutions using Microsoft Fabric, Power BI, Power Query, and Azure services. Oscar has led enterprise-scale data projects and saved organizations significant costs through strategic implementations. He is a Microsoft Fabric Analytics Engineer Associate and Power BI Data Analyst Associate. Oscar founded bibb.pro, creating the #1 global Power BI Theme Generator and writing educational blog posts. Passionate about teaching, he trains both beginners and advanced learners in Power Query, Power BI and other data topics.

First, I would like to thank Kathrin, my wife, not only for supporting me throughout this project but for actively contributing to it as a technical reviewer. She is the inspiration for Quinn, the book's main character: any resemblance between Quinn, who relentlessly works to make things better with a smile on her face, and Kathrin is no coincidence.

Big thanks to Alex and David, my children, for their patience during all the hours this project took from our time together.

Thanks to Aditya, who is not only an Excel expert but also a warm, humorous, and selfless person; the book could not have had a better technical reviewer.

Finally, I want to thank the entire Packt team for their support, especially Tejashwini, who has been with this project since the earliest discussions about the book's topic, and Akanksha, for her thorough reviews and feedback throughout the writing process.

About the reviewers

Aditya Kumar Darak is a three-time Microsoft MVP (Excel and Copilot) who focuses on using AI and automation to transform financial processes into enterprise-deployable solutions. His core philosophy is that systems should be designed so finance professionals can spend their time on strategy, judgment, and decision making, rather than wrestling with Excel at night. Power Query sits at the heart of that work, turning messy, manual data preparation into clean and repeatable workflows. He has previously built end-to-end solutions for finance teams, including a Procurement-to-Pay system and a lease modeling application with built-in approvals.

He is also a gamer and previously ranked first in the Indian Chapter of the Microsoft Excel World Cup.

I would like to thank my family for their patience while review drafts took over my evenings and weekends. A special thanks to the author for trusting me with this book. I am also grateful to the wider Excel and Power Query community which has taught me more than any course ever could and I am glad to give a little of that back.

Kathrin Siegrist is a certified Executive Assistant with extensive experience supporting senior leaders in international, public, and private sector organizations. Her career spans executive search, government, diplomacy, and industry, with roles at Jörg Lienert AG, the Swiss Federal Office of Police (fedpol), the Embassy of Switzerland in Mexico, and ABB. With her strong organizational skills, multilingual communication, and service-oriented approach, she streamlines operations, builds trusted relationships, and delivers high-quality support in fast-paced, dynamic environments.

I am very grateful for the opportunity to review this book. Too often, data courses are either overly technical or fragmented, making it difficult to gain a complete understanding. Working with Oscar and Akanksha was a pleasure, and I am honored to have been part of this network and to have connected with such accomplished professionals. Beyond contributing as a reviewer, I gained valuable insights, making this a rewarding experience.

About the reviewers

Table of Contents

Chapter 7: Combine and Reshape Multiple Files Into a Tidy Long Table 217

Chapter 10: Automate Repetitive Processes 303

Preface

Hello, and welcome! For years, I have trained non-technical people in Power Query, including team assistants, office managers, and business professionals. This book is written for them, and for everyone like them: people who would never call themselves "data people" yet, without consciously knowing it, deal with data every day.

Power Query is the data preparation engine built into modern versions of Excel (2016 or later). It turns repetitive manual cleanup into queries you build once and refresh forever. This book teaches it from the ground up, entirely inside Excel: connecting to files and folders, cleaning and standardizing messy data, combining and merging tables, automating with parameters, and finishing with the Excel Data Model and your first DAX measures.

Rather than a catalog of features, this is a casebook. You follow Quinn, a newly hired data analyst at **Northbridge Office Group** (**NOG**), a fictional UK office-supplies and services firm. Each chapter opens with a real stakeholder request and closes with a refreshable deliverable, and the work accumulates into a single workbook, the `NOG-DataHub`.

Everything is taught through the Power Query user interface. You'll also learn to read the M formula language. Along the way you build important habits including clear query names, early data types, protected keys, and a short "trust loop" of checks after every refresh. You will also find practical guidance for using **Large Language Models** (**LLMs**) such as ChatGPT, with template prompts and one firm guardrail: the AI drafts, you validate against your data.

By the end, you will replace hours of manual spreadsheet work with one-click refreshes, and you will have strong Power Query foundations that carry directly into Power BI or Fabric Dataflows should you decide to take that next step.

Who this book is for

If you work with data in your day-to-day (whether or not you think of yourself as "an Excel person"), this book is for you:

- Excel users and analysts who spend hours cleaning, combining, and reshaping spreadsheets and want that time back. You will learn to turn every recurring cleanup into a refreshable query.

- Assistants, office managers, and coordinators who maintain contact lists, registrations, orders, and other operational data. You will learn low-friction techniques that make lists reliable without formulas or code.
- Finance, HR, and operations professionals who consolidate exports from other systems and track KPIs. You will learn to combine files from folders, merge tables safely, and validate results before sharing them.
- Anyone curious about AI-assisted data work who wants practical prompt templates and guardrails for pairing tools such as ChatGPT with dependable, repeatable data preparation

Only basic Excel skills are assumed: formulas, tables, and file management. No prior Power Query, database, data modeling, or Power BI experience is required; everything is introduced from the ground up.

What this book covers

Chapter 1, Power Query Basics in Excel (ETL + UI Tour), establishes the shared baseline for the whole book. It explains what Power Query is (and what it isn't) using a plain-English Extract, Transform, Load (ETL) framing, tours the Power Query Editor and its key panes, and introduces the core loop of queries, Applied Steps, and refresh. You will complete two small, safe practice loads, compare load destinations (Table versus Connection Only), and run your first trust check.

Chapter 2, Transform Daily Excel Tasks with Power Query, delivers your first end-to-end business win. Helping Amira, the Executive Assistant, you import a messy contacts CSV and build Master_Contacts: trimming whitespace, fixing casing, setting data types, and using Add Column from Examples to create a display name. The chapter establishes the NOG-DataHub workbook you will grow throughout the book, builds passive literacy of the formula bar, and instills the refresh-and-validate habit.

Chapter 3, Connect and Standardize Common Business Sources, extends that success to a folder of monthly Excel exports. Working with Tom, the Events Coordinator, you combine four monthly sessions files using the Folder connector (SharePoint or local), promote headers safely, standardize session types and labels with targeted value replacements, and tame messy facilitator names with a mapping table instead of scattered replacements. The result is Master_Sessions, your first reference table, with light governance to keep it trustworthy.

Chapter 4, Build Reliable Step Chains and Read M Passively, shows how Power Query "thinks". You stabilize Marcus's fragile weekly KPI workbook by connecting to it through the folder connector, choosing the named Excel Table over the raw sheet, and building a robust query, then learn to read the Applied Steps and formula bar: spotting brittle steps, reordering, and repairing them, and protecting the key column (SessionID) and table grain that later chapters depend on.

Chapter 5, Build Reusable Reports with PivotTables, turns a clean query into an aggregated story management can act on. You build a weekly reporting pack of PivotTables that update on refresh, learn to choose implicit measures deliberately (Sum versus Count versus Distinct Count), add slicers for reuse, and apply layout conventions that keep the pack stable and safe to hand over.

Chapter 6, Combine and Clean Multiple Files into One Clean Table, tackles the classic office problem: a folder that fills up with monthly registration exports. Using the Combine Files experience, you turn the whole folder into one refreshable table, apply practical cleanup (types, text, emails, status values), implement a simple and explainable de-duplication rule, and finish with a 30-second trust loop. The output, Registrations_Combined, feeds the rest of the book.

Chapter 7, Combine and Reshape Multiple Files into a Tidy Long Table, applies the same folder pattern to attendance logs, which arrive with multiple session IDs crammed into single cells. You learn the reshaping pattern business users reuse most (Split Column by Delimiter to Rows) to land on a tidy long table with one row per attendee-session, with clean join keys and a validated grain.

Chapter 8, Merge Tables to Build an Enriched Master List, is the master-list payoff. You merge registrations (Chapter 6) with attendance (Chapter 7) using a safe left join workflow: choosing merge keys, picking the join type that matches the question, expanding only the columns you need, and preventing the row-multiplication surprises that silently corrupt merged data. Amira gets the single attendee list she has been assembling by hand every month.

Chapter 9, Join and Lookup Data Safely Without a Data Model, deepens your join skills through a payments reconciliation with Priya from Finance. You use left, inner, and anti joins to match payments to registrations, build exception queries that keep mismatches visible instead of silently dropping them, and derive a clear PaymentStatus, producing Master_Payments and a repeatable reconciliation pattern.

Chapter 10, Automate Repetitive Processes, turns the workbook you have built into something a colleague could open, understand, and maintain. Guided by Hannah, the Senior BI Analyst, you organize queries into named groups, create parameters for values that change (session type, folder path), build a parameter-driven scoped view without touching the master query, and replace a hard-coded source path with a parameter: one change updates every query.

Chapter 11, Build Your First Events Data Model in Excel, connects the master tables into an actual data model. You load Master_Sessions, Master_Attendees, and Master_Payments into the Excel Data Model, define keys and one-to-many relationships in Diagram View, understand cardinality and filter direction, and test the model with implicit measures, answering cross-table business questions that flat tables cannot.

Chapter 12, Answer Questions with Your First DAX Measures, answers the question implicit measures cannot: what percentage of registered people actually showed up? You write three DAX measures that build on each other: [Total Registrations] (COUNTROWS), [Total Attendees] (FILTER), and [Attendance Rate] (DIVIDE). You learn the difference between columns and measures and between implicit and explicit measures, and deliver an Events Performance page Marcus can refresh every quarter.

To get the most out of this book

You need only basic Excel skills: working with formulas, tables, and files. No prior Power Query, M, database, or Power BI experience is required.

Software/hardware covered in the book	Operating system requirements
Microsoft Excel 2016 or later with Power Query (Microsoft 365 desktop version recommended)	Windows

The book's screenshots were taken in the Microsoft 365 desktop version of Excel on Windows. Power Query for Mac offers only a reduced feature set, so a Windows environment is strongly recommended for following along.

All exercises use the `NOG-DataHub` exercise files, which you can store either in a SharePoint document library or in a local folder; both paths are shown throughout the book. The chapters build on each other: from *Chapter 2* onwards you grow a single workbook, so work through the chapters in order and complete each chapter's exercises before starting the next.

A few habits and considerations will save you real frustration along the way:

> **Caution**
>
> **After each chapter, save your workbook as a new file named for the chapter you have just completed** (for example, `NOG-DataHub_Ch04.xlsx`). If you ever need it, this gives you a close starting point to fall back on instead of rebuilding from scratch.

- **Power Query is case sensitive and needs exact writing.** Text matching is exact: "attended" is not the same as "Attended", and an invisible trailing space silently breaks a match; a filter returns zero rows, or a condition never comes true, with no error message. Type values into dialog boxes rather than copy-pasting them, and if a filter or condition unexpectedly returns nothing, reopen the dialog box and check for a stray space.

- **Close & Load versus Close & Load To.** Throughout the book you will sometimes use **Close & Load** and sometimes **Close & Load To...**. **Close & Load** loads the query immediately using the default or last-used destination (usually a table on a new sheet); **Close & Load To...** opens the **Import Data** dialog box so you choose the destination explicitly (table, Connection Only, or the Data Model). Whichever you click, the query is what matters: your steps are safely stored either way, and you can change the load destination at any time from the **Queries & Connections** pane without redoing any work.
- **Refresh often and validate every time.** The trust loop you learn in *Chapter 1* (plausible row count, key columns present, correct types, no unexpected errors) takes seconds and catches almost everything before it reaches a report.
- **If you have questions about the book, head to its GitHub Discussions page.** Follow the instructions in the next section to access the GitHub repo. On the *Discussions* page, ask about the exercises, share what you built, and get help if a step does not work as expected.

Download the example code files

This book includes a complete downloadable code bundle containing all the example projects and files used throughout the chapters. We recommend downloading the bundle so you can follow along smoothly and experiment with the examples.

Use the bundle as a practical starting point. Modify it, extend it, and apply what you learn by creating your own variations as you progress through the chapters.

Get the code bundle

If you bought the book directly from Packt:

1. Go to `https://www.packtpub.com/`
2. Click your **profile picture** and select **Your Orders**
3. Find this book and click **Download Code**

If you bought this book from Amazon or any other channel partner:

1. Go to `https://www.packtpub.com/unlock` or scan the following QR code
2. Search for this book
3. Sign up or log in to your free Packt account
4. Upload your proof of purchase and download the code bundle locally

Usage note: You're free to use and modify this code for personal learning and non-commercial projects.

Free benefits with your book

This book includes free benefits designed to support your learning and help you apply what you learn effectively. Activate them now for instant access (see the *How to unlock* section for instructions).

Here's a quick overview of what you can instantly unlock with your purchase:

Complete Code Bundle

Download the full source code for this book's examples and projects.

DRM-Free PDF Version

Download DRM-free PDF and ePub copies of this book.

7-Day Packt Library Access

Get 7-day unlimited access to 8,000+ books and videos. No credit card required.

Available for first-time Packt+ trial users only.

Next-Gen Reader Access

Read this book on Packt Reader with progress sync, dark mode and note-taking.

How to unlock

Scan the QR code (or go to `packtpub.com/unlock`). Search for this book by name, confirm the edition, and then follow the steps on the page.

UNLOCK NOW

Note: Have your invoice handy. Purchases made directly from the Packt website don't require an invoice.

Share your thoughts

Once you've read *Power Query for Excel Users*, we'd love to hear your thoughts! Scan the QR code below to go straight to the Amazon review page for this book and share your feedback.

`https://packt.link/r/1807427730`

Your review is important to us and the tech community and will help us make sure we're delivering excellent quality content.

Introduction

This book follows Quinn, who has been newly hired at **Northbridge Office Group** (**NOG**).

After high school, Quinn studied business and marketing. Additionally, she's completed some Excel and data management courses, but she doesn't consider herself a data professional.

During her data management courses, Quinn first came across **Power Query**, a feature built into Excel for automating the kind of repetitive data wrangling she'd always done by hand. She used it briefly on a university project and filed it away as something worth mastering properly one day. In her first week at NOG, watching colleagues copy-paste rows between spreadsheets and rebuild the same reports from scratch each Monday, she realized that day had come.

Figure 0.1 – Introducing Quinn

Quinn joined the NOG group with a bold ambition: to drive the team's data and analytics transformation. The NOG group is a successful mid-sized UK office supplies business. One of the NOG CEO's goals is to improve processes and better understand the business.

For Quinn, this is the opportunity of a lifetime. Within the chapters of this book, we will accompany Quinn on this new, exciting, and challenging journey.

Setting up your NOG-DataHub

Throughout this book, you'll work with exercise files that simulate the data environment at NOG. We've organized these files into a folder structure called the `NOG-DataHub`, a shared data repository that mirrors how real organizations store and manage their data.

Download and setup

Follow this step-by-step guide to download and set up the project files:

1. **Download the exercise files**: Download the files from the book's GitHub repository. To access the repository link, follow the steps in the *Download the example code files* section in the *Preface*.
   Once you have the link, open it in your browser. You will land on the GitHub file page for `NOG-DataHub.zip`. Look for the **Download raw file** button. It is a small downward-arrow icon near the top-right of the page. Click it. Your browser will save `NOG-DataHub.zip` to your `Downloads` folder (or wherever your browser saves files by default).

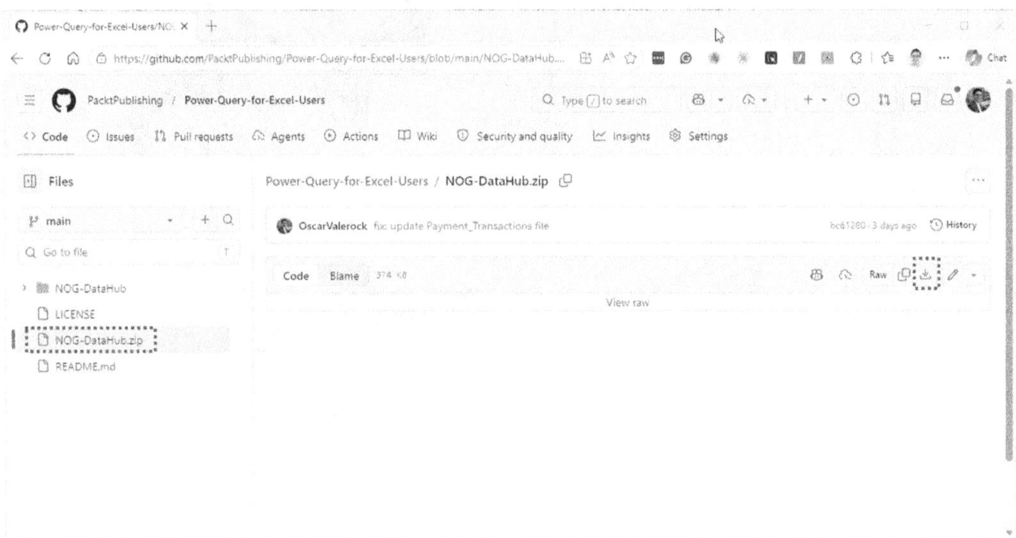

Figure 0.2 – The NOG-DataHub.zip file on GitHub; click the Download raw file button to save it

2. **Extract the ZIP file:** Open **File Explorer** and navigate to the folder where `NOG-DataHub.zip` was saved (usually `Downloads`). Right-click on `NOG-DataHub.zip` and choose **Extract All...** from the context menu.

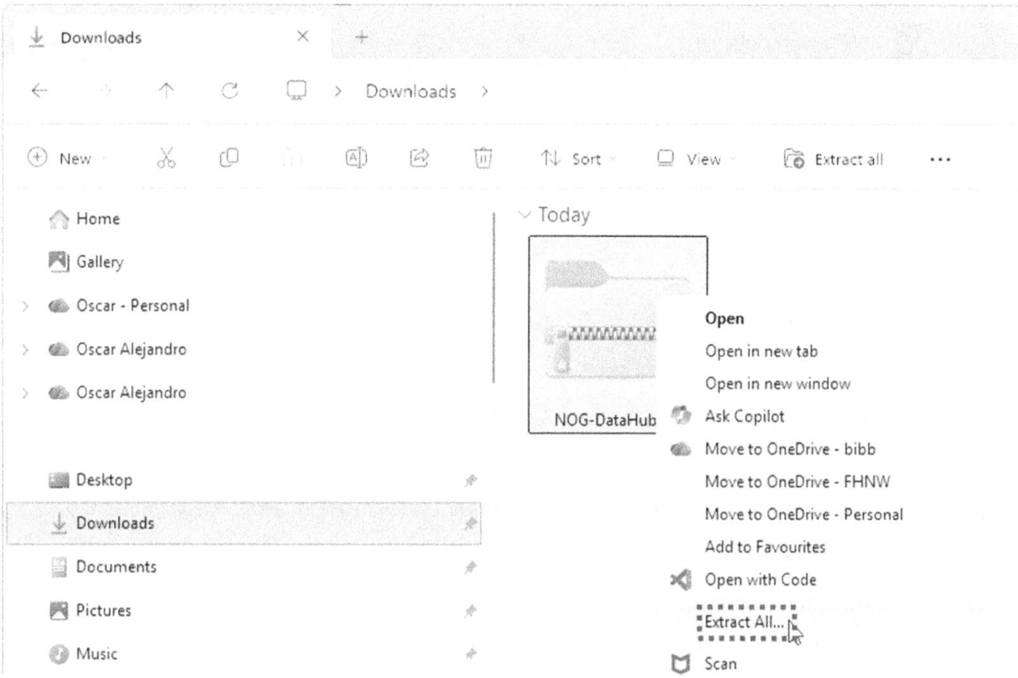

Figure 0.3 – Right-click NOG-DataHub.zip and choose Extract All to unzip the exercise files

A dialog will appear asking where to extract the files. You can leave the default destination for now; you will move the folder in the next step. Click **Extract**.

3. **Place the NOG-DataHub folder:** Once extracted, you will have a folder called `NOG-DataHub`. Move it to one of these two locations:

    - **Recommended — SharePoint**: Upload the `NOG-DataHub` folder to a SharePoint Document Library (for example, under `Documents/NOG-DataHub/`). To upload the folder, open your SharePoint Document Library in a web browser. Select **+ New**, then choose **Upload**, and then **Folder**. Navigate to where you extracted `NOG-DataHub`, select the folder, and click **Upload**. SharePoint will upload the folder and all its contents in one go. This mirrors how files are shared in most real workplaces and makes the exercises more realistic.

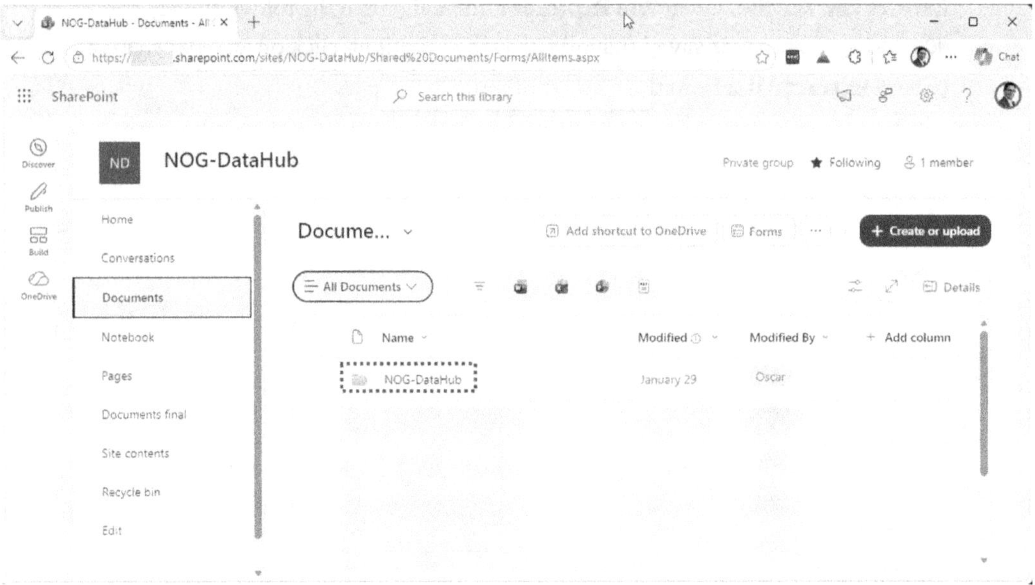

Figure 0.4 – Uploading the NOG-DataHub folder to a SharePoint Document Library

- **Alternative — Local folder**: Copy and paste the `NOG-DataHub` folder to a location you can easily find, such as `C:\Users\YourName\Documents\NOG-DataHub\`

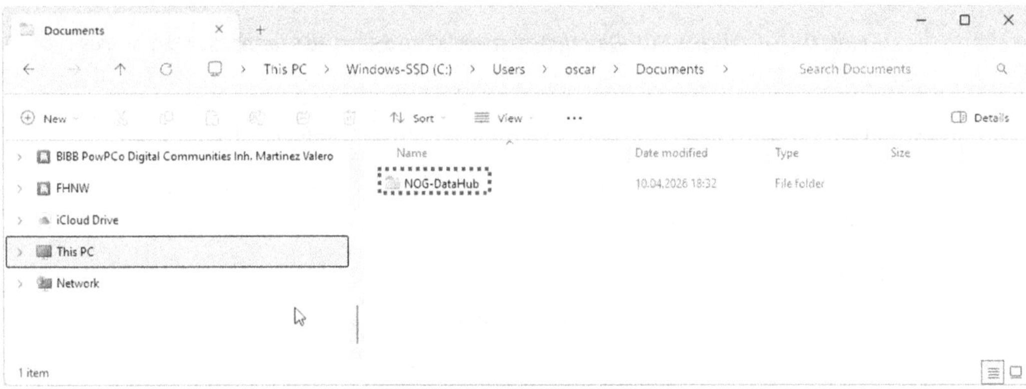

Figure 0.5 – The NOG-DataHub folder is placed in a local Documents folder

Tip

Why SharePoint? We recommend SharePoint because it makes the exercises more business-realistic. It is widely used across organizations and serves as a standard

> platform for file sharing among millions of teams. However, all exercises work perfectly with local folders too.

Folder Structure

Once you have extracted the files, your `NOG-DataHub` should look like this:

```
NOG-DataHub/
├── Quick Tour/         ← Chapter 1: Demo files for first Power Query practice
├── Reference/          ← Chapter 2: Contacts and lookup tables
└── Events/
    ├── Sessions/       ← Chapter 3: Session metadata files
    ├── KPIs/           ← Chapter 4: Weekly event KPIs workbook
    ├── Registrations/  ← Chapter 6: Monthly registration exports
    ├── Attendance/     ← Chapter 7: Attendance logs
    └── Payments/       ← Chapter 9: Payment transactions
```

The `NOG-DataHub` contains files and folders designed for specific exercises covered across the book's chapters; the files contain intentional "messiness" that you'll address using Power Query. The files build on one another, and by the end of the book, you will have transformed these disparate sources into a well-structured data model.

Before you begin

Make sure you do the following:

- **Note your NOG-DataHub location**. You'll need to navigate to it during exercises:
    - For local folders: the full path (e.g., `C:\Users\YourName\Documents\NOG-DataHub\`)
    - For SharePoint: the root site URL (e.g., `https://yourcompany.sharepoint.com/sites/YourSite`)
- **Open Excel** and create a new blank workbook; this will be your working file
- **Don't modify the source files directly**. Power Query connects to them, so keep the originals intact

You're now ready to begin your Power Query journey alongside Quinn.

Part 1

Foundation and Mindset

In this part, you will make the mindset shift that everything else in this book builds on: from manual, repetitive Excel cleanup to structured queries that you build once and refresh with one click. You will start with a safe, low-stakes tour of Power Query itself: what it is, where it lives in Excel, and the core loop of queries, Applied Steps, and refresh. You will then create your first real query and experience the full import-clean-refresh loop, combine monthly exports from a folder into a single reference table and standardize its names, types, and labels, learn to read the Applied Steps and formula bar so your queries stay reliable when source data changes, and turn a clean query into a reusable PivotTable reporting pack that updates on refresh. By the end of this part, you will have working master tables in your `NOG-DataHub` workbook and the habits (clear naming, early data types, protected keys, and a quick validation loop) that keep them trustworthy.

This section contains the following chapters:

- *Chapter 1, Power Query Basics in Excel*
- *Chapter 2, Transform Daily Excel Tasks with Power Query*
- *Chapter 3, Connect & Standardize Common Business Sources*
- *Chapter 4, Build Reliable Step Chains & Read M Passively*
- *Chapter 5, Build Reusable Reports with PivotTables*

1

Power Query Basics in Excel (ETL + UI Tour)

Figure 1.1 – Quinn refreshes her Power Query basics on the first day at her new job

Today is Quinn's first day on the job, and, like many first days in a new job, it's quiet. Quinn uses this time to go over Power Query's interface elements, since it's been some time since she used them, and she feels Power Query will come in handy in her new job.

Before diving into real work, Quinn decides to practice the basics. She grabs two demo files from the company's shared data hub: a simple product list in Excel and a CSV file that contains a small order sample. Quinn uses these files to refresh her memory of Power Query.

In this chapter, you'll learn to -

- Describe what Power Query is and how the **ETL** (**Extract, Transform, Load**) model applies to everyday spreadsheet work
- Navigate the **Power Query Editor** and identify its key areas: the **Queries** pane, the data preview, the Applied Steps panel, and the Formula Bar
- Build a simple query, apply safe transformations, and choose the right load destination: Table, Connection Only, or Data Model
- Run a lightweight post-refresh check to confirm your data loaded correctly; a trust loop you'll reuse throughout the rest of the book

> Note
>
> **Download the code bundle and the PDF version of this book**
>
> Your purchase includes a DRM-free PDF copy of this book, the code bundle, and a range of exclusive benefits. To unlock everything, follow the *Free benefits with your book* section in the *Preface*.

Technical requirements

To follow along with this chapter, you will need:

- **Microsoft Excel 2016 or later** with Power Query available (via **Data** | **Get & Transform Data**)
- The `NOG-DataHub` exercise files set up as described in the *Setting Up Your NOG-DataHub* section of the *Introduction*, specifically the `Quick Tour` folder, which contains:
    - `Demo_ProductList.xlsx`
    - `Demo_OrderSample.csv`

What Power Query is (and what it isn't)

Power Query is a tool built into Excel that connects to a data source, cleans and shapes the data, and loads the result automatically every time you click **Refresh**.

Power Query is like an engine, and most engines are worthless on their own. To make them useful, you need to pair them with something else, for example: an engine paired to a bicycle turns it into a motorcycle, a wagon paired to an engine is a locomotive, and a glider with an engine, is a plane. Cool!

Power Query is an **ETL** (**Extract**, **Transform** and **Load**) engine, which, broadly speaking, is an engine that deals with data. Something great about Power Query's engine is that since its inception, it has not stopped evolving, and today it can be used across multiple Microsoft applications: Excel, Power BI, and Fabric dataflows.

> Note
>
> Since 2016, Power Query has been built into Excel via **Data** | **Get & Transform**. Nowadays, Power Query is available in most versions of Excel. If you're unsure whether your license includes Power Query, check with your IT team.

The ETL mindset: extract, transform, load

At its core, Power Query is an ETL tool. **ETL** is a basic data concept that stands for **Extract**, **Transform**, and **Load**. These are data processes that we will use over and over throughout this book, and they will also be used repeatedly in your work with Power Query.

Fancy? Complicated? Not at all! Without noticing, you already perform ETL processes in your daily life. We extract (E), transform (T) and load (L) data all the time, such as in the following cases:

- **Email summary for your boss:** You extract information from one or many messages, transform it by summarizing the key points, and load it into a summary that you send in a short message
- **Shopping list from recipes:** You extract ingredients from multiple TikTok videos, transform by consolidating duplicates and adjusting quantities, and load into your shopping list on your mobile phone
- **Expense tracking:** You extract purchase tickets and expenses from your credit card, transform them by categorizing and totaling by type (meals, travel, supplies), and load them into your monthly budget spreadsheet

Whether you use Power Query, a notebook, or another tool, you're constantly doing ETL. Understanding this simple pattern will make Power Query feel intuitive.

In short, Power Query allows us to extract (E) data from various sources, transform (T) it in different ways, and load (L) it into different destinations:

- **Cleaning a monthly export:** removing duplicates, fixing inconsistent labels, and trimming spaces before sending a mail merge or sharing a report
- **Combining files from multiple sources:** pulling together weekly or monthly files from different teams into a single, consistent table

- **Refreshing a recurring report:** rebuilding a KPI or summary view automatically each week without touching the steps
- **Standardizing data from different systems:** aligning date formats, department names, or product codes that arrive differently from each source

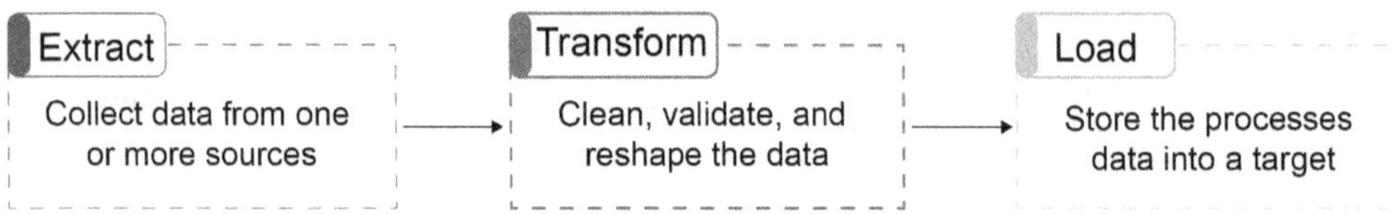

Figure 1.2 – The ETL process: Extract, Transform, Load

What Power Query is not

Before we go further, let's clear up a common misconception. Power Query is not:

- **A replacement for Excel formulas:** Power Query prepares and shapes data; Excel formulas and PivotTables analyze it. They're better together!
- **A programming language you need to master:** While Power Query has a language called M, this book's focus is entirely on using Power Query by clicking buttons and menus (M Code is written by itself).
- **A one-time tool:** The power of Power Query comes from the reusability of the transformations as they are saved and can be refreshed automatically when source data changes.

With the ETL pattern in mind, let's look at where Power Query lives inside Excel and how to find it.

Where Power Query lives in Excel

Power Query is available across different applications in the Microsoft data ecosystem. This book focuses exclusively on Excel and Power Query, but you can also find Power Query in Power BI and Fabric.

Power Query is not a standalone tool or app; you launch it from Excel. This may sound a bit counterintuitive, but we are going to spend most of our time not in the Excel interface, but in Power Query.

Exercise: launching the Power Query Editor

The Power Query editor is the place where we will build and tweak our instructions.

There are several ways to launch the Power Query Editor, which we will explore throughout Quinn's journey. In this case, we will launch Power Query from an Excel table.

Important

For the following exercise, we will use the `Demo_ProductList.xlsx` file from the `Quick Tour` folder.

Open the `Demo_ProductList.xlsx` file and execute the following:

1. Click on any cell within the **Products** table
2. Click on the **Data** tab
3. On the **Get & Transform** group, select **From Table/Range**

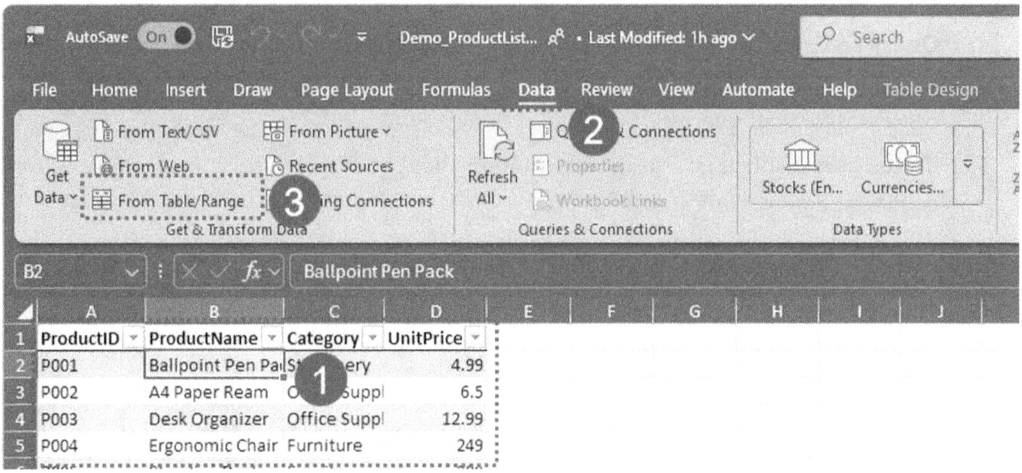

Figure 1.3 – From Table/Range on the Data tab

After you click on the **From Table/Range** button, the Power Query editor will open. Let's spend some time understanding the Power Query editor user interface.

The Power Query editor is where you'll create, modify, and manage your queries. Here you will shape the data, adjust query steps, and preview your data. The interface has five main components, as visible in *Figure 1.4*:

1. **Ribbon:** Provides multiple tabs with buttons for transforms, data transformations and query options:
   - **Home:** Common transformations and table-level operations
   - **Transform:** Operations focused on individual columns

   - **Add Column:** Tools for adding new columns
   - **View:** Provides options for customizing the editor layout and data profiling tools
2. **Queries pane:** Displays all your available queries. Think of a query as a single extract (E) process.
3. **Current view:** This section shows a limited row preview of the selected query

> **Note**
>
> Power Query loads only a preview of your data, not the full dataset. This is by design: it keeps the editor responsive and avoids pulling potentially large datasets into memory before your query is ready.
>
> The preview is typically limited to the first 1,000 rows.

4. **Query settings:** Shows the selected query's properties, including its name, description, and applied steps. Applied steps is where you will find all the transformation (T) processes for your queries.
5. **Status bar:** Displays important information about your query, such as column and row counts, and processing status

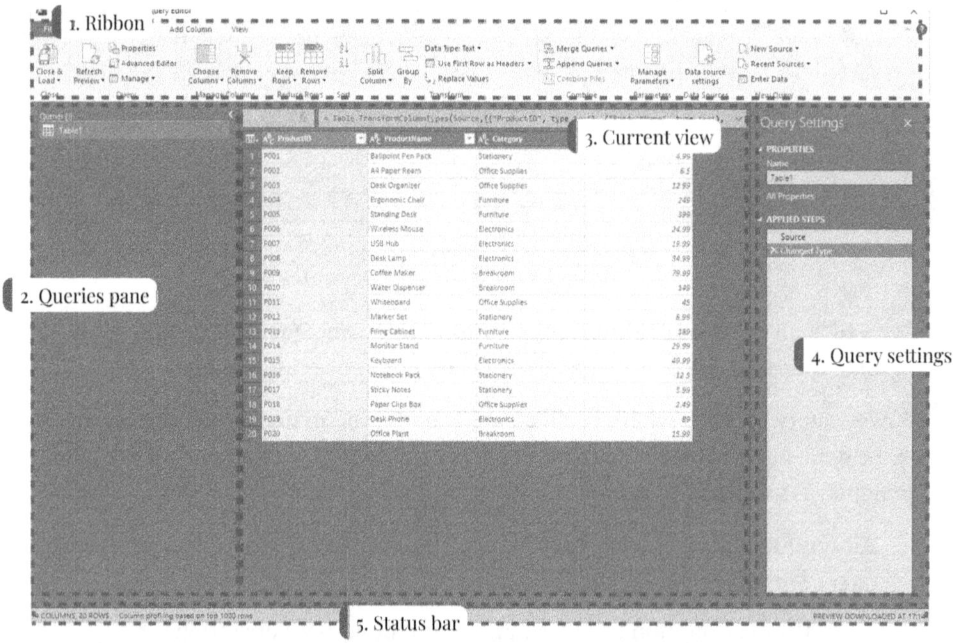

Figure 1.4 – Power Query Editor interface

> **Tip**
>
> The Current view changes depending on the applied step you select. This way, you can see how your data is being transformed.

At this moment, you may feel a bit overwhelmed looking at all the buttons in the Power Query interface, but I assure you, there is no reason to worry. Most of the time, you will use only a handful of them, and through Quinn's journey, we will explore the most common scenarios.

For now, let's close the Power Query editor without loading data into the worksheet:

1. Click the **Home** tab
2. Click the **Close & Load** dropdown arrow
3. Select **Close & Load To...**

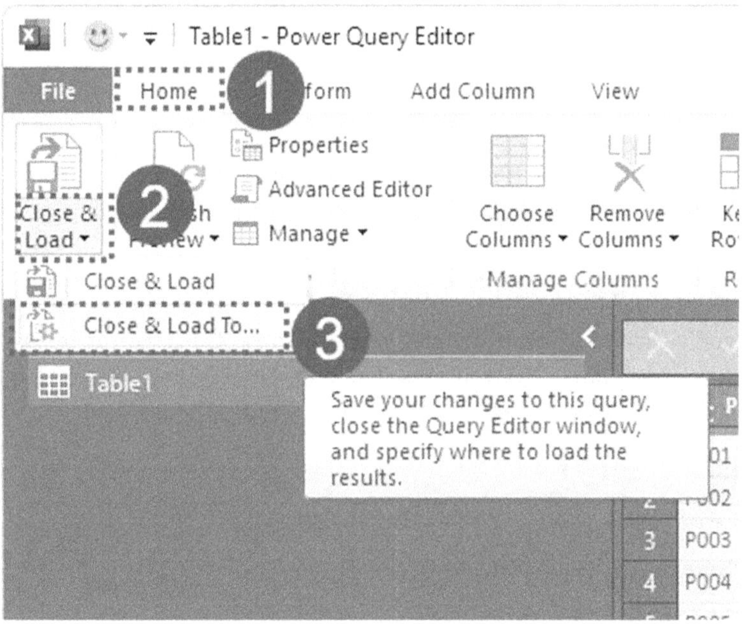

Figure 1.5 – Close and Load dropdown menu

4. In the **Import Data** dialog, select **Only Create Connection**
5. Click **OK**

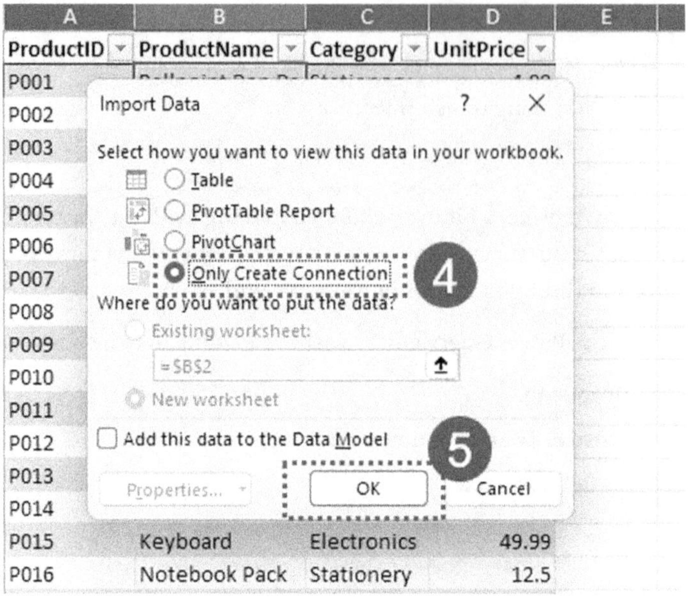

Figure 1.6 – Import Data dialog with Only Create Connection selected

This keeps our query (the set of steps Power Query has recorded) available without loading it anywhere. Save your workbook now to preserve the query connection.

Queries, steps, and refresh: the core loop

Now that you've had your first encounter with the Power Query editor, it is a good time to pause and understand the three concepts that make Power Query so useful: queries, steps, and refresh.

What is a query?

A **query** is a set of instructions that tells Power Query:

1. **Where** to get the data (the source)
2. **How** to transform it (the steps)
3. **Where** to put the result (the destination)

What are applied steps?

Every action you perform in the Power Query editor through its intuitive interface (renaming a column, changing a data type, removing rows) is recorded as a step. These steps appear in the **Applied Steps** pane on the right side of the editor.

This is one of Power Query's superpowers: your transformations are transparent, repeatable, and easy to adjust. You can do any of the following:

- Click any step to see what your data looked like at that point
- Delete a step to undo that transformation
- Reorder steps carefully to change the sequence of operations
- Add new steps anywhere in the chain

The refresh loop

Refreshing data sometimes feels like magic. Once you've built a query and loaded it to Excel, your source data won't stay static for long: new rows arrive, values get updated. The magic is that you don't need to redo any work: Just click **Refresh**, and Power Query re-runs your entire recipe on the updated data.

This makes Power Query an essential tool for anyone who works with recurring data, and as we have already seen, that includes all of us.

Exercise: build your first query with steps

> **Important**
>
> For this exercise, we will continue from the query we created in the previous exercise in the `Demo_ProductList.xlsx` file from the `Quick Tour` folder.

Let's open our existing query and observe how steps are recorded:

1. Open the `Demo_ProductList.xlsx` file (if not already open). Click the **Data** tab.
2. Click **Queries & Connections** to open the **Queries & Connections** pane
3. Double-click the query we created before to open it in the **Power Query Editor**

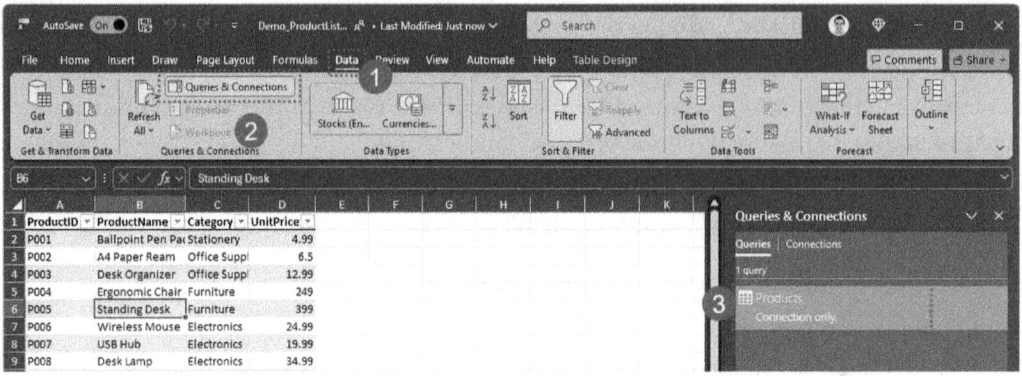

Figure 1.7 – Queries and Connections pane showing the Products query

You should see your product data in the preview pane, and in the **Applied Steps** pane, you'll see steps like **Source** and possibly **Changed Type**.

Now let's apply a few transformations:

1. **Rename a column:** Double-click on the **UnitPrice** column header and rename it to Price

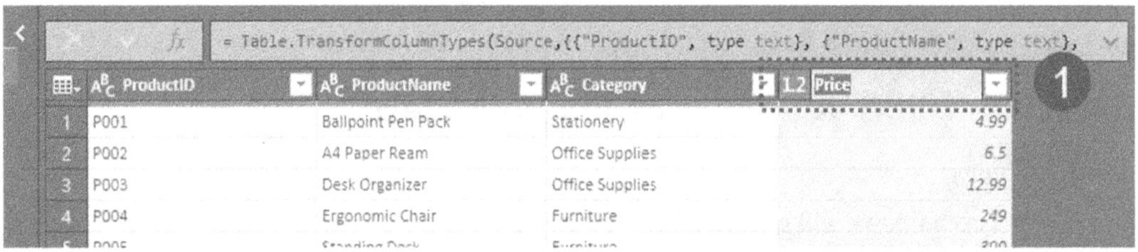

Figure 1.8 – Renaming UnitPrice to Price

Notice a new step appeared, that is, **Renamed Columns**:

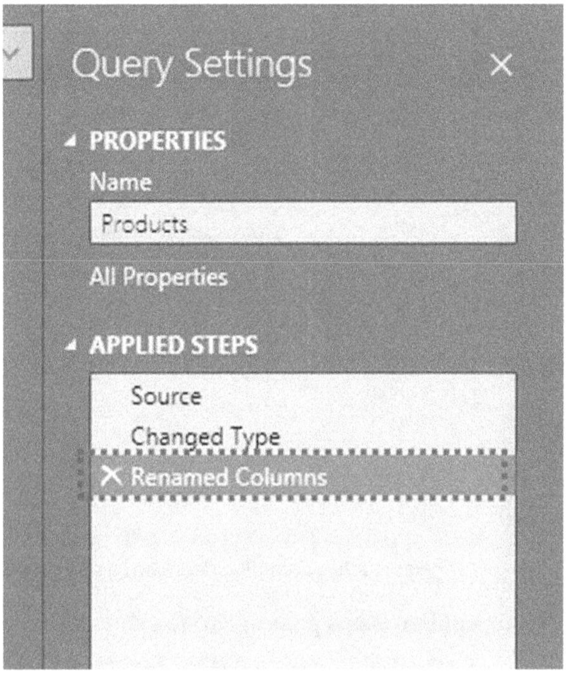

Figure 1.9 – Renamed Columns step in Applied Steps

2. **Change the data type**:
    1. Click on the **Price** column header
    2. Click the **Transform** tab
    3. Click **Data Type**
    4. Select **Currency**

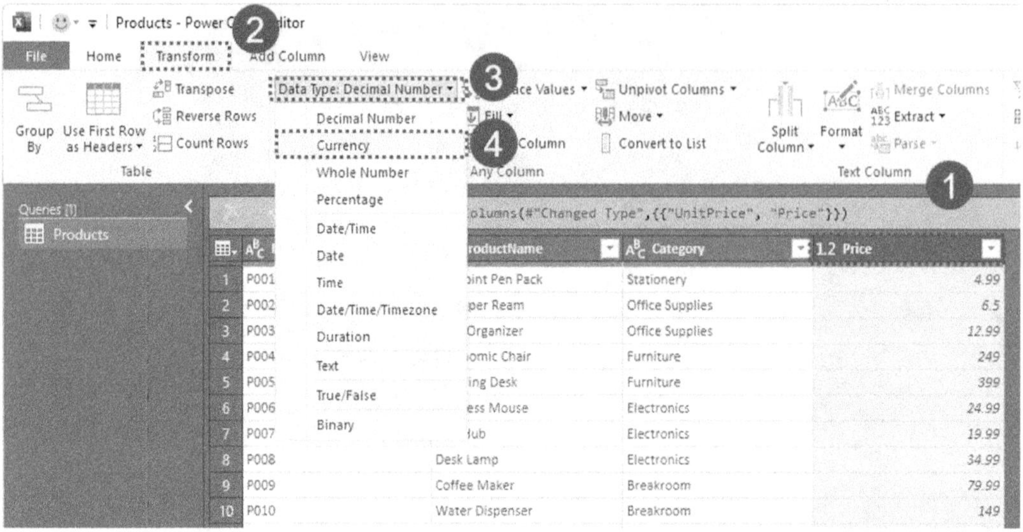

Figure 1.10 – Changing Price data type to Currency

Now look at your **Applied Steps** pane again. You should see something like this:

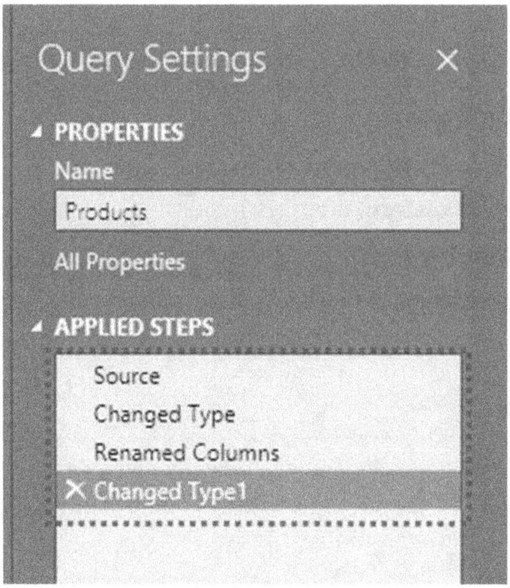

Figure 1.11 – Applied Steps pane showing transformation history

> **Tip**
>
> Click on each step to see how the data preview changes. This is how you can "travel through time" in your data transformation!

3. Rename the query to something meaningful. In the **Query Settings** pane on the right, under **Properties**, change the name from **Products** to `Product_List`.

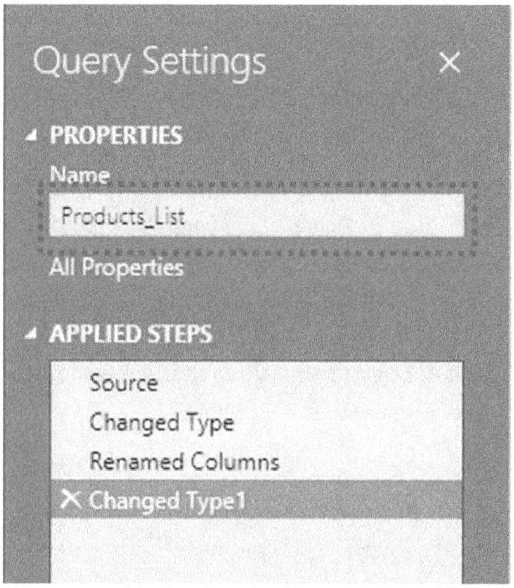

Figure 1.12 – Renaming the query to Product_List

Load options: table vs. connection only

When you're done building a query, you need to decide if and how to load it back to Excel. Loading the data is the "L" in ETL. Clicking **Close & Load** creates a connection to the query and gives you several options for loading the results:

- **Only Create Connection:** This keeps the query available, but the data is not loaded anywhere visible. This is helpful for intermediate queries that feed into other queries or for testing queries.
- **Table:** Loads data as an Excel table on a worksheet. Use this when you want to see and work with the data directly.
- **PivotTable Report:** Loads data directly into a PivotTable, ready for analysis.

- **PivotChart:** Loads data into a PivotChart for visualization.
- **Add to Data Model:** Loads data into Excel's internal data model, enabling relationships between tables. We will explore this option in later chapters.

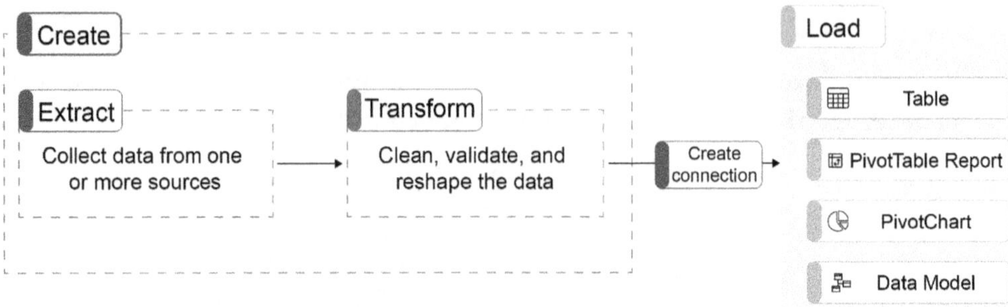

Figure 1.13 – Import Data load options

For our first query, we will load the data as a table. Since the query was originally created as a connection only, we need to change its load destination:

1. Click **Home** | **Close & Load** to save your changes and return to Excel

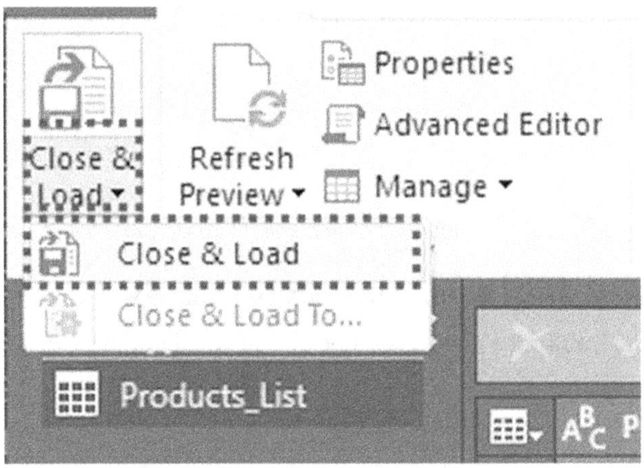

Figure 1.14 – Close and Load button

2. Open the **Queries & Connections** pane if it isn't visible:
   - Click the **Data** tab
   - Click **Queries & Connections**

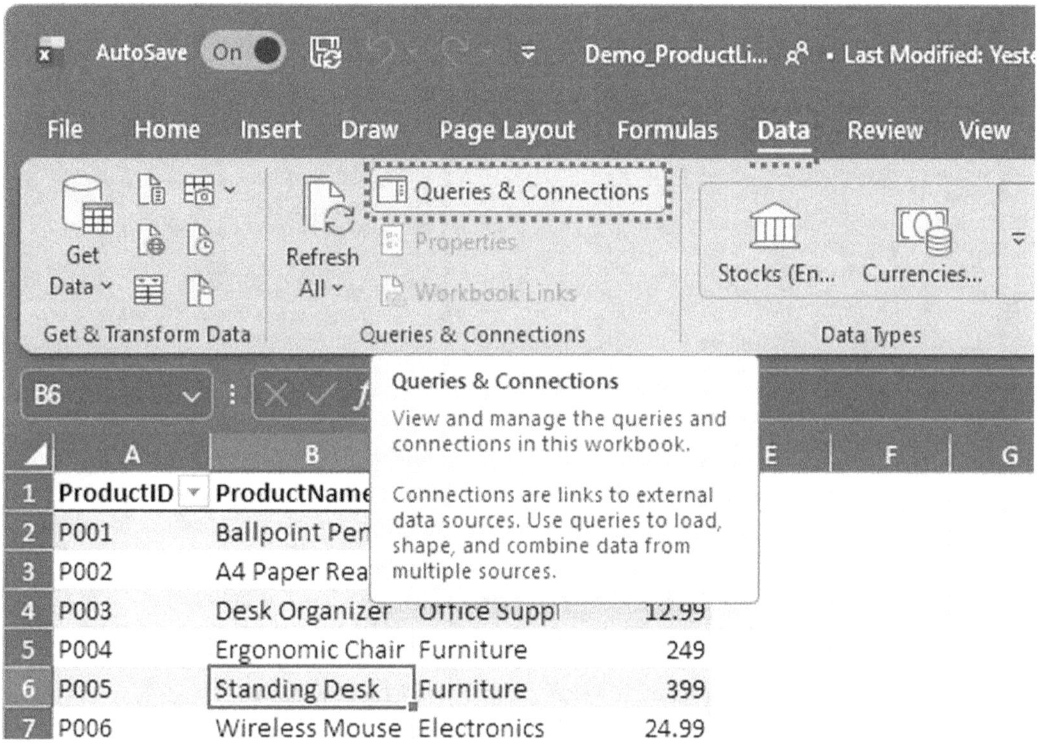

Figure 1.15 – Queries and Connections button on the Data tab

3. Right-click on the **Products** query
4. Select **Load To...**

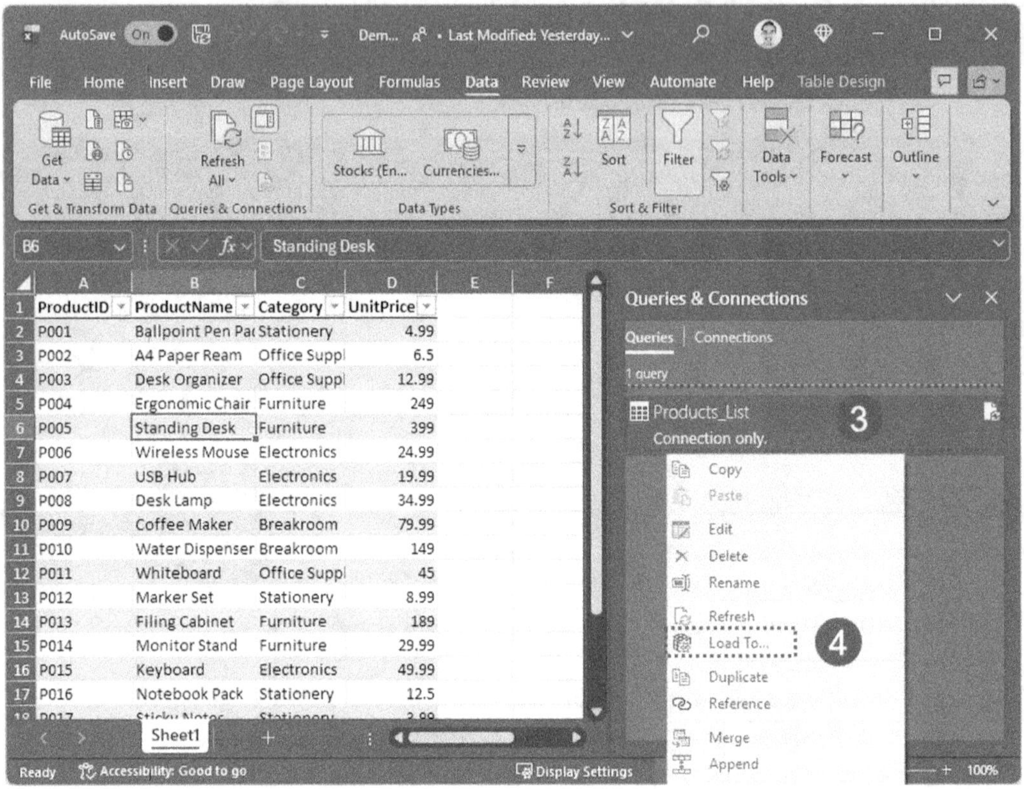

Figure 1.16 – Right-click menu with Load To option

5. In the **Import Data** dialog, select **Table**
6. Choose where to place the table (new worksheet or existing)
7. Click **OK**

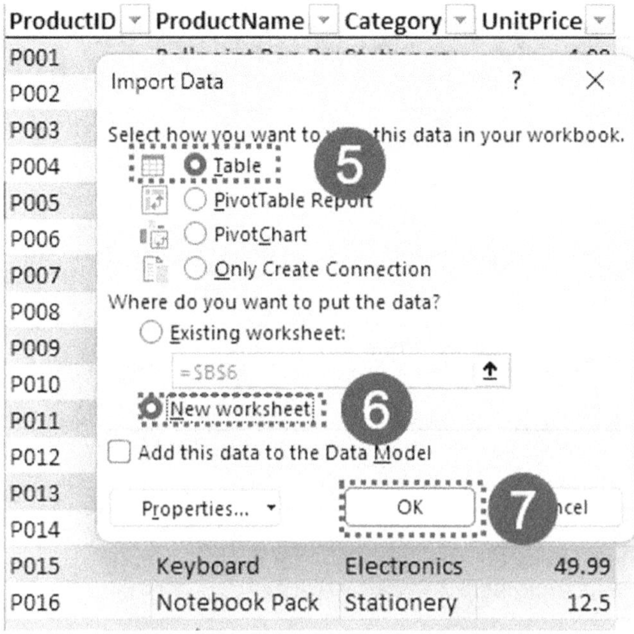

Figure 1.17 – Import Data dialog with Table selected

Your transformed data now appears as a table in Excel. Notice that the **Queries & Connections** pane shows your query with a row count. This means the table is connected to your query; it's not just a copy of data.

Testing refresh

Let's test the refresh loop by making a change to the source data.

1. Go back to the original sheet with your source *Products* table
2. Change one of the product names or prices. For example, in the first row, rename the **ProductName** and change the **UnitPrice**.

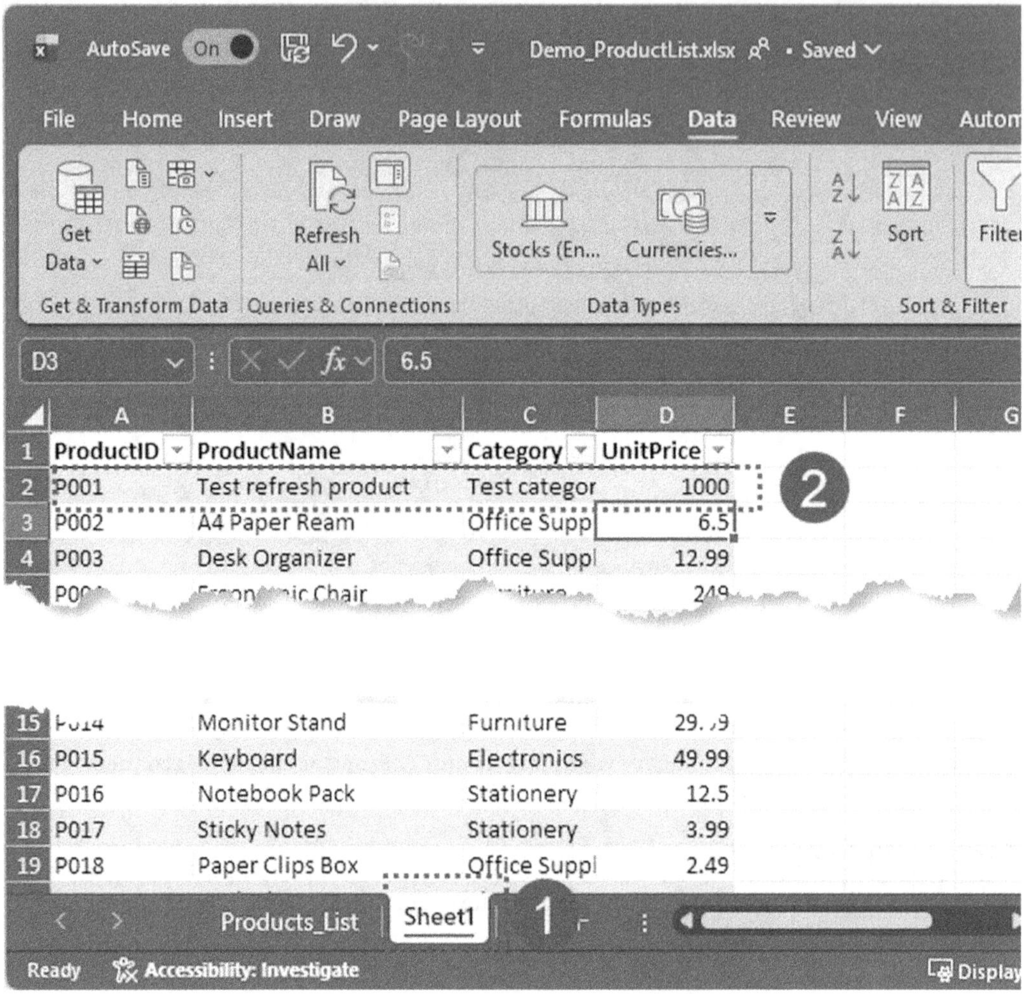

Figure 1.18 – Modifying source data to test refresh

3. Navigate to the sheet with your loaded *Products* table
4. Right-click on the table and select **Refresh**, or click **Data** | **Refresh All**

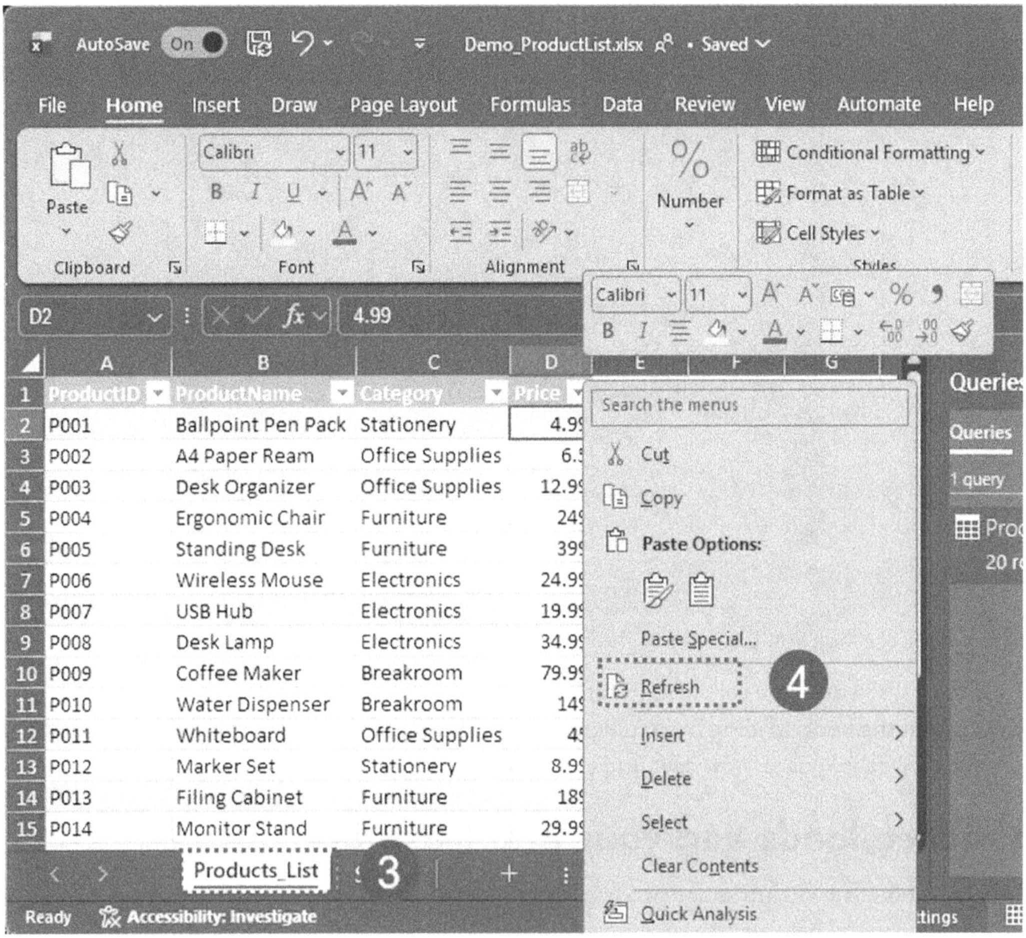

Figure 1.19 – Refreshing via right-click context menu

5. Observe that your change flows through automatically and all your transformations (rename, data type) are reapplied to the updated data

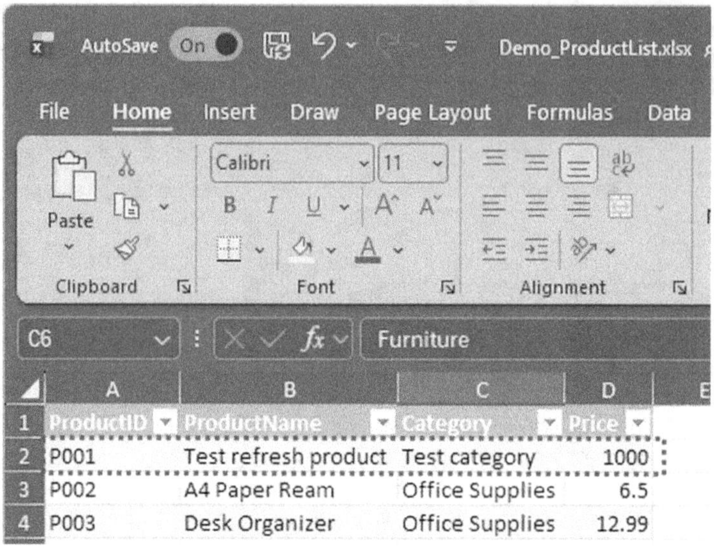

Figure 1.20 – Refreshed data reflecting source changes

This is the core loop you'll use throughout this book: connect, transform, load, and refresh.

Now that you've seen the core loop in action, let's put it to work with two patterns you'll use throughout the book: loading from folders and running a quick check to make sure your data arrived correctly. You can now save and close the file.

Practice loads and your first trust loop

In this section, we will introduce two patterns that are useful in real-world business environments and help elevate trust in your data: loading data from folders and trust loops.

Why folders?

In the previous exercises, we loaded data directly from a table. That works fine for quick demos, but it is different from real work scenarios:

- Files often sit in shared folders (SharePoint or local network drives)
- New files arrive regularly in the same folder
- You may need to combine multiple files from the same location

By connecting to a folder rather than a standalone file, Power Query can see all files in that location. You can then filter for the specific file you need or later, combine them all.

Exercise: load a CSV from a folder

In this exercise, we'll work with a CSV file, but this time using the folder connector. Choose the option that matches your setup.

> **Important**
>
> This exercise will use the `Demo_OrderSample.csv` file from the Quick Tour folder. Do not open the file; we will connect to it.

Option A: from SharePoint folder (recommended)

If you uploaded the `NOG-DataHub` to SharePoint:

1. Open a new Excel workbook
2. Click the **Data** tab
3. Click **Get Data**
4. Click **From File**
5. Click **From SharePoint Folder**

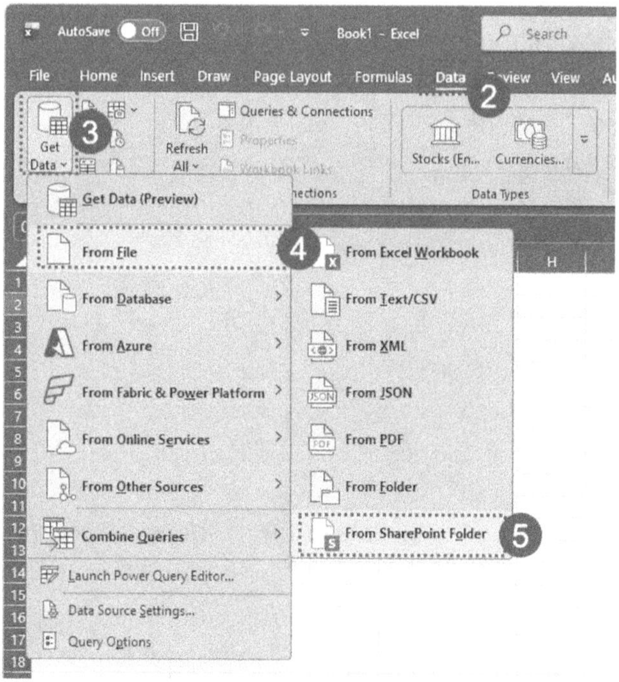

Figure 1.21 – Get Data | From SharePoint Folder

6. Paste your SharePoint site URL (e.g., `https://yourcompany.sharepoint.com/sites/YourSite`) and click **OK**

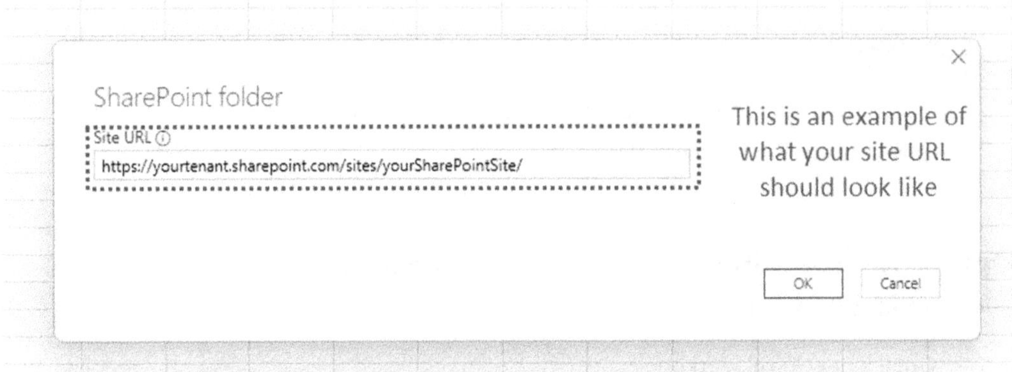

Figure 1.22 – Entering the SharePoint site URL

7. If prompted, sign in with your Microsoft account and connect

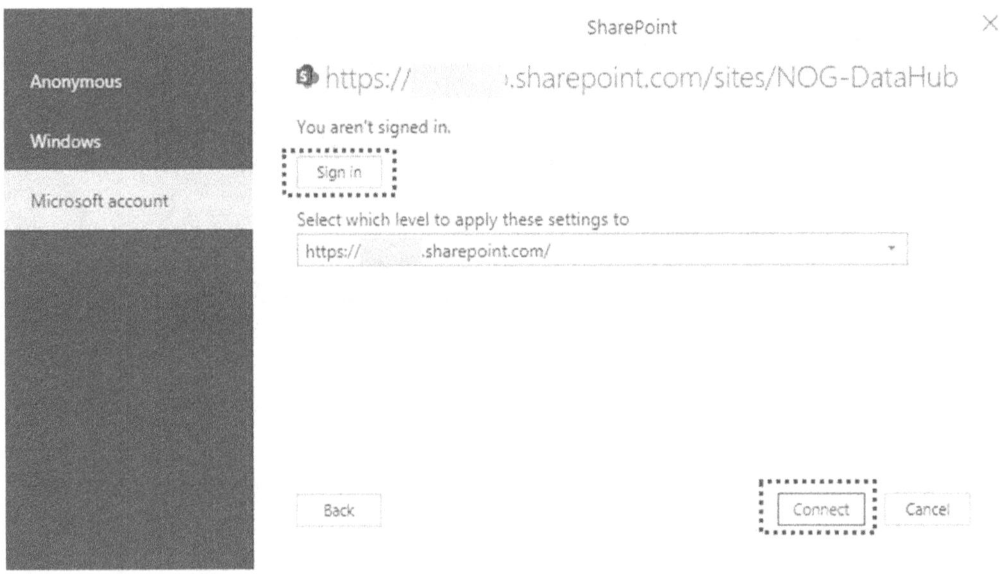

Figure 1.23 – Signing in with Microsoft account

8. Power Query shows all files in the SharePoint site. Click **Transform Data** to open the editor

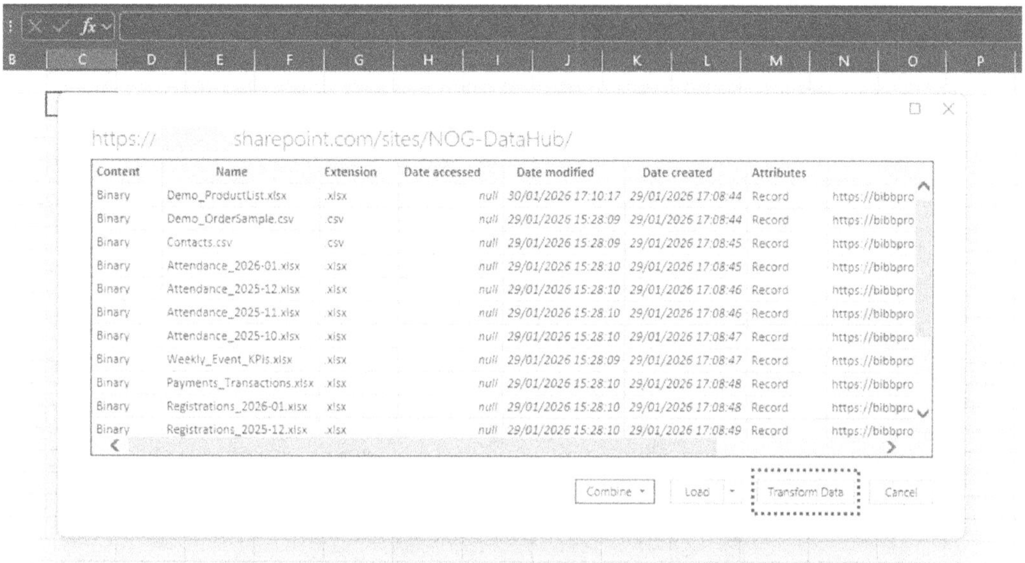

Figure 1.24 – SharePoint file listing with Transform Data

Option B: from local folder

If you extracted the `NOG-DataHub` to a local folder:

1. Open a new Excel workbook
2. Click the **Data** tab
3. Click **Get Data**
4. Click **From File**
5. Click From **Folder**

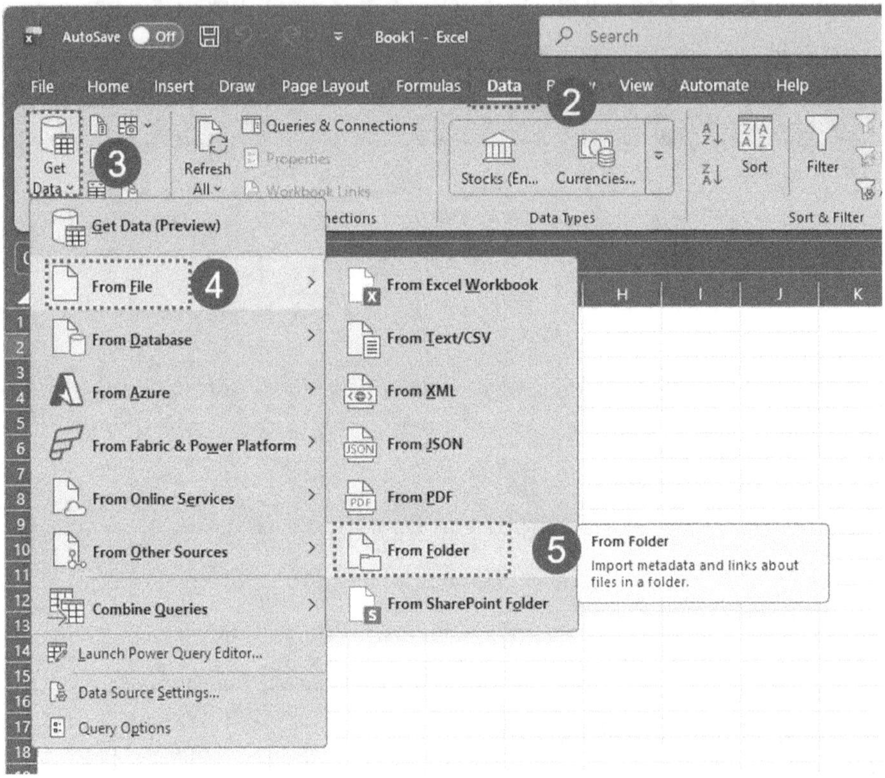

Figure 1.25 – Getting data from a local folder

6. Browse to your `NOG-DataHub` folder (e.g., `C:\Users\YourName\Documents\NOG-DataHub`) and click **OK**

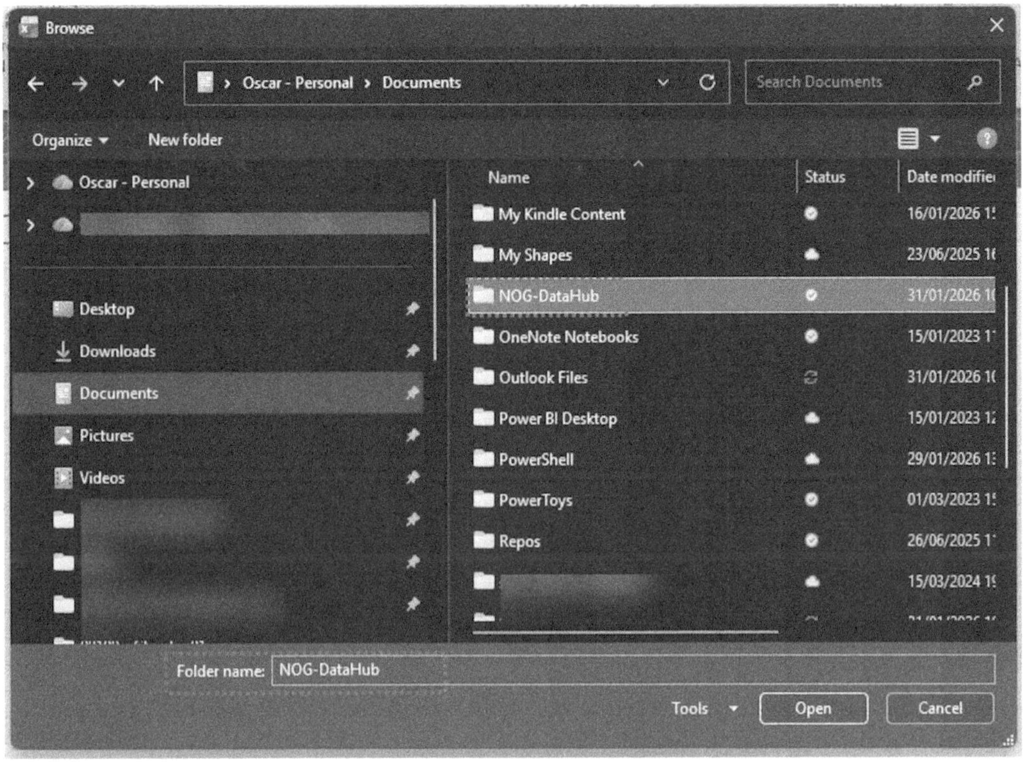

Figure 1.26 – Browsing to the NOG-DataHub folder

7. Power Query shows all files in the folder. Click **Transform Data** to open the editor

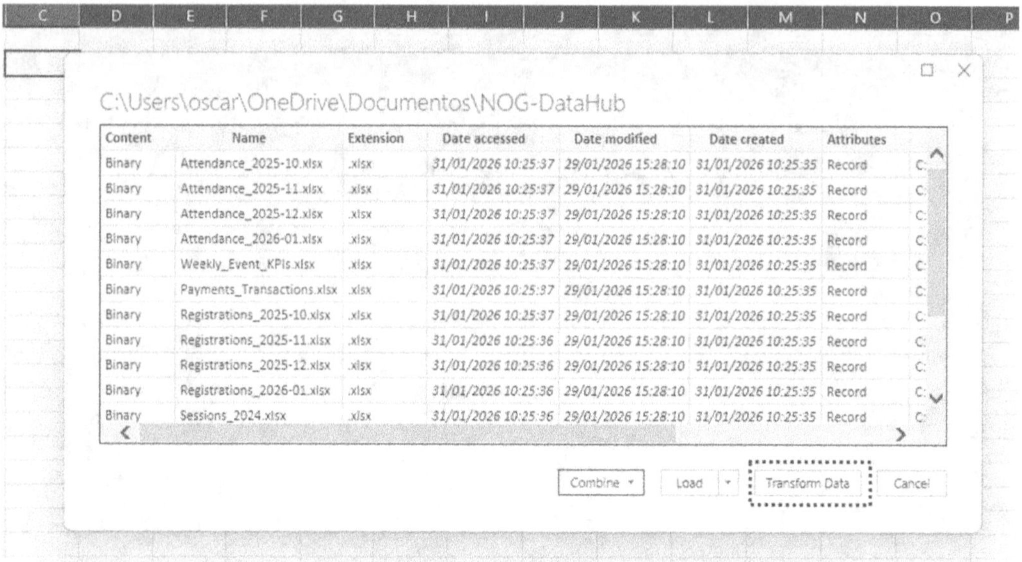

Figure 1.27 – Local folder file listing with Transform Data

Filter to your file

Whether you used SharePoint or Local Folder, you'll now see a list of all files. Let's filter to the one we need:

1. In the **Folder Path** column (you may need to scroll right to find it), click the filter dropdown
2. Click **Text Filters**
3. Click **Contains**

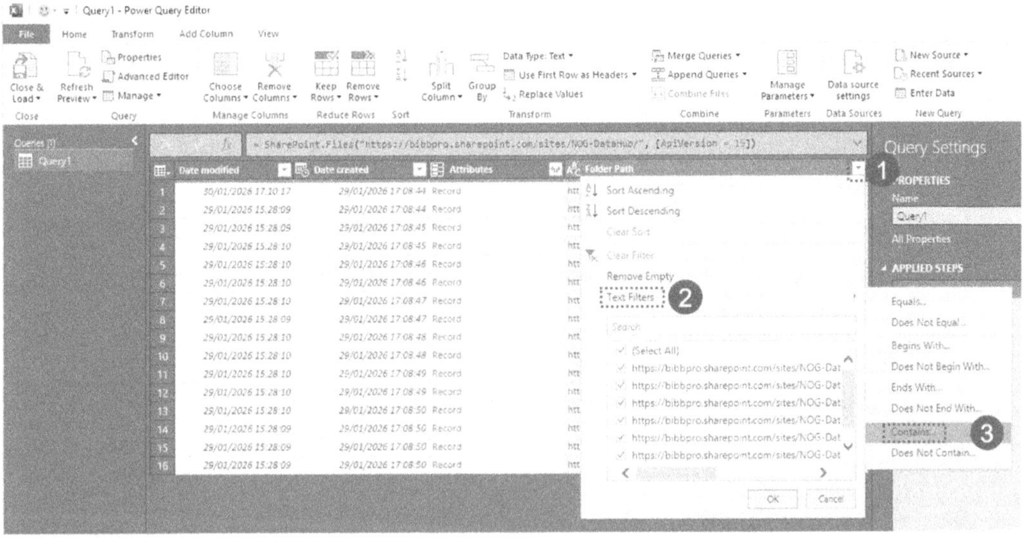

Figure 1.28 – Text Filters | Contains on Folder Path

4. Enter **Quick Tour**
5. Click **OK**

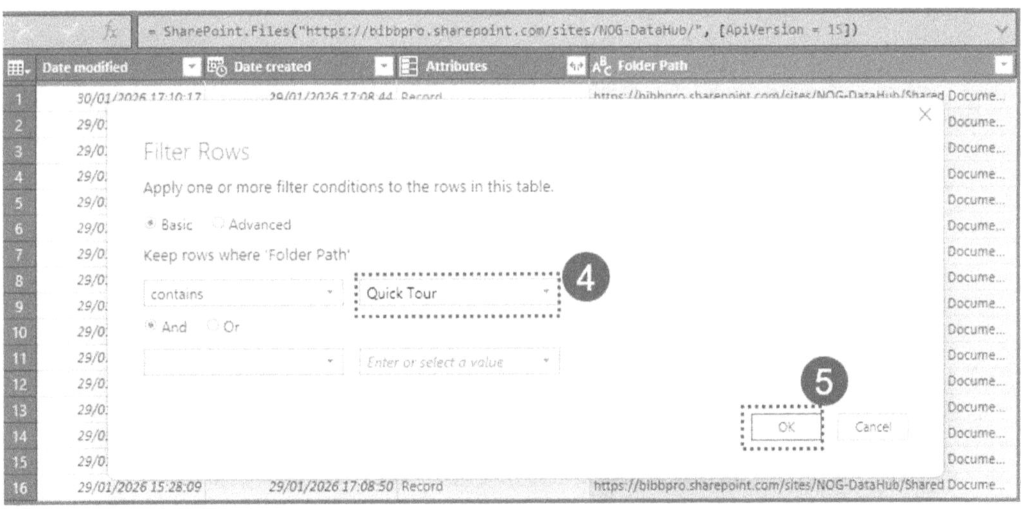

Figure 1.29 – Entering "Quick Tour" as the filter value

6. In the **Name** column, click the filter dropdown
7. Select only `Demo_OrderSample.csv`
8. Click **OK**

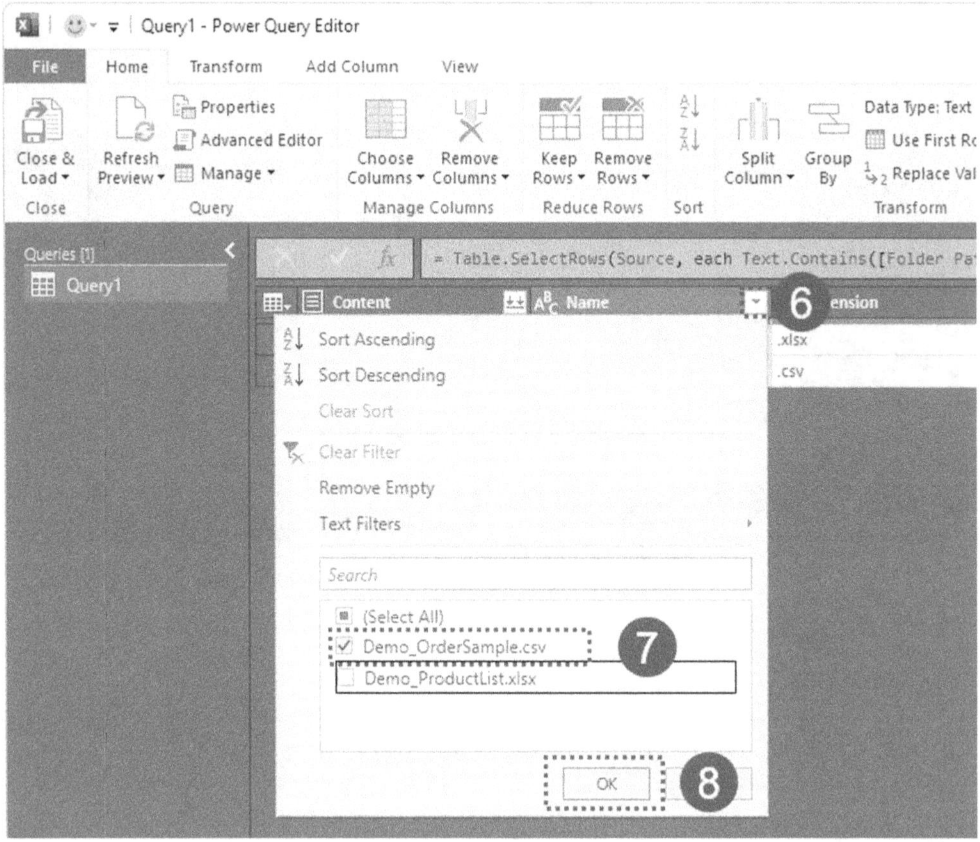

Figure 1.30 – Filtering the Name column to Demo_OrderSample.csv

9. You should now see a single row. Click on the **Binary** link in the **Content** column to open the file

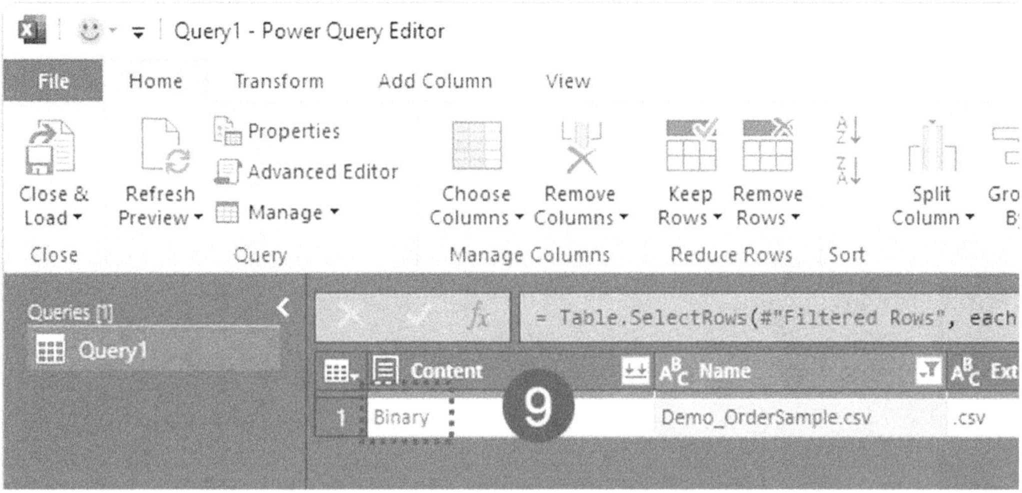

Figure 1.31 – Clicking the Binary link to open the file

Power Query now shows your CSV data.

Apply transformations

Now let's clean the data as before. Look at the **CustomerName** column and you'll notice extra spaces and inconsistent casing. Let's fix it:

1. Select the **CustomerName** column by clicking its header
2. Go to the **Transform** tab
3. Click **Format** | **Trim** to remove leading and trailing spaces
4. Click **Format** | **Clean** to remove non-printable characters
5. Click **Format** | **Capitalize Each Word** to standardize the casing

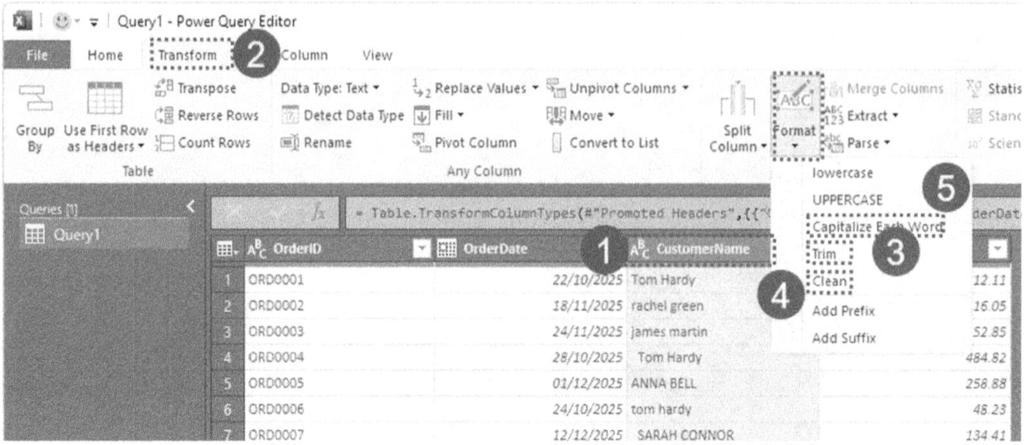

Figure 1.32 – Format menu: Trim, Clean, and Capitalize Each Word

6. Rename the query to **Order_Sample** in the **Query Settings** pane

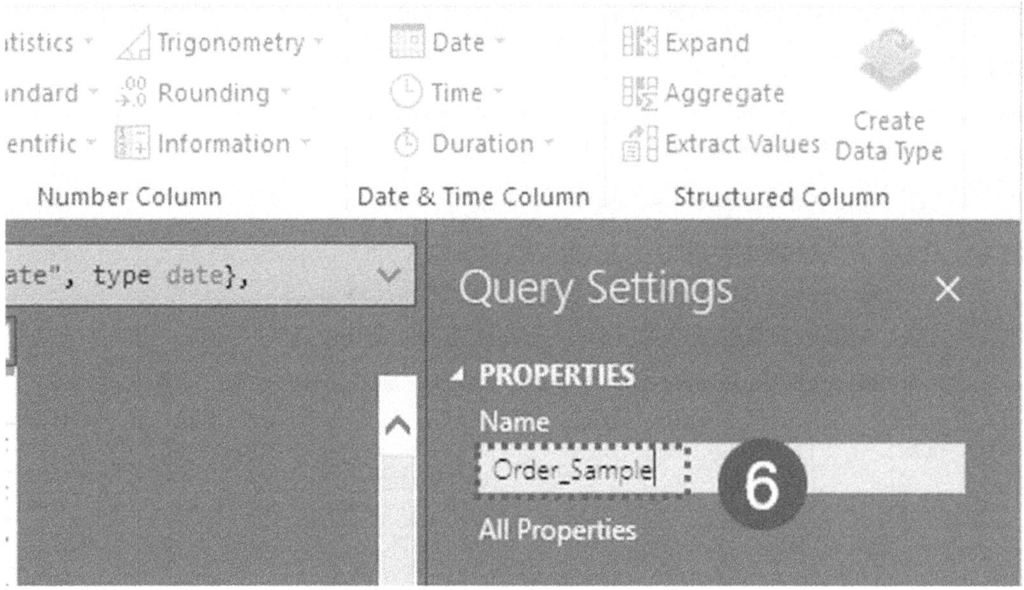

Figure 1.33 – Renaming the query to Order_Sample

Load as Connection Only

Follow these steps:

1. Click the **Home** tab
2. Click the **Close & Load** dropdown arrow

3. Click **Close & Load To...**

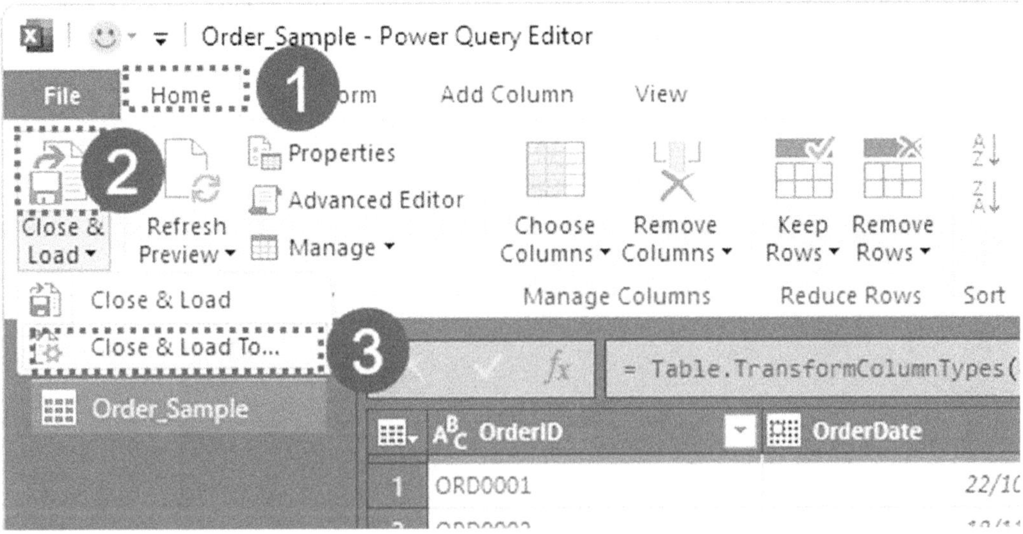

Figure 1.34 – Close & Load To

4. In the dialog, select **Only Create Connection**. Click **OK**

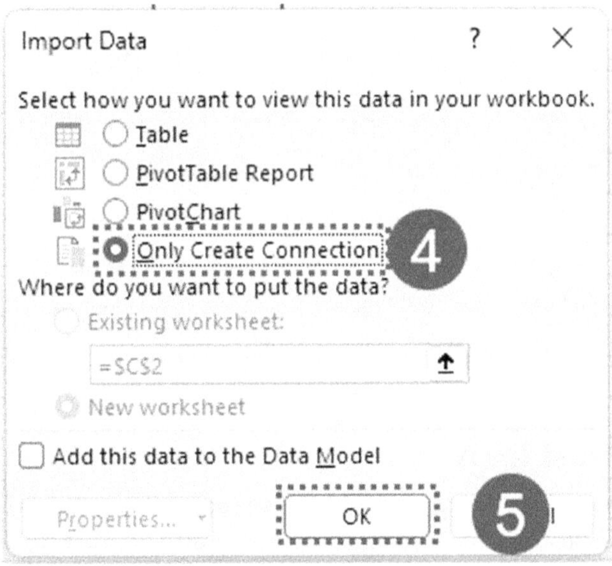

Figure 1.35 – Import Data dialog with Only Create Connection selected

Notice that no new sheet is created, but you can see the query in the **Queries & Connections** pane. The query exists and can be refreshed, but it doesn't take up space in your workbook with a visible table. This is useful for:

- Intermediate queries that feed into other queries
- Queries you want to load to a PivotTable instead of a table
- Keeping your workbook clean when you have many queries

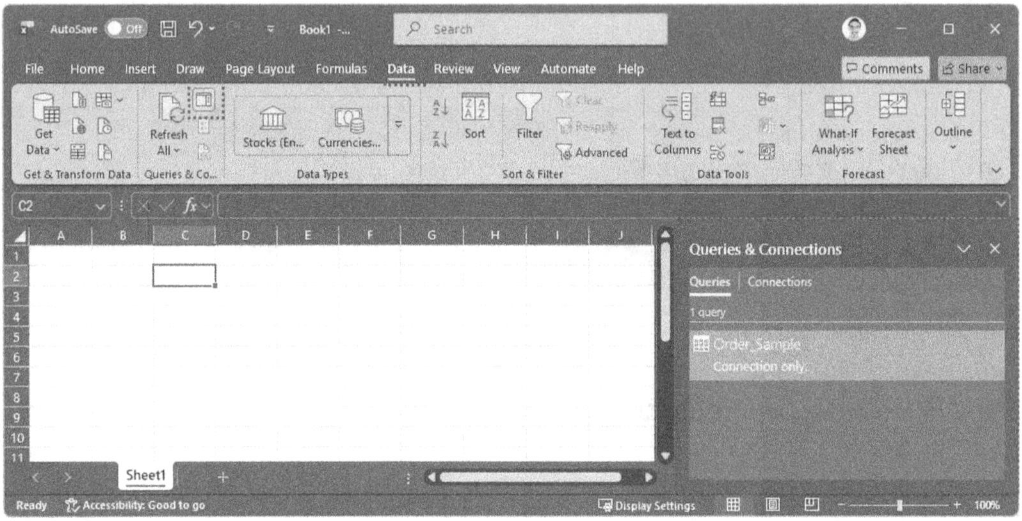

Figure 1.36 – Query visible in Queries and Connections pane as connection only

Next, we'll validate the query to ensure that it's reliable.

> **Note**
>
> This folder-based pattern is what we'll use throughout the book. Whether loading from SharePoint or a local folder, the steps after connecting are identical. This consistency makes it easy to switch between environments.

Your first trust loop

A **trust loop** is a routine you run before relying on something. Within a loop you do not instantly and blindly trust that something works correctly; you verify it each time. Trust loops are embedded in many disciplines and in data work, a trust loop means making some "sanity" checks to your data before you start using it to take important decisions.

It is highly recommended that, after creating your queries, loading data, and refreshing the data, you run this quick validation checklist. Over time, you will run through it automatically without even noticing. It takes 30 seconds and builds confidence that your data is correct:

Check	What to look for
Row count	Does the number of rows look plausible? Check the status bar or table size.
Key columns present	Are all the important columns there? No missing headers?
Data types correct	Are numbers showing as numbers, dates as dates, text as text?
No errors	Scan for error values (shown in red) or unexpected blank cells.

Table 1.1 – Post-refresh trust loop checklist

Let's practice this on our **Order_Sample** query:

1. Click the **Data** tab
2. Click **Queries & Connections** to open the pane
3. Double-click the **Order_Sample** query to open it in the editor

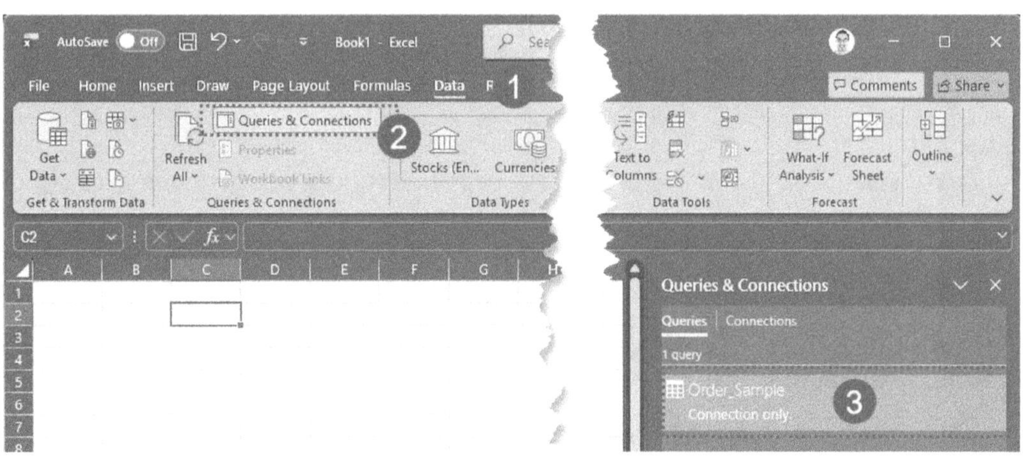

Figure 1.37 – Opening the Order_Sample query from Queries and Connections

4. Check that all expected columns are present: **OrderID**, **OrderDate**, **CustomerName**, **Amount**
5. *Figure 1.38* – Look at the bottom status bar: it should show the row and column count

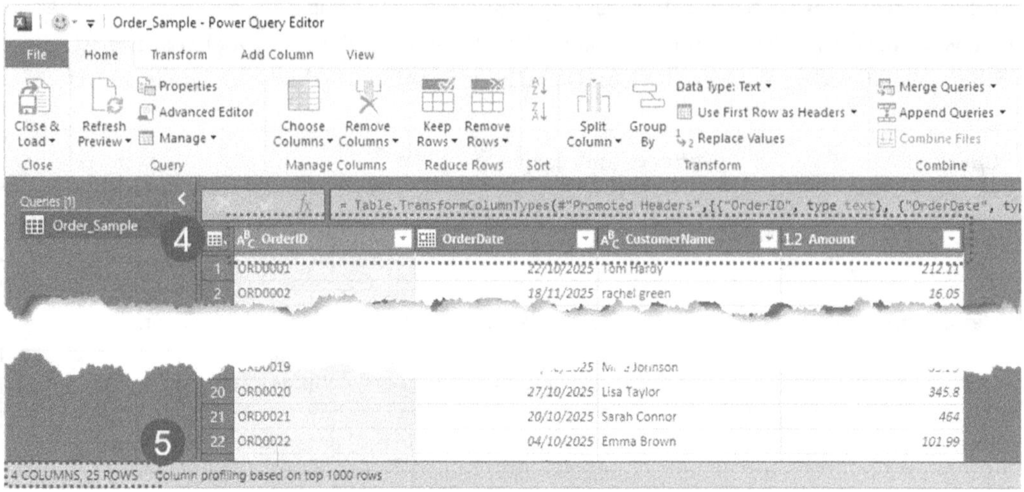

Figure 1.38 – Check that all the status bar columns are present

6. Click on the column headers to see the detected data type (shown by the icon to the left of the column name):
   - **OrderID**: Text (ABC icon)
   - **OrderDate**: Date (calendar icon)
   - **CustomerName**: Text (ABC icon)
   - **Amount**: Number (1.2 icon)

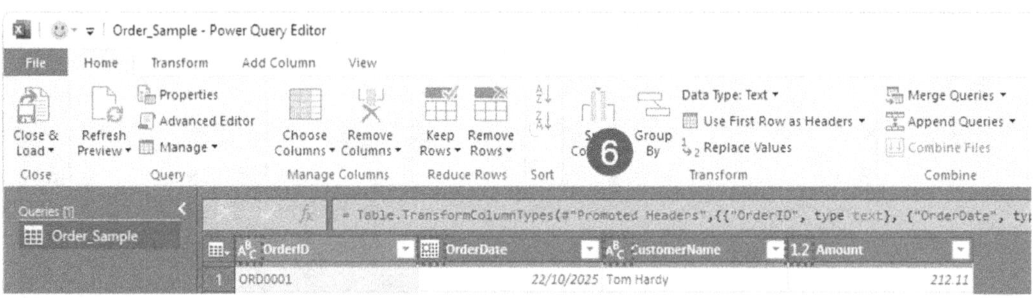

Figure 1.39 – Verifying data types via column header icons

7. Scan through the preview for any error values (cells with red backgrounds) or unexpected blanks

If everything looks good, your data is ready to use. You can click **Close & load** | **Close & Load**, and save the file in your preferred location (`NOG-DataHub_CH01`).

Summary

In this chapter, you learned:

- **Power Query is an ETL engine** built into Excel—Extract, Transform, Load
- **The Power Query Editor** is your workspace for building transformations
- **Applied Steps** record every action—transparent, repeatable, and adjustable
- **Refresh** re-runs all your steps on updated source data automatically
- **CSV files load the same way** as Excel files—the patterns are consistent
- **Trim and Clean** text fields to remove invisible problems
- **Load options** lets you choose **Table** (visible data) vs **Connection Only** (query saved, no sheet)
- **Run a Trust Loop** after every refresh to verify your data

In this chapter you built two queries: **Product_List**, loaded as a Table, and **Order_Sample**, loaded as **Connection Only**.

In the next chapter, you'll put these skills to work on a real business problem: cleaning and standardizing a messy contacts list that Amira has been fixing by hand every month.

2

Transform Daily Excel Tasks with Power Query

Figure 2.1 – Amira takes Quinn's help to clean up her Contacts file, once and for all

It is Quinn's second week at Northbridge Office Group, and by now the team knows her better; this has led to her first business request.

Amira is the Executive Assistant to NOG's upper management team. Having been with the company for many years and well acquainted with everyone, she is ideally positioned to manage the company's master contact list.

"I've got a problem," Amira says, catching Quinn in the kitchen. "I have a contacts file that is driving me mad. Mike told me you could help me out. Can I pick your brain later during the day?"

Quinn joins Amira at her desk and glances at the file on Amira's screen. Amira explains that multiple people across the company feed the list: reception adds visitors, sales adds prospects, and events add attendees. At first glance, Quinn identifies several issues and suspects there may be more: random capitalization, trailing spaces in data, and departments spelled all over the place.

As they keep talking, Amira starts to show her frustration: "Every time I need to send out invitations or run a mail merge, I have to spend at least two hours cleaning this up... and by next week, I have to do it all over again."

Quinn smiles, knowing that this is precisely the kind of problem Power Query can easily solve. "What if I told you there is a way to set this cleaning process once," Quinn says, "and then just click **Refresh** whenever the file changes?" Amira raises an eyebrow. "I'm listening."

In this chapter, you'll learn to -

- Recognize which everyday Excel tasks Power Query can replace, and understand when a repeatable query workflow is a better fit than formulas or manual cleanup
- Import a CSV file, apply core transformations (trim whitespace, fix casing, set data types, and use Column from Examples) then trigger a one-click refresh
- Navigate the Power Query interface (Queries pane, Data preview, Applied Steps, and the formula bar), and reorder or remove steps safely
- Read formula bar expressions to understand what each action in Power Query generates, and run a quick validation check after every refresh to confirm row counts, column presence, and data types

Technical requirements

To follow along with this chapter, you will need:

- Microsoft Excel 2016 or later with Power Query available (via **Data** | **Get & Transform Data**)
- Your `NOG-DataHub` workbook from *Chapter 1*, which should already contain the Power Query Basics sandbox queries created during that chapter's exercises.
- The exercise file `Contacts.csv`, located in the `NOG-DataHub/Reference/` folder of the exercise file pack. If you have not yet set up this folder, refer to *Setting Up Your NOG-DataHub* in the *Introduction* for instructions.

Why Power Query changes everyday Excel work

Amira's problem is not unique. Across every department such as sales, HR, finance, and operations, people spend hours each week doing the same cleanup tasks. Copy data, fix formatting, run a mail merge, then do it all again next week.

Power Query offers a different approach: set up your cleanup steps once, then refresh with a single click whenever the source data changes.

From Manual Cleanup to Repeatable Workflows

Quinn spends some time listening to Amira and learning how she currently cleans the contact list. In doing so, she identifies the process as repeatable and structured, following a defined set of steps:

1. Open the CSV file
2. Use **Find & Replace** to fix department names
3. Add helper columns with `=TRIM()` and `=PROPER()` formulas
4. Copy and paste values to remove the formulas
5. Manually scan for remaining issues
6. Repeat everything next week

Amira acknowledges that her current approach has several problems:

- **Time-consuming**: Several hours spent every month in this process
- **Error-prone**: It is easy to miss something or make inconsistent fixes, which has happened several times
- **No audit trail**: No record of what was changed or why
- **Not reusable**: The entire process must be repeated from scratch

Quinn knows that with Power Query, each transformation we perform becomes a recorded step. These steps are saved with your workbook and applied automatically whenever we refresh it.

Manual Approach	**Power Query Approach**
Repeat every time	Set up once, refresh forever
No record of changes	Every step is visible and editable
Easy to make mistakes	Consistent, repeatable results

Manual Approach	Power Query Approach
Knowledge stays in your head	Logic saved in the workbook

Table 2.1 – Manual approach versus Power Query approach

Recognizing tasks suited for Power Query

But we need to be careful as not every Excel task needs Power Query. Here's a simple rule of thumb: **if you'll do it more than once a week, query it**.

Power Query works well for:

- **Repetitive imports**: Weekly sales exports, monthly reports, regular data dumps
- **Data with consistent structure**: Files that do not often change their headings, columns, or sheet names
- **Data from external sources**: CSV files, other Excel workbooks, SharePoint lists
- Consistent cleanup patterns: Fixing casing, trimming spaces, standardizing values
- **Combining multiple files**: Merging monthly files into one table

Power Query is less suited for:

- **One-off analysis**: If you'll never touch the data again, manual cleanup may be faster
- **Highly irregular data**: Files that change structure unpredictably: new columns, changing column names, changing data formats
- **Real-time calculations**: Power Query in Excel refreshes on demand, not continuously

> **Note**
>
> Power Query in Power BI and Fabric can refresh on a schedule.

The NOG-DataHub: your data workspace

Quinn opens the `NOG-DataHub` folder and confirms the structure she'll be working with:

```
NOG-DataHub/
├── Reference/
└── Events/
    ├── Sessions/
    ├── Registrations/
    ├── Attendance/
```

```
├── KPIs/
└── Payments/
```

Note

The `NOG-DataHub` folder and its structure are introduced at the start of the book. If you haven't set yours up yet, refer to the *Introduction* for the full walkthrough.

Why does structure matter?

Quinn is happy that NOG has a defined structure for some of its data; having data ordered in a logical way makes the process easier to work with in these ways:

- **Reliable file paths**: Queries connect to specific locations; data which is organized in folders prevents broken links
- **Easier maintenance**: When files have logical homes, updates are straightforward
- **Team collaboration**: Everyone knows where to find (and where to put) data files (and where to put them)

The **Master_Contacts** query will be the first building block in Quinn's `NOG-DataHub` workbook.

Your first query: import, clean, refresh

"Let me show you," Quinn says, pulling up a chair next to Amira. "We'll build a query that cleans your contacts file automatically."

Over the next few minutes, Quinn walks Amira through creating her first Power Query: from connecting to the CSV file to loading clean data back into Excel.

Important

For this exercise, use the `Contacts.csv` file from the `Reference` folder in your `NOG-DataHub`.

Connecting to Amira's contacts file

We will start by connecting to our `NOG-DataHub` using the folder connector pattern from *Chapter 1*. Choose the option that matches your setup:

Option A: from SharePoint folder (recommended)

I'd recommend the option to connect from SharePoint folder:

1. Open a new Excel workbook (this will become your `NOG-DataHub` workbook) and save it in your preferred location (e.g. `NOG-DataHub_CH02.xlsx`)
2. Click on the **Data** tab on the ribbon
3. Click **Get Data**
4. Click **From File**
5. Click **From SharePoint Folder**

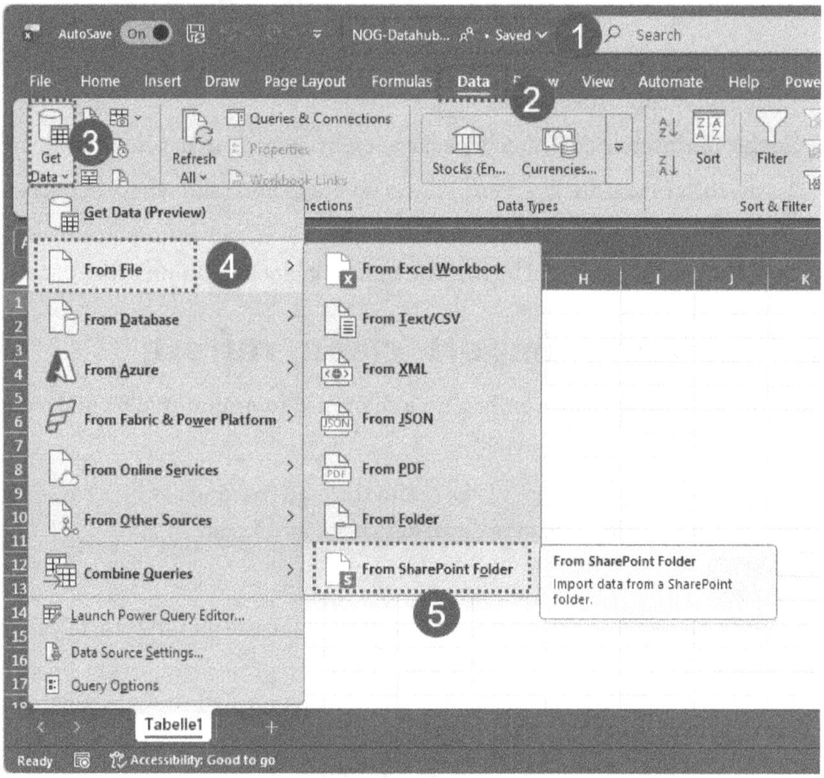

Figure 2.2 – Get Data menu expanded to From SharePoint Folder

6. Paste your SharePoint site URL and click **OK**

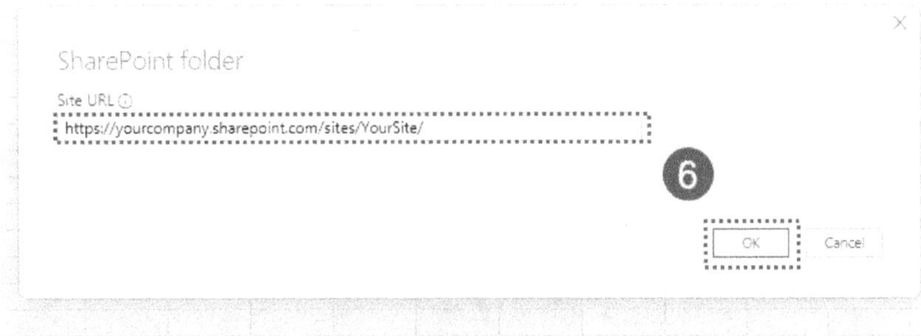

Figure 2.3 – SharePoint Folder connection dialogue

7. If prompted, sign in with your Microsoft account and connect
8. Power Query shows all files in the SharePoint site. Click **Transform Data** to open the editor

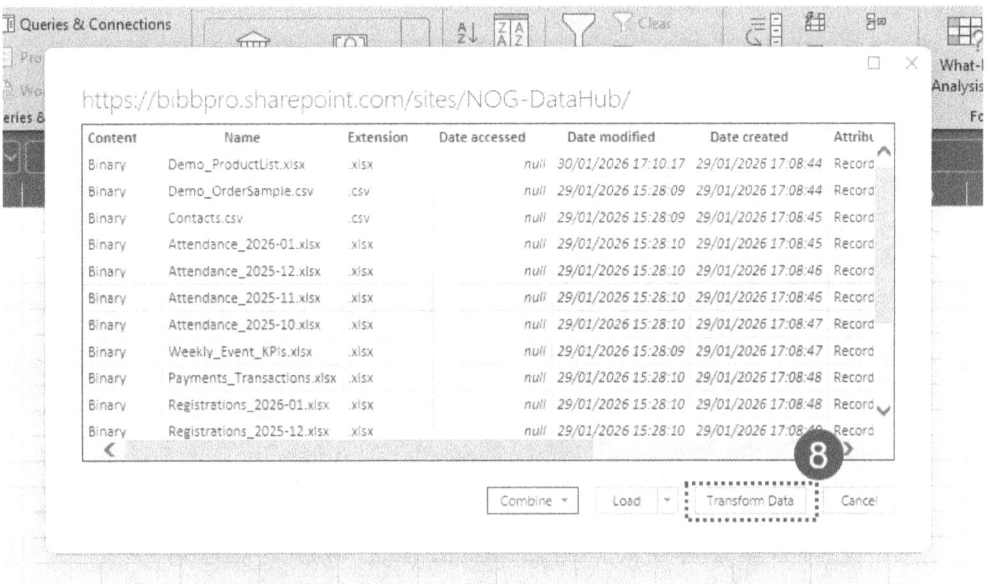

Figure 2.4 – SharePoint file listing with Transform Data button

Option B: from local folder

Here are the steps if you want to connect from a local folder:

1. Open and save (e.g. `NOG-DataHub_CH02.xlsx`) a new Excel workbook (this will become your `NOG-DataHub` workbook)
2. Click the **Data** tab on the ribbon

3. Click **Get Data**
4. Click **From File**
5. Click **From Folder**

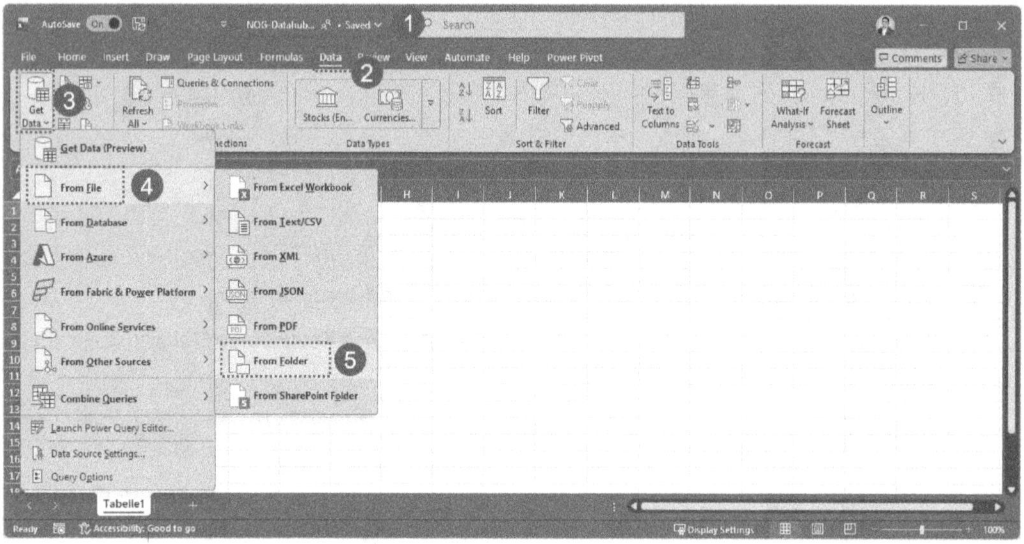

Figure 2.5 – Get Data menu expanded to From Folder

6. Browse to your `NOG-DataHub` folder and click **Open**

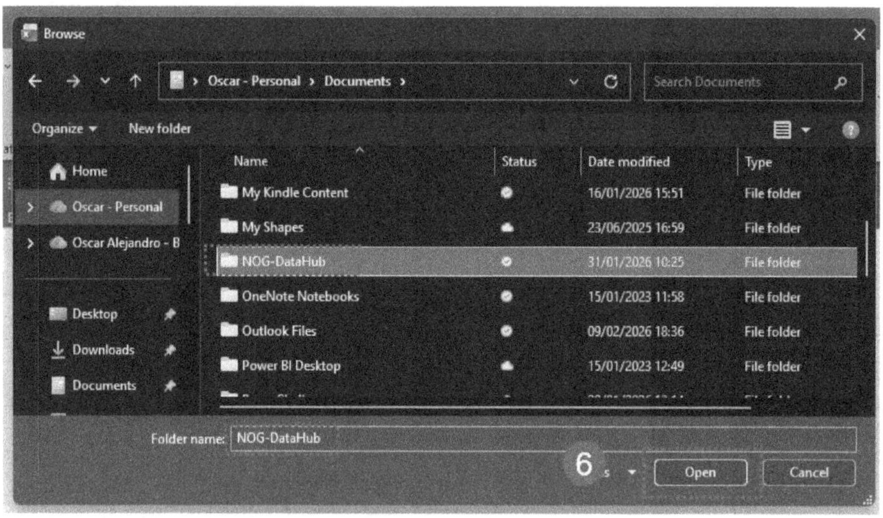

Figure 2.6 – Folder browser dialog

7. Power Query shows all files in the folder. Click **Transform Data** to open the editor

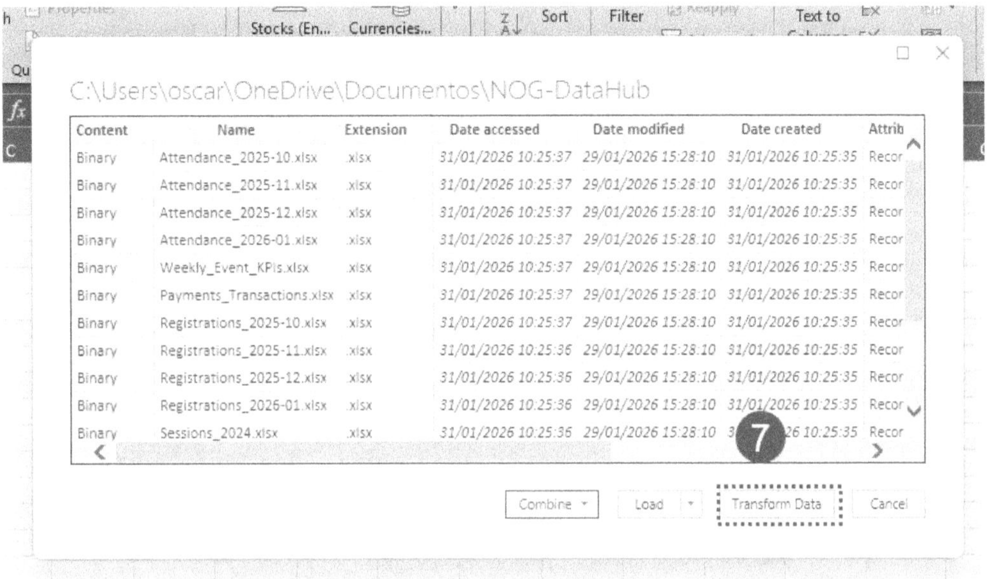

Figure 2.7 – Local folder file listing with the Transform Data button

Tip

Always click **Transform Data** rather than **Load** when starting a new query. This lets you inspect the files and, if needed, filter them before loading them into Excel.

Filter to the contacts file

Whether you used SharePoint or a local folder, you'll now see a list of all files. Let's filter to the one we need.

If you cannot see all columns, scroll to the right of the Power Query Editor window; the Folder Path column sits toward the right.

1. In the **Folder Path** column, click the filter dropdown
2. Click **Text Filters**
3. Click **Contains**

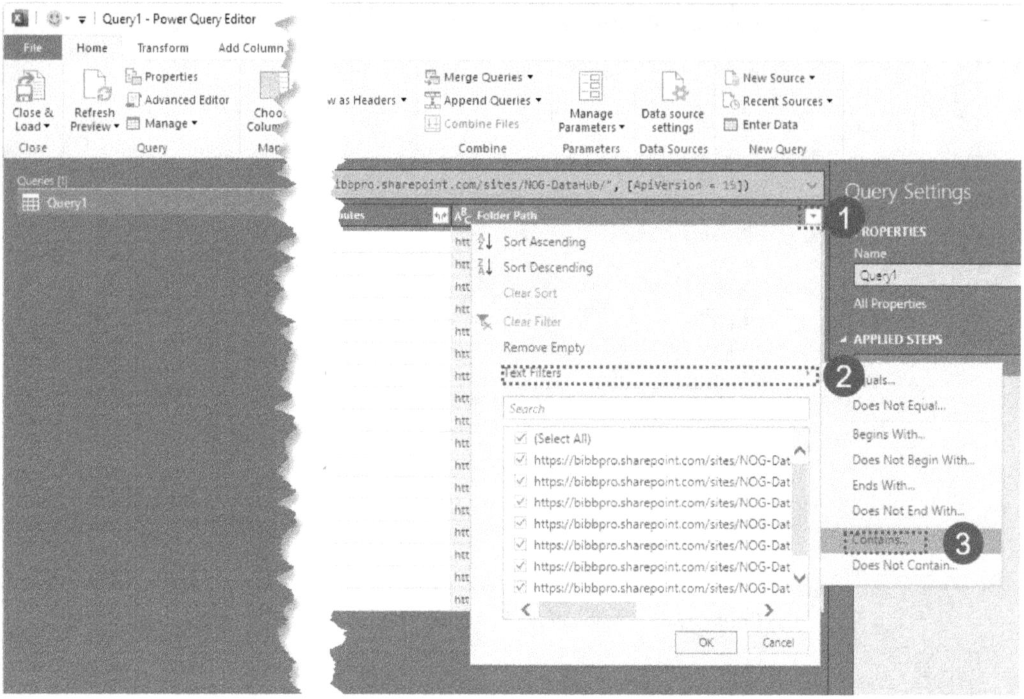

Figure 2.8 – Text Filters Contains option in the filter dropdown

4. Type `Reference` and click **OK**

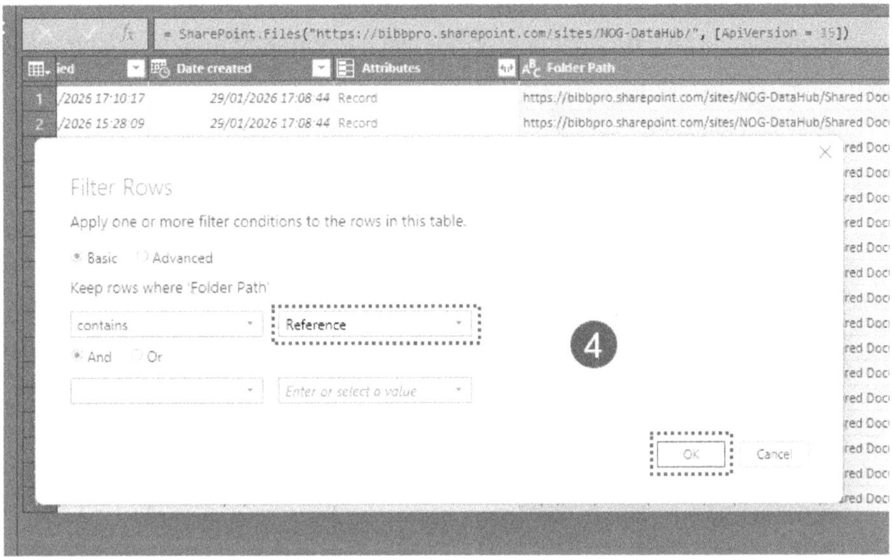

Figure 2.9 – Text Filters Contain dialogue with Reference entered

> **Tip**
>
> Keep in mind that you can filter by several columns to narrow your search. For example, filter by Folder Path first, then by Name. This is especially useful on large document libraries and when files share the same name but sit in different folders.

After filtering, two files remain; we will focus on `Contacts.csv`. To open it:

5. Click the **Binary** value in the **Content** column

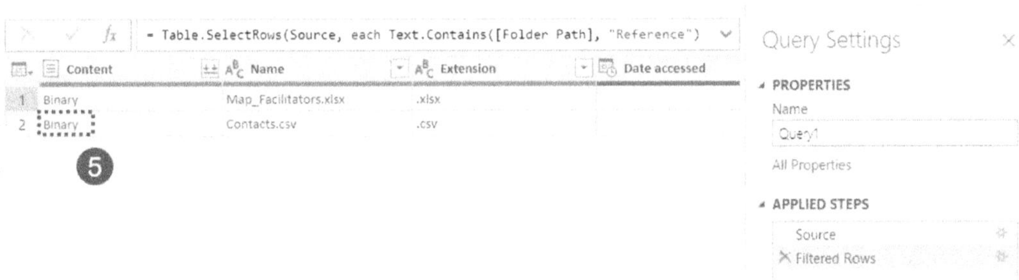

Figure 2.10 – Content column showing a binary link for the filtered file

The first thing Quinn does is rename the query, as clear, meaningful naming of our objects makes it easier to understand their contents and find them later.

6. In the **Query Settings** pane (right side), find the **Name** field. Change it to `Master_Contacts`

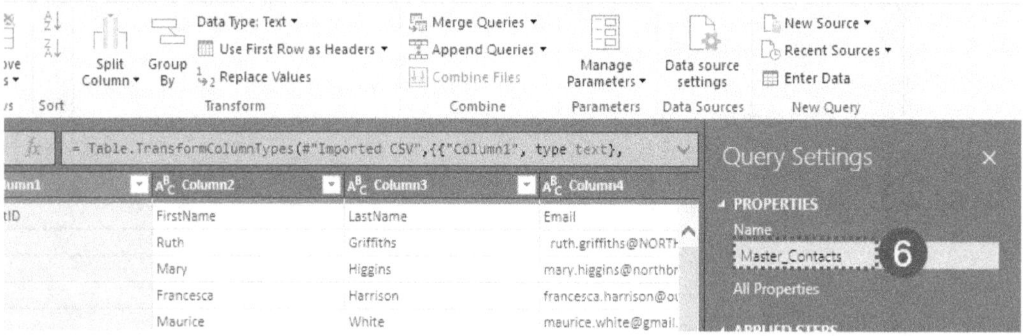

Figure 2.11 – Query Settings pane with query renamed to Master_Contacts

Power Query loads the CSV data, but we can observe that the first row contains the column headers (or column names) rather than data. Let's fix that.

7. Click the **Transform** tab on the ribbon
8. Click **Use First Row as Headers**

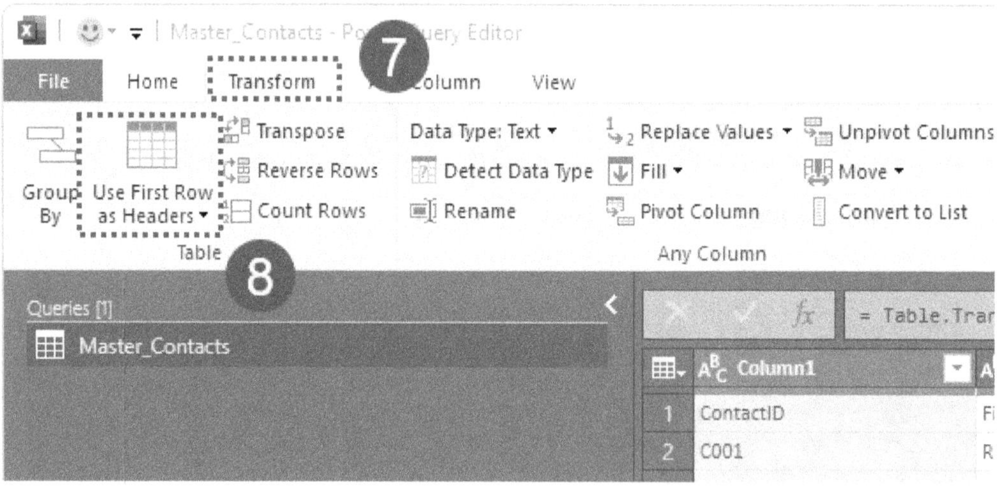

Figure 2.12 – Transform tab with Use First Row as Headers button

The columns now show meaningful names such as **FirstName**, **LastName**, and **Email** instead of generic Column1, Column2 labels.

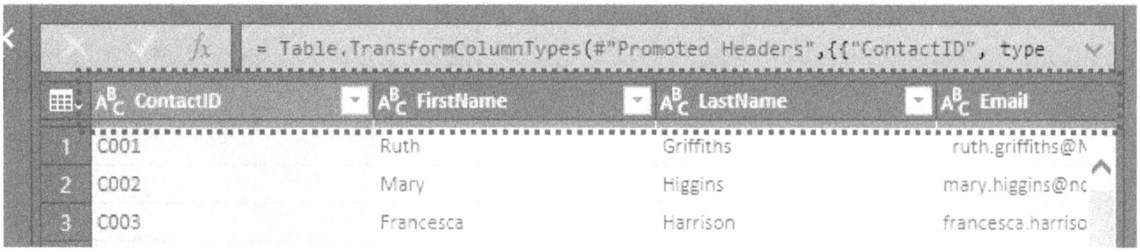

Figure 2.13 – Data preview after promoting the first row as headers

Cleaning up text

Looking at the data preview, Quinn immediately spots the first problem: names have inconsistent casing. Some are "JOHN", others "smith", others "Jane".

Fix the casing

Follow these steps:

1. Click the **FirstName** column header to select it
2. Click the **Transform** tab on the ribbon
3. Click **Format**
4. Click **Capitalize Each Word**

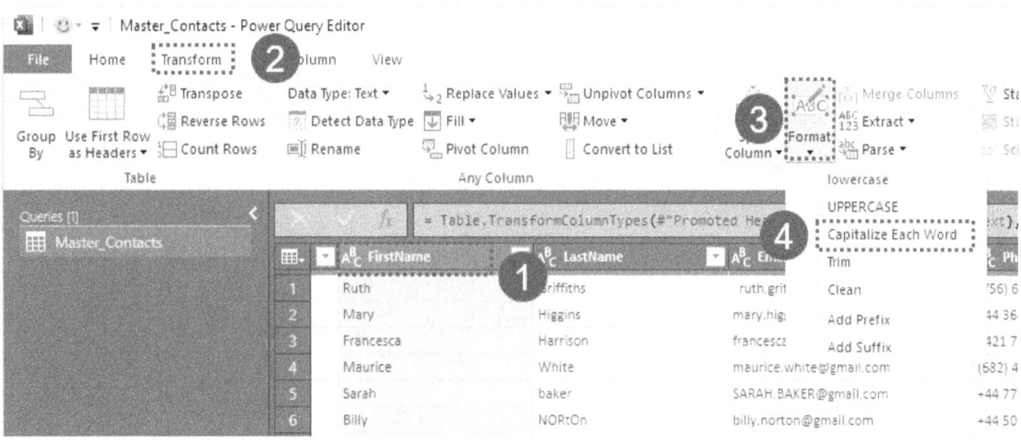

Figure 2.14 – Transform tab showing Format dropdown with Capitalise Each Word

5. Repeat for the **LastName** column
6. Notice the **Applied Steps** pane on the right; these actions have created one **Capitalized Each Word** step for both columns

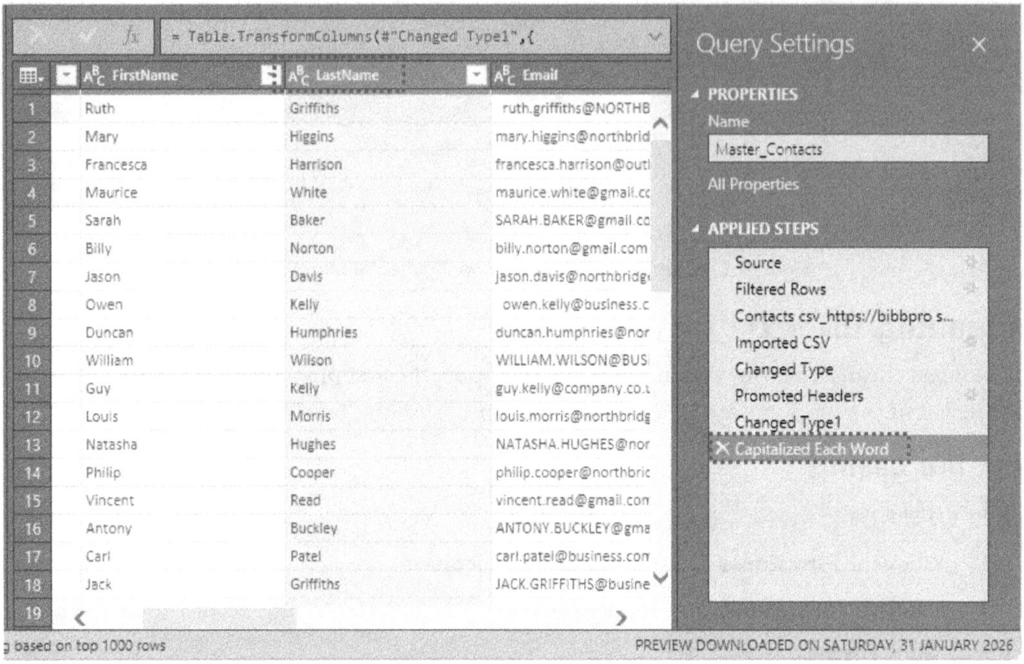

Figure 2.15 – Applied Steps pane showing Capitalized Each Word steps

Next, we will make the email addresses lowercase for consistency and to avoid duplicate issues when matching:

1. Select the **Email** column
2. Click the **Transform** tab on the ribbon
3. Click **Format**
4. Click **lowercase**

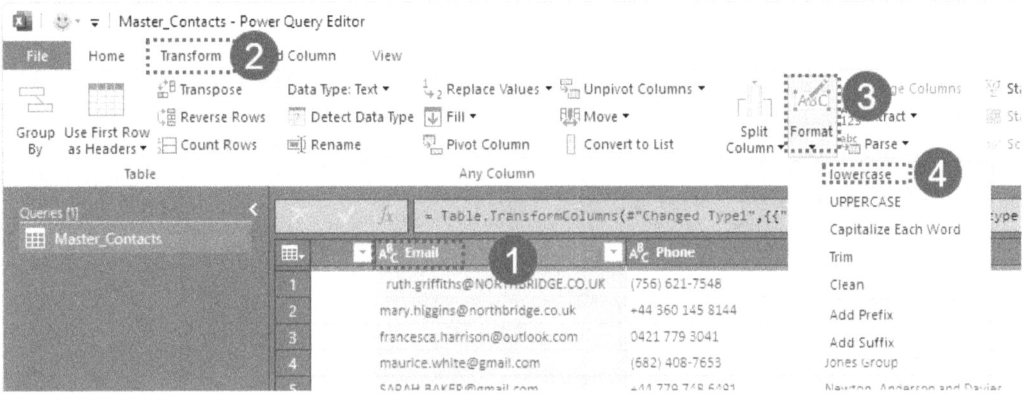

Figure 2.16 – Format dropdown with lowercase option

Trim whitespace

Trailing and leading spaces are troublemakers. They cause filters to miss matches and other types of failures.

In Power Query, you can often apply the same transformation to multiple columns in one go:

1. Hold *Ctrl* and click to select **Email**, **Company**, and **Department** columns

Figure 2.17 – Selecting multiple columns with Ctrl + click

2. Click the **Transform** tab on the ribbon
3. Click **Format**
4. Click **Trim**

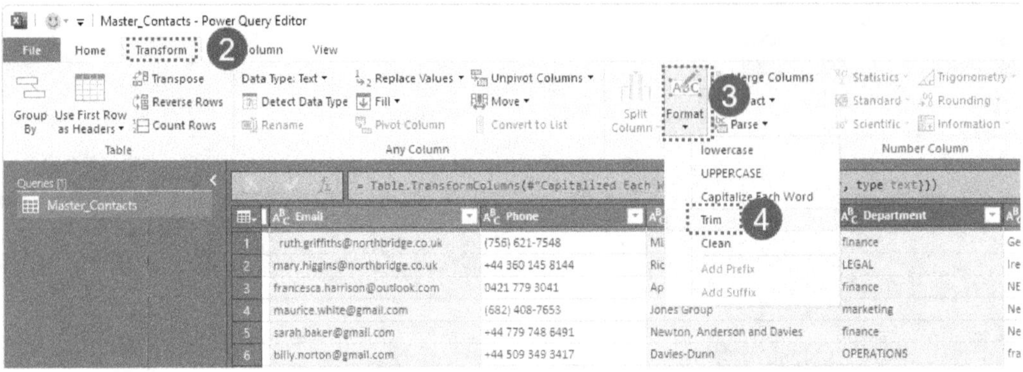

Figure 2.18 – Format dropdown with Trim option on selected columns

Each transformation adds another step. Quinn points to the **Applied Steps** pane: "See, Amira, Power Query records all the actions we do. When the data in the source file changes, these exact steps will run again automatically, in the same order."

Standardizing inconsistent values

Quinn scrolls through the **Department** and **Country** columns. The values are all over the place: "finance", "LEGAL", "Sales", "OPERATIONS" in Department, and "france", "GERMANY", "united kingdom", "UK" in Country.

Capitalize the **Department** and **Country** columns:

1. Hold *Ctrl* and click to select the **Department** and **Country** columns
2. Click the **Transform** tab on the ribbon
3. Click **Format**
4. Click **Capitalize Each Word**

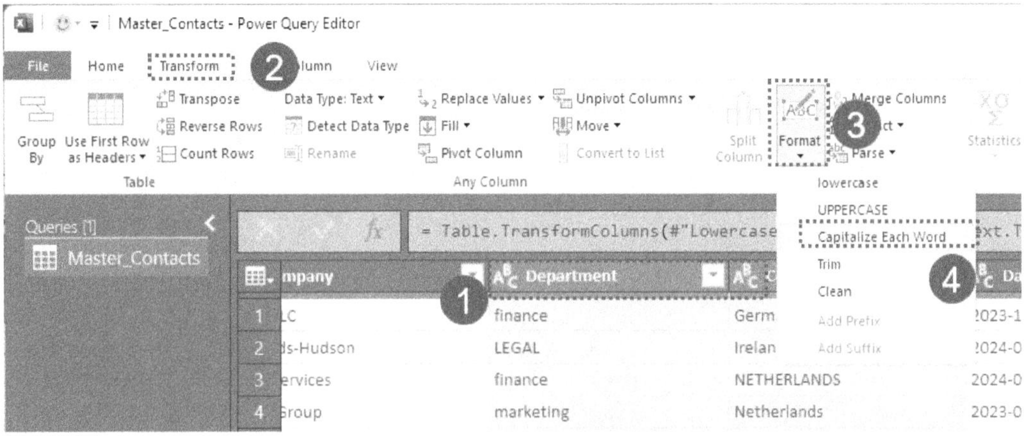

Figure 2.19 – Format Capitalise Each Word applied to Department and Country columns

That fixes the casing, but there's still one problem: some rows say "Uk" (the capitalized form of "UK") instead of "United Kingdom." Let's replace "Uk" with "United Kingdom".

5. Select the **Country** column
6. Click **Replace Values** on the **Transform** tab

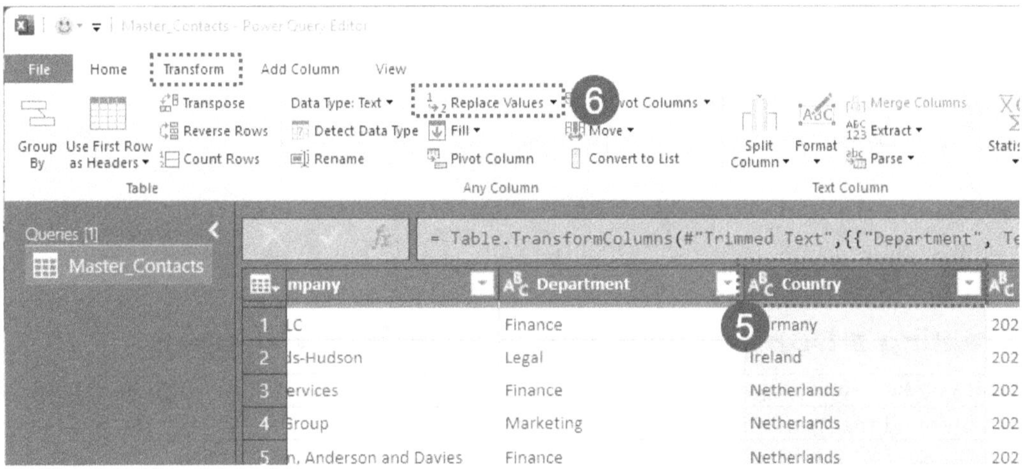

Figure 2.20 – Replace Values button on the Transform tab

7. In the dialog:
    - **Value to Find**: `Uk`
    - **Replace With**: `United Kingdom`

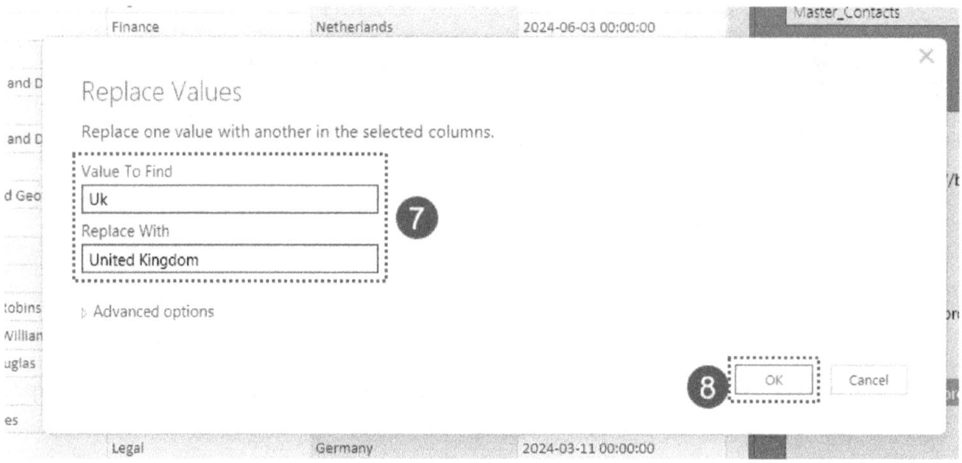

Figure 2.21 – Replace Values dialog with UK replaced by United Kingdom

8. Click **OK**

> **Tip**
>
> Before replacing values, click the filter dropdown on a column to see all unique values. This helps you spot variants you might have missed.

For larger cleanup tasks with many variants, *Chapter 3* will show you how to use small mapping tables instead of multiple **Replace Values** steps.

Creating a DisplayName with column from examples

"This is great," Amira says, "but for mail merges I need names in *FirstName, LastName* format. I usually build that with a formula column."

Power Query has a built-in feature that can figure out the pattern for you. Instead of writing a formula, you show it a few examples, and it does the rest.

1. Click the **Add Column** tab on the ribbon
2. Click **Column From Examples**
3. Click From **All Columns**

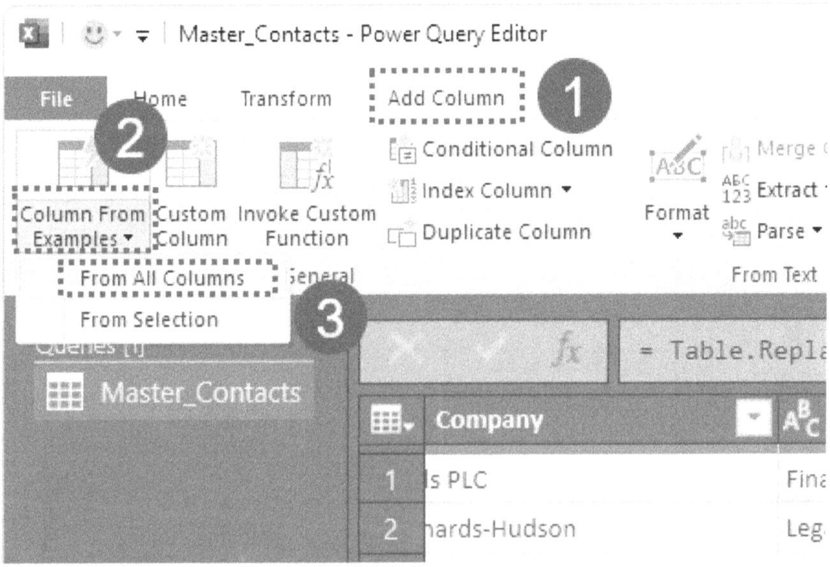

Figure 2.22 – Add Column tab showing Column from Examples dropdown with From All Columns

A new blank column appears on the right side of the data preview, with an input area at the top.

4. In the first row, type the expected result; for example, if the row shows **FirstName** = Ruth and **LastName**= Griffiths, type Ruth, Griffiths and press *Enter*

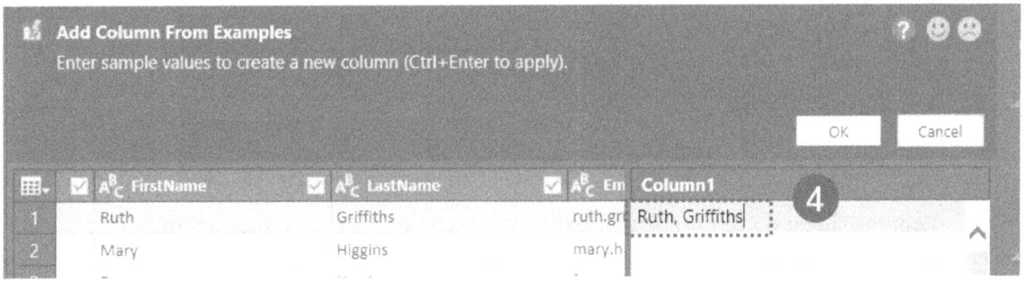

Figure 2.23 – Column from Examples with typed example and auto-filled suggestions

Power Query analyzes the pattern and fills in the remaining rows automatically. Check a few rows to confirm the results look correct.

5. If the suggestions look right, click **OK**

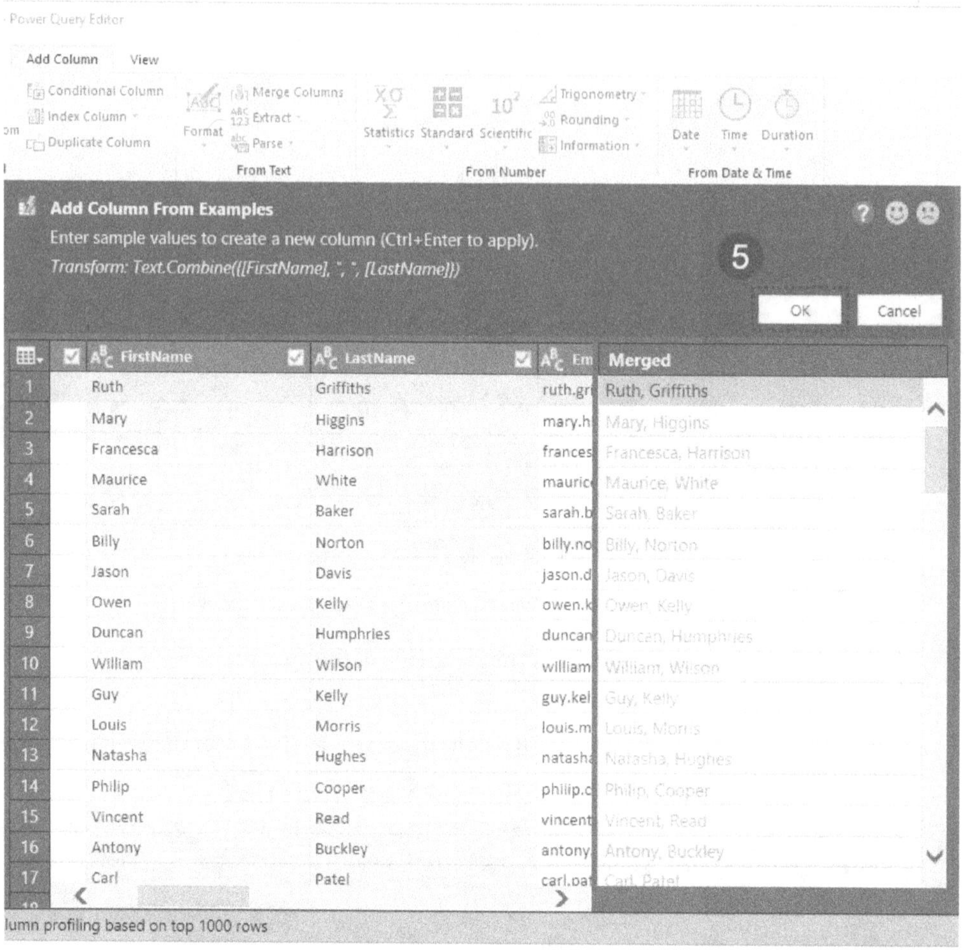

Figure 2.24 – Data preview showing the new DisplayName column generated from examples

6. Rename the new column from **Merged** to `DisplayName` by double clicking on the column's header

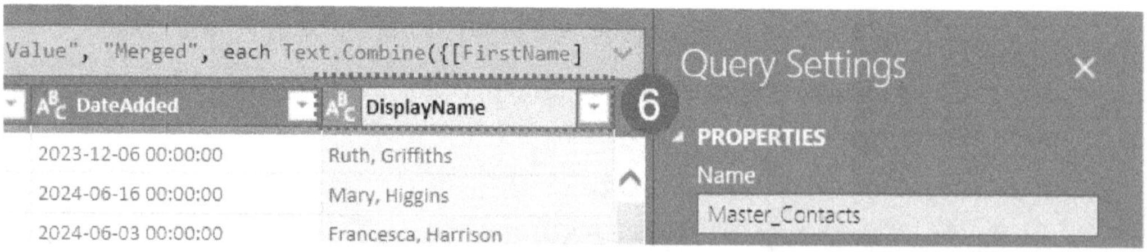

Figure 2.25 – Renaming the column to DisplayName

Amira leans in. "Did it work out the pattern from just one example?"

"Exactly. Power Query looked at the columns available and figured out how to combine them. Instead of writing a formula, you just had to show it what you wanted."

> **Tip**
>
> If Power Query doesn't get the pattern right from one example, type a second example in another row. Two or three examples are usually enough for it to understand the pattern.

Setting data types and handling blanks

Data types tell Power Query (and Excel) how to interpret each column. Getting them right prevents problems downstream.

Look at the icons in each column header:

- **ABC** = Text
- **123** = Whole number
- **1.2** = Decimal number
- **Calendar** = Date

For a contacts list, all columns should be text.

> **Note**
>
> Power Query often adds an automatic **Changed Type** step when you first connect. Review what it assumes. Sometimes, it guesses wrong (e.g., treating a phone number as a whole number, which removes leading zeros).

If Power Query guessed incorrectly:

1. Click the type icon in the column header to see the data type options
2. Select the correct type for that column (for example, text for the ContactID)

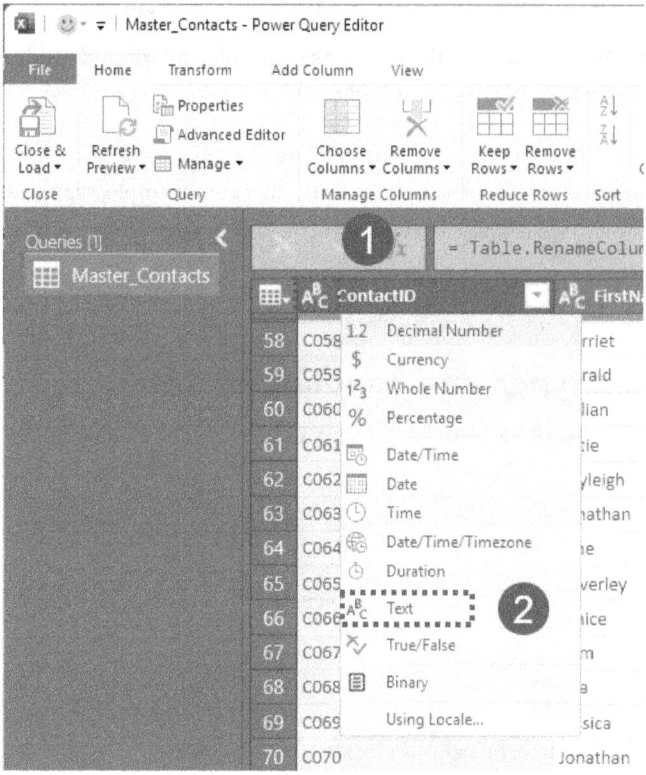

Figure 2.26 – Column header type icon dropdown showing data type options

Loading and testing the refresh loop

The query is ready. Time to load it back into Excel.

1. Click the **Home** tab on the ribbon
2. Click **Close & Load**
3. Select **Close & Load To...**

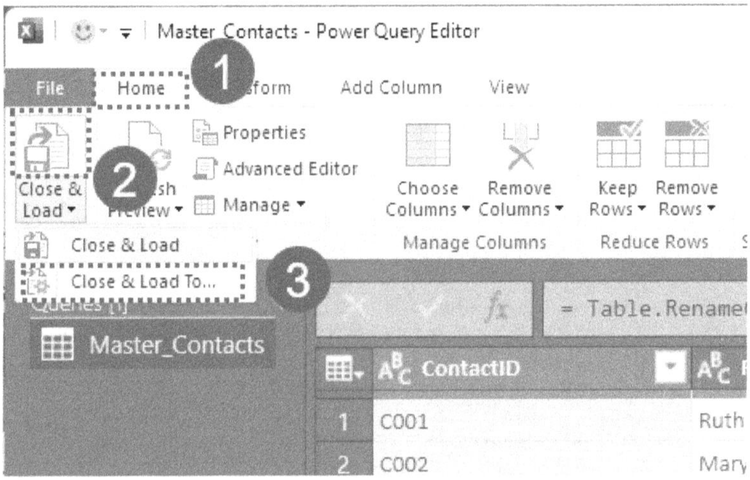

Figure 2.27 – Close and Load drop-down menu

4. In the **Import Data** dialog, select **Table** and **New worksheet**
5. Click **OK**

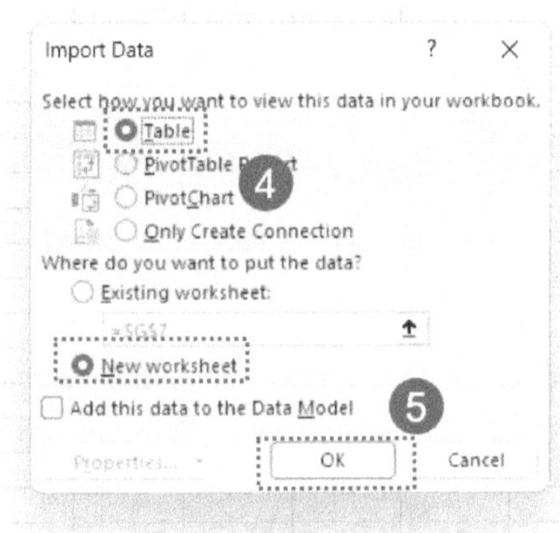

Figure 2.28 – Import Data dialog with Table and New worksheet selected

Power Query creates a new worksheet with your cleaned data in an Excel Table.

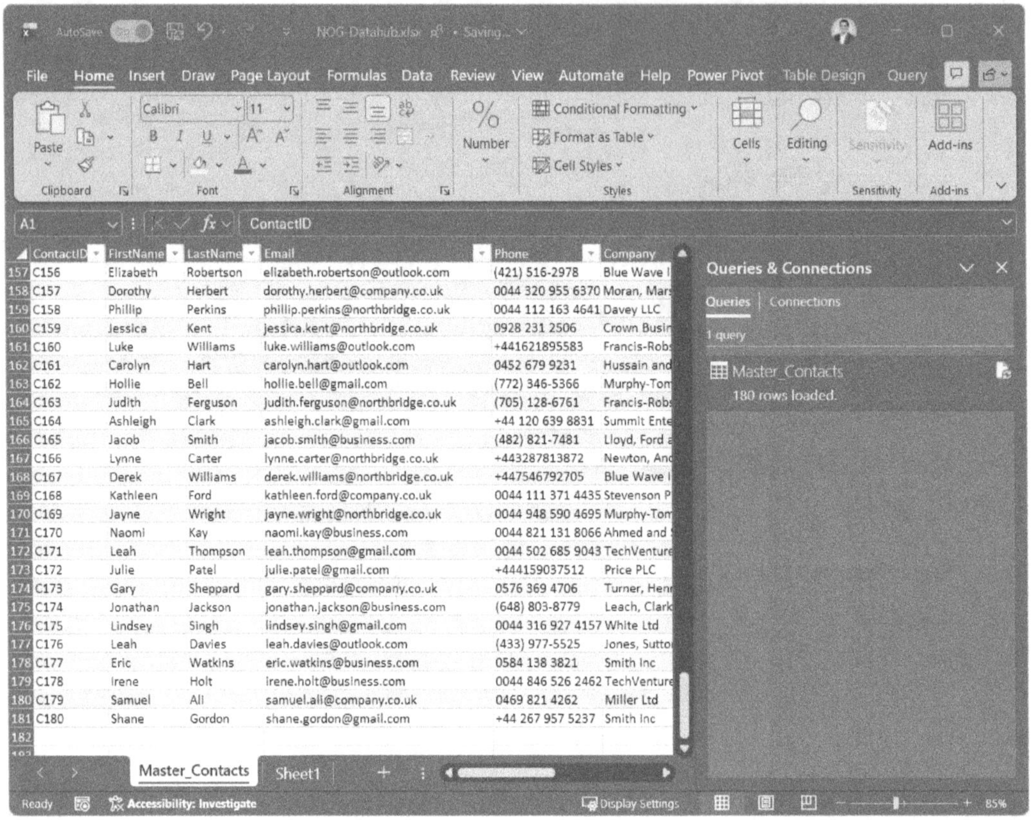

Figure 2.29 – Clean contacts table loaded in Excel

"That's it?" Amira asks.

"That's it. But watch this." Quinn asks Amira to open the original `Contacts.csv` file and add a messy row to demonstrate that the query automatically cleans new data.

Applied steps and the Power Query interface

"How did it know what to do?" Amira asks, still looking at the refreshed table.

Quinn reopens the Power Query Editor to show her what's happening behind the scenes. To edit an existing query:

1. Click the **Data** tab on the ribbon
2. Click **Queries & Connections** (a pane appears on the right)
3. Double-click **Master_Contacts** to open it in the editor

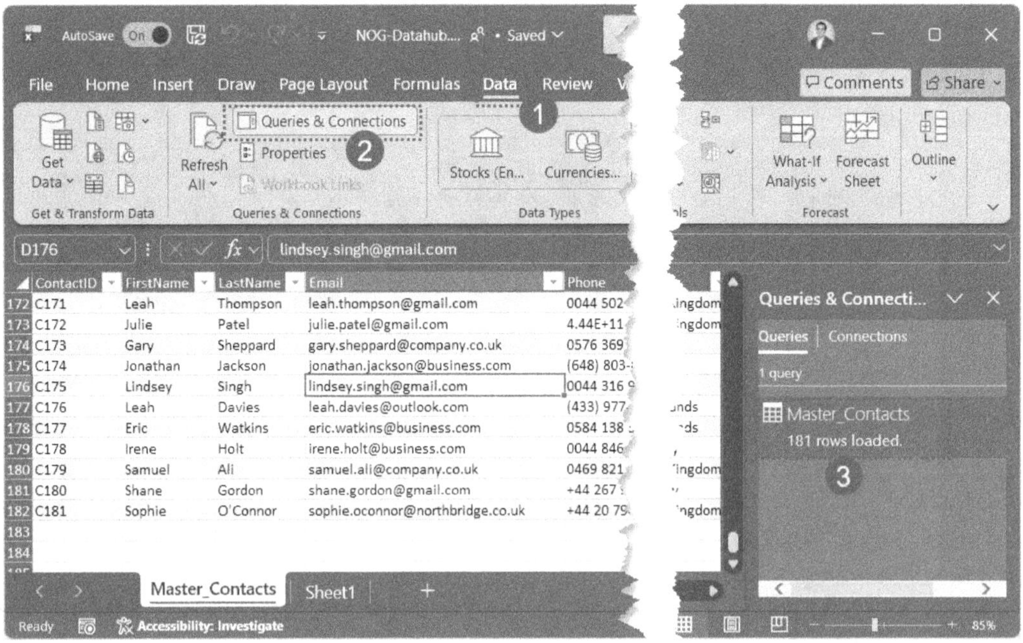

Figure 2.30 – Queries and Connections pane with Master_Contacts query

Working with applied steps

You already met the Power Query Editor interface in *Chapter 1*. The key area to focus on now is the **Applied Steps** pane on the right. It records every transformation you built in this chapter. Each step shows the data at that point in the process.

Navigate through steps:

1. Click on the **Source** step. You'll see the raw CSV data as it was imported
2. Click on **Capitalized Each Word**. Now the names are properly cased
3. Click the last step. You'll see the final, clean result

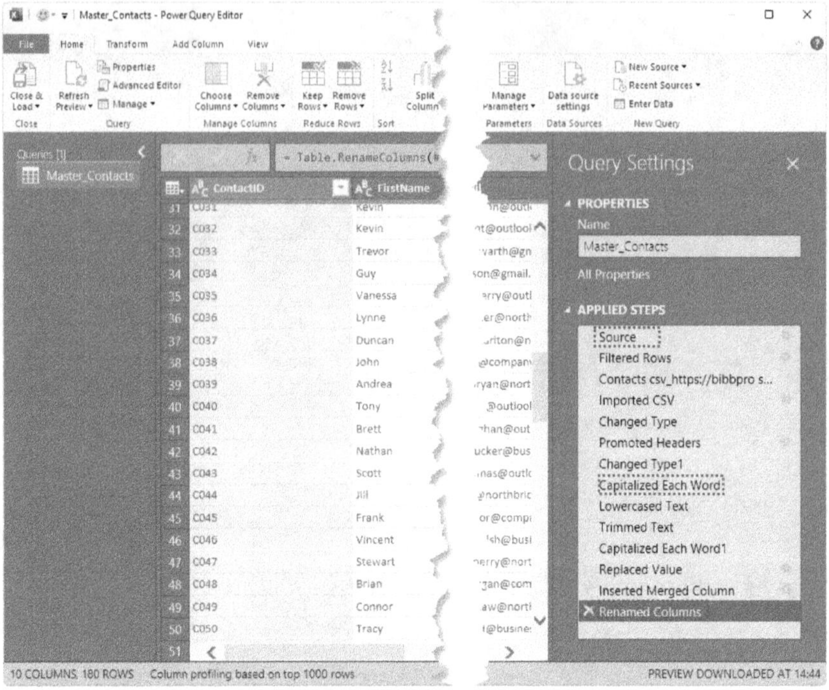

Figure 2.31 – Applied Steps pane with a step selected and data preview showing the data at that point

This is powerful for debugging. If something looks wrong in your final data, click through the steps to find where the problem started.

Caution

There is no *Ctrl* + *Z* undo in Power Query. Once you delete a step, it is gone and you will need to recreate it manually. Also, deleting a step in the middle can break the steps that follow it. Power Query will warn you if this might happen.

Why step order matters

Think of Applied Steps as a recipe. You can't frost a cake before you've baked it.

In Power Query terms:

- You can't filter by a column that hasn't been renamed yet
- You can't trim spaces in a column that's been removed
- You can't set data types on columns that don't exist

Each step builds on the previous one. If you delete or modify an early step, everything after it may break.

For example, your query has these steps:

1. Source (load the CSV)
2. Promoted Headers (use first row as column names)
3. Capitalized FirstName
4. Filtered rows where Department = "Sales"

If you delete *step 2* (Promoted Headers), *steps 3* and *4* will fail. They reference column names like **FirstName** and **Department** that only exist after promoting headers.

> **Tip**
>
> When a query suddenly shows errors, check if someone (or you) modified an earlier step. Click through the steps from the bottom up to find where the query first broke.

Passive M literacy: reading the formula bar

You don't need to write M code to use Power Query effectively. But being able to read it, even at a basic level, helps you understand what's happening and troubleshoot problems.

What each step actually does

Every step in **Applied Steps** has a corresponding M expression in the formula bar. If the formula bar is not visible:

1. Click the **View** tab on the ribbon
2. Tick the **Formula Bar** checkbox

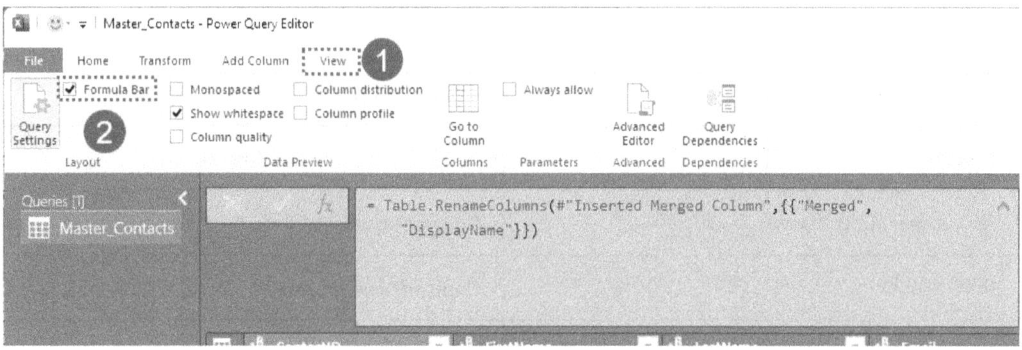

Figure 2.32 – View tab with Formula Bar checkbox enabled

Click on any step to see its code. For example, click on the **Capitalized Each Word** step. The formula bar shows:

```
= Table.TransformColumns(#"Changed Type1",{{"FirstName", Text.Proper, type text},
{"LastName", Text.Proper, type text}})
```

Let's break this down:

Part	Meaning
`Table.TransformColumns`	The function being used (transform columns in a table)
Changed Type1	Reference to the previous step's output
`"FirstName", "LastName"`	The columns being transformed
`Text.Proper`	The Transformation (Capitalize Each Word)
`type text`	The resulting data type

Table 2.4 – Breakdown of the Capitalized Each Word M expression

You don't need to memorize these. Just notice the pattern: Function (Previous Step, Details).

Here are common M functions you'll encounter:

Function	What it does
`Table.TransformColumnTypes`	Changes data types
`Table.RenameColumns`	Renames columns
`Table.ReplaceValue`	Find and replace values
`Text.Trim`	Removes leading/trailing spaces
`Text.Lower/Text.Upper`	Changes case
`Text.Proper`	Capitalizes each word
`Table.SelectRows`	Filters rows

Function	What it does
`Table.RemoveColumns`	Removes columns

Table 2.5 – Common M functions you will encounter

When you see these in the formula bar, you'll know what that step is doing without needing to write a single line of code.

Spotting steps that might cause trouble

Power Query sometimes creates steps automatically. These auto-generated steps can cause problems if you're not aware of them.

Watch out for changed type

When you connect to a data source, Power Query often guesses the data types and adds a **Changed Type** step automatically. Sometimes it guesses wrong:

- Product codes treated as dates
- Text that looks like dates converted unexpectedly
- Decimal values are missing because only whole numbers appear in the first 200 rows

Always review any automatic **Changed Type** step. Click on it and check what it assumed for each column. If you prefer to control type assignments yourself, you can disable this behavior entirely: in the Power Query Editor, go to **File** | **Options and settings** | **Query options** | **Data Load**, and set **Type detection** to **Never detect column types and headers for unstructured sources**.

Multiple changed type steps

If you have several **Changed Type** steps scattered through your query, they can conflict. It's cleaner to remove the automatic ones and set types deliberately at the end of your transformations.

Hardcoded values in filters

If you filter rows using **Replace Values** or **Filter Rows** with specific text, that text is hardcoded. If the source data changes (e.g., "Uk" is corrected to "United Kingdom" in the source file), your **Replace Values** step still runs; it just won't find a match, which is harmless. But a **Filter Rows** step looking for a value that no longer exists would return no results.

Column references by name

Steps like **Removed Columns** reference columns by their exact name. If someone renames a column in the source file, the query breaks.

> **Tip**
>
> Rename auto-generated steps to something meaningful. Right-click a step and select **Rename**. *Lowercased Emails* is clearer than *Changed Type1* when you're debugging months later.

Validate before you celebrate

Power Query makes automation easy. But automation without validation can propagate errors just as easily as it propagates correct data.

Quinn shows Amira a simple routine: after every refresh, spend thirty seconds checking that the data looks right. This quick habit catches problems before they cause bigger issues downstream.

Your quick validation checklist

After refreshing a query, check these five things:

1. **Row count**: Does the number of rows match what you expect? (Check the status bar at the bottom of the Power Query Editor, or the Excel status bar when viewing the table)
2. **Column count**: Are all expected columns present? Did any get dropped or added unexpectedly?
3. **Data types**: Do the column header icons show the correct types? (**ABC** for text, **123** for numbers, calendar for dates)
4. **Error values**: Are there any cells showing "Error"? Click the filter dropdown on any column to check for error values quickly.
5. **Spot-check**: Scroll through a few rows. Do names look properly capitalized? Are departments standardized? Anything obviously wrong?

This takes about thirty seconds. Make it a habit: **Refresh** → **Quick check** → **Use data**.

If something looks off, investigate before sharing results with others.

Running the trust loop on Master_Contacts

Let's run through the checklist with **Master_Contacts**:

Check	What to look for	Expected result
Row count	Number of rows in preview	Matches source CSV (minus header row)
Columns	ContactID, FirstName, LastName, Email, Phone, Company, Department, Country, DateAdded, DisplayName	All present
Data types	All columns show ABC (text)	Correct for contacts
Errors	No "Error" values	None visible
Spot-check	Names capitalized, emails lowercase, departments consistent, DisplayName in "Last, First" format	Looks clean

Table 2.6 – Validation checklist for Master_Contacts

Documenting your work

As your workbook grows with more queries, documentation becomes essential. A few seconds now save confusion later.

Add a query description

Follow these steps:

1. In the **Power Query Editor**, click the **View** tab on the ribbon
2. Tick the **Query Settings** checkbox (if not already visible)
3. At the top of the **Query Settings** pane, click **All Properties**

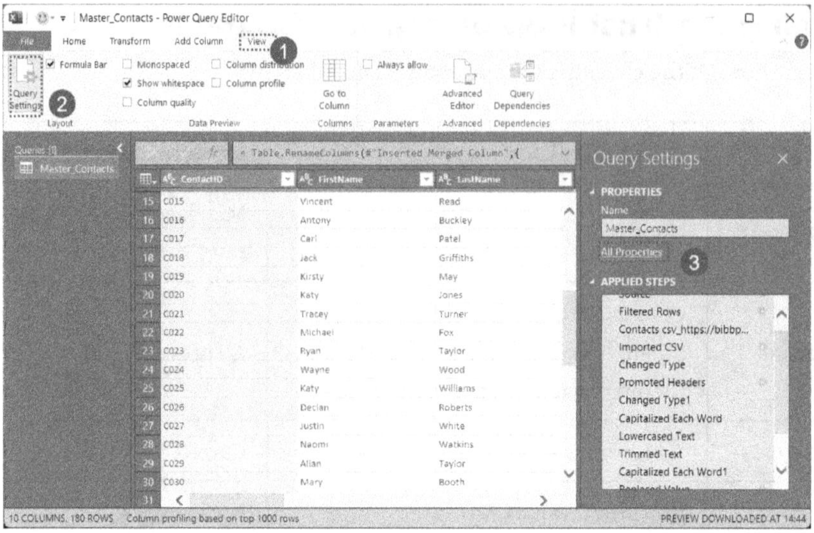

Figure 2.33 – Query Settings pane with All Properties link highlighted

4. In the **Query Properties** dialog, type a description and click **OK**

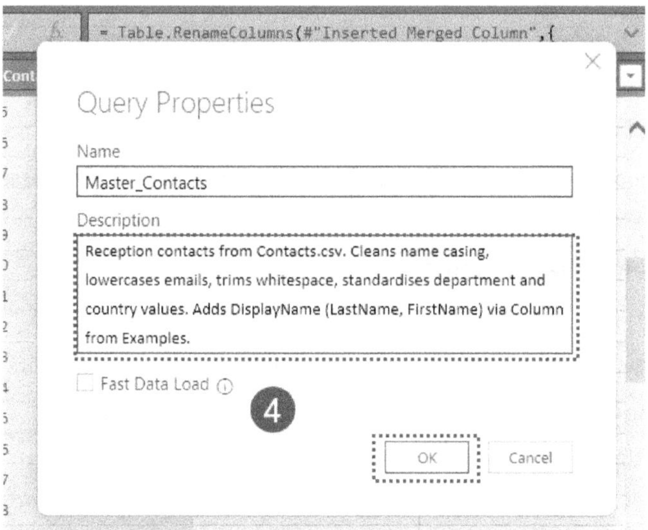

Figure 2.34 – Query Properties dialog with description field

For **Master_Contacts**, we can add something like:

```
Reception contacts from Contacts.csv. Cleans name casing, lowercases emails,
trims whitespace, standardizes department and country values. Adds DisplayName
(FirstName, LastName) via Column from Examples.
```

Rename your steps

Generic step names like "Lowercased Text" or "Replaced Value" don't help when you're debugging months later. You can change the names with these steps:

1. Right-click any step
2. Select **Rename**
3. Give it a meaningful name like `Lowercased Emails`, `Standardized Country`

Close, load and save

Now, you can click on the **Close and Load** button and save your file.

> **Tip**
>
> Future you will thank present you for taking thirty seconds to document your queries. So will colleagues who need to maintain them.

Summary

In this chapter, you've built your first complete Power Query workflow:

- **Mindset shift**: From manual, repetitive cleanup to "build once, refresh forever"
- **Your first query**: Connected to a CSV, applied transformations, used Column from Examples to create DisplayName, loaded clean data to Excel
- **Interface confidence**: Navigated the editor, understood Applied Steps, worked with the formula bar
- **Passive M literacy**: Read (not wrote) M code to understand what each step does
- **Trust habit**: Established a quick validation checklist to run after every refresh

Amira's hour-long cleanup task is now a five-second refresh. The query remembers every transformation and applies them consistently, every time.

In *Chapter 3*, Quinn helps Tom combine four monthly session exports into a single, reliable sessions catalog using the Folder connector and a mapping table. The cleanup patterns you've learned here will carry forward.

3

Connect and Standardize Common Business Sources

Figure 3.1 – Quinn helps Tom standardize his data

Quinn is at the coffee machine when Tom from the Events team approaches her.

"Hey Quinn, Amira told me you did something clever with her contacts file. I think I've got a similar mess, but worse."

"Sure," says Quinn. "Let me come back to you after lunch." Tom manages NOG's training and events calendar. Every month, the booking system exports a new spreadsheet with that month's session details: titles, facilitators, dates, locations. Because the system uses free-text fields rather than controlled dropdowns, different staff members enter the same values in different ways. The exports land in a shared folder, one file per month.

After lunch, Quinn meets Tom in the meeting room. "The problem," Tom says, while sharing his screen on the monitor, "is that each month the data is slightly different. One file says 'Workshop', another says 'WORKSHOP'. Facilitators are listed as 'John Smith' in one month and 'J. Smith' the next. I end up copying everything into a separate spreadsheet by hand and fixing it all manually."

Quinn looks at the four files on Tom's screen, October through January, and sees a pattern. It's true that this is a very similar problem to the one he had, but multiplied across files and folders.

"This seems to be something that we can fix. We can set up Power Query to pull the files together automatically," Quinn says, "and clean them up in one go."

Tom raises an eyebrow. "All four? At once?"

"All four. And when February's file arrives, you just click Refresh."

In this chapter, you'll learn to -

- Connect to authoritative data sources and identify which business lists should become reference tables
- Use the Folder connector to combine multiple monthly Excel exports into a single, refreshable table
- Shape raw session data into a clean **Master_Sessions** reference table by renaming, pruning, and enforcing one row per **SessionID**
- Standardize names and categories using casing fixes, Replace Values, and mapping tables merged into the main query
- Implement lightweight governance for reference tables: check for duplicate keys, validate row counts, and document query purpose

> Note
>
> **Download the code bundle and the PDF version of this book**
>
> Your purchase includes a DRM-free PDF copy of this book, the code bundle, and a range of exclusive benefits. To unlock everything, follow the *Free benefits with your book* section in the *Preface*.

Technical requirements

The chapters in this book build on each other. Make sure you have completed all exercises in the previous chapter before starting this one.

To follow along with this chapter, you will need:

- Microsoft Excel 2016 or later with Power Query available (via **Data** | **Get & Transform Data**)
- Your `NOG-DataHub` workbook from *Chapter 2*, which should already contain the following query:
  - **Master_Contacts_** the cleaned contacts reference table loaded as **Connection Only**
- The following exercise files from your `NOG-DataHub` folder:
  - `Events/Sessions`
    - `Sessions_2025-10.xlsx`
    - `Sessions_2025-11.xlsx`
    - `Sessions_2025-12.xlsx`
    - `Sessions_2026-01.xlsx`
  - `Reference/`
    - `Map_Facilitators.xlsx`

From scattered files to a single source of truth

Tom's situation is a common business scenario. Data arrives in regular batches, like monthly exports, weekly reports, quarterly dumps, and someone has to stitch them together. The manual approach creates problems:

- **Version drift**: Each month's copy gets slightly different fixes
- **Missed updates**: A correction in October's file never reaches the master spreadsheet
- **Inconsistent labels**: Without a single standard, every month invents its own naming

The solution is to connect directly to the source files and let Power Query combine and clean them. Instead of copying data out of files, we can make Power Query point at the folder where the files live. When new files (or even folders) appear, a refresh picks them up.

This is where the concept of a **reference table** comes in. A reference table is a single, reliable list that other reports can depend on. For Tom, that's a sessions catalog: one table with every session, every facilitator, every date, standardized and trustworthy. We'll call it **Master_Sessions**.

Quinn opens the `NOG-DataHub` and navigates to the `Events` folder.

It has four monthly files, each containing session metadata: IDs, names, types, facilitators, dates, durations, capacities, locations, and statuses.

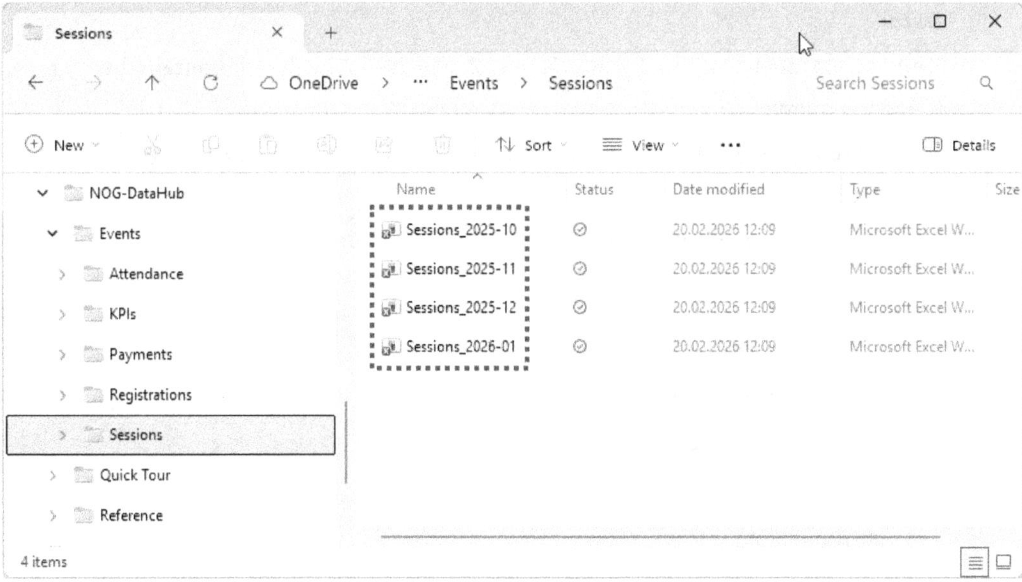

Figure 3.2 – The Events/Sessions/ folder with four monthly session export files

"These files are the source of truth," Quinn tells Tom. "We won't copy or move the data out of them; we'll connect to the folder itself. That way, when your system exports a new month, Power Query sees it automatically."

In *Chapter 1* and *Chapter 2*, you connected to a folder and filtered to a single file. This time, you'll connect to a folder and combine all the files inside it. The cleanup patterns from *Chapter 2*, that is casing, trimming, and replacing values, still apply. The new skill is combining multiple files into one table.

Connecting to the sessions folder

> **Important**
>
> For this exercise, use the four files in the `Events/Sessions/` folder in your `NOG-DataHub`:
>
> - `Sessions_2025-10.xlsx`
> - `Sessions_2025-11.xlsx`
> - `Sessions_2025-12.xlsx`
> - `Sessions_2026-01.xlsx`

Connect to the NOG-DataHub folder

By now you've connected to the `NOG-DataHub` folder twice: once in *Chapter 1* and once in *Chapter 2*. Follow the same pattern:

Connect to a folder (SharePoint or local)

Follow these steps:

1. Continue in your `NOG-DataHub` workbook from *Chapter 2*
2. Click the **Data** tab
3. Click **Get Data**
4. Click **From File**
5. Choose one of the following:
    - **From SharePoint Folder** (for cloud files)
    - **From Folder** (for local files)
6. Provide the location:
    - If using **SharePoint** → paste your **SharePoint site URL** and click **OK**
    - If using **Local Folder** → browse to your `NOG-DataHub` folder and click **OK**
7. If prompted (SharePoint only), sign in with your Microsoft account
8. Click **Transform Data** to open the Power Query Editor

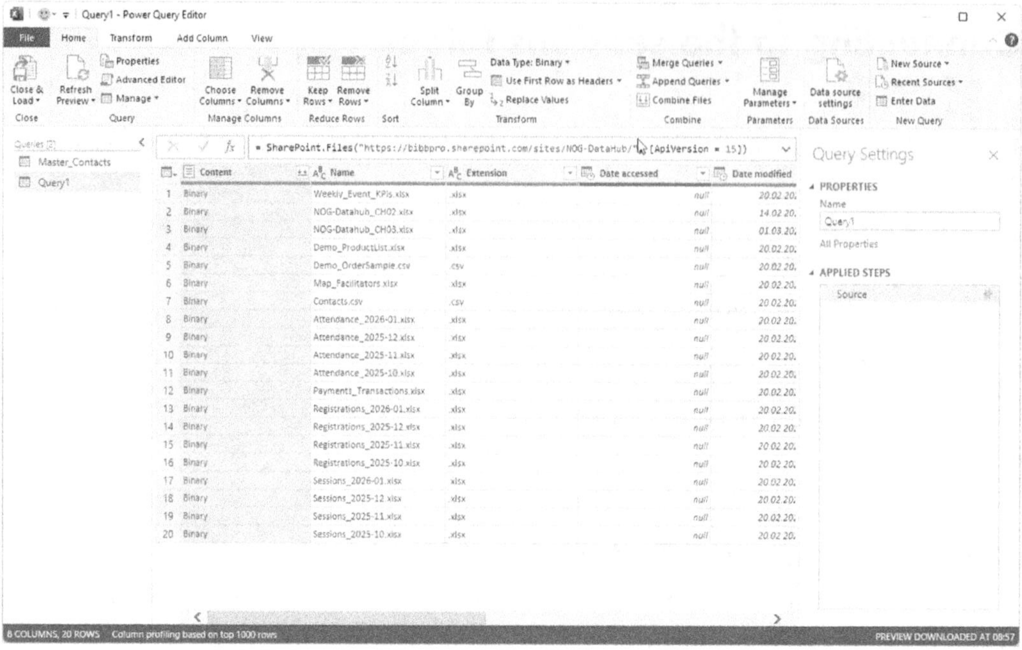

Figure 3.3 – File listing after connecting to the NOG-DataHub folder

Filter to the sessions folder

Power Query shows all files in the `NOG-DataHub`. We need to narrow it down to the `Sessions` folder:

1. In the **Folder Path** column, click the filter dropdown
2. Click **Text Filters**
3. Click **Contains**

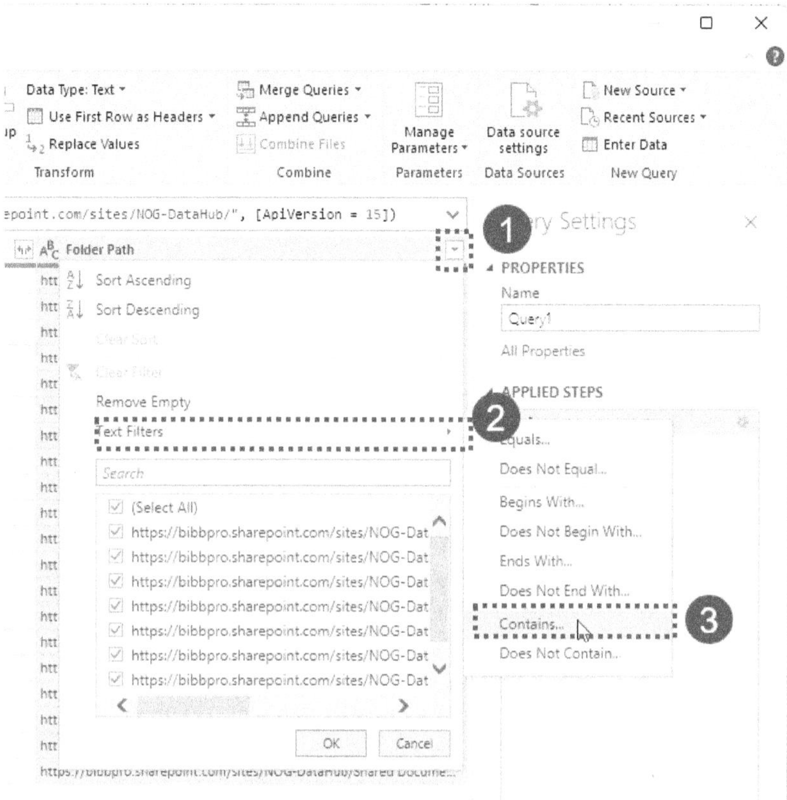

Figure 3.4 – Text Filters menu expanded to show the Contains option

4. Type `Sessions`
5. Click **OK**

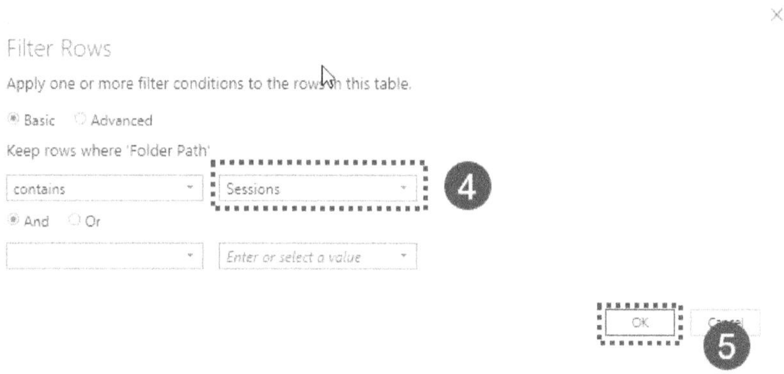

Figure 3.5 – Filter Rows dialog with Sessions typed in the value field

You should now see four rows, one for each monthly file.

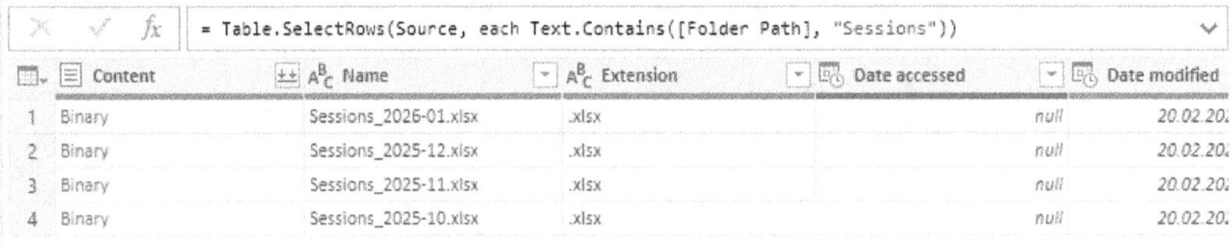

Figure 3.6 – Four Sessions files after filtering

Combine the files

In Chapters 1 and 2, you filtered down to a single file and clicked the `Binary` link in the Content column to open it. This time, you have four files and you want to combine them all into one table:

1. In the **Query Settings** pane on the right, rename the query to `Master_Sessions`

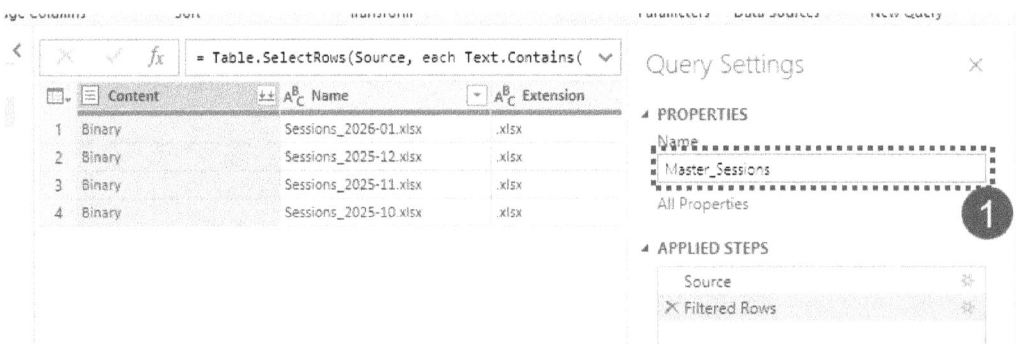

Figure 3.7 – Renaming the query to Master_Sessions

2. Click the **Combine Files** button (the double-arrow icon) at the top of the **Content** column.

   If you cannot see the **Content** column, drag the Power Query Editor window wider or scroll right; it is the last column on the right.

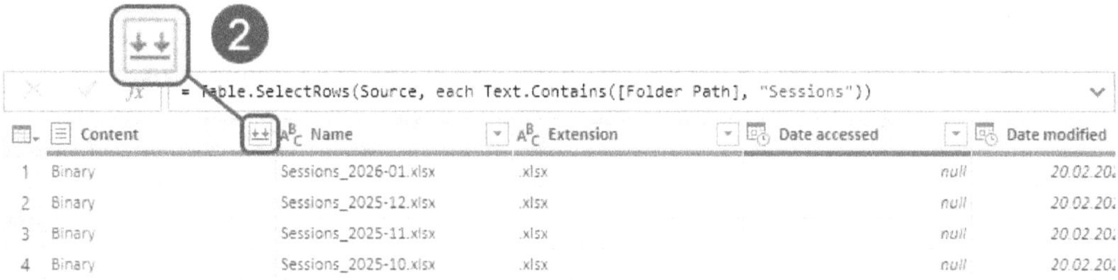

Figure 3.8 – Combine Files button in the Content column

3. In the **Combine Files** dialog, select the sheet or table to use. Click **Sheet1** in the left panel to select it as the sample
4. Verify that the preview shows the expected columns: **SessionID**, **SessionName**, **SessionType**, and so on
5. Click **OK**

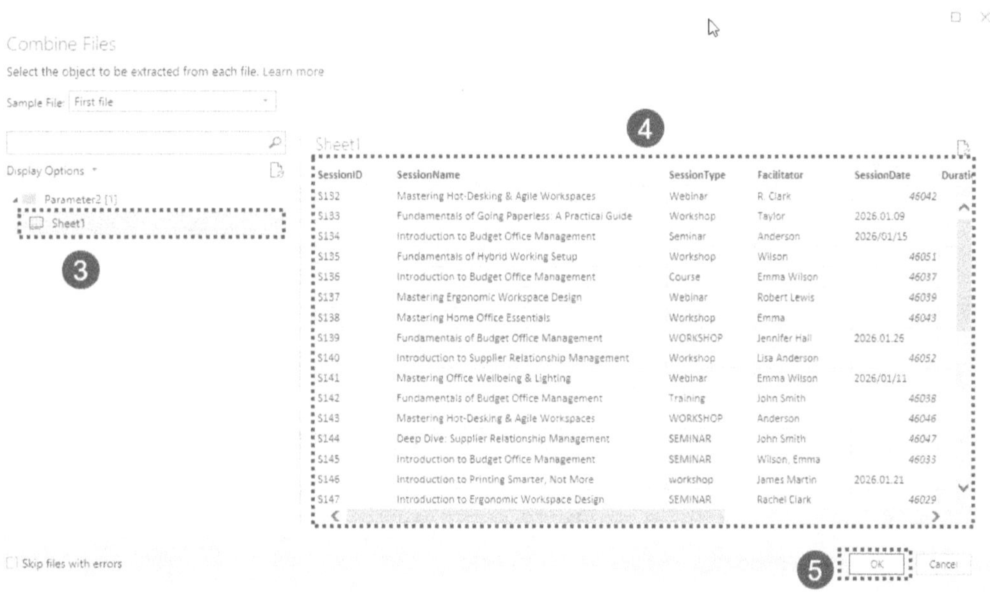

Figure 3.9 – Combine Files dialog with the Sessions object selected and preview visible

Caution

This approach only works when all files in the folder have **the same column structure**: identical column names, in the same order, across every file. If one month's export has an extra column, a renamed header, or columns in a different order, the combined table will have misaligned data or errors. Always verify the preview before clicking **OK**, and check with whoever produces the exports that the structure is consistent.

Power Query combines all four files into a single table. Notice the **Source.Name** column on the left. It shows which file each row came from (e.g., "`Sessions_2025-10.xlsx`").

Figure 3.10 – Combined data with Source.Name column showing file origins

When Tom's system exports February's file to the `Sessions` folder, he will just need to click **Refresh**. Power Query will scan the folder again and pick up the new file automatically, no manual copy-paste needed.

Note

After combining files, Power Query creates several helper queries in the **Queries** pane (you may see names like **Transform File**, **Transform Sample File**, and a parameters query). These are part of the combine machinery; leave them as they are. We'll focus on the main **Master_Sessions** query.

Shaping raw Sessions into Master_Sessions

The combined data is raw. Before standardizing values, let's shape the table into a clean structure.

Check the headers

Look at the column names in the preview. After combining, Power Query should have promoted the first row of each file as headers. Verify you see columns like **SessionID**, **SessionName**, **SessionType**, **Facilitator**, **SessionDate**, **Duration**, **MaxCapacity**, **Location**, and **Status**.

If the first row shows generic names (`Column1`, `Column2`, etc.), the headers need to be promoted in the Transform Sample File query, not here. In the **Queries** pane, click **Transform Sample File**, then click the **Transform** tab and click **Use First Row as Headers**. Switch back to **Master_Sessions**; the column names should now appear.

correctly.

Remove extra columns

The combine process added a **Source.Name** column showing which file each row came from. It is useful for debugging, but **Master_Sessions** is a reference table. It does not need file provenance. Follow these steps to remove the extra columns:

1. Right-click the **Source.Name** column header
2. Click **Remove**

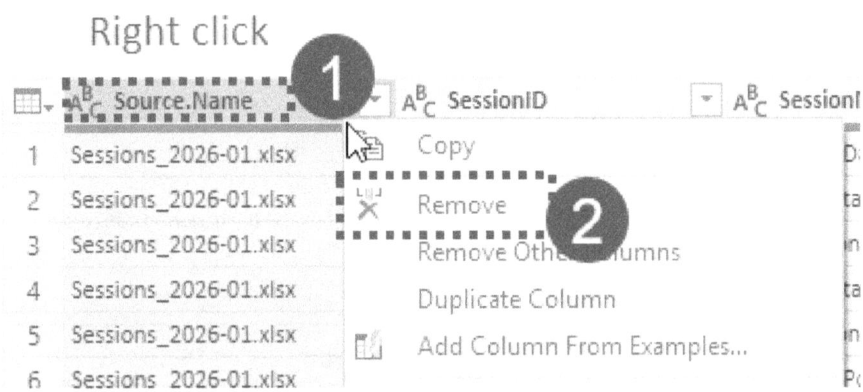

Figure 3.11 – Removing the Source.Name column added by the combine step

> **Tip**
>
> If you ever need to trace which file a row came from, for example, to investigate a data quality issue; keep **Source.Name** temporarily and remove it once you've finished debugging. Rename it to `SourceFile` first so it stands out clearly in the column list.

Set data types

Power Query may have guessed data types during the *combine* step. Let's set them deliberately:

1. Click the type icon in the **SessionID** column header
2. Select **Text**

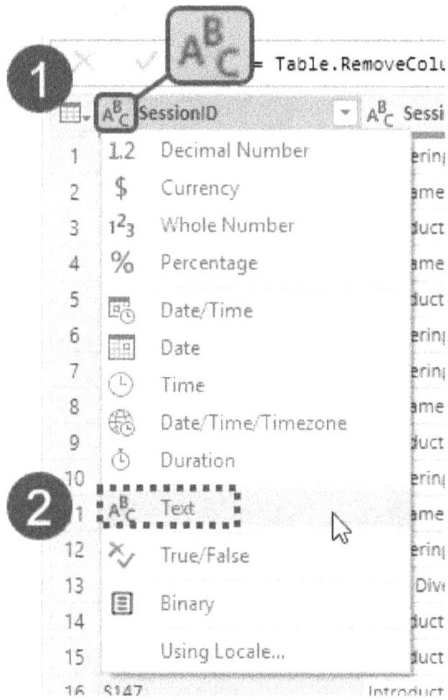

Figure 3.12 – Column header icons showing the assigned data types

Repeat for each column:

Column	Data Type
SessionID	Text
SessionName	Text

Column	Data Type
SessionType	Text
Facilitator	Text
SessionDate	Date
Duration	Decimal Number
MaxCapacity	Whole Number
Location	Text
Status	Text

Table 3.1 – Data types for Master_Sessions columns

Note

After changing the data type for **SessionDate** to **Date**, you may see a few error values. Some rows in the source files store dates as text strings (e.g., "2025-10-11" without time information), which Power Query handles slightly differently. Don't worry about these for now. Note the pattern. We'll address data type issues more thoroughly as we progress through the book.

Quick validation

Before moving on, run a quick trust loop:

Check	Expected
Row count	~167 rows (status bar at the bottom)
Columns	9 columns: SessionID through Status
Data types	Icons match Table 3.1
Errors	A few possible in SessionDate (noted above)

Table 3.2 – Validation checkpoint after shaping

The column and row count is visible on the status bar at the bottom:

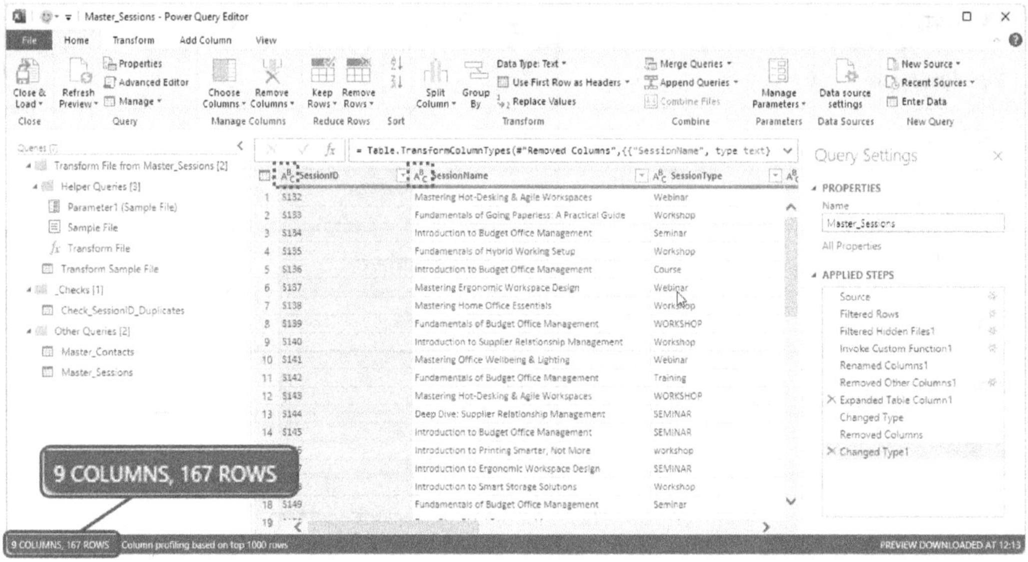

Figure 3.13 – Status bar showing row and column count after shaping

Standardizing names, types, and labels

The data is shaped, but the values inside it are still messy. This is where the real cleanup happens.

Discover the mess

Before transforming anything, take a moment to explore the data. Click the filter dropdown on a few columns to see what you're dealing with:

1. Click the filter dropdown on the **SessionType** column. You'll see values like `Workshop`, `workshop`, `WORKSHOP`, `Seminar`, `SEMINAR`, `Course`, `Training`, `Webinar`, that is, the same type spelled in different ways.

Figure 3.14 – Filter dropdown on SessionType showcasing variants

2. Click the filter dropdown on the **Location** column. You'll see values like `Online`, `online`, `ONLINE`, `Virtual`, along with physical locations like `London`, `Office`, `Manchester Hub`, and `Birmingham Centre`.
3. Click the filter dropdown on the **Status** column. You'll see values like `Active`, `active`, `Confirmed`, `CONFIRMED`, `Scheduled`.
4. Click the filter dropdown on the **Facilitator** column. This one is the worst. You'll see variants like `John Smith`, `J. Smith`, `John, Smith`, all referring to the same person. There are 38 different values for just 10 facilitators.

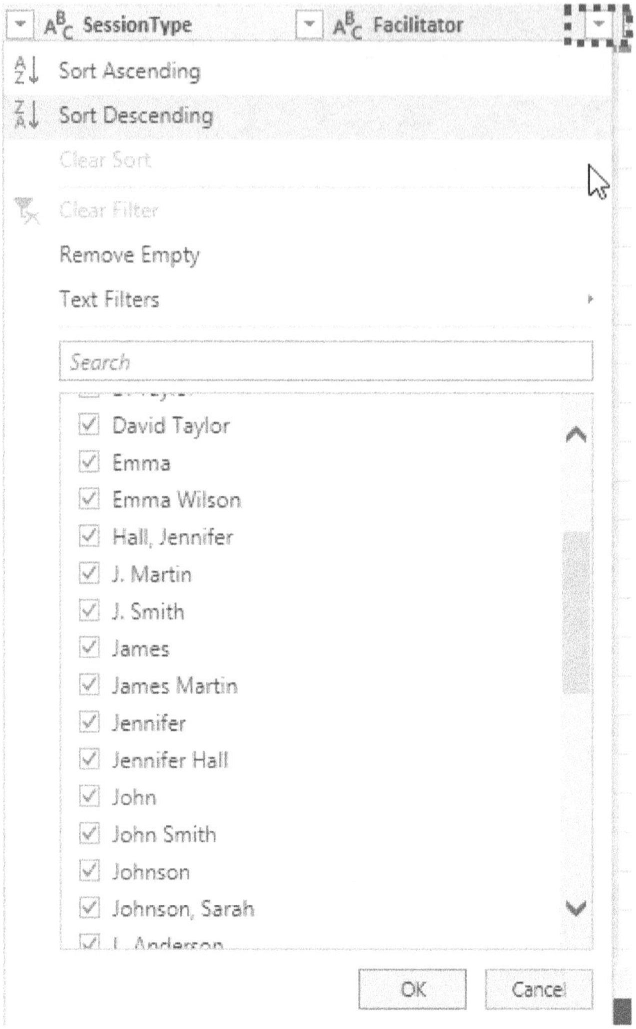

Figure 3.15 – Filter dropdown on Facilitator showing name variants

Tip

Always explore your data with filter dropdowns before you start transforming. You need to see the problem clearly before you can fix it properly. Bear in mind that Power Query only loads a preview of the data (typically the first 1,000 rows), so the filter dropdown reflects that sample rather than the full dataset. If your data is larger, Power Query will show a warning directly in the filter menu as a reminder to verify with the full load before drawing conclusions.

Click *Cancel* to close the filter dropdown before continuing.

Quick wins: session type, location, and status

The casing variants in **SessionType**, **Location**, and **Status** are easy to fix. These are the same patterns you used in *Chapter 2*. You can apply casing to all three columns at once.

Fix casing for all three columns:

1. Click the **SessionType** column header
2. Hold *Ctrl* and click the **Location** column header
3. Hold *Ctrl* and click the **Status** column header
4. Click the **Transform** tab
5. Click **Format**
6. Click **Capitalize Each Word**

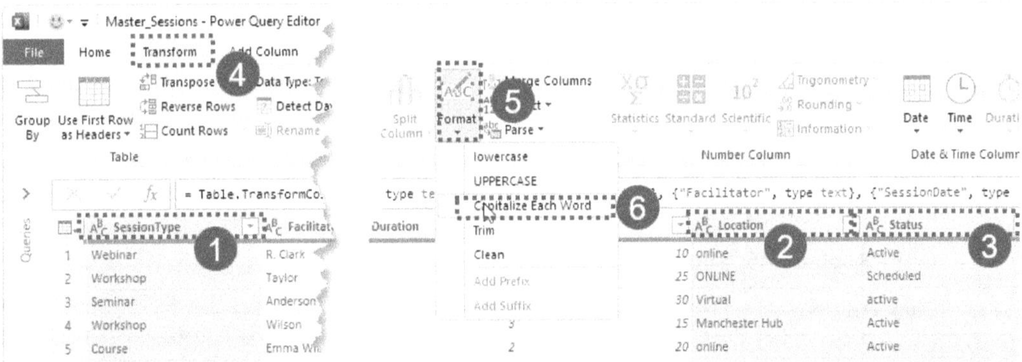

Figure 3.16 – Applying Capitalize Each Word to SessionType, Location, and Status in one step

This converts all three columns in a single step: `workshop` and `WORKSHOP` become `Workshop`, `online` and `ONLINE` become `Online`, `active` becomes `Active`, and so on. Now fix Location synonyms. `Virtual` is still a separate value from `Online`. Let's consolidate it.

7. Right-click the **Location** column header
8. Click **Replace Values**

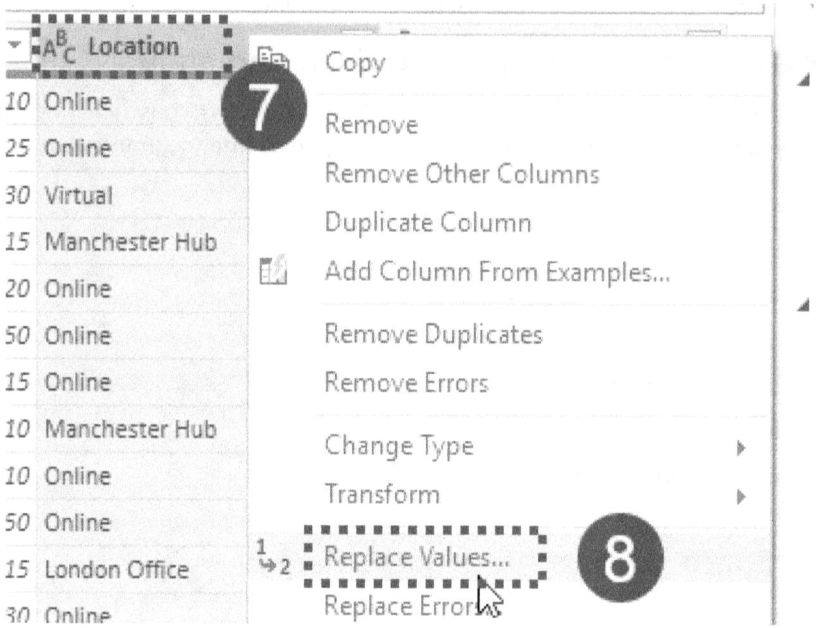

Figure 3.17 – Replace Values in the Location column right-click context menu

9. In the **Value to Find** box, type `Virtual`
10. In the **Replace With box**, type `Online`
11. Click **OK**

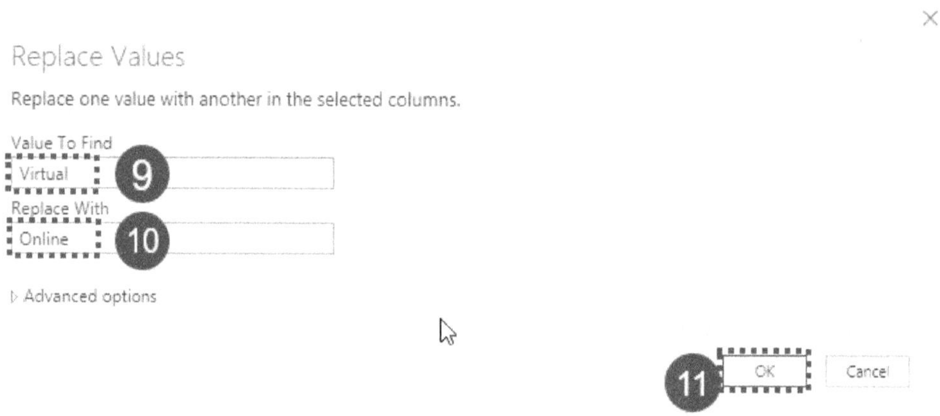

Figure 3.18 – Replace Values dialog replacing Virtual with Online

`Virtual` now maps to `Online`, giving you one consistent value for remote sessions.

Click the filter dropdowns on **SessionType**, **Location**, and **Status** again to verify. You should now see clean, consistent values:

Column	Before	After
SessionType	Workshop, workshop, WORKSHOP, Seminar, SEMINAR, Course, Training, Webinar	Workshop, Seminar, Course, Training, Webinar
Location	Online, online, ONLINE, Virtual, London Office, Manchester Hub, Birmingham Center	Online, London Office, Manchester Hub, Birmingham Centre
Status	Active, active, Confirmed, CONFIRMED, Scheduled	Active, Confirmed, Scheduled

Table 3.3 – SessionType, Location, and Status before and after standardization

The facilitator problem: why casing alone isn't enough

If you apply **Capitalize Each Word** to the **Facilitator** column, `john smith` becomes `John Smith` but `J. Smith`, `Smith`, and `John` remain separate values. These aren't casing variants; they're entirely different strings that all refer to the same person.

For this kind of problem, you need a **mapping table**: a small lookup that maps each messy value to a clean, standard name.

Here are the ten facilitators in Tom's data, along with the variants that appear across the four monthly files:

Standard Name	Variants in the Data
John Smith	John Smith; J. Smith; John, Smith
Sarah Johnson	Sarah Johnson; Johnson, Sarah; Johnson, Sarah
Michael Brown	Michael Brown; M. Brown; Brown; Brown, Michael
Emma Wilson	Emma Wilson; Emma, Wilson; Wilson, Emma

Standard Name	Variants in the Data
David Taylor	David Taylor; D. Taylor; Taylor; Taylor, David
Rachel Clark	Rachel Clark; R. Clark; Rachel, Clark; Clark, Rachel
James Martin	James Martin; J. Martin; Martin James
Jennifer Hall	Jennifer Hall; Jennifer, Hall; Jennifer
Robert Lewis	Robert Lewis; Robert Lewis; Lewis, Robert
Lisa Anderson	Lisa Anderson; L. Anderson; Anderson

Table 3.4 – Facilitator name variants across the session files

That's 38 different values for 10 people. No amount of **Capitalize Each Word** or **Replace Values** steps will sort this out cleanly. A mapping table solves it in one go.

AI Helper

Building a mapping table from your own data

In real projects, you will need to build this mapping table yourself. If you have access to an AI assistant (such as ChatGPT, Copilot, or Claude), it can help you draft it. Copy the list of unique Facilitator values from the filter dropdown and paste them into a prompt like: `Given these facilitator name variants: [paste values], create a mapping table with two columns, OriginalValue and StandardName, that maps each variant to the most complete version of the name.` The AI will suggest a mapping. **Always verify the suggestions against your actual data**: check that every **OriginalValue** matches a real value in your Facilitator column and that the **StandardName** is correct. AI suggestions are a starting point, not a final answer.

Load the mapping table

The mapping table is already prepared for you in the exercise files. You will find it at:

```
NOG-DataHub/
└── Reference/
    └── Map_Facilitators.xlsx
```

It has two columns: **OriginalValue** (every name variant from the session files) and **StandardName** (the clean, canonical version):

OriginalValue	StandardName
J. Smith	John Smith
John	John Smith
Smith	John Smith
Johnson, Sarah	Sarah Johnson
M. Brown	Michael Brown

Table 3.5 – Sample rows from Map_Facilitators.xlsx (38 rows total, one per variant)

To load it, follow the same folder connector pattern from earlier in this chapter but this time, you add the connection from inside the Power Query Editor, without closing it first.

Until now, you started new queries from the Excel ribbon (**Data | Get Data**). The Power Query Editor has its own **New Source** button on the **Home** tab that does the same thing. This lets you add a second query while you are already working in the editor, keeping both queries in the same session.

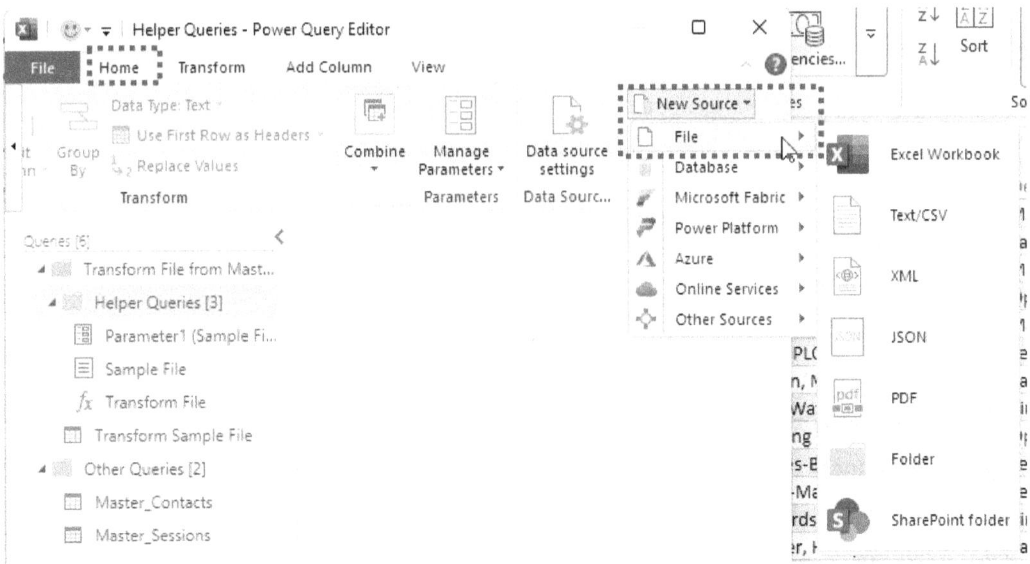

Figure 3.19 – The New Source button on the Home tab of the Power Query Editor

> **Important**
>
> For this exercise, we will connect to the `Map_Facilitators.xlsx` file from the `Reference/` folder in your `NOG-DataHub`.

Connect to the folder

Follow these steps:

1. In the Power Query Editor, click the **Home** tab
2. Click **New Source**
3. Click **File**
4. Choose one of the following:
    - **From SharePoint Folder**
    - **From Folder**
5. Provide the location
    - If using **SharePoint Folder** → Paste your SharePoint site URL and click **OK**
    - If using **Local Folder** → Browse to your `NOG-DataHub` folder and click **OK**
6. If prompted, sign in with your Microsoft account
7. Click **Transform Data**

Filter to the file

Follow these steps:

1. In the **Folder Path** column, click the filter dropdown
2. Click **Text Filters**
3. Click **Contains**
4. Type `Reference`
5. Click **OK**
6. In the **Name** column, click the filter dropdown
7. Click **Text Filters**
8. Click **Equals**
9. Type `Map_Facilitators.xlsx`
10. Click **OK**

> **Tip**
>
> Filtering on both the folder path and the filename is good practice. In SharePoint environments, it is common to have files with the same name in different folders. Filtering on path alone could return multiple matches, and filtering on filename alone would too. Combining both filters pins the query to exactly one file.

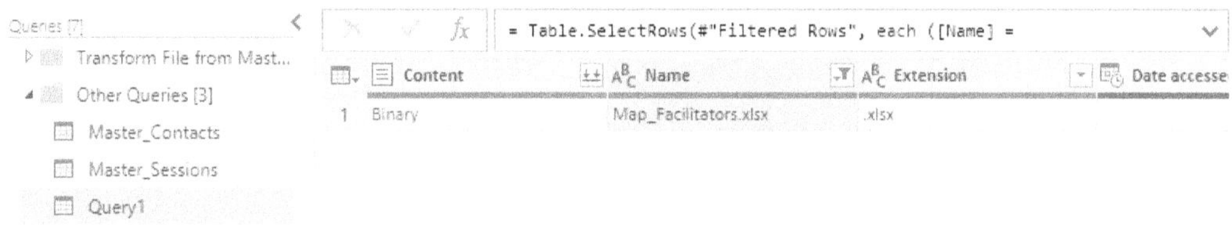

Figure 3.20 – Folder listing filtered to Map_Facilitators.xlsx in the Reference folder

11. Click the **Binary** link in the **Content** column to open the file

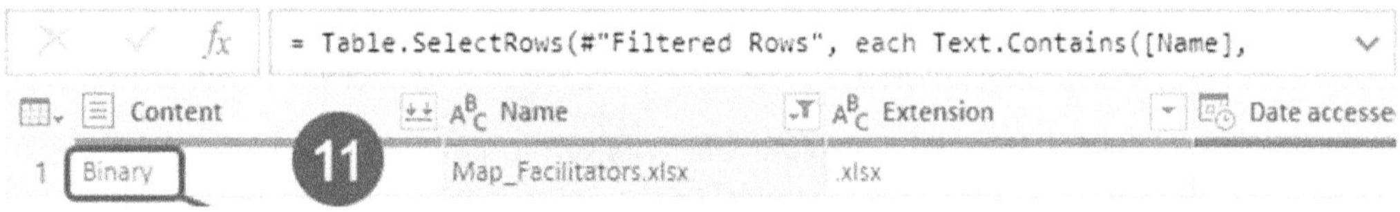

Figure 3.21 – Binary link in the Content column for Map_Facilitators.xlsx

12. In the navigation table, find the row where **Kind** is **Table** and click the **Table** link in its **Data** column

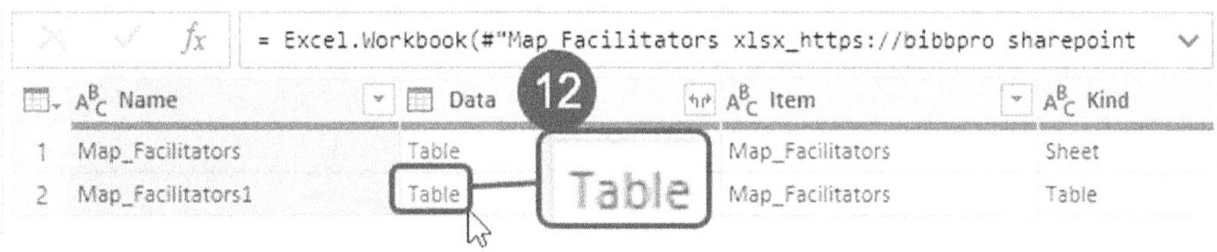

Figure 3.22 – Navigation table showing the Table row for Map_Facilitators

Power Query opens the file and displays the **OriginalValue** and **StandardName** columns.

	OriginalValue	StandardName
1	John Smith	John Smith
2	J. Smith	John Smith
3	John	John Smith
4	Smith	John Smith
5	Sarah Johnson	Sarah Johnson
6	Johnson	Sarah Johnson
7	Sarah	Sarah Johnson
8	Johnson, Sarah	Sarah Johnson
9	Michael Brown	Michael Brown

Figure 3.23 – Map_Facilitators query showing OriginalValue and StandardName columns

13. In the **Query Settings** pane, rename the query to `Map_Facilitators`

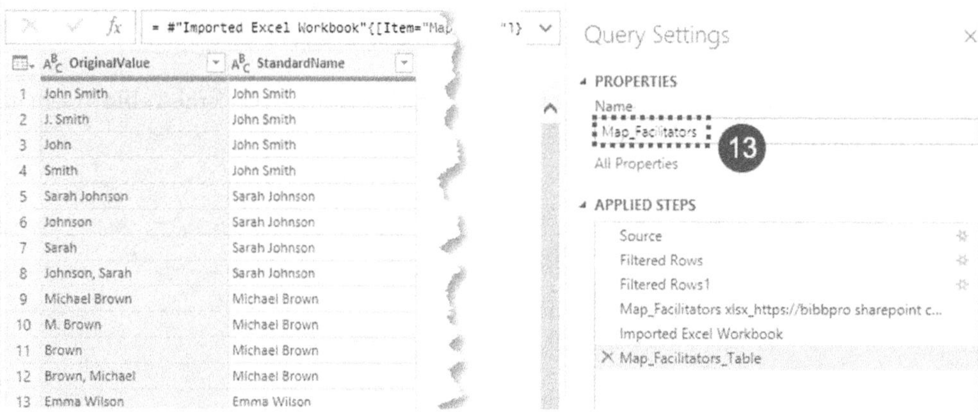

Figure 3.24 – Map_Facilitators query visible in the Queries pane

> **Tip**
>
> For a smaller mapping table (five to ten rows), **Home | Enter Data** lets you type values directly in the editor without a separate file. For 39 rows, loading from a file is far more practical. Bear in mind that values entered via **Enter Data** are embedded in the query

itself; if the mapping ever needs updating, you will have to re-enter the values manually in the editor. For anything you expect to reuse or maintain, a separate file is always the better choice.

Merge the mapping table into Master_Sessions

Now let's join the mapping table to **Master_Sessions** so that each messy **Facilitator** value is replaced with its standard name:

1. In the **Queries** pane, click **Master_Sessions** to switch back to it
2. Click the **Home** tab
3. Click **Merge Queries**

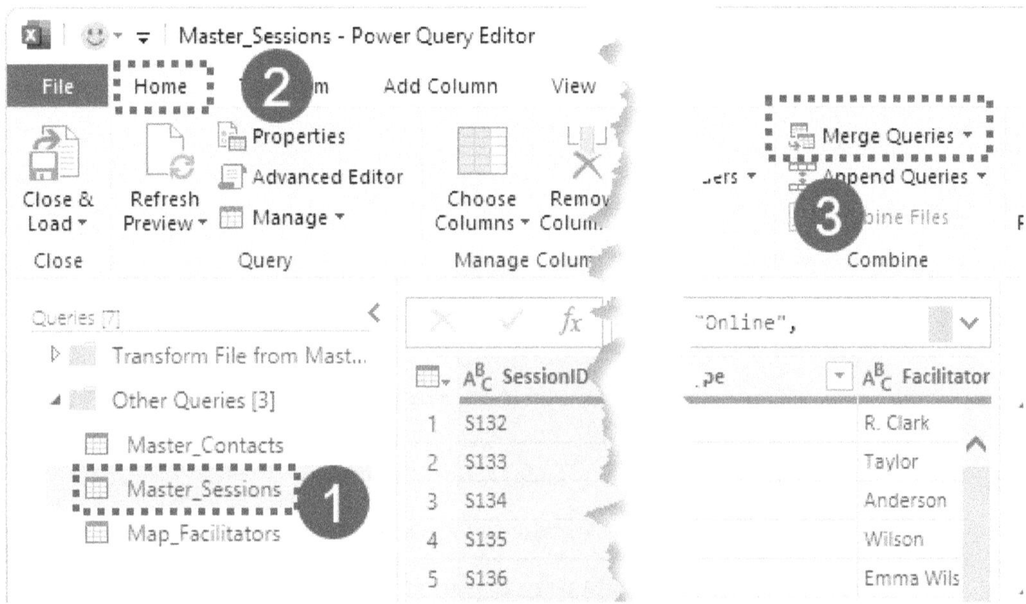

Figure 3.25 – Merge Queries button on the Home tab

4. In the **Merge** dialog, click the **Facilitator** column in the **Master_Sessions** table (top half)
5. Select **Map_Facilitators** from the dropdown (bottom half)
6. Click the **OriginalValue** column in the **Map_Facilitators** table
7. Leave the **Join Kind** as **Left Outer** (all from first, matching from second)
8. Click **OK**

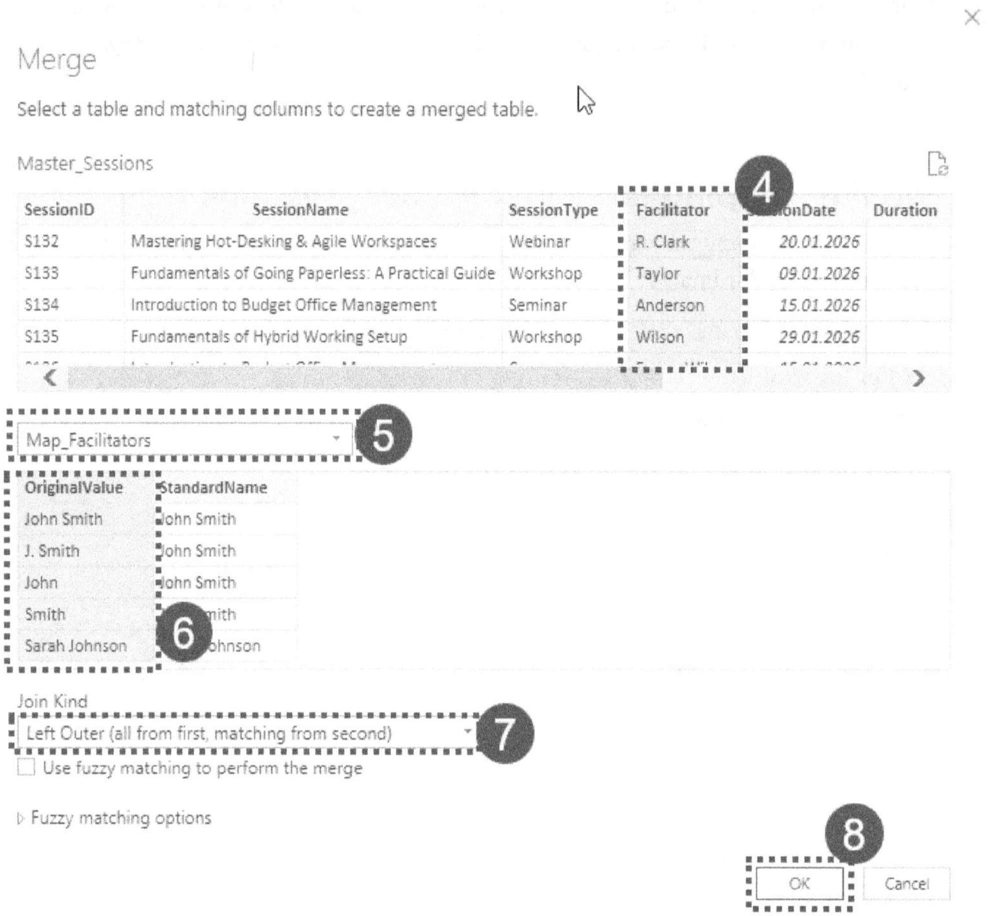

Figure 3.26 – Merge Queries dialog with Facilitator matched to OriginalValue

A new column called **Map_Facilitators** appears at the right side of the table, showing `Table` in each cell. We need to expand it to get the **StandardName** values.

9. Click the expand button (the double-arrow icon) on the **Map_Facilitators** column header
10. Untick **OriginalValue** (we don't need it; we already have the Facilitator column)
11. Keep only **StandardName** ticked
12. Untick Use original column name as prefix
13. Click **OK**

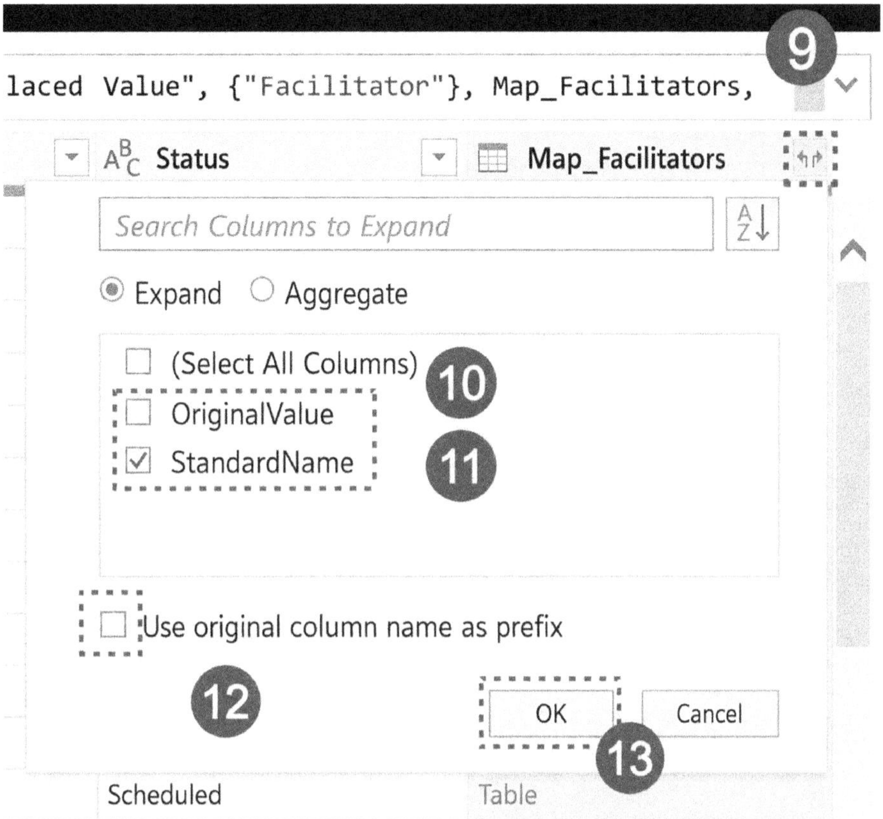

Figure 3.27 – Expanding the Map_Facilitators column to show StandardName

You should now see a **StandardName** column with clean facilitator names.

14. Right-click the original **Facilitator** column header
15. Click **Remove**

Figure 3.28 – Removing the original Facilitator column

16. Double-click the **StandardName** column header
17. Rename it to **Facilitator**

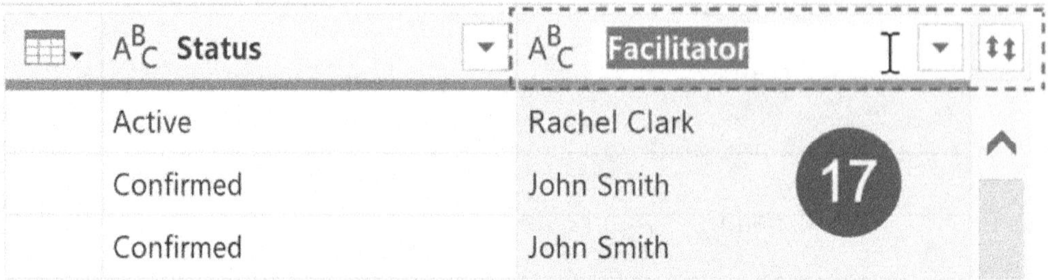

Figure 3.29 – Renaming StandardName to Facilitator

Click the filter dropdown on the **Facilitator** column. Instead of 38 messy variants, you should now see 10 clean, consistent names.

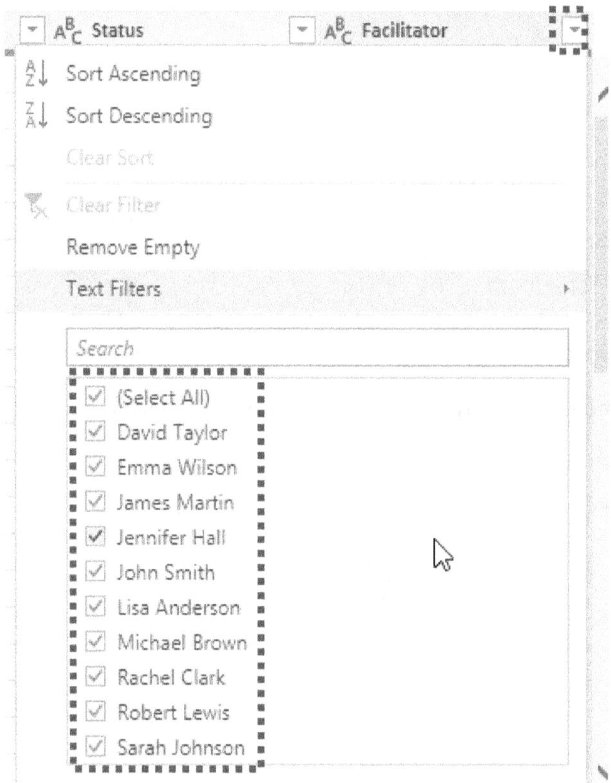

Figure 3.30 – Filter dropdown on Facilitator showing 10 standardised names

Tom looks at the list and grins. "That's exactly what I need: ten names, no duplicates, no guessing."

Why mapping tables beat scattered Replace Values

You could achieve the same result with 28 individual **Replace Values** steps: one for each variant that differs from the standard name. But a mapping table is better in almost every way:

- **Easier to maintain**: When a new variant appears, add one row to the mapping table instead of inserting a new step in the middle of your query
- **Reusable**: The same **Map_Facilitators** query can feed other queries that also use facilitator names
- **Self-documenting**: The mapping table **is** the documentation. Anyone can open it and see exactly how names are standardized
- **Stakeholder-friendly**: You can show Tom the mapping table and ask, "Is this correct?" It would be much harder to validate 28 Replace Values steps

> Tip
>
> **Column from Examples callback**
>
> If you'd like to create facilitator initials (e.g., "JS" from "John Smith"), try the **Column from Examples** feature you learned in *Chapter 2*. Click **Add Column** | **Column from Examples** | **From All Columns**, type one or two examples like "JS" for John Smith, and let Power Query figure out the pattern.

Protecting your reference tables

Master_Sessions is now clean and standardized. But a reference table carries responsibility; other reports and queries will depend on it. A few quick governance checks help ensure it stays reliable.

Check for duplicate keys

SessionID should be unique: one row per session. If two monthly files accidentally share a **SessionID**, you'd have silent duplicate rows in **Master_Sessions**.

Rather than running the check inside **Master_Sessions** (which would require undoing steps afterwards), create a throwaway **reference query** that points at **Master_Sessions**. The check runs on the reference; **Master_Sessions** is never touched.

Create the reference query:

1. In the **Queries** pane, right-click **Master_Sessions**
2. Click **Reference**

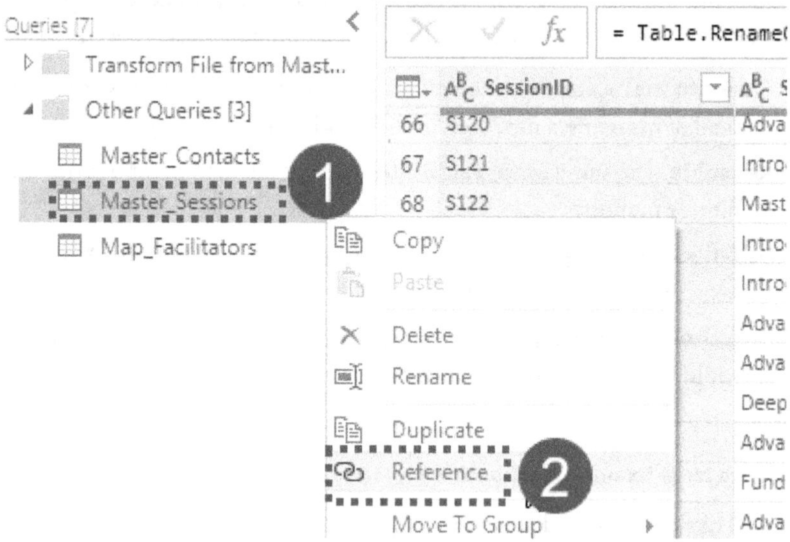

Figure 3.31 – Reference option in the Master_Sessions right-click menu

A new query appears, already pointing at **Master_Sessions**. Rename it immediately:

3. Click the **Query Settings** pane and rename the query to `Check_SessionID_Duplicates`

Run the duplicate check

Follow these steps:

1. Click the **SessionID** column header
2. Click the **Home** tab
3. Click **Group By**

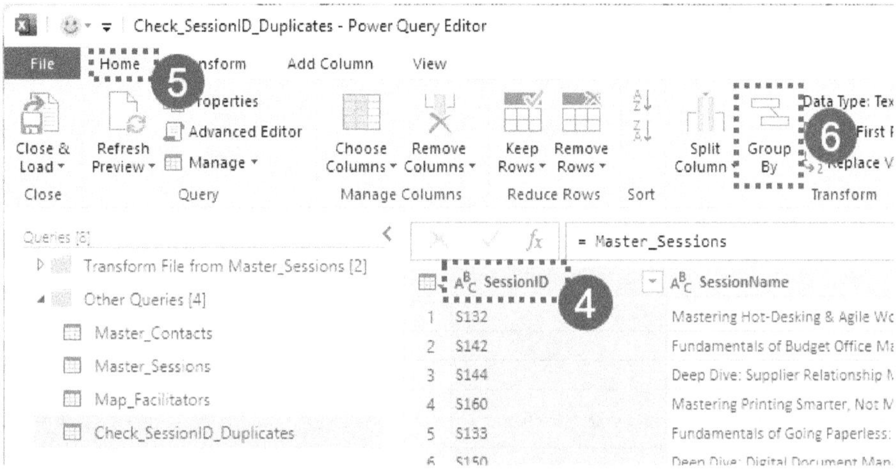

Figure 3.32 – Group By button on the Home tab

4. In the **Group By** dialog, select the fields as follows:
   - **Group by**: `SessionID`
   - **New column name**: `Count`
   - **Operation**: Count Rows
5. Click **OK**

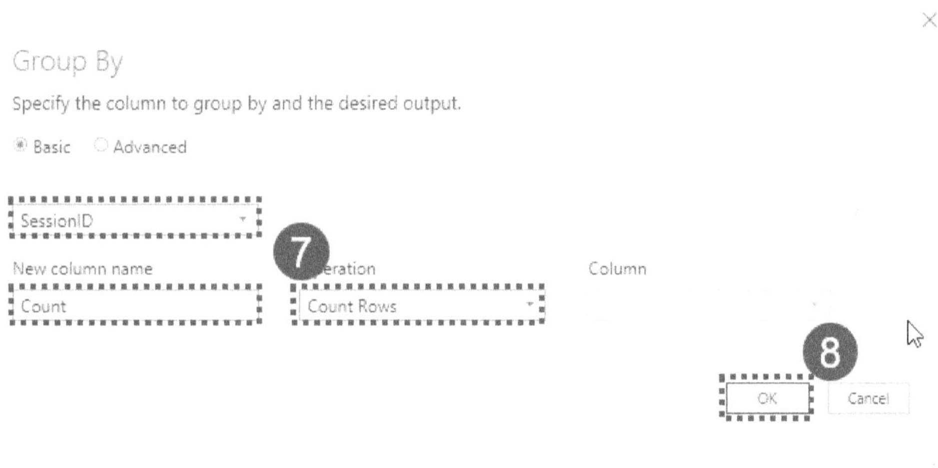

Figure 3.33 – Group By dialog configured to count rows per SessionID

6. Click the filter dropdown arrow on the **Count** column header
7. Click **Number Filters**

8. Click **Greater Than**

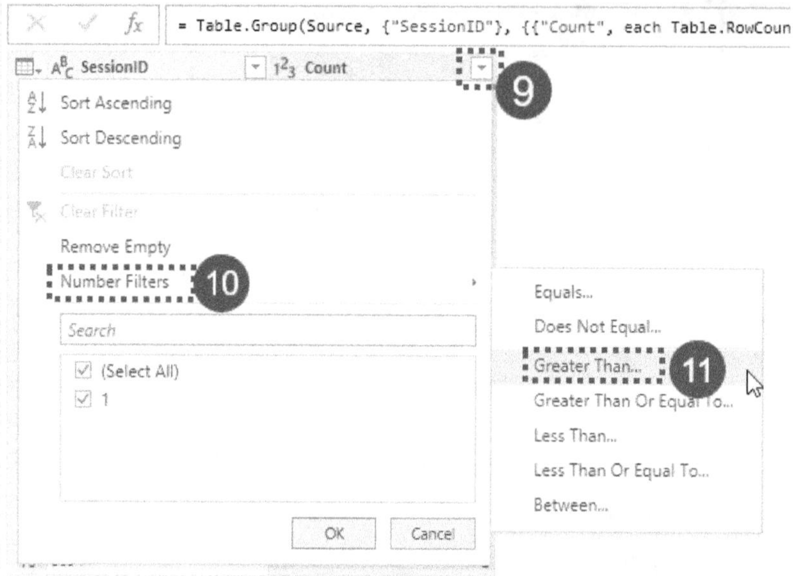

Figure 3.34 – Number Filters | Greater Than on the Count column

9. Type 1
10. Click **OK**

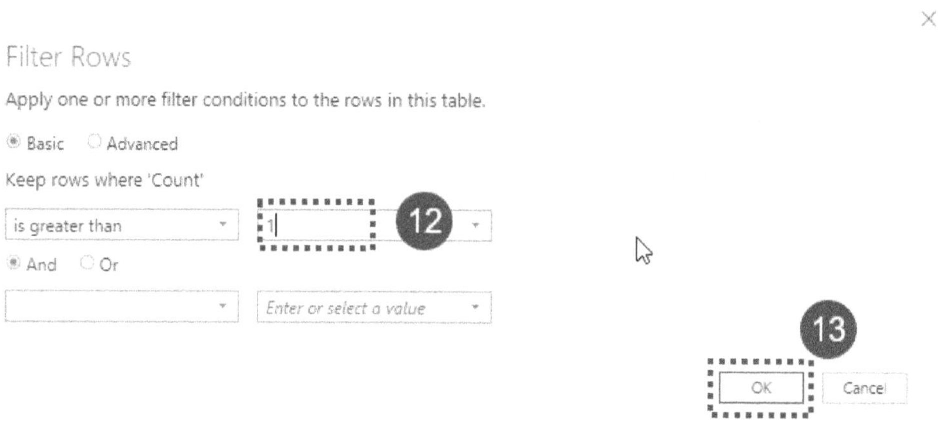

Figure 3.35 – Filter Rows dialog with value set to greater than 1

If the result shows zero rows, your SessionIDs are unique, no duplicates.

Figure 3.36 – Filtered result showing no duplicate SessionIDs

Move the check query to a group.

Rather than deleting it, keep it as a permanent data quality asset. Power Query lets you organize queries into named groups. An **_Checks** group separates quality monitors from your main data queries without cluttering the **Queries** pane.

1. In the **Queries** pane, right-click **Check_SessionID_Duplicates**
2. Click **Move to Group**
3. Click **New Group**

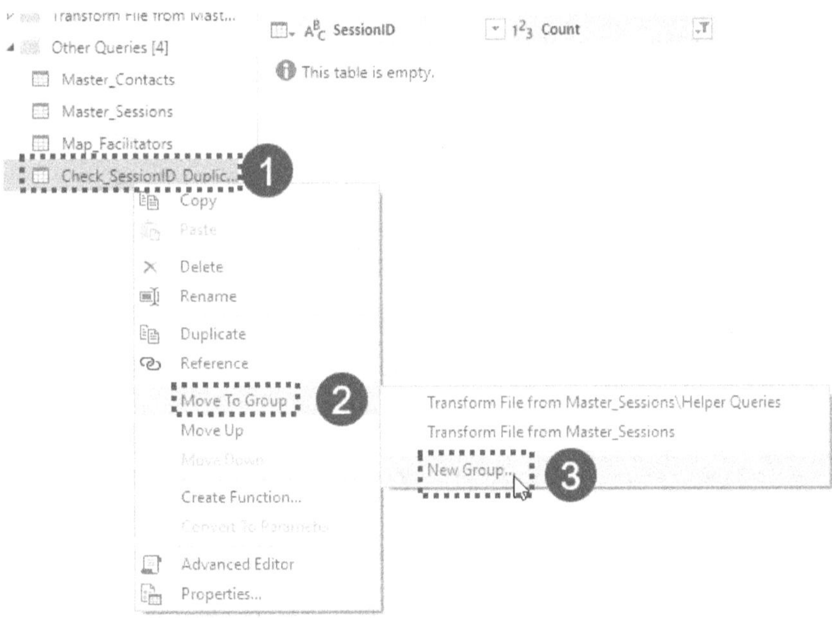

Figure 3.37 – Move to Group | New Group in the right-click menu

4. Type `_Checks`
5. Click **OK**

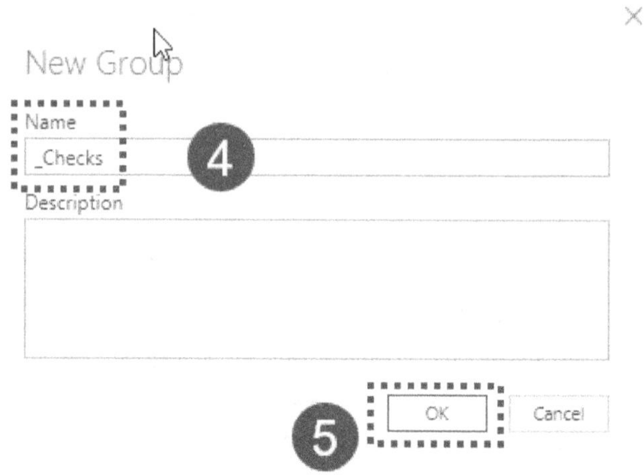

Figure 3.38 – Naming the new group _Checks

The query moves into the **_Checks** group at the bottom of the **Queries** pane. It refreshes automatically with the rest of the workbook. If duplicates ever appear after a new monthly file is added, this query will catch them immediately.

As the book progresses, each chapter that introduces a new data quality check will add it to the same **_Checks** group, building a lightweight validation layer alongside your main queries.

Document your queries

As your workbook grows, documentation prevents confusion. Add a description to Master_Sessions using the same pattern from *Chapter 2*:

1. In the **Queries** pane, click **Master_Sessions**
2. In the **Query Settings** pane, click **All Properties**
3. In the description field, type something like:

```
Combined sessions metadata from monthly files in Events/Sessions/.
Standardized SessionType, Location, Status, and Facilitator names via
Map_Facilitators lookup. Key field: SessionID (unique).
```

4. Click **OK**

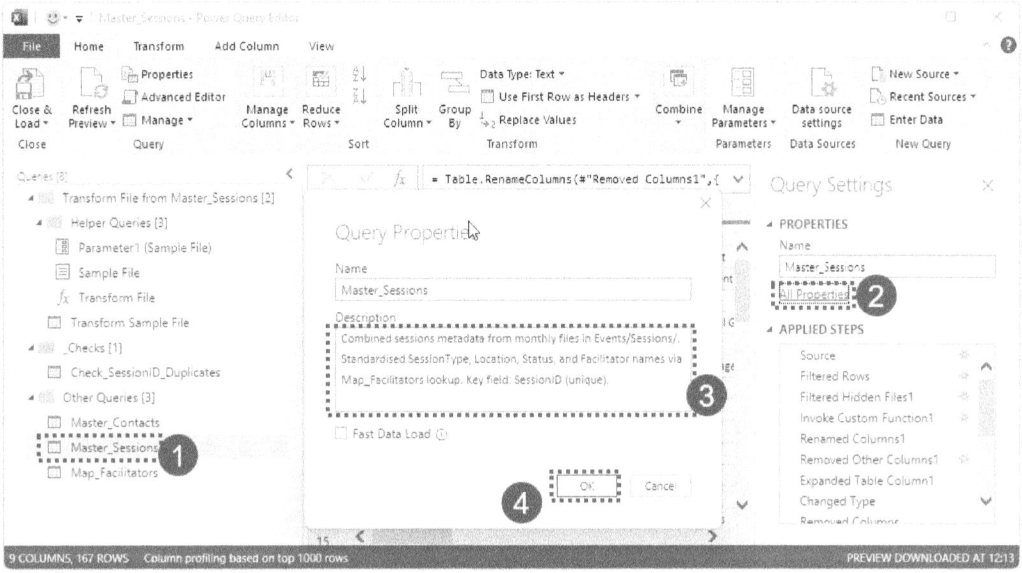

Figure 3.39 – Query Properties dialog with description for Master_Sessions

Load as connection only

Master_Sessions will feed later chapters. It doesn't need its own worksheet right now. Load it as a connection:

1. Click the **Home** tab
2. Click the **Close & Load** dropdown arrow
3. Click **Close & Load To...**

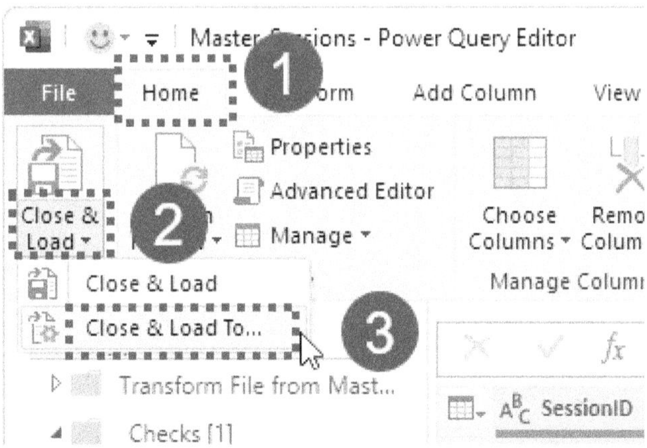

Figure 3.40 – Close and Load To option in the dropdown menu

4. Select **Only Create Connection**
5. Click **OK**

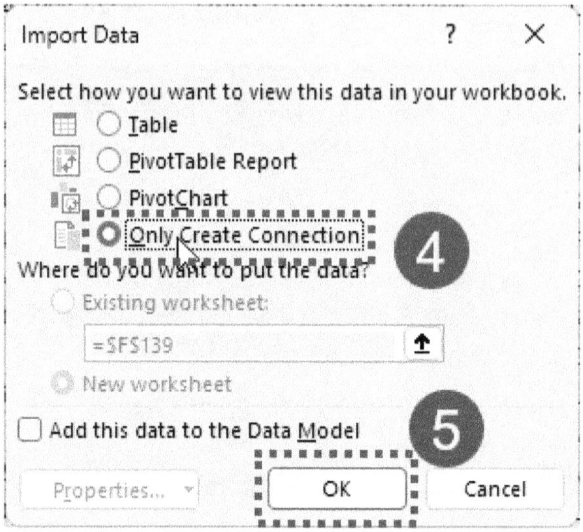

Figure 3.41 – Import Data dialog with Only Create Connection selected

The **Queries & Connections** pane shows **Master_Sessions** and **Map_Facilitators** as connection-only queries.

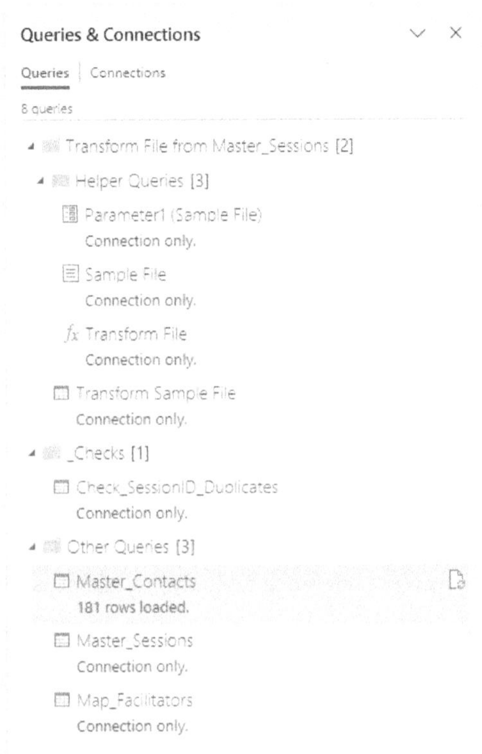

Figure 3.42 – Queries & Connections pane showing Master_Sessions and Map_Facilitators

Final trust loop

Run through the checklist one last time:

Check	Expected
Row count	~167 rows
Columns	SessionID, SessionName, SessionType, Facilitator, SessionDate, Duration, MaxCapacity, Location, Status
SessionType	5 clean values: Workshop, Seminar, Course, Training, Webinar
Facilitator	10 clean names (no variants)

Check	Expected
Location	4 values: Online, London Office, Manchester Hub, Birmingham Centre
Status	3 values: Active, Confirmed, Scheduled
Duplicate Session IDs	None

Table 3.6 – Final validation checklist for Master_Sessions

"This is brilliant," Tom says, scrolling through the clean list. "One table, everything is consistent. And when February's file lands in the folder?"

"Just click **Refresh**."

Summary

In this chapter, you built a complete reference table from multiple source files:

- **Folder connector for multiple files**: Connected to the `Events/Sessions/` folder and combined four monthly Excel exports into one table using **Combine & Transform**
- **Column pruning**: Removed unnecessary columns early to keep the query focused
- **Quick standardization**: Used **Capitalize Each Word** and **Replace Values** to fix **SessionType**, **Location**, and **Status**. We used these same patterns in *Chapter 2*
- **Mapping table**: Loaded `Map_Facilitators.xlsx` from the `Reference` folder via the Folder connector and merged it into **Master_Sessions** to standardize 38 name variants down to 10 clean facilitator names
- **Governance basics**: Verified **SessionID** uniqueness with Group By, documented the query, and loaded as **Connection Only**

In this chapter, we created **Master_Sessions** query (connection only), which is Tom's reliable sessions catalog and **Map_Facilitators** query (connection only), which is the reusable facilitator name lookup.

In *Chapter 4*, Quinn helps Marcus build reliable step chains for tracking weekly event KPIs. The patterns you've built here — folder connections, reference tables, and mapping lookups — will carry forward throughout the book.

4

Build Reliable Step Chains and Read M Passively

Figure 4.1 – Marcus explains to Quinn that every few weeks, someone renames a header, and the entire report breaks as a result.

It is Monday morning. Quinn arrives at her desk to find a message from Marcus, the Marketing Manager, already waiting for her.

"Hey Quinn, my KPI report is broken again. I'm presenting to leadership in two hours."

Quinn pulls up Marcus's workbook. In the **Queries & Connections** pane, the KPIs query shows a yellow warning triangle, *"Download did not complete."* She clicks through to the source file and sees what happened: someone tidied up the weekly KPIs spreadsheet over the weekend and deleted a column they no longer needed. That column was still referenced in Marcus's query. The moment it disappeared from the source, the query had nothing to find.

This is not the first time it has happened. Marcus explains to Quinn that every few weeks, someone renames a header, and the entire report breaks as a result. He spends half an hour each time trying to fix it or just copies the numbers into his slide deck by hand.

In this chapter, you'll learn to -

- Identify why fragile step chains break and what makes a query reliable for recurring reports
- Build a clean, refreshable **Weekly_Event_KPIs** query from a messy, informal range using the Power Query UI
- Read the **Applied Steps** pane and formula bar to understand, repair, and reorder transformations without writing M code
- Protect key columns and the query grain, and apply a step-by-step debugging workflow when a refresh fails

Technical requirements

The chapters in this book build on each other. Make sure you have completed all exercises in the previous chapter before starting this one.

To follow along with this chapter, you will need:

- Microsoft Excel 2016 or later with Power Query available (via **Data** | **Get & Transform Data**)
- Your `NOG-DataHub` workbook from *Chapter 3*, containing the following queries in the **Queries & Connections** pane:
    - **Master_Contacts** — loaded to a worksheet (built in *Chapter 2*)
    - **Master_Sessions** — connection only (built in *Chapter 3*)
- The exercise file `Weekly_Event_KPIs.xlsx`, located in the `Events/KPIs/` folder of your NOG-DataHub

Files are available in the book's GitHub repository. Download and extract the `NOG-DataHub` folder, following the instructions in the *Setting Up Your NOG-DataHub* section of the *Introduction*; make sure you have completed the exercises of the previous chapters before starting.

Why reliable step chains matter for everyday reports

The problem has a name: a **fragile query**. A fragile query is one that depends on things outside its control: the column order in the source, a manually formatted range, the assumption that nobody will ever adjust the layout. When any of those assumptions break, the query breaks along with them.

The opposite is a **reliable step chain**: a query whose steps are explicit, named, and tolerant of minor changes in the source. It knows which column to look for by name, not by position. It deliberately handles blank rows and fill-down patterns. It survives a refresh without Quinn's help.

Fragile query	**Reliable step chain**
References columns by position	References columns by name
Breaks if a column is inserted or moved	Tolerates column order changes
Errors are hard to trace	Applied Steps make errors easy to find
Only one person knows how to fix it	Anyone can read the steps and understand what they do

Table 4.1 – Fragile query versus reliable step chain

Think of a step chain as a recipe. Each step takes what the previous step produced and slightly transforms it: filter out blank rows, fill in a date, and rename a column. If an early step changes (or breaks), every step that follows it is affected. A good recipe is clear and explicit: "take the column named WeekEnding" is a reliable instruction; "take the third column from the left" is not.

The other half of the solution

Building a better query is one half of the fix. The other half is people.

Marcus's workbook is updated every week by several people on the Events team. They are not doing anything wrong; they are adding data, adjusting layouts, and inserting columns as the team's needs evolve. But they may not realize that a query somewhere else depends on that spreadsheet staying consistent.

This is a **data ownership** question. Someone, ideally Marcus or a nominated person on the Events team, needs to be responsible for keeping the source file's structure stable. Everyone who updates the file should understand the basic rules: do not insert columns, do not rename headers, and do not remove the blank-row pattern that separates weeks.

That is a training and communication task, not a Power Query task. Quinn's query will be far more robust after this chapter's work, but it will only stay reliable if the people who touch the source file understand why structure matters.

Excel offers tools to help protect a file's structure. You can lock specific columns so they cannot be deleted, or add data validation rules to key fields (for example, requiring that a SessionID always be a number). These are not Power Query features; they sit on the Excel side, but they are part of the same solution.

> AI Helper
>
> **Protecting your source file's structure**
>
> Ask an AI assistant (such as ChatGPT, Copilot, or Claude): `How do I protect the column structure of an Excel Table so that users cannot insert or delete columns?` and `What data validation rule can I add to a column to prevent free-text entries and only allow values starting with a specific prefix?` Test any suggestions in a copy of the file before applying them to the live source. Always verify the result works as expected before rolling it out to the team.

With the people's side acknowledged, Quinn turns back to the workbook. Let's build Marcus a query that lasts.

From messy weekly range to a structured query

Quinn opens the file Marcus has been maintaining, `Weekly_Event_KPIs.xlsx`, in the `Events/KPIs/` folder. The data tells a familiar story.

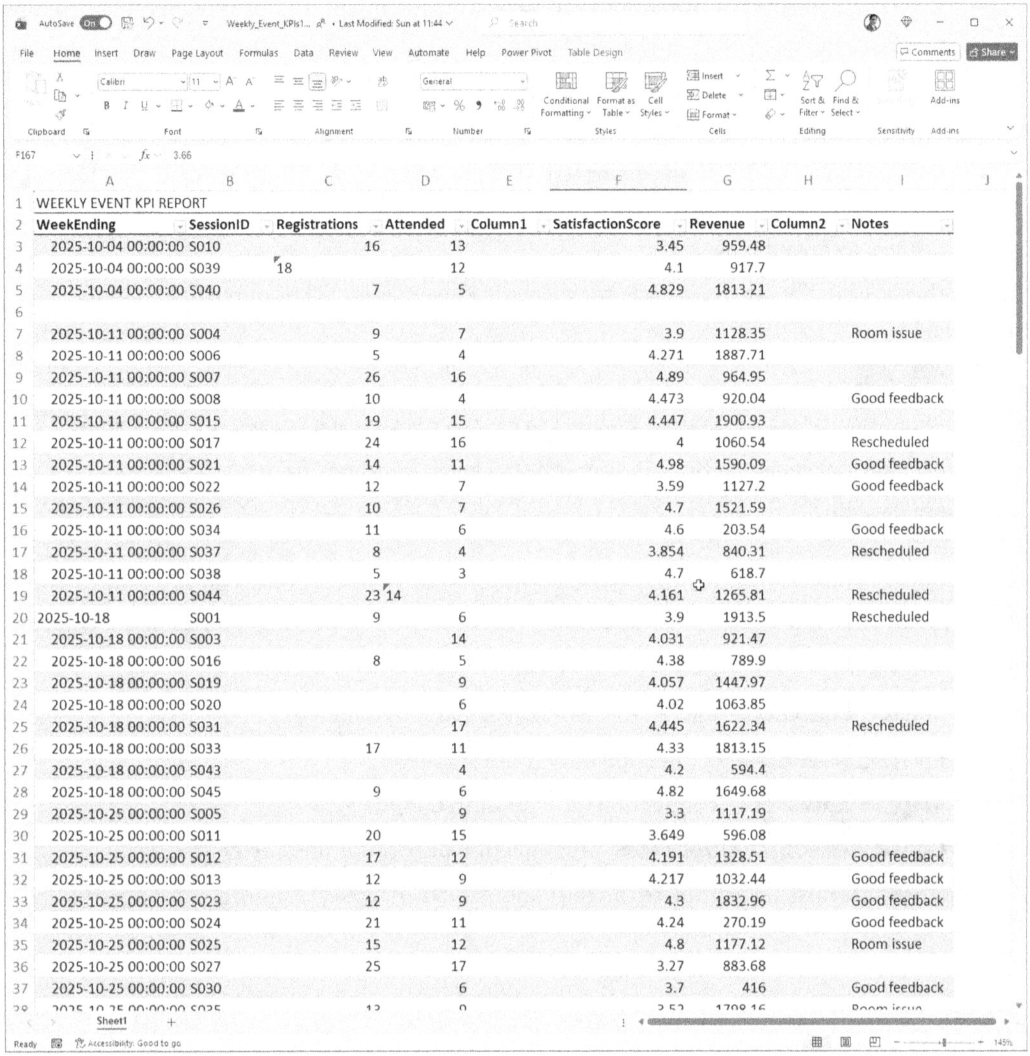

Figure 4.2 – The Weekly_Event_KPIs.xlsx source file showing the loosely structured layout

The layout has several problems that will cause a query to break or produce unreliable results:

- **Inconsistent WeekEnding formats**: most dates are stored as 2025-10-04 00:00:00, but some rows use dots (2025.11.01) or slashes (2025/12/13), and some are plain dates without a time component. Power Query cannot silently reconcile these into a single Date type.
- **Blank rows separate each weekly group**: These are visual separators that make the spreadsheet readable but break a query.

- **A TOTALS row at the bottom of the data**: This is a manual summary row that has no place in a query built for row-level analysis.
- **Two unnamed gap columns**: There are two gap columns between Attended and Satisfaction, and between Revenue and Notes.
- **Registrations and Attended stored as text in some rows**: These are cells that look like numbers but were entered in text-formatted cells, causing Power Query to read the column as mixed type.

Each of these is a deliberate fix we will make inside Power Query. The source file remains untouched.

> **Important**
>
> For this exercise, use the `Weekly_Event_KPIs.xlsx` file from the `Events/KPIs/` folder in your `NOG-DataHub`. Continue in your `NOG-DataHub workbook` from *Chapter 3*; do not open a new file.

By this point, your `NOG-DataHub` workbook should contain the following queries in the **Queries & Connections** pane:

- **Master_Contacts** — loaded to a worksheet (built in *Chapter 2*)
- **Master_Sessions** — connection only (built in *Chapter 3*)
- **Map_Facilitators** — connection only (built in *Chapter 3*)
- **Check_SessionID_Duplicates** — connection only (built in *Chapter 3*)

If any of these are missing, complete the relevant chapter before continuing.

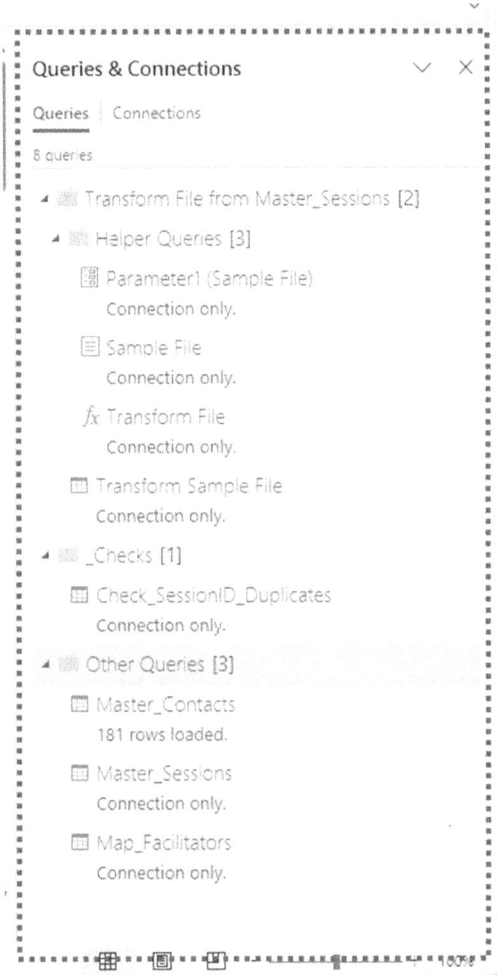

Chapter 4">

Figure4.3-Queries& Connections pane showing the expected queries before starting Chapter 4

Connect to the NOG-DataHub folder

Follow the same folder connector pattern from the **previous chapters:** go to **Data** | **Get Data** | **From File**, choose **From SharePoint Folder** or **From Folder**, navigate to your `NOG-DataHub`, and click **Transform Data** to open the Power Query Editor.

Filter to the KPIs file

Power Query lists every file in the `NOG-DataHub`. Filter down to the one you need: Use the same two-step filter pattern from the previous chapters to narrow the listing down to the file you need:

- Filter the **Folder Path** column: **Text Filters** | **Contains** | **KPIs**
- Filter the **Name** column: **Text Filters** | **Equals** | **Weekly_Event_KPIs.xlsx**

You should see a single row for the file.

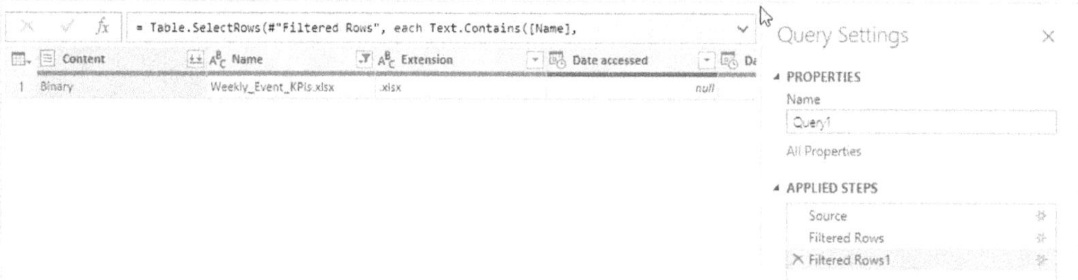

Figure 4.4 – Folder listing filtered to Weekly_Event_KPIs.xlsx in the Events/KPIs folder

In the **Query Settings** pane, rename the query to `Weekly_Event_KPIs`.

> **Important**
>
> Rename the query before doing anything else. The query name appears in the **Queries** pane, in any error messages, and in the formula bar of other queries that reference this one. A meaningful name ("Weekly_Event_KPIs") makes all three far easier to read than an auto-generated one ("Query1").

Next, follow these steps:

1. Click the **Binary** link in the **Content** column to open the file

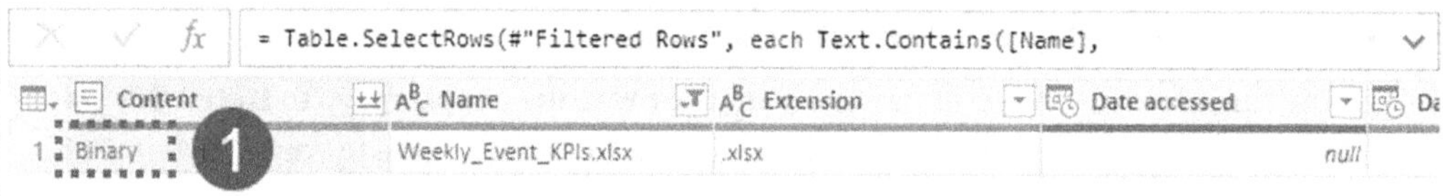

Figure 4.5 – Binary link in the Content column for the KPIs file

When Power Query opens an Excel workbook, it presents a **Navigator,** which can show up to three types of objects (though in Marcus's file, Named Ranges are not present):

- **Sheets**: the raw worksheet tab, including everything on it: title rows, blank cells, merged cells, whatever the user has put there
- **Named Tables**: a structured Excel Table (created with **Insert** | **Table**). Power Query reads only the table data, starting from the header row
- **Named Ranges**: a named selection of cells; it is less common, but occasionally used for small reference lists

Choosing a **named Table** is almost always the right call. Because a Table has a defined start and end, Power Query ignores anything outside it, including title rows like **WEEKLY EVENT KPI REPORT**. Choosing the Sheet instead would include the title row, requiring an extra removal step.

> **Note**
>
> In Marcus's file the Table already exists. If you ever apply this pattern to your own files, make sure the data is a proper Excel Table, not just a formatted range. Select any cell in the data and press *Ctrl* + *T* (or go to **Insert** | **Table**) to convert a range into a Table. Excel Tables have a defined header row and boundary, which is what Power Query uses to connect cleanly.

Marcus's file already has a named **Table**. In the **Navigator**, you will see a couple of entries of various kinds: `Table` and `Sheet`.

Figure 4.6 – Navigator dialog showing a Sheet entry and a Table entry for the same workbook

2. In the Navigator, click the **Table** hyperlink (look for the row where Kind = Table)

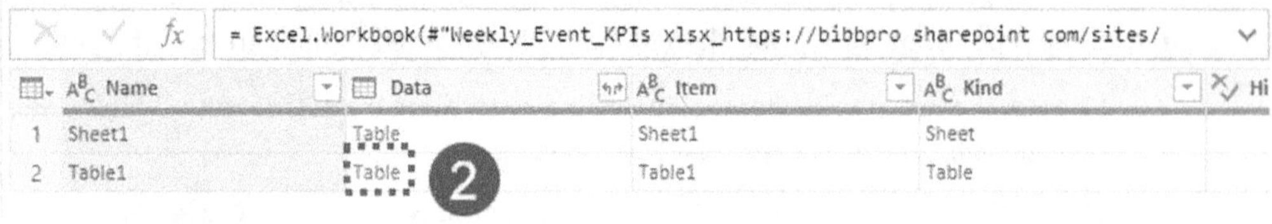

Figure 4.7 – Navigator with the Table entry selected and the data preview showing correct headers

3. Verify the preview shows the correct headers: WeekEnding, SessionID, Registrations, Attended, Satisfaction, Revenue, and Notes; with two unnamed columns (Column1 and Column2) sitting between them as gap columns. This is expected; you will remove them in the next step.

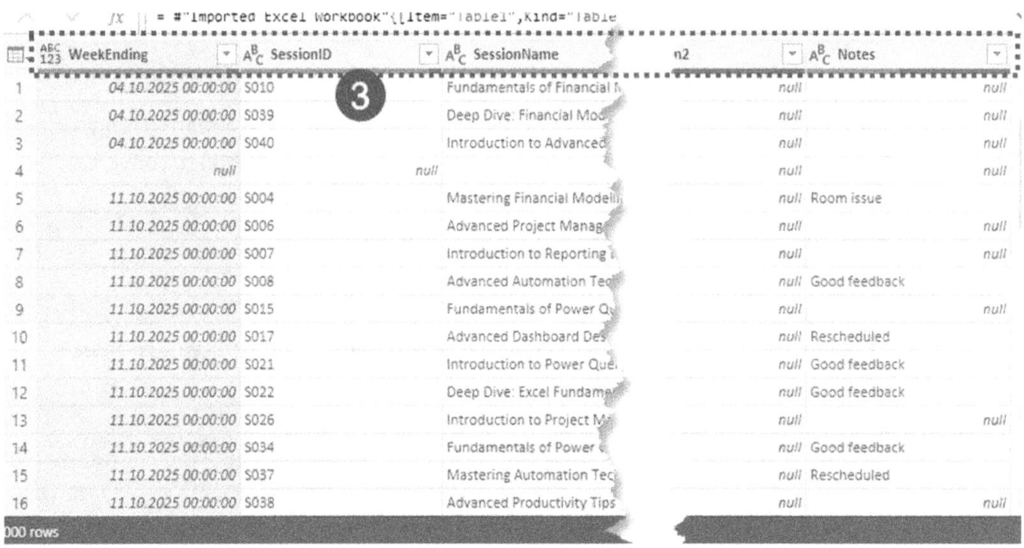

Figure 4.8 – Navigator preview confirming the correct column headers for the KPIs Table

Note

If you were to select the Sheet instead of the Table, the preview would show the title row (**WEEKLY EVENT KPI REPORT**) as the first row, with the real headers appearing in row two. You will need an extra **Remove Top Rows** step to skip the title. Selecting the named `Table` avoids this entirely.

Remove gap columns

The two unnamed columns between **Attended** and **Satisfaction**, and between **Revenue** and **Notes**, have no data and no purpose. Remove them before doing anything else; it keeps the column list clean for every step that follows. Execute these steps:

1. Click the **Home** tab
2. Click **Choose Columns**

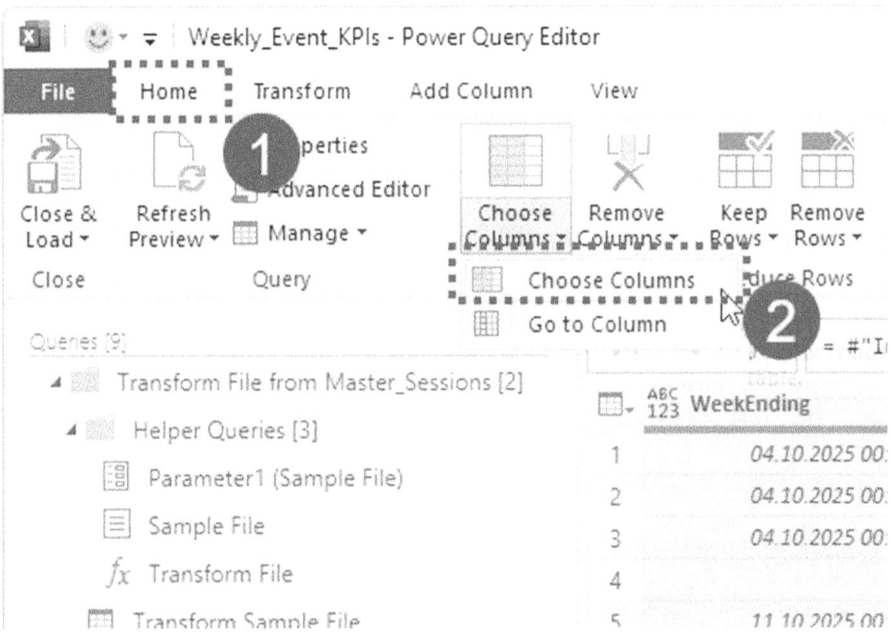

Figure 4.9 – Choose Columns button on the Home tab

3. In the dialog, untick the two unnamed columns (shown as **Column1** and **Column2**, or similar)
4. Click **OK**

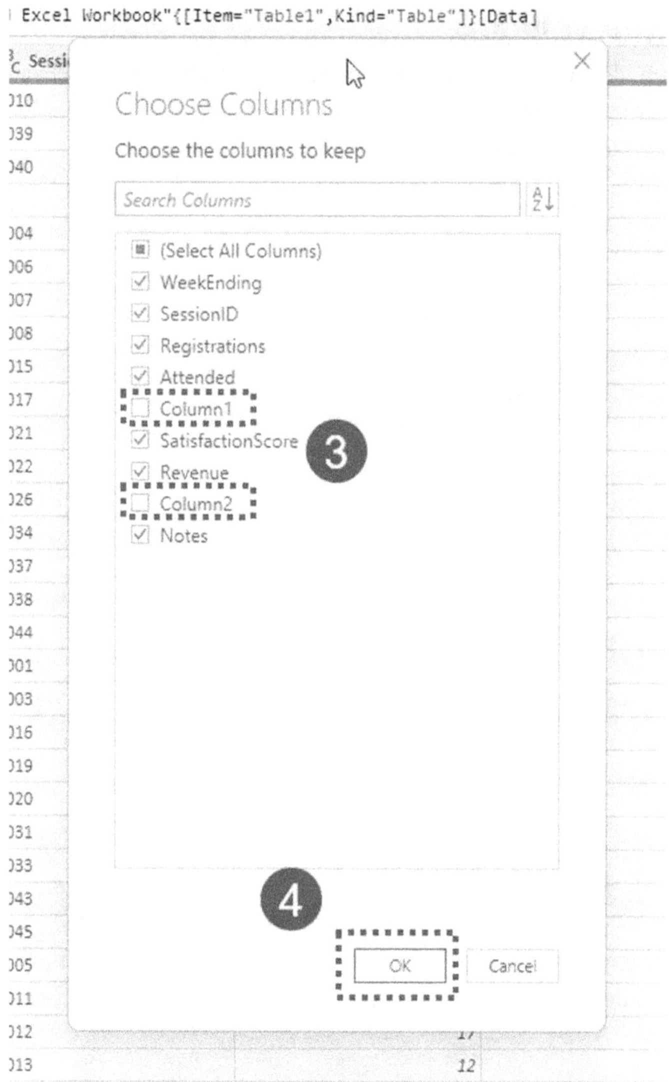

Figure 4.10 – Choose Columns dialog with the two unnamed gap columns unticked

Tip

Keeping only the columns you need, rather than removing the ones you don't, is good practice early in the step chain. Every subsequent step uses a simpler table, and if the source file later gains a new column, it will be automatically excluded. There is no risk of a later step accidentally picking up a column you did not intend to keep.

Remove blank rows and the TOTALS row

The blank rows between weekly groups are visual separators; useful for reading the spreadsheet, but noise for a query. There is also a **TOTALS** row at the bottom of the data, which is a manually entered summary. Neither belongs in a query built for row-level analysis.

Remove the blank separator rows first:

1. Click the **Home** tab
2. Click **Remove Rows**
3. Click **Remove Blank Rows**

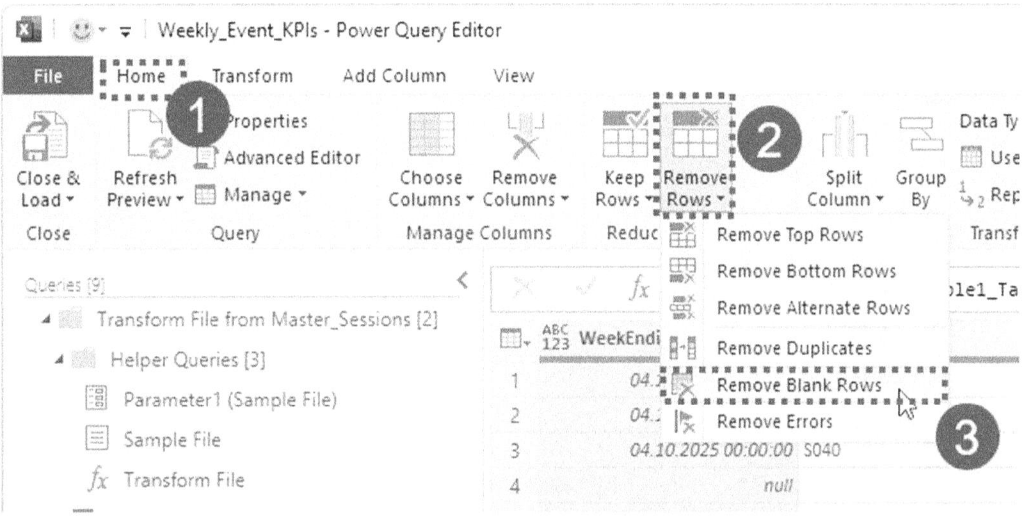

Figure 4.11 – Remove Rows menu expanded to show Remove Blank Rows

Power Query removes any row where every cell is null. The blank weekly separators disappear.

Now let's remove the **TOTALS** row. The **TOTALS** row has a blank SessionID; it is a summary row, not a session record. The cleanest way to remove it is to filter the **SessionID** column to keep only rows where a SessionID is present.

4. Click the filter dropdown on the SessionID column header
5. Hover over Text Filters
6. Click **Does Not Equal**

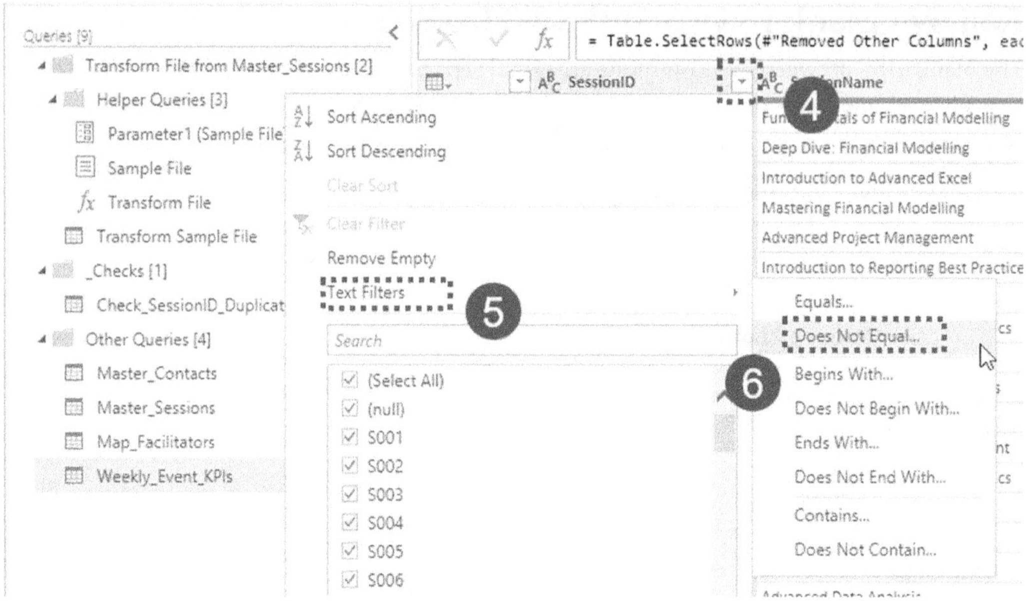

Figure 4.12 – Text Filters menu on the SessionID column header with Does Not Equal selected

7. In the value field, type `null`
8. Click **OK**

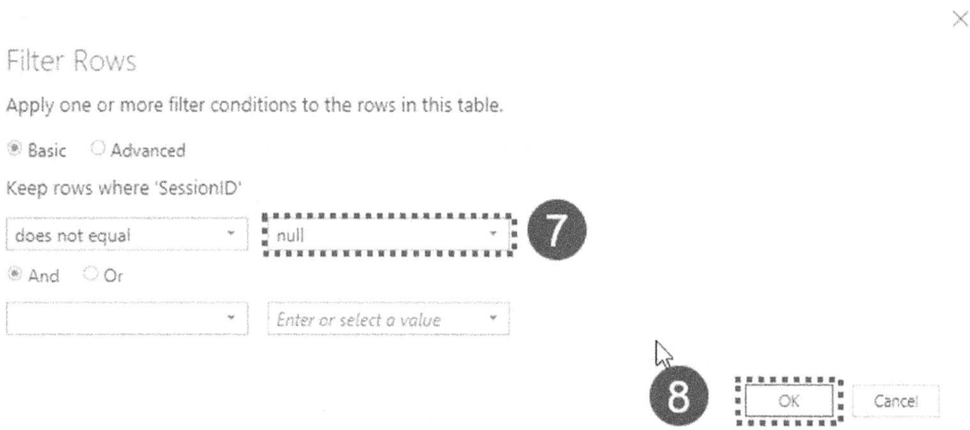

Figure 4.13 – Filter Rows dialog with the value field left blank to remove rows with no SessionID

The **TOTALS** row disappears. Every remaining row now represents a real session record.

Tip

Filtering by a key column like SessionID is more robust than filtering the label "TOTALS" in another column. If the label changes ("Total", "Grand Total"), the filter still works because a real session record will always have a SessionID.

Set data types

The last structural step is setting types deliberately. Power Query may have guessed some types, but guesses are not guaranteed; set them explicitly so the query behaves the same on every refresh.

Fixing the WeekEnding type and errors

Set the type for each column using the type icon to the left of the column header. Here is how to change one, **WeekEnding**, to Date:

1. Click the type icon to the left of the **WeekEnding** column header (it shows **ABC123** if Power Query has read it as text)
2. Click **Date**

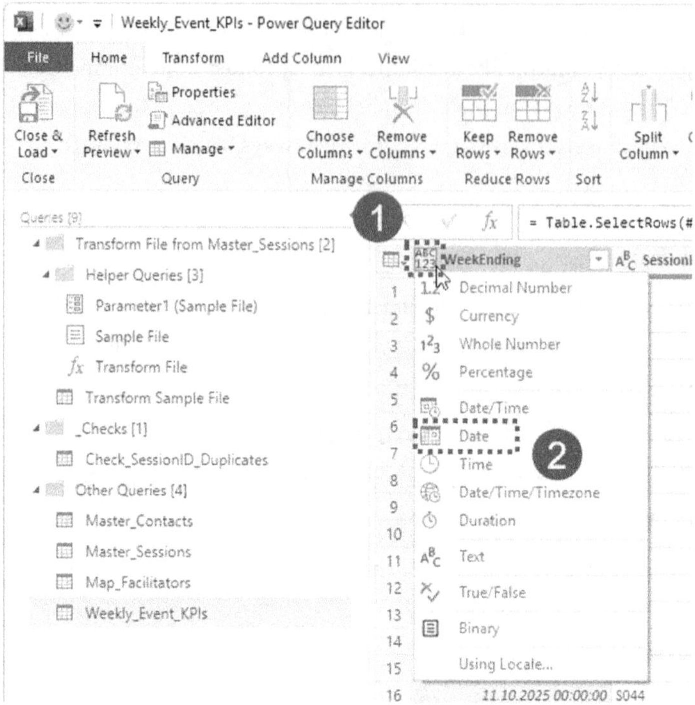

Figure 4.14 – Clicking the type icon on WeekEnding and selecting Date from the dropdown

Repeat for every column in the table:

Column	Data Type
WeekEnding	Date
SessionID	Text
Registrations	Whole Number
Attended	Whole Number
Satisfaction	Decimal Number
Revenue	Decimal Number
Notes	Text

Table 4.2 – Data types for Weekly_Event_KPIs columns

After setting all column types from *Table 4.2*, the column header icons update to reflect each type. Check that every header now shows the correct symbol before moving on:

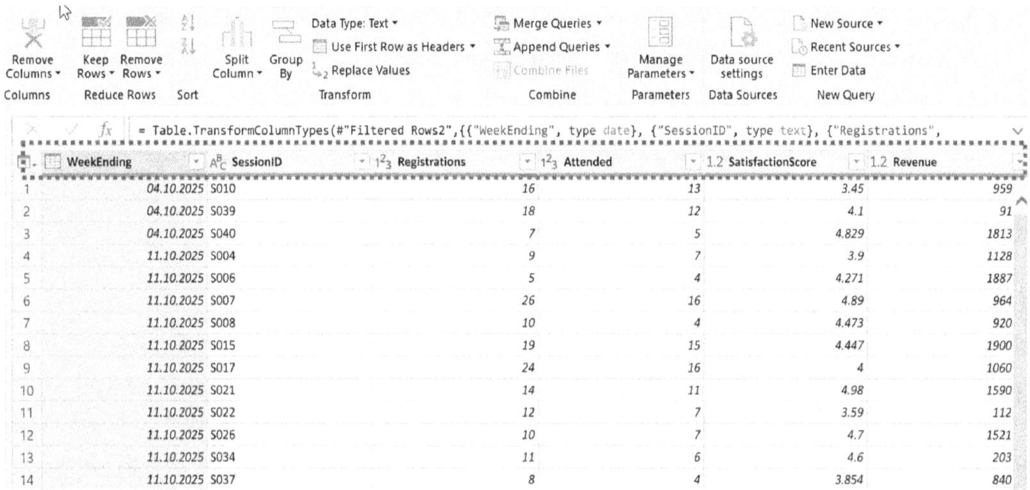

Figure 4.15 – Column header type icons after setting all data types

After setting **WeekEnding** to **Date**, you may see a small number of error values in that column. These correspond to rows where the date was typed as text using a non-standard separator like dots (2025.11.01) or slashes (2025/12/13) instead of dashes. Power Query cannot automatically convert these formats when setting the type through the UI.

These errors are a data quality signal, not a Power Query failure. The correct fix is at source: the person entering the data used an inconsistent format. This connects directly to the change management point from earlier in the chapter; format consistency in the source file is the responsibility of the people who maintain it.

For now, note the affected rows (you can click an error cell to see which value caused it). A full data-entry standard for the Events team that includes one date format applied consistently prevents this from recurring.

Newer versions of Power Query, particularly in Excel 365 and recent Power BI updates, handle locale-aware type inference more reliably and manage the datetime-to-date truncation more cleanly. However, they do not automatically resolve genuinely mixed formats, such as a mix of dashes, dots, and slashes in the same column. That still requires an explicit fix at source.

AI Helper

Locking down your source file

Ask an AI assistant: `How do I use data validation in Excel to restrict a column to dates in a specific format, and how do I protect a worksheet so that users can only edit certain columns?`

Use the suggestions to add guardrails to the source file before rolling it out to the team. Always test any protection or validation rules in a copy of the file first.

Handling mixed types

Some rows in **Registrations** contain blank values (sessions for which registration or attendance data were not recorded). After you set these columns to **Whole Number**, you will see **null** appear in those cells; this is expected. Valid numbers convert correctly, and blank cells become `null`: an explicit *no data* value rather than an ambiguous blank. When Power Query reads a column containing a mix of numbers and blanks, it may assign a mixed type; explicitly setting the type resolves this.

If any cells were entered as text (rather than as numbers) in the source, they will show as errors after the type change. The same principle applies: the fix is at the source, and the errors are useful signals.

Caution

When you change a data type, Power Query typically replaces the previous type-change step rather than adding a new one, unless the previous step was something other than a type change. If you change your mind about a type and set it again, check the **Applied Steps** pane to confirm you have one clean type step, not two conflicting ones stacked on top of each other.

Bring in the session name

The KPIs table is now clean and correctly typed, but it only carries a SessionID. Without the session name, Marcus cannot read the report at a glance. That name already exists in **Master_Sessions**, the query you built in *Chapter 3*.

You have already used **Merge Queries** in *Chapter 3* to standardize facilitator names. The same pattern applies here: match SessionID to bring in the session name from **Master_Sessions**.

> **Important**
>
> **Master_Sessions** must be available in your workbook. If you have not completed *Chapter 3*, make sure the `NOG-DataHub` workbook contains a **Master_Sessions** query before continuing.

Follow these steps:

1. In the **Power Query Editor**, click the **Home** tab
2. Click **Merge Queries**

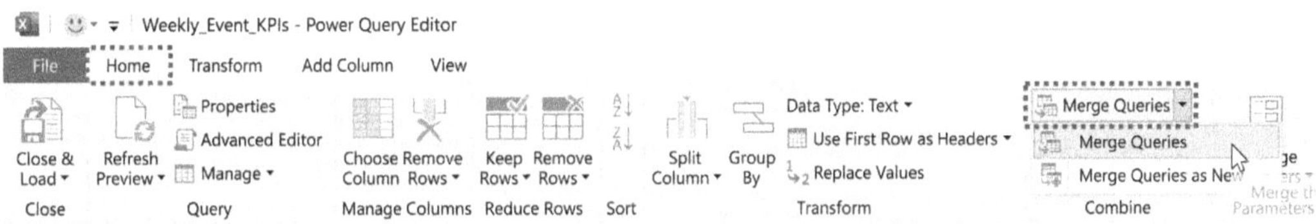

Figure 4.16 – Merge Queries button on the Home tab

3. In the **Merge** dialog, confirm the top table is **Weekly_Event_KPIs**
4. Click the **SessionID** column in the top table to select it as the join key
5. In the dropdown below, select **Master_Sessions**
6. Click the **SessionID** column in the **Master_Sessions** table
7. Confirm the **Join Kind** is set to **Left Outer** (all from first, matching from second)
8. Click **OK**

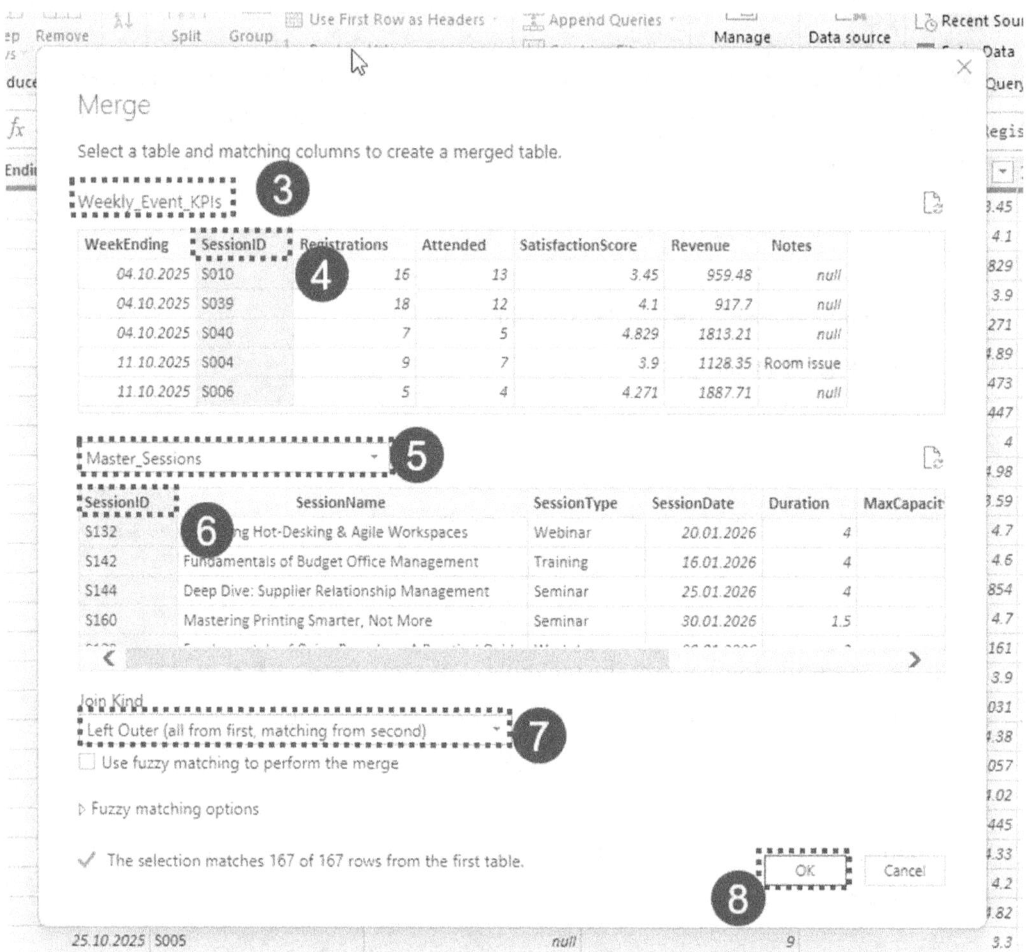

Figure 4.17 – Merge dialog with SessionID matched between Weekly_Event_KPIs and Master_Sessions

Note

A **Left Outer join** keeps every row in **Weekly_Event_KPIs** regardless of whether a matching SessionID exists in **Master_Sessions**. Any KPI row with no match will show a `null` in the **SessionName** column; a useful signal that the source data may be out of sync.

Power Query adds a new **Master_Sessions** column containing a nested table for each row. You only need one field from it: **SessionName**.

9. Click the expand icon in the **Master_Sessions** column header

10. Tick **SessionName** only
11. Untick **Use original column name as prefix**
12. Click **OK**

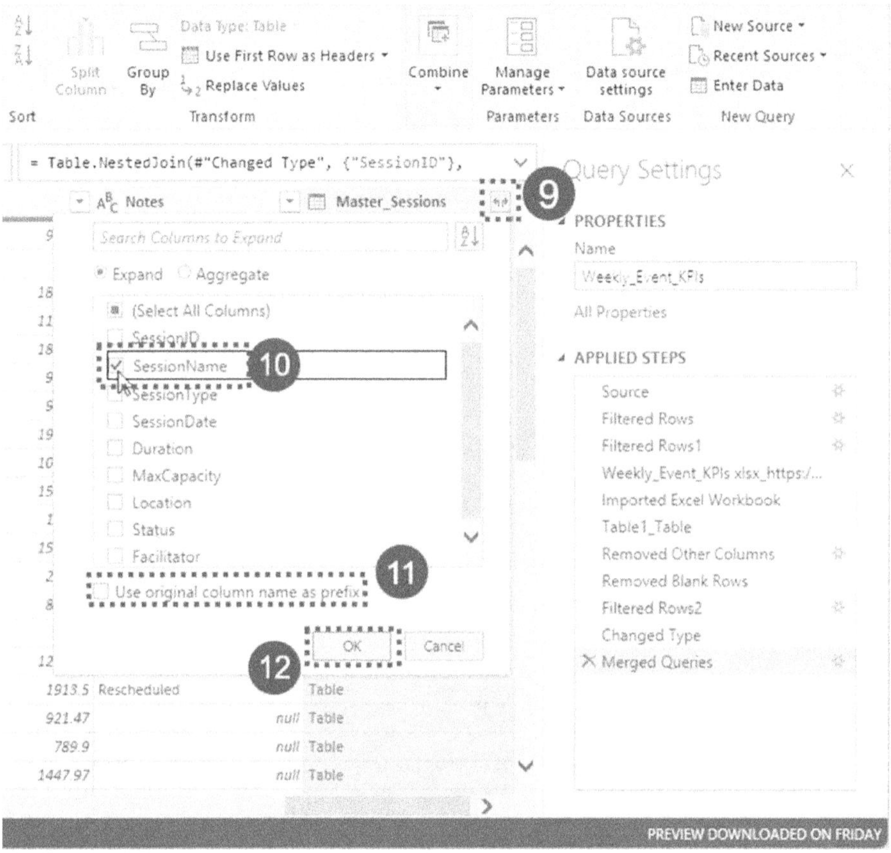

Figure 4.18 – Expanding the merged column to bring in SessionName only

The **SessionName** column appears on the right-hand side of the table. Each KPI row now shows the full session name alongside its figures.

Load to a worksheet

Marcus needs this data on a sheet he can use for his Monday report. Let's prepare that:

1. Click the **Home** tab
2. Click the dropdown arrow next to **Close & Load**
3. Click **Close & Load To...**

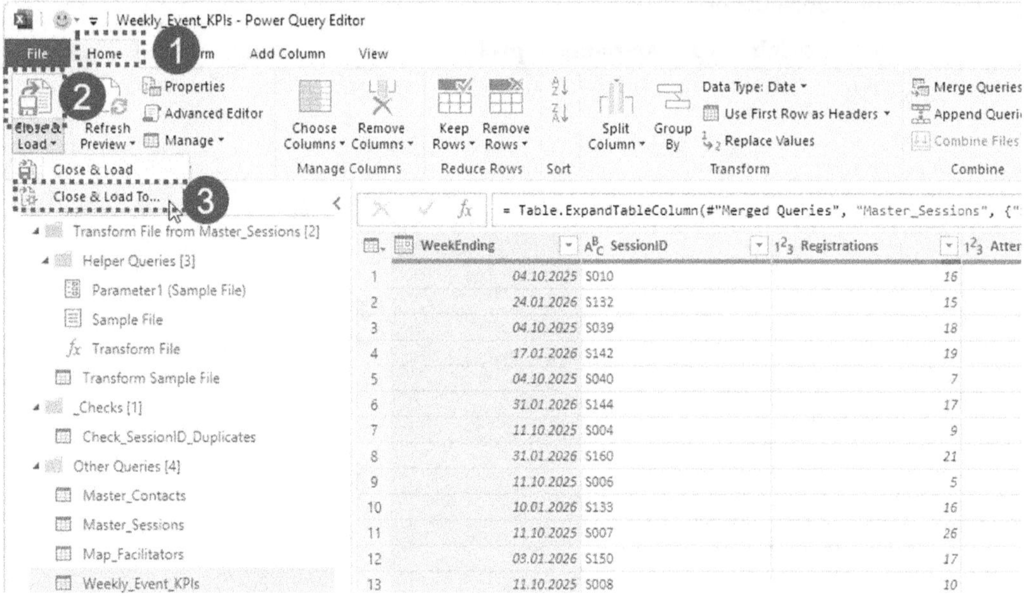

Figure 4.19 – Close and Load dropdown with Close & Load To… selected

4. In the **Import Data** dialog, select Table
5. Select **New worksheet**
6. Click **OK**

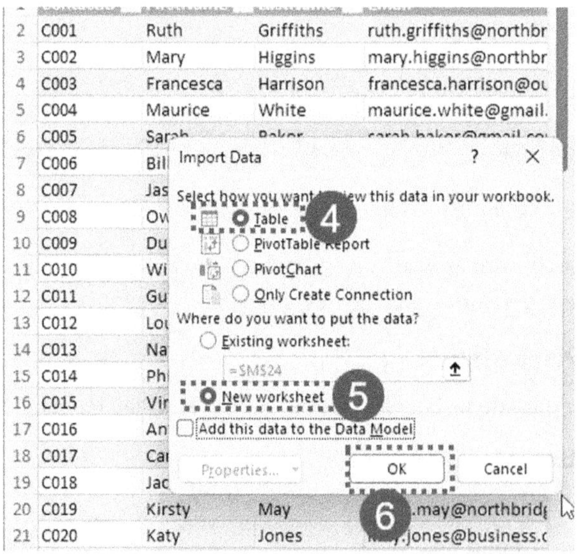

Figure 4.20 – Import Data dialog set to load as a Table to a new worksheet

Power Query loads the clean **Weekly_Event_KPIs** table to a new sheet in your `NOG-DataHub` workbook.

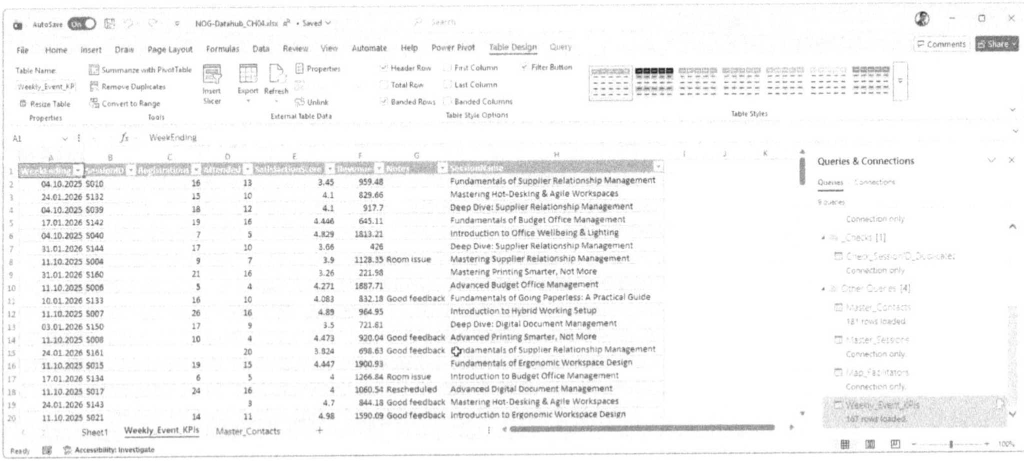

Figure 4.21 – Weekly_Event_KPIs query loaded to a worksheet in the NOG-DataHub workbook

Marcus looks at the clean table. Every row has a date, there are no blank rows, and the column names are exactly what his PivotTable expects.

"That's it," he says. "That's what it should look like."

> **Tip**
>
> This is a good moment to save your workbook. Press *Ctrl* + *S* before continuing. The query and its steps are stored inside the workbook file; saving now means you can close and reopen without losing anything.

A working query is only half the story; the other half is being able to read it.

Reading the applied steps and formula bar

The query works. But right now, if Marcus refreshes it in three months and something goes wrong, he, or whoever is looking after the workbook, will not know where to start.

This is where the **Applied Steps** pane becomes your most useful tool. Every transformation you performed left a record: a named step with a formula behind it. You do not need to write M code to read these records. You just need to know what to look for.

Reopening the Power Query editor

After closing the editor, you can return to it at any time:

1. Click the **Data** tab
2. Click **Queries & Connections** to open the pane (if it is not already visible)
3. In the **Queries & Connections** pane, double-click **Weekly_Event_KPIs**

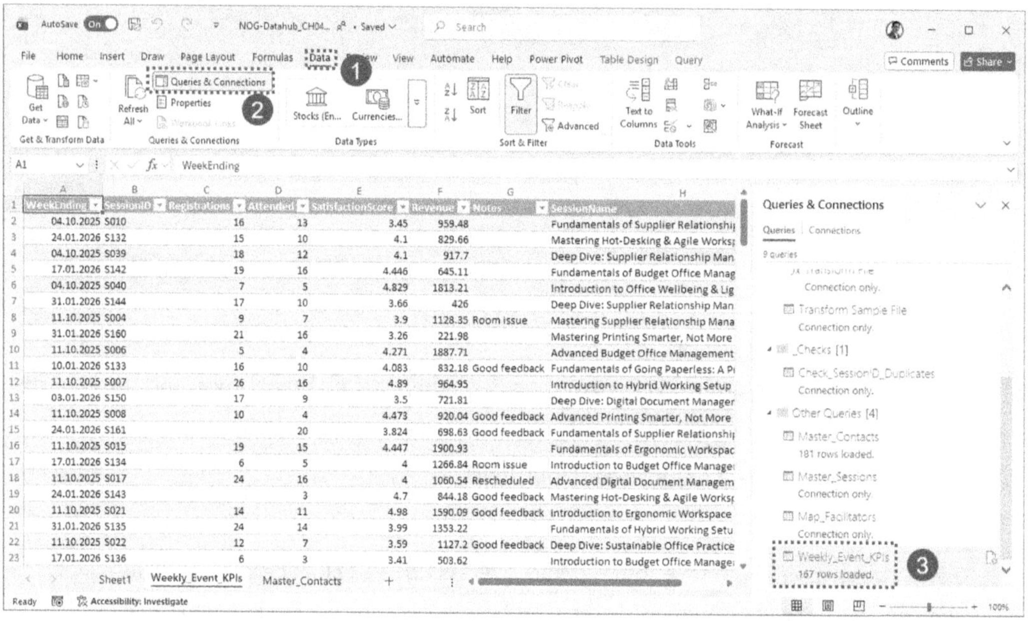

Figure 4.22 – Double-clicking a query in the Queries & Connections pane to reopen the Power Query Editor

The Power Query Editor reopens with the query exactly as you left it: **Applied Steps**, formula bar, and all.

Navigating the applied steps pane

Look at the **Applied Steps** pane on the right-hand side of the Power Query Editor. Your steps will look something like:

- Source
- Filtered Rows
- Filtered Rows1
- Imported Excel Workbook
- Table1_Table
- Removed Other Columns
- Removed Blank Rows
- Filtered Rows2
- Changed Type
- Merged Queries
- Expanded Master_Sessions

> Note
>
> Your step names may differ slightly depending on whether you connected via SharePoint Folder or Local Folder, and on which version of Excel you are using. The important thing is the shape: filtering steps at the top narrowing down to the file, then the cleanup steps, then the merge at the bottom.

Click **Source**. The data preview updates to show the raw folder listing, every file in the `NOG-DataHub`. Click **Filtered Rows** and the list narrows to the KPIs file only. Click **Removed Other Columns** and the gap columns are already gone. Click each step in turn and watch the preview change.

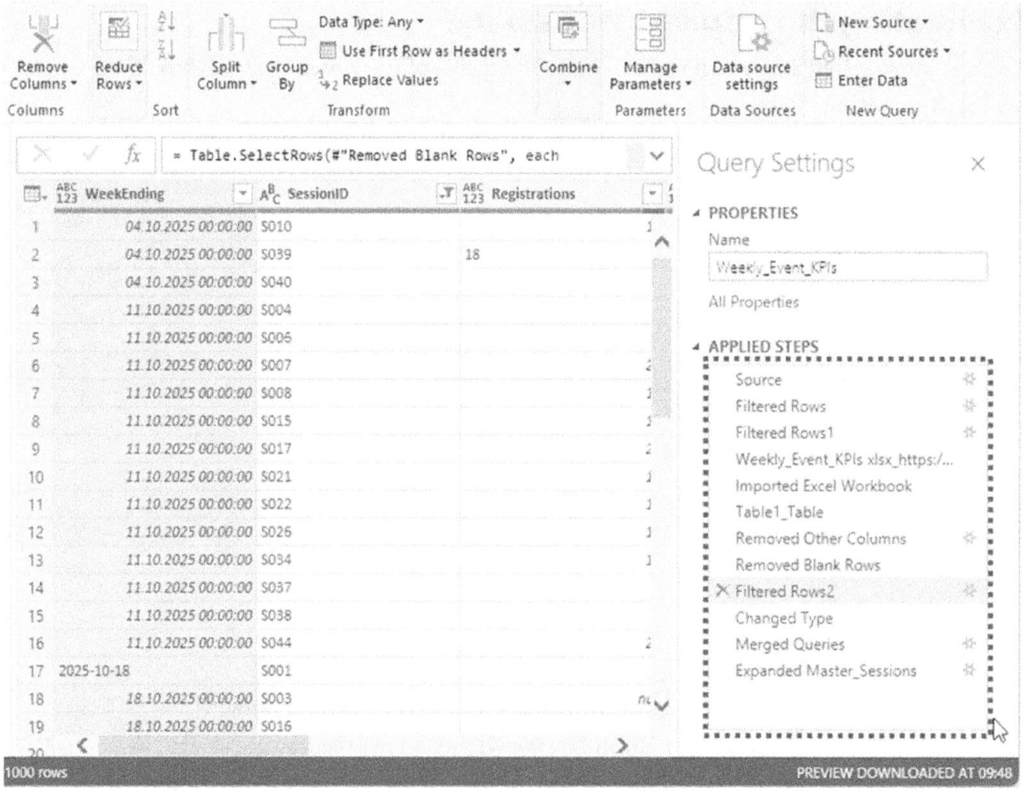

Figure 4.23 – Applied Steps pane showing the full step chain for Weekly_Event_KPIs

This is the recipe. Each step hands its output to the next. If you click a step halfway down the list, every step above has already been applied. Every step below has not yet run.

> **Tip**
>
> Give every step a meaningful name. Double-click a step name in the **Applied Steps** pane to rename it. `Filled Down WeekEnding` is immediately clear; **FilledDown1** is not. Well-named steps turn the **Applied Steps** pane into documentation you can read at a glance.

Reading the formula bar

Click any step in the **Applied Steps** pane and look at the **formula bar** at the top of the editor. You will see the M expression that Power Query generated for that step.

You do not need to understand M to get value from the formula bar. Focus on a few readable patterns. For example, here's what you'll see when you click the **Changed Type** step:

```
= Table.TransformColumnTypes(#"Filtered Rows2",{{"WeekEnding", type date},
{"SessionID", type text}, {"Registrations", Int64.Type}, {"Attended",
Int64.Type}, {"SatisfactionScore", type number}, {"Revenue", type number},
{"Notes", type text}})
```

You can read this even without knowing M. It says: take the result of the previous step (**Filtered Rows2**), and change the types of these named columns. Notice that columns are referenced by *name*, not by position. If someone inserts a column before **WeekEnding** in the source file, this step still finds **WeekEnding** correctly.

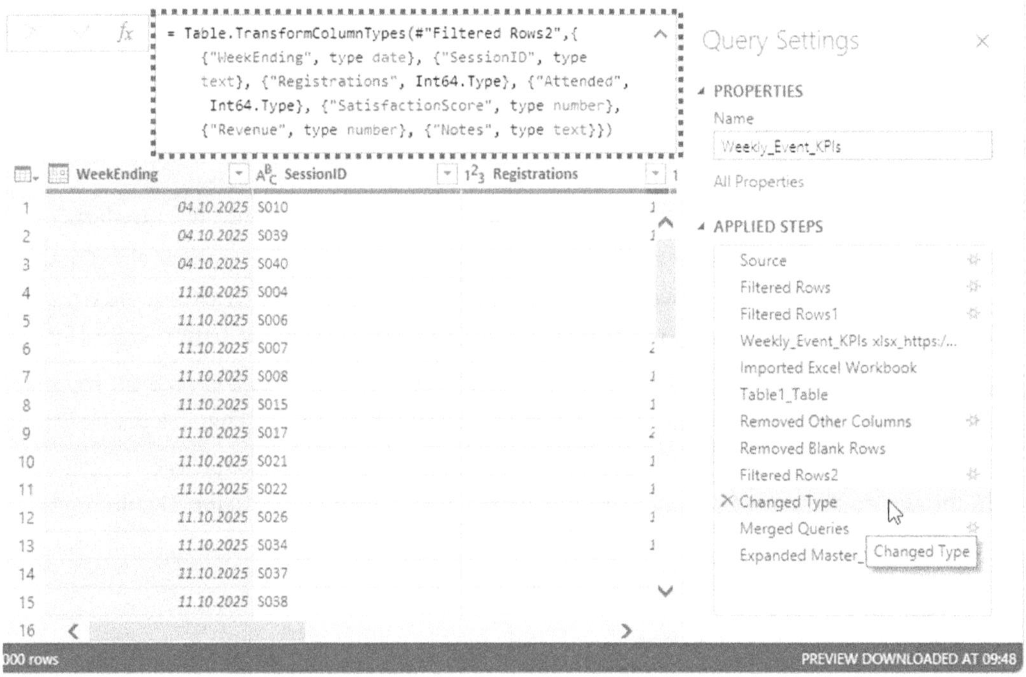

Figure 4.24 – Formula bar showing the Changed Type step with named column references

Readable steps are necessary but not sufficient.

Protecting key columns and grain

A clean query is not enough on its own. You also need to understand what the table represents and make sure no transformation step accidentally destroys that meaning.

Grain: what does one row represent?

The **grain** of a table is the answer to: what does one row in this table describe?

In **Weekly_Event_KPIs**, one row represents one session in one week. A session can appear in multiple weeks (if it runs repeatedly), and a week contains multiple sessions. The combination of WeekEnding + SessionID uniquely identifies each row.

Getting the grain right matters because it determines what you can calculate and how the table will join to other data in later chapters. If a transformation accidentally duplicates rows or drops weeks, your calculations will be wrong, and you may not notice immediately.

SessionID: the key column

SessionID is the key column for this table. It identifies which session a row belongs to, and it is the field you will use to join **Weekly_Event_KPIs** to other tables in *Chapters 8* and *9*.

Key columns need to be treated with care throughout the step chain:

- **Never drop them**: Check every **Remove Columns** step to confirm SessionID is not in the list.
- **Keep them typed as Text**: SessionID values like `S010` are identifiers, not numbers. Typing them as **Whole Number** would cause errors; Power Query cannot convert a value like `S010` to a number. Even for IDs that look purely numeric, setting the type to Whole Number risks silently stripping leading zeros (for example, "010" becomes 10), which would break any later join that relies on exact matching.
- **Never silently transform them**: A step that trims whitespace or changes casing should not touch SessionID. Inconsistent IDs break joins.

Click through to the final step in the **Applied Steps** pane. Confirm the **SessionID** column is present, typed as **Text**, and has no `null` values.

> Note
>
> **AttendeeEmail: A Note for Later**
>
> **Weekly_Event_KPIs** does not contain an **AttendeeEmail** column; that information lives in the registration and attendance files, which you will work with in *Chapters 6* and 7. It is worth flagging now because **AttendeeEmail** will become a key column in those chapters, joining registrations to attendee records.
>
> For now, note the pattern: each chapter builds tables with defined keys, and those keys carry forward into joins. The care you take with SessionID here pays off in *Chapters 8* and *9* when you merge these tables together.

Marcus's query now works reliably. The final habit to build is making it maintainable: for Marcus, for Quinn, and for whoever comes next.

Documenting and debugging your query

This section covers four habits that keep a query maintainable: naming steps clearly so anyone can follow the transformation at a glance, writing a short query description that records the source and key decisions, applying a reliable debugging workflow for when a refresh fails, and running a final validation checklist before handing the query back to Marcus.

Naming your steps

You have already seen that step names make the **Applied Steps** pane readable. Go through each step now and rename any that are unclear:

1. In the **Applied Steps** pane, select the step and then right-click the **Filtered Rows** step
2. Click **Rename**

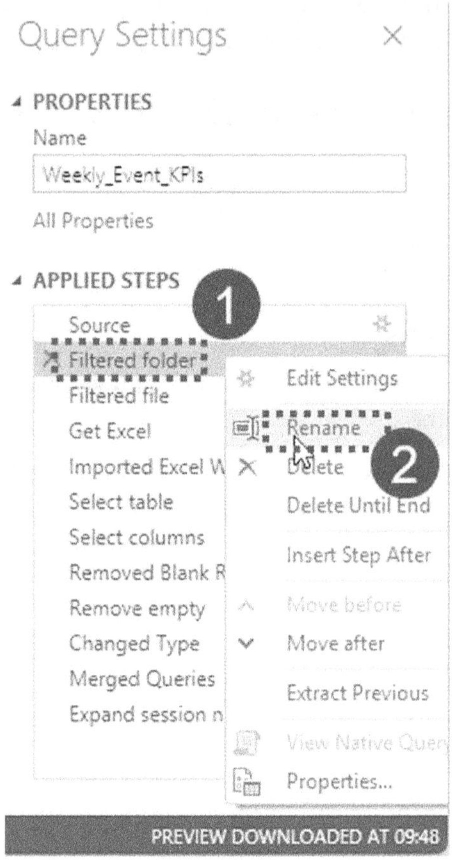

Figure 4.25 – Right-click menu on a step showing the Rename option

3. Type a more specific name, for example, `Filter folder`
4. Press *Enter*

Repeat for any other step with a generic name. When you are done, the **Applied Steps** pane should read like a plain-language description of what the query does. Depending on your version of Excel and connection type, your steps may look something like:

- Source
- Filtered folder
- Filtered file
- Get Excel
- Imported Excel Workbook
- Select table

- Select columns
- Removed Blank Rows
- Remove empty
- Changed Type
- Merged Queries
- Expand session name

> **Note**
>
> Your step names and the number of steps may differ. What matters is that each step name clearly describes what it does; anyone reading the list should be able to follow the transformation without opening the formula bar.

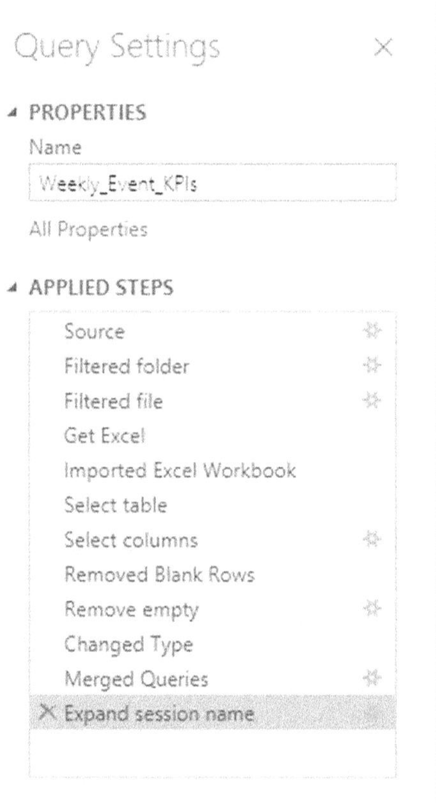

Figure 4.26 – Applied Steps pane with descriptive step names

Writing a query description

Step names describe the *how*. The query description covers the *what* and *why*.

1. In the **Queries** pane, right-click **Weekly_Event_KPIs**
2. Click **Properties**

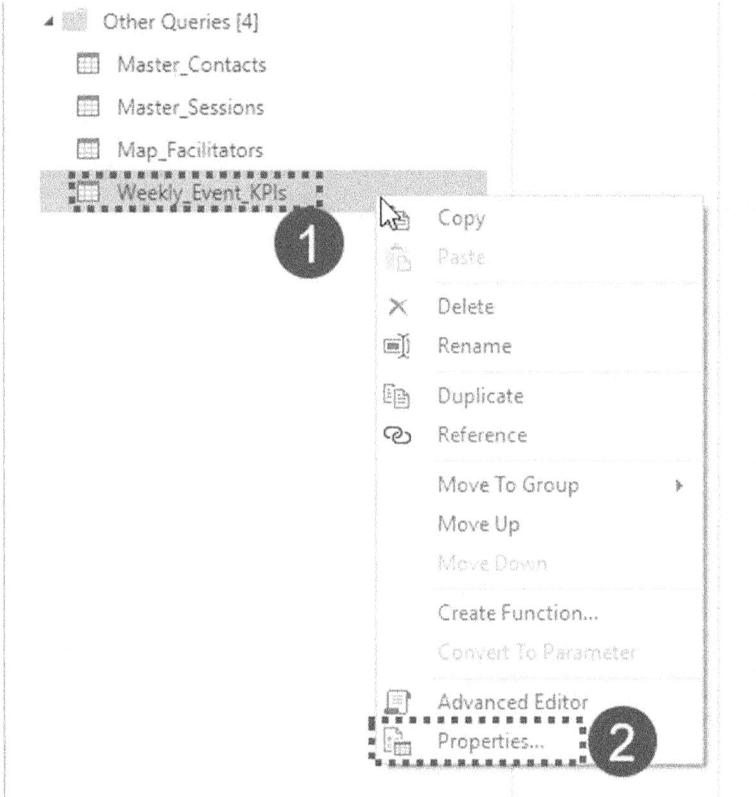

Figure 4.27 – Query Properties option in the right-click menu

3. In the **Description** field, type something like
   `Weekly KPIs per session from Events/KPIs/Weekly_Event_KPIs.xlsx. Cleaned: removed gap columns, blank rows, filled WeekEnding, set types. Merged SessionName from Master_Sessions on SessionID. Key column: SessionID (Text). Grain: one row per session per week.`
4. Click **OK**

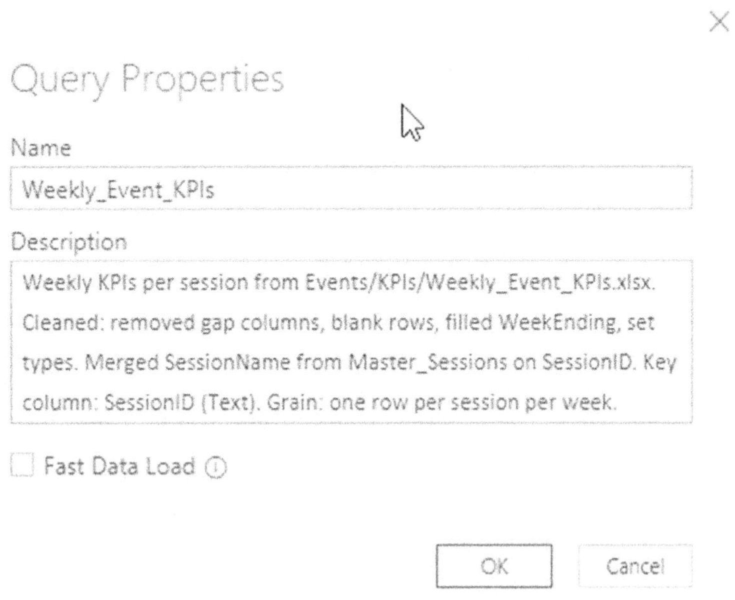

Figure 4.28 – Query Properties dialog with a description for Weekly_Event_KPIs

> **Tip**
>
> You can also add a description to individual steps. In the **Applied Steps** pane, right-click any step and click **Properties**. Type a short note in the **Description** field and click **OK**. Steps that have a description show a small icon next to their name, a quick visual cue that the step has been documented.

5. Click **Close & Load** to save your changes and return to the workbook

AI Helper

Documenting your step chain

To get a plain-language summary of your query, right-click the query name in the **Queries** pane and click **Copy**. This copies the full M code of the query to your clipboard. Paste it into an AI assistant with a prompt like: `Here is a Power Query M query. Summarize what it does in three bullet points for a colleague who does not know Power Query.` . The AI will produce a readable summary. Treat it as a first draft, read it against your actual **Applied Steps** to make sure it is accurate before you share it. AI summaries can miss nuances, especially if step names are not descriptive.

A debugging workflow for when things break

At some point, Marcus will refresh this query and see a red error. Here is a reliable approach to diagnosing if something went wrong:

1. Open the query in the Power Query Editor. In the **Queries & Connections** pane, double-click **Weekly_Event_KPIs**
2. Walk through the **Applied Steps** from the top:
    a. Click the first step: **Source**
    b. Click each step in turn, moving downwards
    c. Watch for the first step where the preview shows an error, a blank table, or unexpected data

    The first step showing an error is usually where the problem begins. Errors in the steps below are often just downstream effects caused by that initial issue.
3. Read the formula bar on the broken step by clicking the broken step to select it and looking at the formula bar
    The most common cause is a column name that no longer exists in the source. For example, if someone renamed "Attended" to "Attendees" in the source file, any step that references "Attended" will fail. You will see something like:

    ```
    Expression.Error: The column 'Attended' of the table wasn't found.
    ```
4. Fix the step, don't rebuild the query:
    a. Double-click the broken step in the Applied Steps pane

   b. Correct the column name to match the new source name

   c. Click **OK**

> **Caution**
>
> Do not delete a broken step and rebuild it from scratch unless you have exhausted all other options. Deleting a step in the middle of a chain breaks every step below it; Power Query will warn you before confirming, but the warning is easy to dismiss. Always try to edit the step first.

Here are the most common causes of refresh failure in source files maintained by multiple people:

Cause	**What you will see in the formula bar**
Column renamed	The column **OldName** was not found
Column deleted	Same error as above
New column inserted before a positional reference	Wrong column being processed, possibly no error
Sheet or table renamed	Navigator path no longer resolves

Table 4.3 – Common refresh failure causes and their symptoms

Final validation checklist

Before closing the editor and handing the query back to Marcus, run through a quick trust loop:

Check	**Expected**
Row count	~160 rows, no blank rows, no **TOTALS** row
WeekEnding	Every row has a date or an error (errors indicate non-standard date formats in the source)
SessionID	Present on every row, typed as Text, no nulls
SessionName	Present on every row after merge; nulls indicate a **SessionID** with no match in **Master_Sessions**

Check	Expected
Registrations/ Attended	Whole Number type; nulls acceptable where data was not recorded; errors indicate text-formatted source cells
Data types	Match *Table 4.2*
Applied Steps	All steps named clearly, including merged session names
Query loads to worksheet	No error on Close & Load

Table 4.4 – Final validation checklist for Weekly_Event_KPIs

Quinn closes the **Power Query Editor** and clicks **Refresh All**. The query runs successfully, and the table updates correctly on Marcus's worksheet.

It is still Monday morning. Marcus has forty minutes before his presentation.

"It works," Quinn says. "And it will keep working, as long as nobody inserts a column in the source file."

"I'll send a note to the team," Marcus says.

That is exactly the right response.

Summary

In this chapter, you built a clean, reliable query for Marcus's weekly KPI report, and you learned how to read what Power Query is actually doing:

- **Reliable step chains**: a query that references columns by name, not position, and handles structural noise (blank rows, fill-down patterns, gap columns) deliberately.
- **Sheets vs. Tables vs. Named Ranges**: why selecting a named Excel Table in the Navigator produces a cleaner starting point than selecting the raw sheet.
- **Applied Steps as a recipe**: each step is readable and clickable; click any step to see the data at that point in the transformation.
- **Formula bar passive literacy**: recognizing named column references versus positional ones, and identifying the most common patterns (type changes, fill down, filters).
- **Key columns and grain**: SessionID is the join key; one row = one session per week. Never drop, retype, or silently transform key columns.

- **Merging to enrich a query**: using **Merge Queries** to bring **SessionName** in from **Master_Sessions** via **SessionID**; the same **Left Outer** join pattern from *Chapter 3*, applied to a new context.
- **Documentation and debugging**: named steps, query descriptions, AI-assisted summaries, and a step-by-step debugging workflow for when refreshes fail.
- **Change management**: a reliable query is one half of the solution; the people who maintain the source file are the other half.

In this chapter, we created the **Weekly_Event_KPIs** query, loaded to a worksheet in the `NOG-DataHub` workbook, ready for Marcus's Monday reports

In *Chapter 5*, Quinn helps Marcus take this clean KPI data further; building a reusable PivotTable summary pack that refreshes automatically alongside the query.

5

Build Reusable Reports with PivotTables

Figure 5.1 – Marcus needs a report to present to management

The following Monday, Marcus stops by Quinn's desk before the morning standup.

"The KPI table is great," he says. "Really clean. But when I present this to the leadership team, I can't just drop a raw table into my slides. I need a proper summary, something that shows the trend at a glance."

Quinn nods. She had expected this. The clean query from *Chapter 4* is the foundation, but Marcus needs a report, something he can hand to twelve people in a meeting room and have them understand it in thirty seconds.

"Give me an hour," Quinn says. "We'll build you two summary pages. They'll refresh automatically whenever the data updates. You won't have to rebuild anything from week to week."

Marcus raises an eyebrow. "And if someone asks to see just the workshops?"

"One click on a **slicer**," Quinn says.

That gets his attention.

A clean query is the prerequisite for a reliable report. When Power Query has removed blank rows, the totals row, and formatting inconsistencies, what remains is a clean table with a consistent and predictable structure: the same columns appear every time, the correct data types, and each session is represented by a single row per session and week. That predictability and consistency are what make PivotTables reliable and stable.

Compare the alternative: building a PivotTable on a manually maintained range. Every time someone adds a row, adjusts a column, or reformats a cell, the PivotTable can behave unpredictably: it may include the wrong rows, miss new data, or break entirely. A Power Query output sidesteps all of that. The query handles the cleaning; the PivotTable handles the aggregation.

In this chapter, Quinn will build two summary views for Marcus:

- **Registrations by Week** — the weekly trend of registrations, one row per week
- **Attended by Session Type** — total attendance grouped by session type (Workshop, Seminar, Training, Webinar, or Course)

Both will update with a single **Refresh All**. Both will respond to the same slicer.

In this chapter, you'll learn to -

- Extend an existing Power Query merge to bring in a new column, and switch the query from loading to a worksheet to Connection Only
- Build stable PivotTables from a query connection, choosing the right fields and avoiding layouts that break on refresh
- Choose and verify the correct aggregation (Sum, Count, or Distinct Count) so each PivotTable value answers the right business question
- Format and package the report for reuse: rename headers, add titles, connect a slicer to multiple PivotTables, and add a refresh note so colleagues can update the data safely

Technical requirements

The chapters in this book build on each other. Make sure you have completed all exercises in the previous chapters before starting this one.

For the exercises in this chapter, continue in your `NOG-DataHub` workbook from *Chapter 4*. Do not open a new file. By this point, your workbook should contain the following queries in the Queries & Connections pane:

- **Master_Contacts** — loaded to a worksheet (*Chapter 2*)
- **Master_Sessions** — connection only (*Chapter 3*)
- **Map_Facilitators** — connection only (*Chapter 3*)
- **Check_SessionID_Duplicates** — connection only (*Chapter 3*)
- **Weekly_Event_KPIs** — loaded to a worksheet (*Chapter 4*)

If any of these are missing, complete the relevant chapter before continuing.

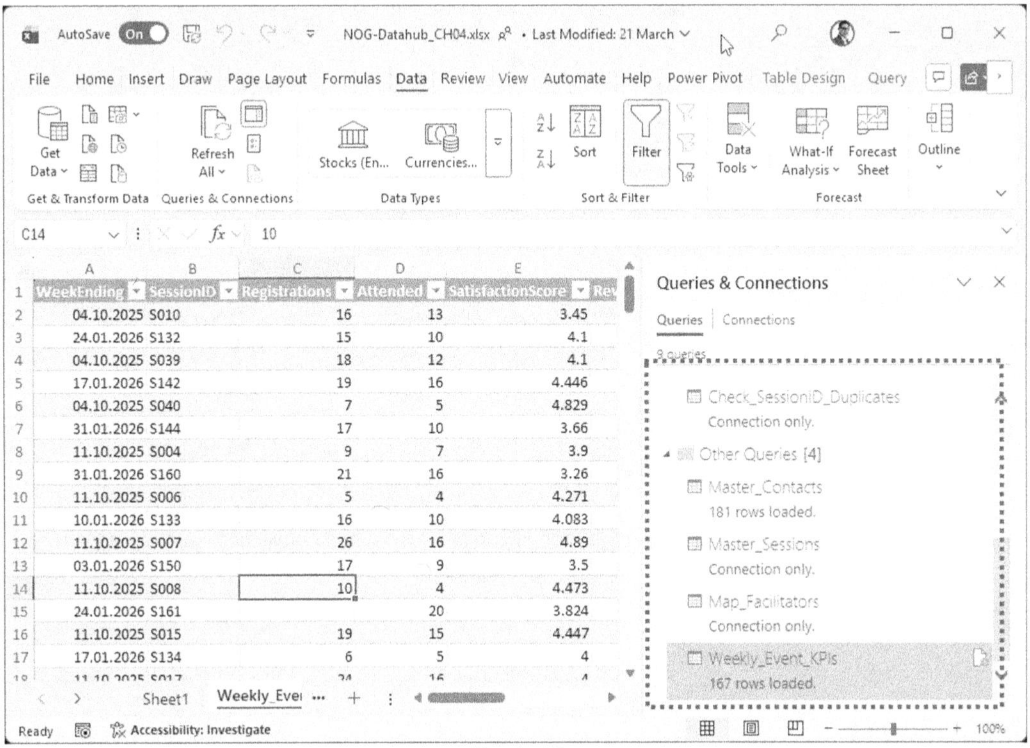

Chapter 5">

Figure5.2–Queries& Connections pane showing the expected queries before starting Chapter 5

Extending the query to include session types

Before building the PivotTables, Quinn recalls Marcus's question: "Can I filter by session type?"

The **Weekly_Event_KPIs** query currently carries a **SessionName** column, which was merged in from **Master_Sessions** in *Chapter 4*. But **SessionType** (`Course`, `Seminar`, `Training`, `Webinar`, `Workshop`) was not included. It exists in **Master_Sessions**. Bringing it in is a small change: reopen the expand step and tick one more column.

1. Click the **Data** tab
2. Click **Queries & Connections** to open the pane if it is not already visible
3. Double-click **Weekly_Event_KPIs** to open the Power Query Editor

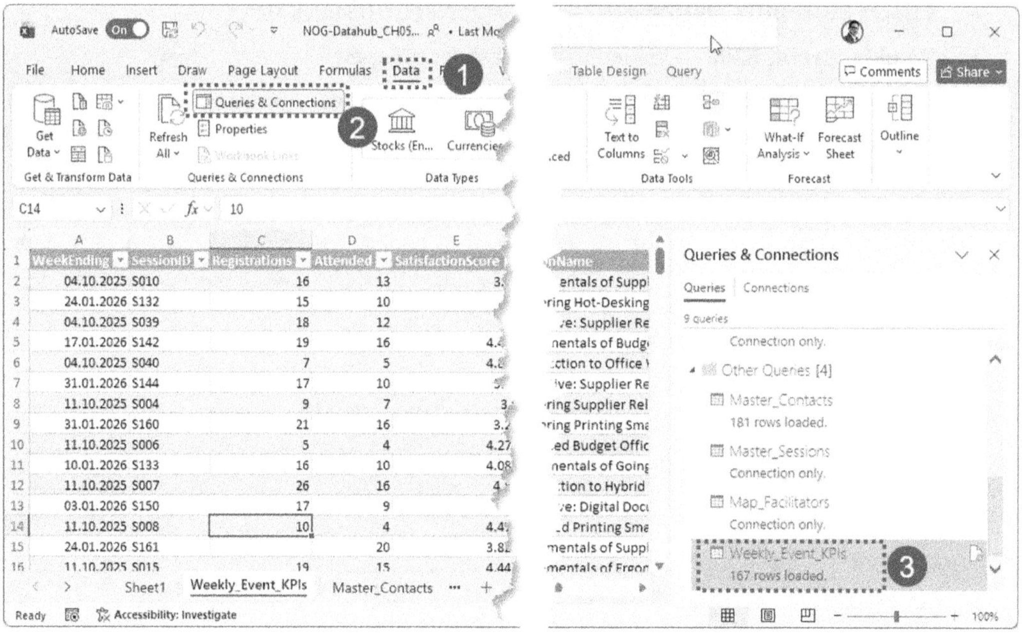

Figure 5.3 – Double-clicking Weekly_Event_KPIs in the Queries and Connections pane to reopen the editor

4. In the **Applied Steps** pane, click the gear icon to the right of the last step (**Expand session name** or something similar), the one that expanded the **Master_Sessions** column:

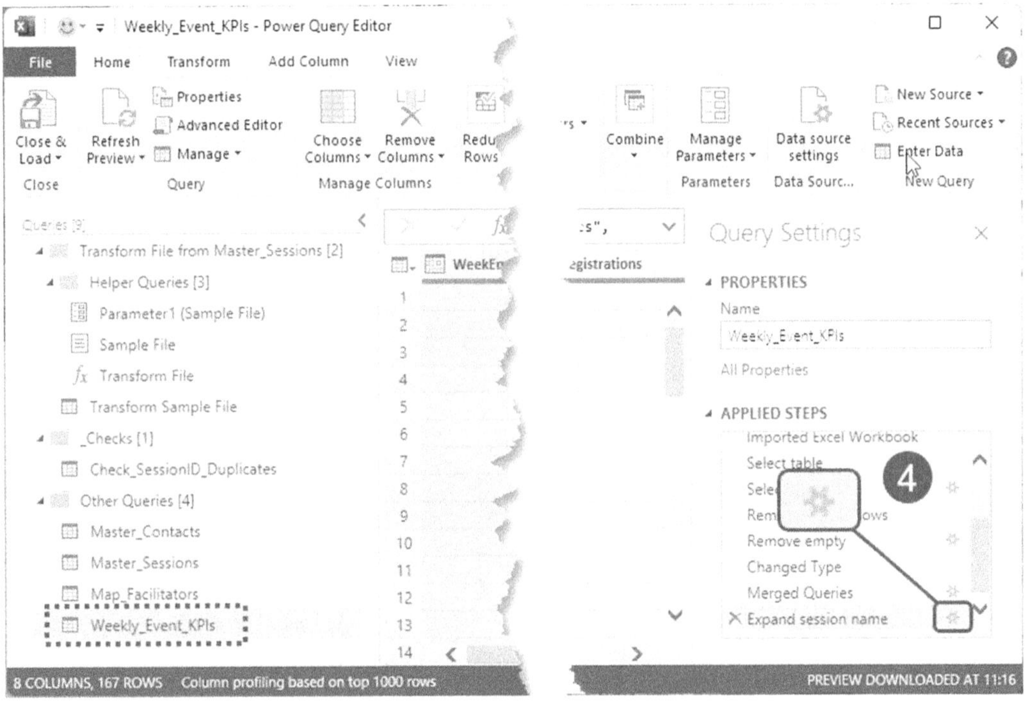

Figure 5.4 – Clicking the gear icon on the Expanded Master_Sessions step to reopen the column selector

The column selector dialog reopens. **SessionName** is already ticked.

5. Tick **SessionType** as well (**SessionName** remains ticked)
6. Click **OK**

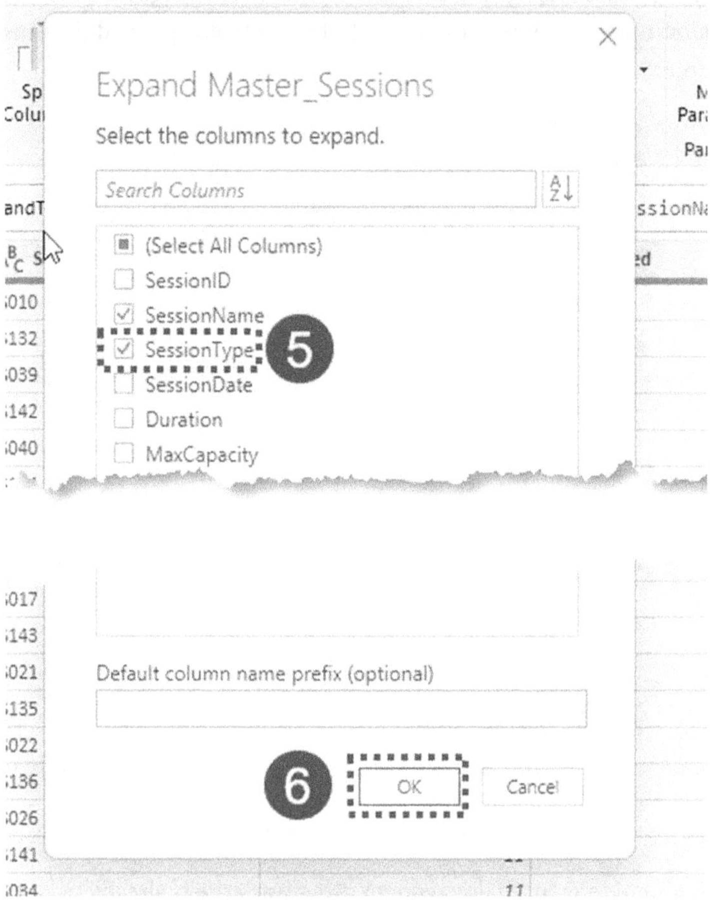

Figure 5.5 – Column selector with both SessionName and SessionType ticked

The **SessionType** column appears to the right of the preview. Each row now shows its session type: Course, Seminar, Training, Webinar, or Workshop.

> **Tip**
>
> When you edit an existing step using the gear icon, Power Query updates that step in place; it does not add a new step. This keeps the **Applied Steps** list clean and avoids stacking redundant steps on top of each other.

Removing the worksheet table

In *Chapter 4*, the query was loaded into a worksheet so Marcus could review the raw data. Now that the PivotTables will serve as his view into the data, the worksheet is no longer needed. Close the **Power Query Editor** first, then delete the sheet:

1. Click the **Home** tab
2. Click **Close & Load**

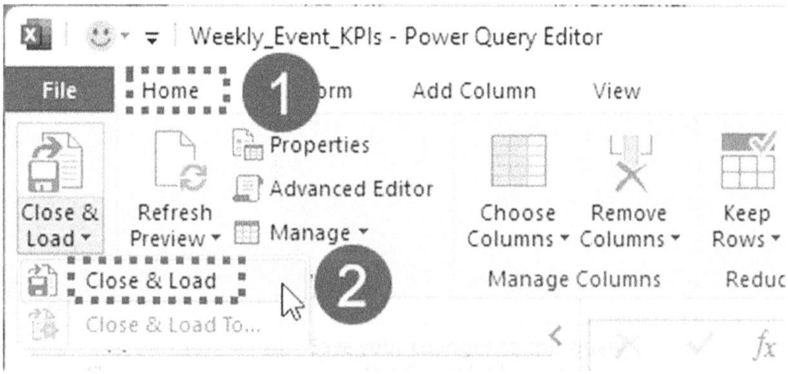

Figure 5.6 – Close & Load button on the Home tab

Excel closes the editor and applies the **SessionType** change to the existing query output. The raw KPI table on the worksheet now includes the new **SessionType** column.

Now delete the worksheet. Deleting it does not delete the query; Power Query will keep **Weekly_Event_KPIs** query in the Excel file and switch it to **Connection only** automatically.

3. Right-click the sheet tab that holds the **Weekly_Event_KPIs** table (the one created in *Chapter 4*)
4. Click **Delete** and click **Delete** again to confirm

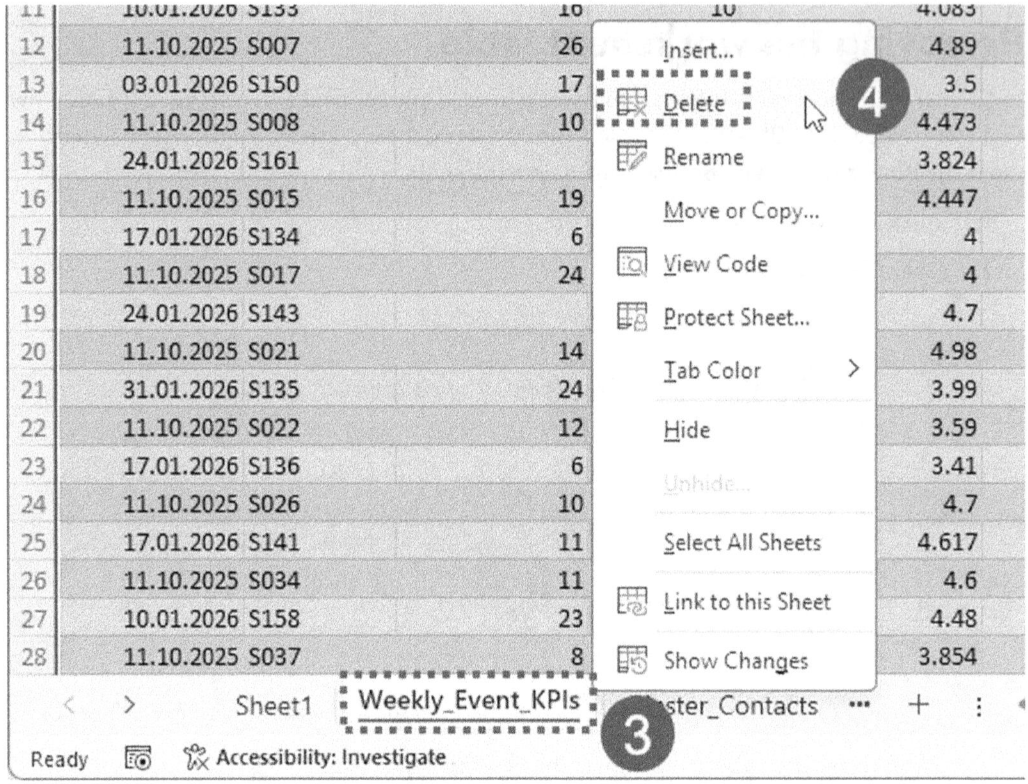

Figure 5.7 – Deleting the Weekly_Event_KPIs worksheet after closing the Power Query Editor

Open the **Queries & Connections** pane and look at the **Weekly_Event_KPIs** entry; it now shows **Connection only**.

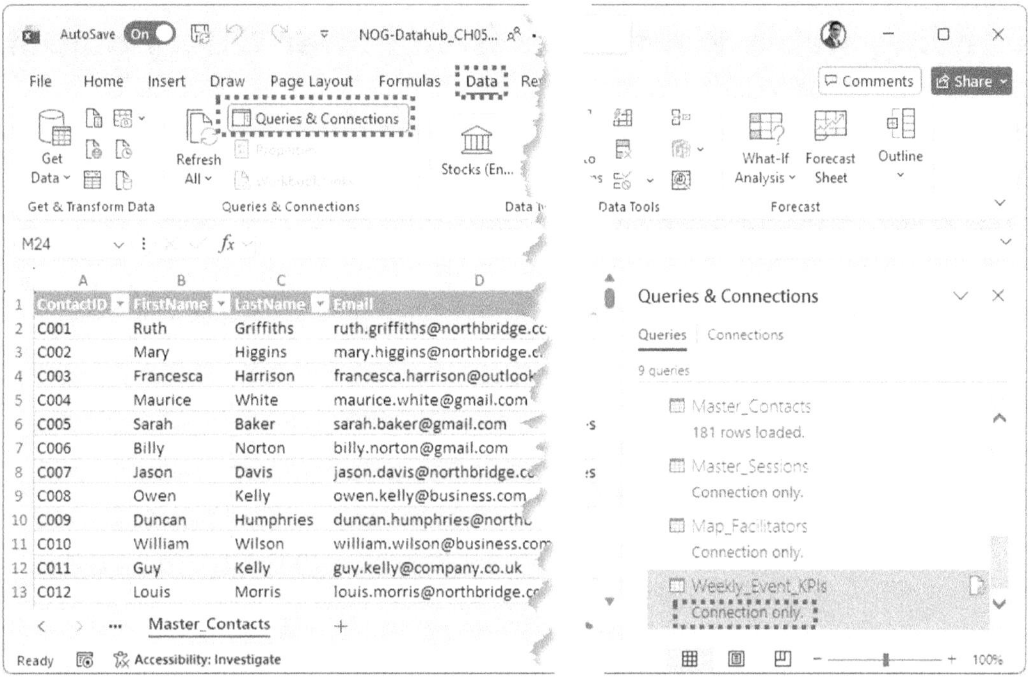

Figure 5.8 – Queries & Connections pane showing Weekly_Event_KPIs as Connection only after deleting the sheet

This is one of the most useful things to know about Power Query: **the query is not the sheet**. Deleting the output sheet does not delete the query. The query remains in the workbook, ready to refresh and feed whatever you connect to it next; in this case, two PivotTables.

> Note
>
> **Connection only** does not mean the query stops working. It still runs every time you press **Refresh All**; it simply delivers its output directly to whatever is connected to it (a PivotTable, the Data Model, or another query), rather than writing rows to a worksheet.

Building stable PivotTables from Power Query output

With the query updated and set to **Connection only**, Quinn is ready to build the first PivotTable. The quickest route is directly from the **Queries & Connections** pane: right-click the connection and load it as a PivotTable in one step.

PivotTable 1: registrations by week

The first PivotTable answers the question Marcus brought to Quinn's desk: how many people registered by date? This is the weekly trend he needs to show the leadership team at a glance. Let's set it up:

1. Click the **Data** tab
2. Click **Queries & Connections**
3. In the **Queries & Connections** pane, right-click **Weekly_Event_KPIs**
4. Click **Load To...**

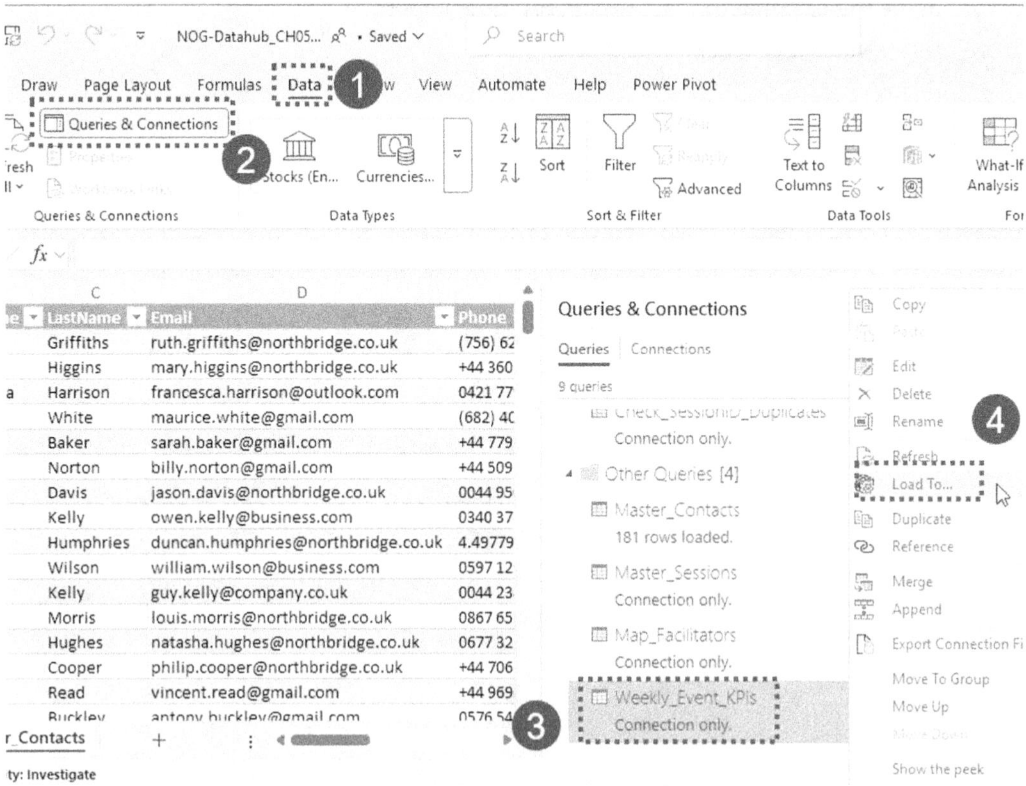

Figure 5.9 – Right-click menu on Weekly_Event_KPIs in the Queries and Connections pane showing Load To...

5. In the **Import Data** dialog, select **PivotTable Report**
6. Select **New worksheet**
7. Click **OK**

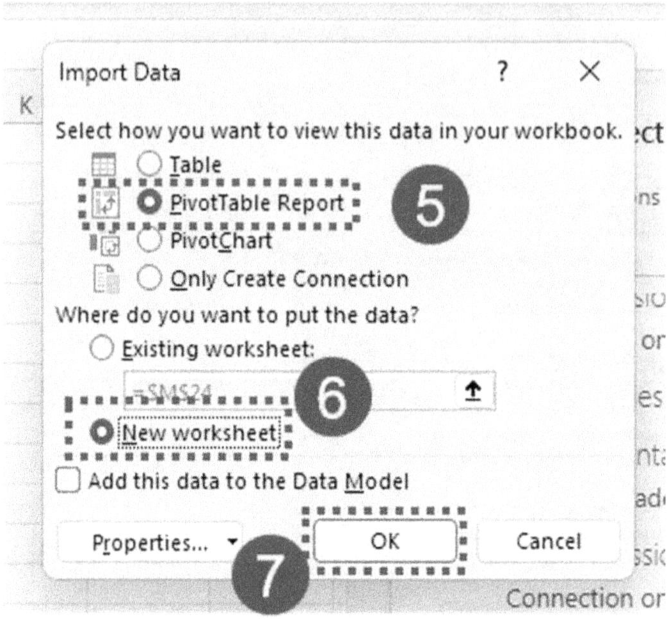

Figure 5.10 – Import Data dialog with PivotTable Report and New worksheet selected

Excel inserts a blank PivotTable on a new sheet. The **PivotTable Fields** pane opens on the right, showing all the columns from **Weekly_Event_KPIs**.

Now build the "Registrations by Week" summary:

8. Drag **WeekEnding** to the **Rows** area
9. Drag **Registrations** to the **Values** area

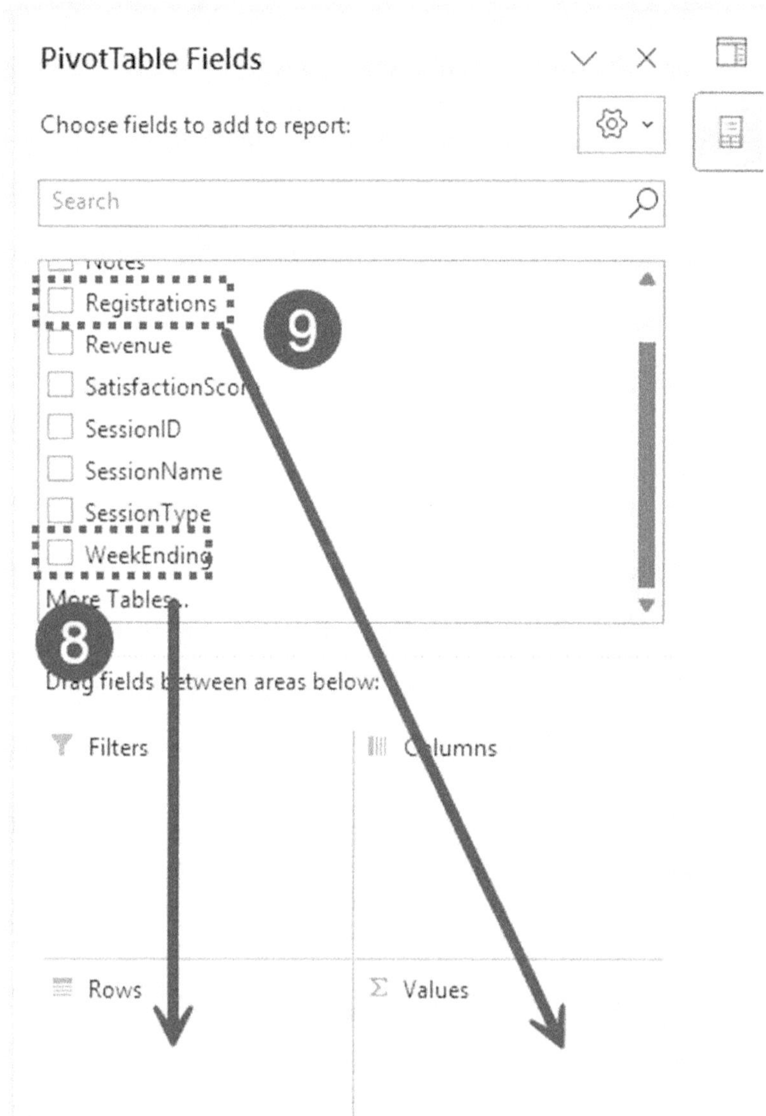

Figure 5.11 – PivotTable Fields pane with WeekEnding in Rows and Registrations in Values

Caution

Excel will almost certainly group your dates automatically. Since Excel 2016, a feature called **Auto Date Grouping** detects date fields and collapses them into Year, Quarter, and Month levels the moment you drop them into Rows. Instead of seeing individual week-ending dates, you will see a hierarchy, and the weekly detail Marcus needs will be hidden.

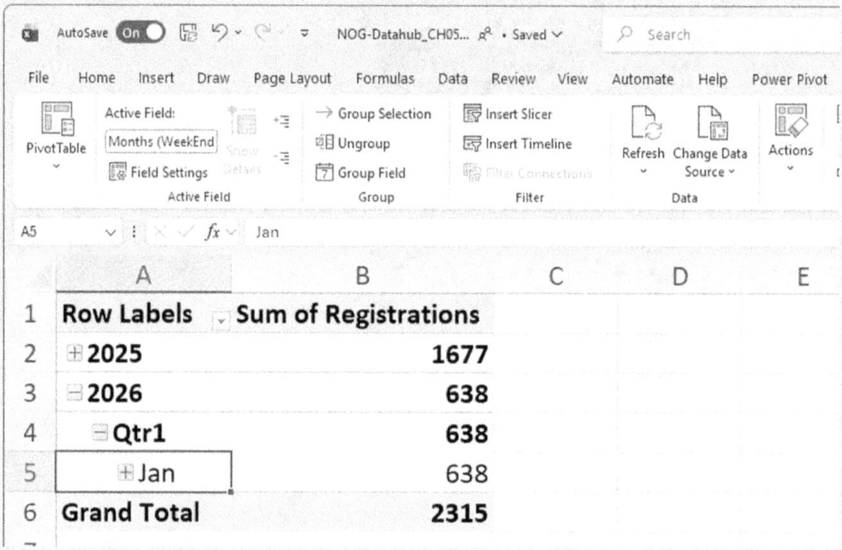

Figure 5.12 – PivotTable showing auto-grouped dates collapsed into Year, Quarter and Month levels

Ungroup the dates before continuing:

a. Right-click any date value in the **Rows** area of the PivotTable
b. Click **Ungroup**

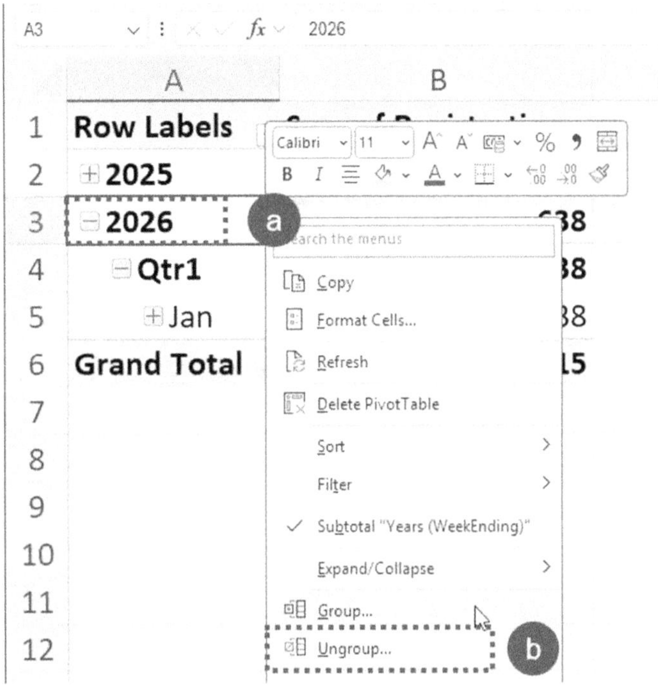

Figure 5.13 – Right-click menu on a grouped date showing the Ungroup option

The PivotTable now shows one row per week: individual WeekEnding dates with total registrations for that week.

Now, rename the sheet tab:

10. Right-click the sheet tab at the bottom of the screen
11. Click **Rename**

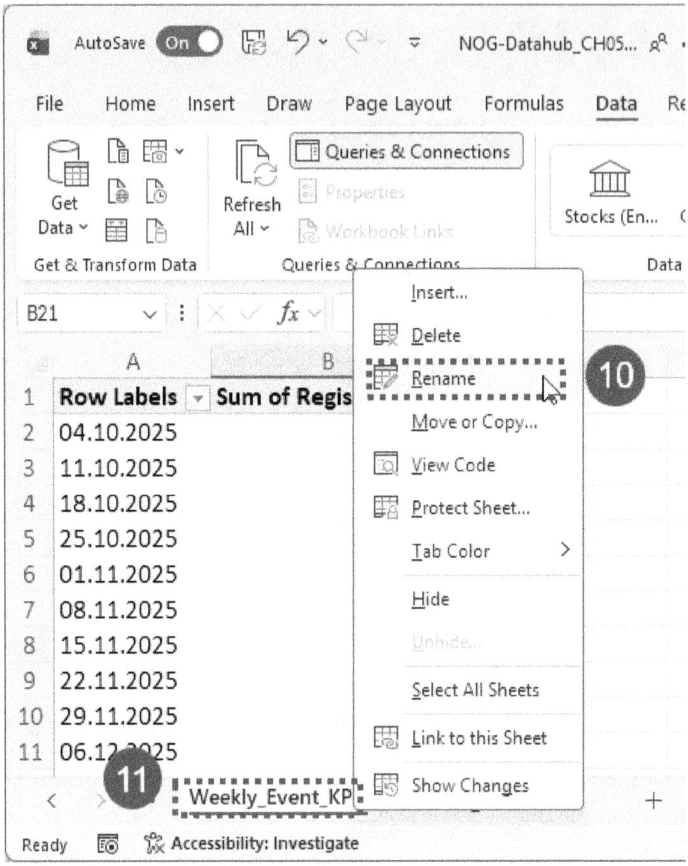

Figure 5.14 – Right-click menu on the sheet tab showing the Rename option

12. Type `KPI - Weekly Summary` and press *Enter*

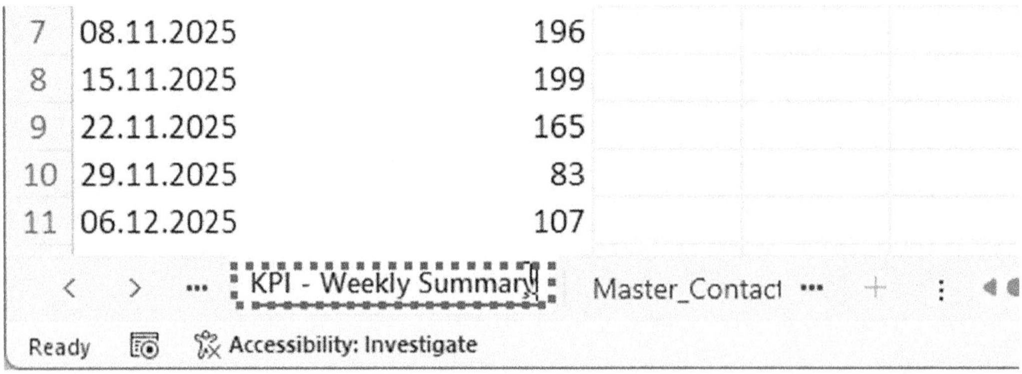

Figure 5.15 – Completed Registrations by Week PivotTable with renamed sheet tab

PivotTable 2: attendance by session type

The second PivotTable answers a different question: across all weeks, how many people attended each session type? This is the view Marcus wants to use to show which session type is generating the highest engagement.

For this second PivotTable, we will use a different method: go to **Insert** | **PivotTable** and point it at the same connection. We will place it on the same sheet, to the right of the first PivotTable, but first make sure there is enough space for it. Scroll to the right to check how many columns the first PivotTable uses, then click a cell that clears it comfortably. **G1** is a good starting point if your date list does not extend that far:

1. Click cell **G1** on the **KPI - Weekly Summary** sheet
2. Click the **Insert** tab
3. Click **PivotTable**
4. Click **From External Data Source**

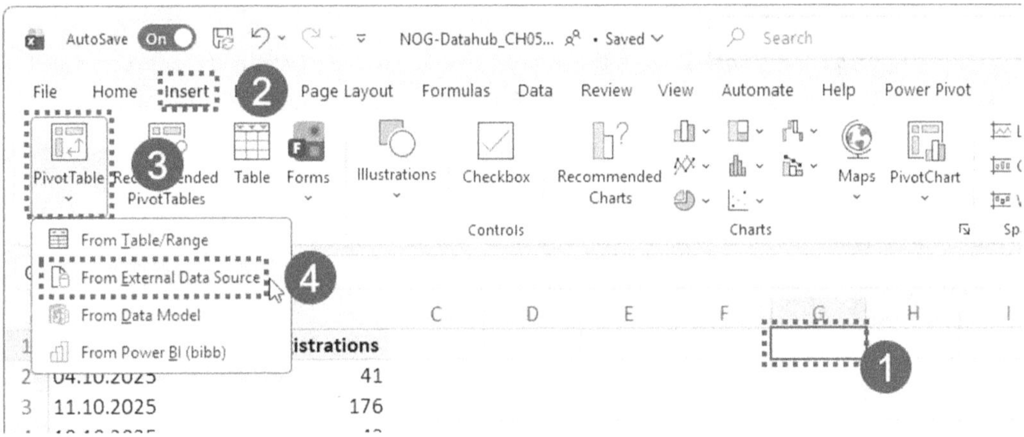

Figure 5.16 – PivotTable button on the Insert tab

5. In the dialog click **Choose Connection**

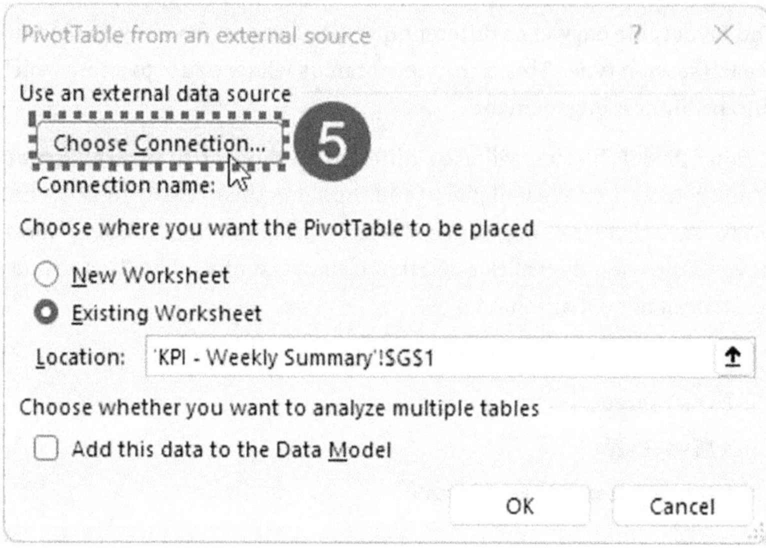

Figure 5.17 – PivotTable dialog with Use an external data source selected and Choose Connection highlighted

6. In the **Existing Connections** dialog, click the **Connections** tab if it is not already active
7. Click on the query **Weekly_Event_KPIs**
8. Click **Open**

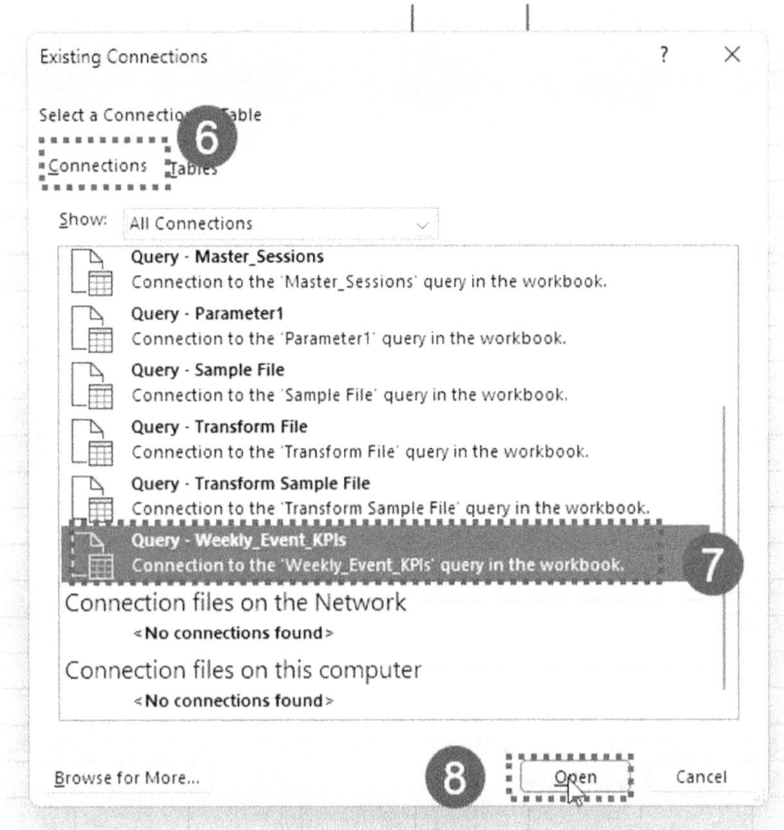

Figure 5.18 – Existing Connections dialog with Weekly_Event_KPIs selected under the Queries tab

9. Back in the PivotTable dialog, select **Existing Worksheet**
10. Confirm the cell reference shows **G1** (or adjust it if needed)
11. Click **OK**

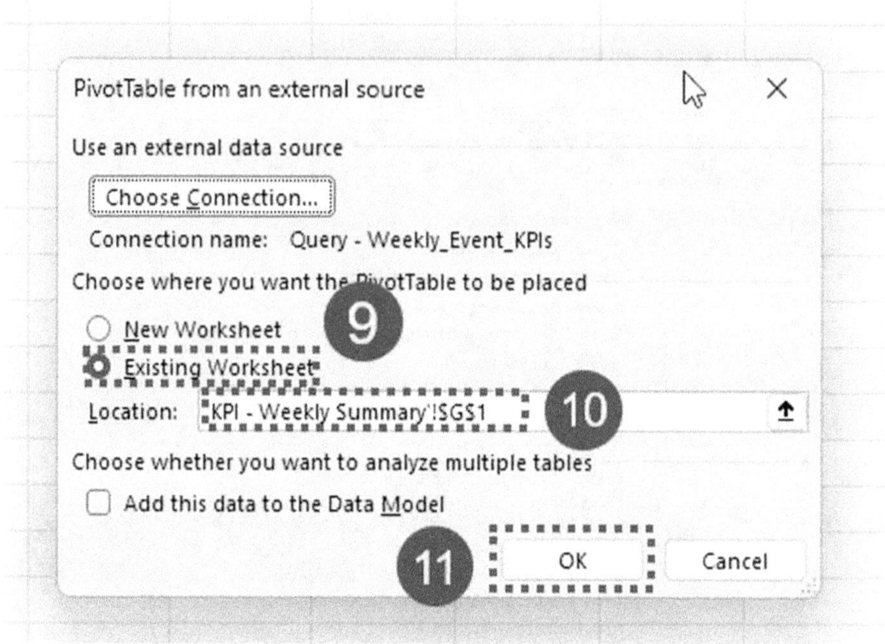

Figure 5.19 – PivotTable dialog set to Existing Worksheet with G1 as the target cell

A second blank PivotTable appears to the right of the first. Now build the "Attended by Session Type" summary.

12. Drag **SessionType** to the **Rows** area
13. Drag **Attended** to the **Values** area

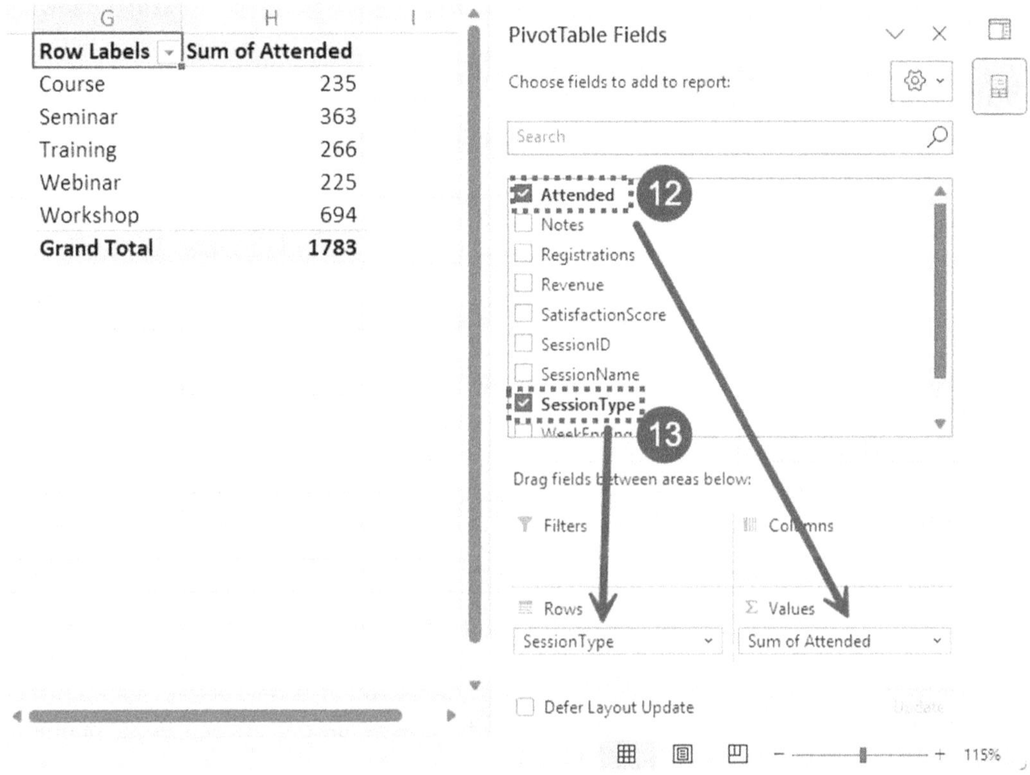

Figure 5.20 – The Attended by Session Type PivotTable, with the PivotTable Fields pane showing SessionType in Rows and Sum of Attended in Values

The second PivotTable shows one row per session type (`Course`, `Seminar`, `Training`, `Webinar`, `Workshop`), each with the total number of attendees across all weeks and sessions.

> **Caution**
>
> When two PivotTables share a sheet, keep enough space (vertically and horizontally) between them. PivotTables expand as data grows; if one sits directly below another, it will collide with it on refresh, and Excel will show an error.

Using implicit measures correctly

Every PivotTable calculation uses an **implicit measure**: the aggregation Excel applies automatically when you drag a field to the **Values** area. For numbers, the default is usually **Sum**. For text fields, it defaults to **Count**.

These defaults are sensible starting points, but they are not always correct. The skill is knowing when to verify and when to override.

Sum, Count, and Distinct Count

There are three aggregations worth understanding at this stage:

Aggregation	What it does	When to use it
Sum	Adds all values in the group	Numeric fields that accumulate: Registrations, Attended, Revenue
Count	Counts every row in the group, including duplicates	Counting records, not unique items
Distinct Count	Counts unique values only	People, IDs, emails; anything where one person can appear more than once

Table 5.1 – The three most common implicit measures and when to use each

The distinction between **Count** and **Distinct Count** catches many people out. Imagine a future report built on a registration table, where each row represents one person registering for one session. If you drag **AttendeeEmail** into the **Values** area and leave the aggregation as **Count**, you get the total number of registrations, not the number of unique attendees. A person who registered for three sessions counts three times.

AttendeeEmail	Count	Distinct Count
sarah@example.com (3 sessions)	3	1
james@example.com (1 session)	1	1
Total	4	2

Table 5.2 – Count versus Distinct Count of AttendeeEmail for the same two attendees

For **Weekly_Event_KPIs**, this risk does not apply directly. Registrations and Attended are already aggregated numbers (one number per session per week), so Sum is correct. But when you later work with row-level registration or attendance data in *Chapters 6* and *7*, this distinction becomes critical.

Checking and changing aggregation

Always verify that the aggregation in the **Values** area matches the business question. The quickest way is directly from the right-click menu:

1. Right-click any value in the **Registrations** or **Attended** column
2. Hover over **Summarize Values By**
3. Confirm **Sum** is ticked, or click the correct aggregation if it is not

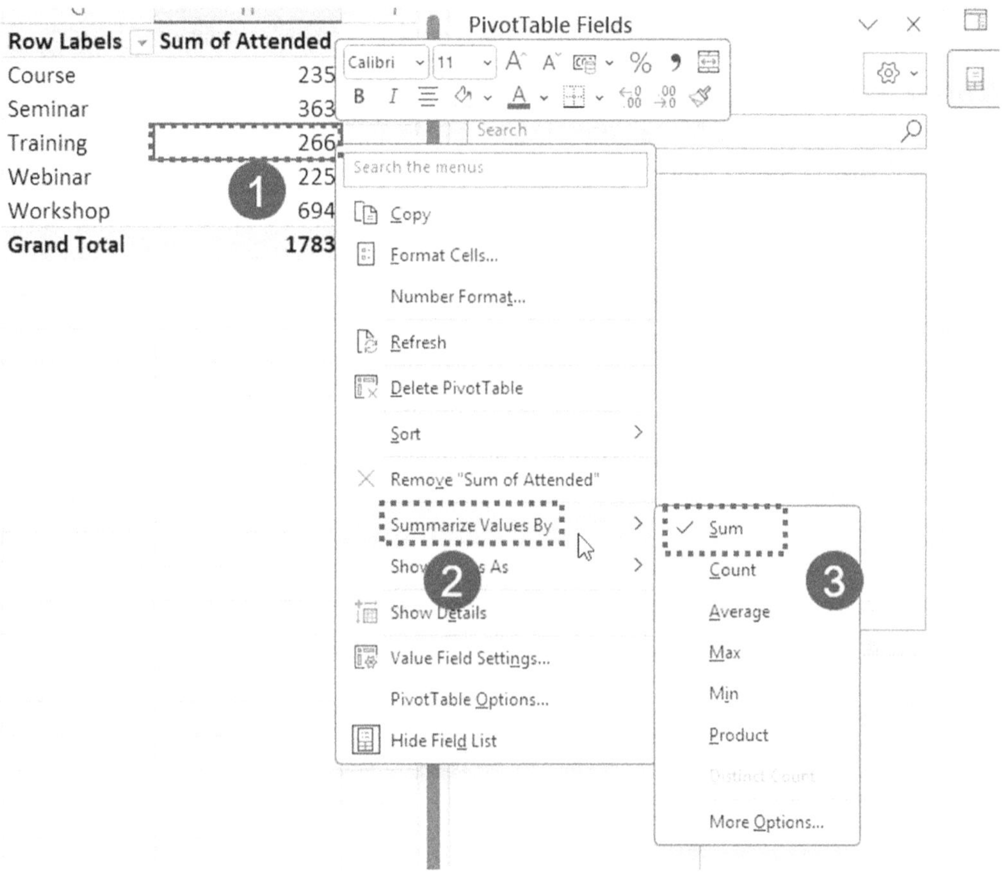

Figure 5.21 – Right-click context menu showing Summarise Values By with Sum ticked

Tip

Make checking **Summarize Values By** a habit whenever you add a field to the **Values** area. The aggregation Excel picks by default is not always what you intend. Two seconds to verify are faster than explaining a wrong number to a manager.

Turning PivotTables into clear, stakeholder-friendly pages

A freshly built PivotTable is functional but uninviting. The column headers say, "Sum of Registrations", row labels may include "(blank)", and the layout defaults to a compact style that is hard to read at a glance. Four straightforward changes transform it into something Marcus can present without apology.

Work through these on both PivotTables, starting with **KPI - Weekly Summary**.

Rename the value field header

In Excel 365, you can rename a value field header directly on the cell: click it, type the new name, and press *Enter*. Let's do it in our file:

1. Click the cell that reads **Sum of Registrations**
2. Type `Registrations` (with a trailing space) and press *Enter*

> **Note**
>
> The trailing space is intentional. Excel does not allow a custom name that exactly matches an existing column name; typing `Registrations` without the space will produce an error. Adding a single space makes the name technically distinct while looking identical in the report.

Repeat for the second PivotTable: click **Sum of Attended**, type `Attended` (with a trailing space), and press *Enter*.

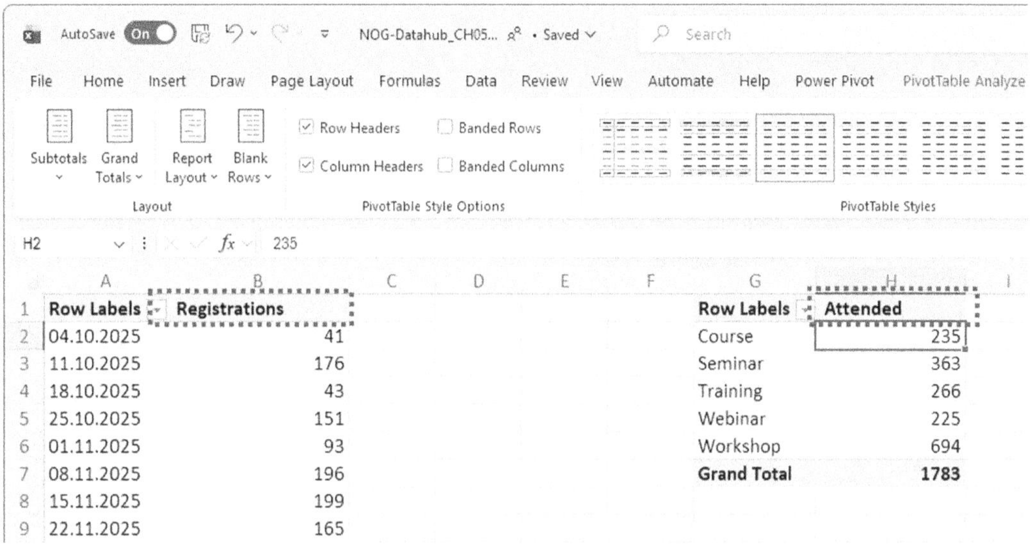

Figure 5.22 – Both PivotTable headers renamed: "Registrations" on the left and "Attended" on the right

Switch to tabular layout

The default compact layout nests row labels, which can look confusing when there are multiple row fields. Tabular layout gives each field its own column. Let's see how:

1. Click anywhere inside the PivotTable
2. Click the **Design** tab
3. Click **Report Layout**
4. Click **Show in Tabular Form**

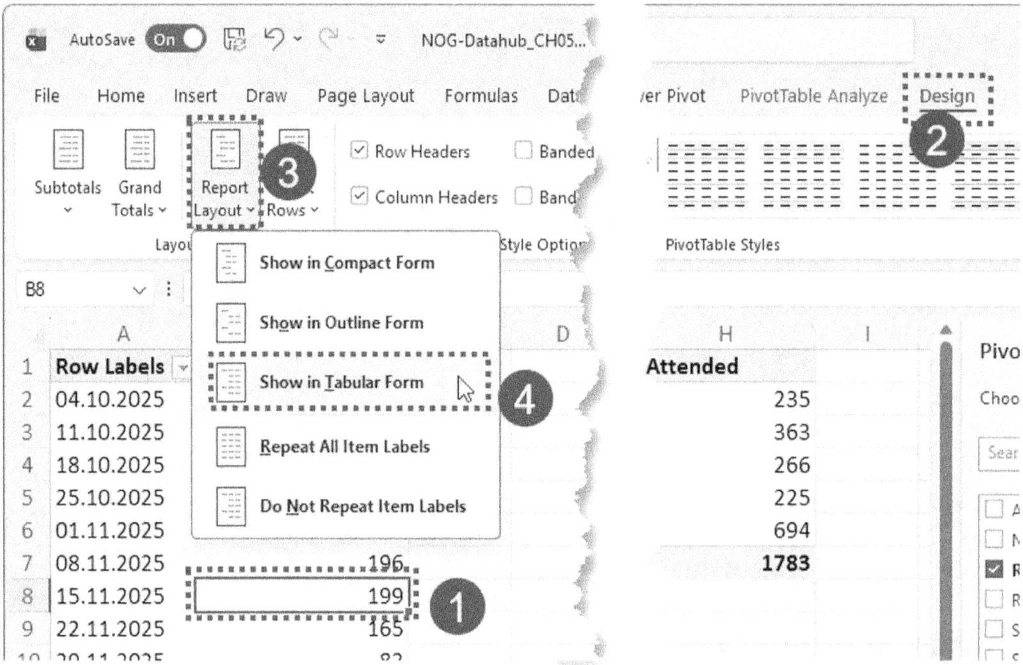

Figure 5.23 – PivotTable Design tab with Report Layout menu expanded to Show in Tabular Form

Remove grand totals (if not needed)

A grand total at the bottom of **Registrations by Week** is a single sum of all registrations across all weeks, which is only meaningful if Marcus needs that number. If the leadership meeting focuses on the trend rather than the cumulative total, the grand total is noise. Let's remove these for now:

1. Click anywhere inside the PivotTable
2. Click the **Design** tab
3. Click **Grand Totals**
4. Click **Off** for **Rows and Columns**

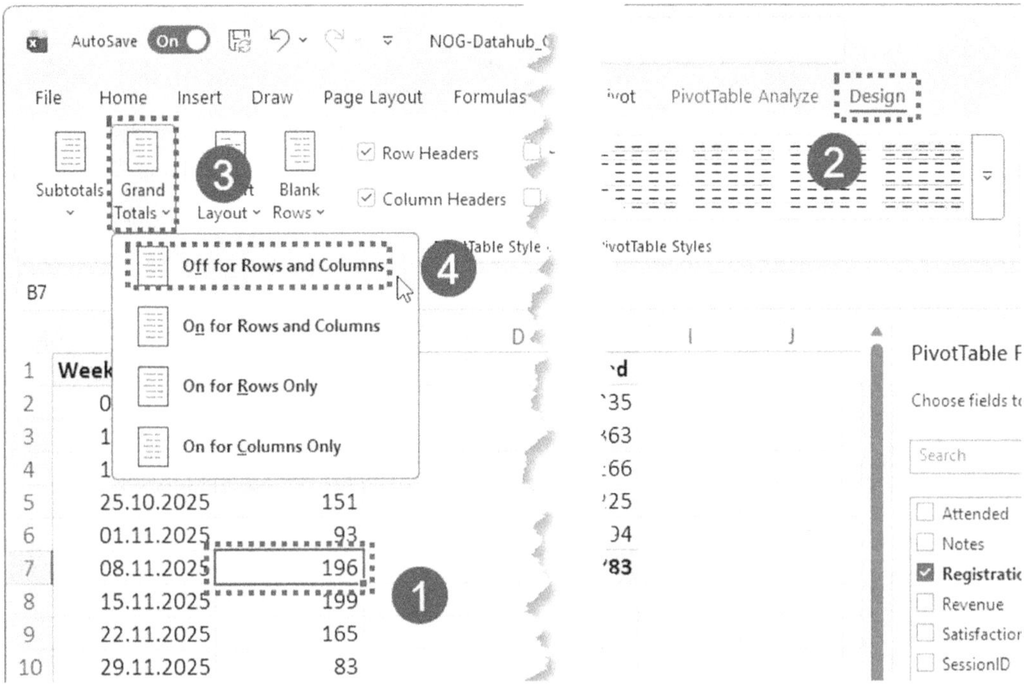

Figure 5.24 – Grand Totals menu with Off for Rows and Columns highlighted

Add clear titles

A **title** here is a plain-text cell label typed directly into the worksheet above each PivotTable, not a PivotTable setting. It tells anyone opening the file what each table shows before they look at the numbers, which matters whenever the workbook is shared or handed off.

Both PivotTables start at row 1, so you need to insert rows above them before adding titles.

1. Right-click the row 1 header to select the entire row and click **Insert**; this pushes both PivotTables down by one row
2. Repeat to insert a second blank row, so you have two clear rows above the data

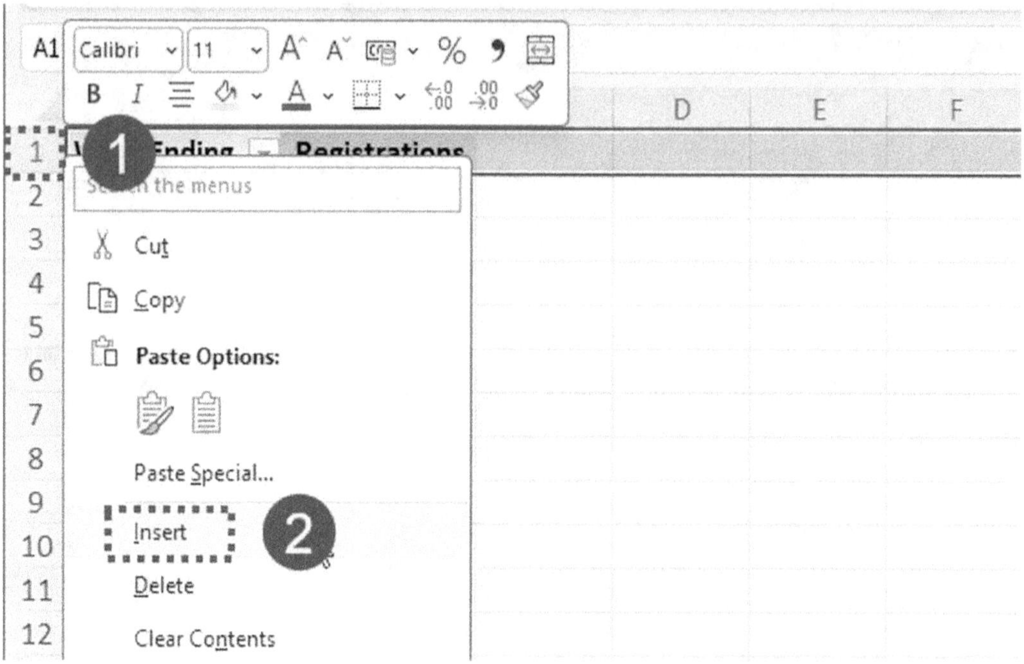

Figure 5.25 – Right-click menu on the row 1 header showing the Insert option

Now add a title for each PivotTable and format them:

3. Click cell **A2** and type `Registrations by Week`
4. Click cell **G2** and type `Attended by Session Type`

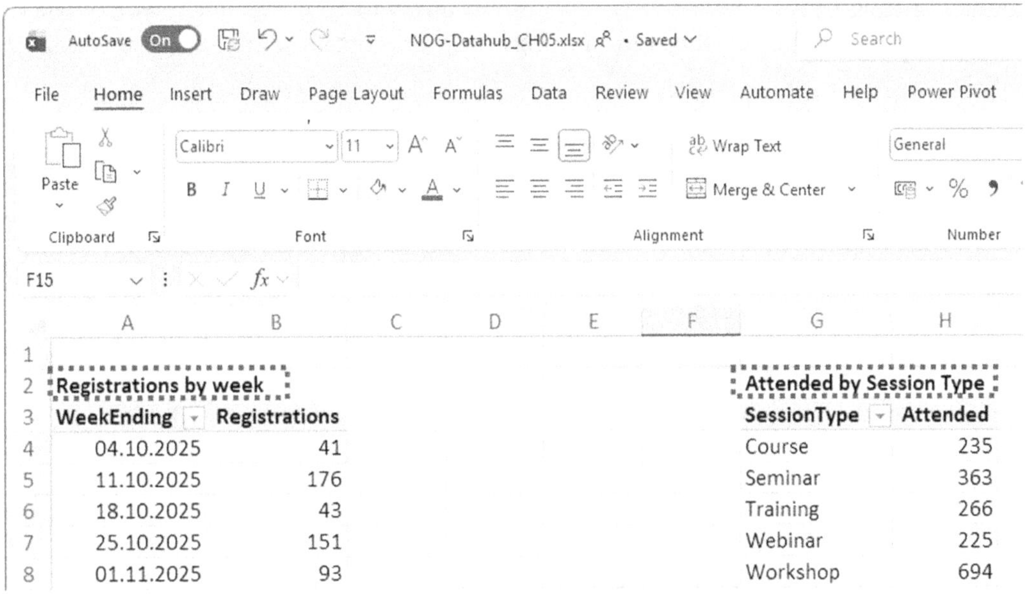

Figure 5.26 – Titles added in row 1 above each PivotTable

Keep titles simple and descriptive of the metric only: do not include the filter state (for example, "All Session Types") in the title. Once a slicer is applied, that wording becomes wrong. The slicer itself makes filtering visible; the title just needs to name what is being measured.

AI Helper

Drafting a report description

Once your PivotTable is formatted, you can use an AI assistant (such as ChatGPT, Copilot, or Claude) to draft a plain-English explanation for colleagues.

Try this prompt: `Here are the fields in my PivotTable: Rows = WeekEnding (weekly dates), Values = Registrations (Sum). The data covers Oct 2025 to Jan 2026 and comes from a Power Query table called Weekly_Event_KPIs. Write a one-paragraph explanation of what this report shows, suitable for a non-technical manager.`

The AI will produce a readable first draft. Before using it, check three things: Does the description mention the right fields? Does it match the actual date range in your data? Does it reflect any slicer filters currently applied? Correct anything that does not match. AI descriptions are a starting point, not a finished product.

Marcus looks at the two PivotTables. The first shows registrations fluctuating week to week. The second shows that Workshops are drawing nearly three times the attendance of Courses.

"This is exactly what I need," he says. "Can I filter just the workshops on the first page?"

"That's what the slicer is for," Quinn says.

Reusing the pack: refresh, slicers, and safe handover

The last step is packaging the report for reuse. Formatting makes it readable. Slicers make it flexible. A refresh note makes it safe to hand off.

Adding a SessionType slicer

A slicer is a visual filter button that any reader can click; no knowledge of PivotTables is required. One slicer can control both PivotTables simultaneously, so Marcus can filter to Workshops and see both the weekly trend and the attendance total update at the same time.

Start on the **KPI - Weekly Summary** sheet:

1. Click anywhere inside the PivotTable
2. Click the **PivotTable Analyze** tab
3. Click **Insert Slicer**

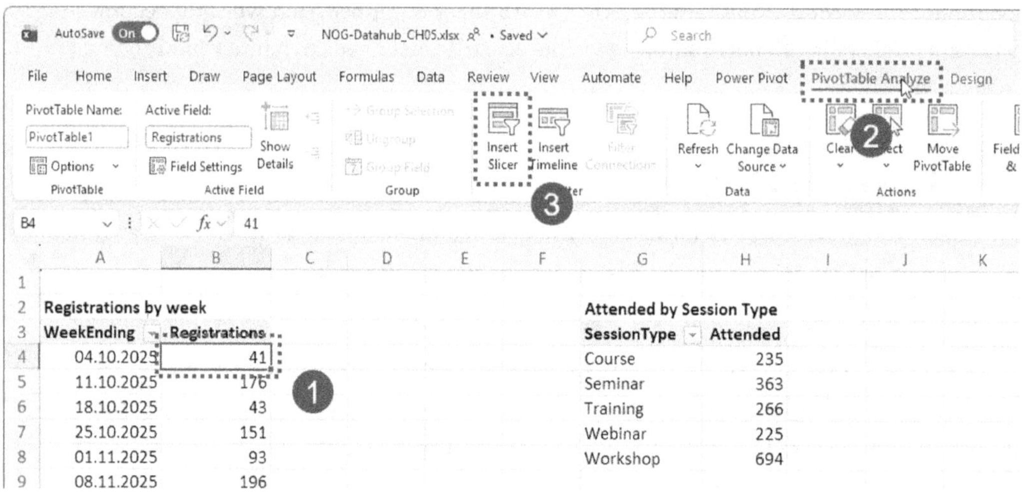

Figure 5.27 – Insert Slicer button on the PivotTable Analyze tab

4. In the **Insert Slicers** dialog, tick **SessionType**
5. Click **OK**

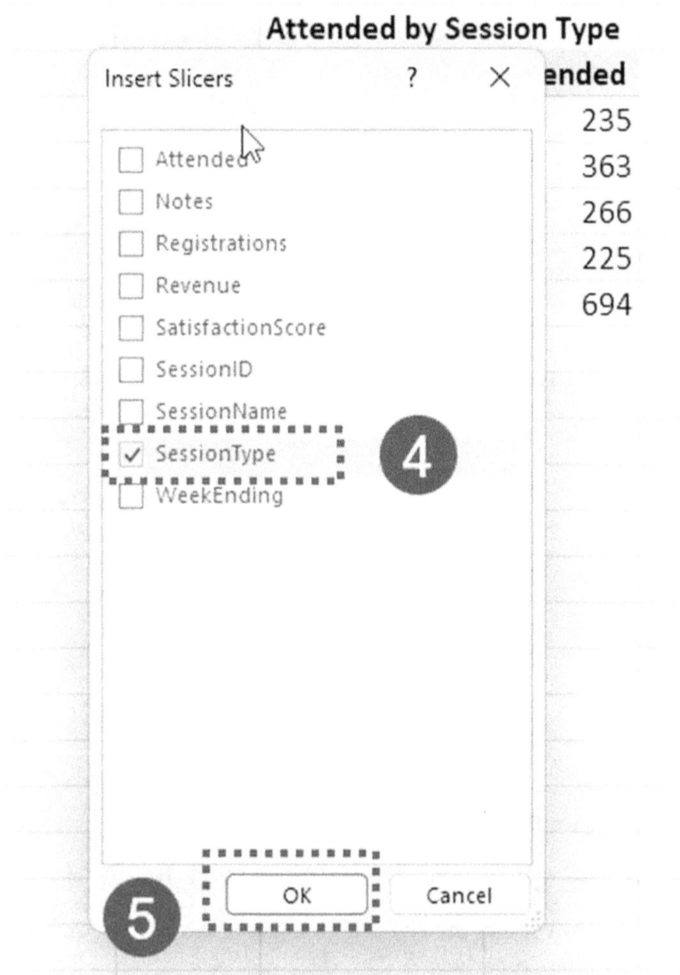

Figure 5.28 – Insert Slicers dialog with SessionType ticked

A slicer panel appears, showing all the session types. Clicking any button instantly filters the PivotTable.

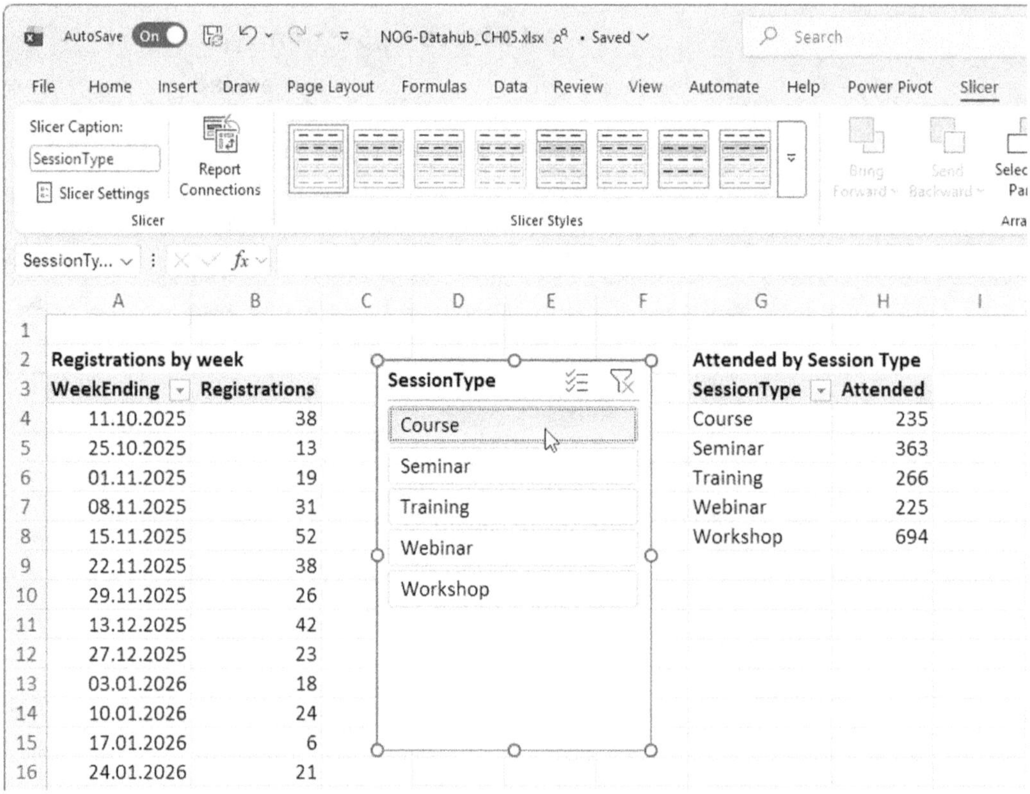

Figure 5.29 – SessionType slicer on the KPI - Weekly Summary sheet

Connecting the slicer to both PivotTables

By default, the slicer only filters the PivotTable it was created from. Connect it to the second PivotTable so both update together.

1. Click the slicer to select it, the **Slicer** tab appears on the ribbon
2. Click the **Slicer** tab if it doesn't open automatically
3. Click **Report Connections**

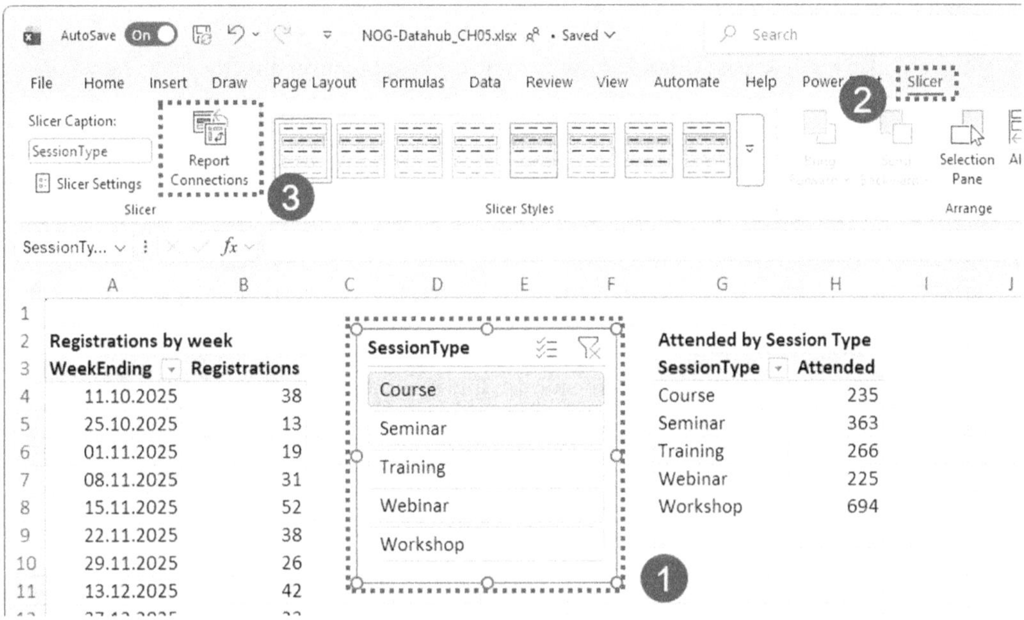

Figure 5.30 – Slicer tab on the ribbon with Report Connections highlighted

4. In the **Report Connections** dialog, tick both PivotTables, they both sit on the **KPI - Weekly Summary** sheet
5. Click **OK**

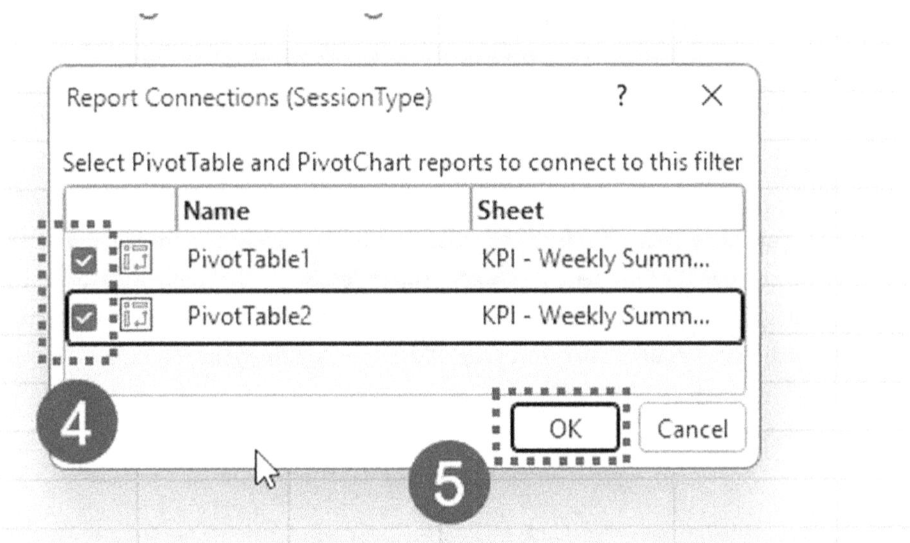

Figure 5.31 – Report Connections dialog with both PivotTables ticked

Tip

You can also reach **Report Connections** by right-clicking the slicer directly; it appears in the context menu alongside other slicer options.

Now, clicking **Workshop** in the slicer filters both Pivot Tables at once. Marcus can switch between session types without touching a single field or formula.

Tip

Move the slicer to a consistent location on the sheet (for example, top right, next to the PivotTable) so that anyone opening the file can find it immediately. Resize it so all five session type buttons are visible without scrolling.

Adding refresh instructions

The report is ready to hand off, but Marcus is not the only person who will use it. His assistant and at least two other managers have access to the workbook. They need to know how to refresh it and what not to touch.

Add a plain-text note in a cell close to the PivotTable title on each report sheet. Keep it to one line:

```
To update this report: go to the Data tab and click Refresh All. Do not edit the PivotTable directly.
```

This is not a callout box or a pop-up; it is a visible, permanent instruction that anyone opening the file will see before they look at the data.

Note

Excel's built-in refresh options are limited: you can set a query to refresh at a regular interval or when the file opens via **Query Properties**, but both require the workbook to be open. For unattended, scheduled refreshes that run without anyone opening the file, tools such as Power BI or Microsoft Fabric Dataflows are the right choice, but they are outside the scope of this book.

Preparing the workbook for a safe handoff

Before sending the file to Marcus, run a quick tidy-up:

- **Delete any scratch or test sheets**: If you created a temporary sheet during this chapter, delete it now. Only the two PivotTables and the workbook's existing query sheets should remain.
- **Rename the sheet tab clearly**: It should already be named **KPI - Weekly Summary**. Confirm that no sheet tab still says "Sheet1" or similar.
- **Check for (blank) rows**: If any PivotTable row shows "(blank)" in the row labels, it means at least one row in the source query has a null value in that field. Go back to the Power Query Editor, investigate the null, and decide whether to filter it out or fill it.

Final validation checklist

Before closing the workbook, run through this checklist:

Check	Expected
Both PivotTables show data after Refresh All	Data visible in both
Slicer connects to both PivotTables (Report Connections)	Both ticked
Registrations and Attended use Sum, not Count	Confirmed in Value Field Settings
Sheet tab is descriptive	KPI - Weekly Summary
Refresh instructions are visible on the sheet	One line above the PivotTable title

Table 5.3 – Final validation checklist for the Weekly KPI Summary Pack

Quinn sends the workbook to Marcus with a brief note: "Two PivotTables: one for the weekly trend, one by session type. Use the slicer to filter by SessionType. To refresh, go to the **Data** tab and click **Refresh All**."

The reply arrives twenty minutes later, from the leadership meeting room.

"Worked perfectly. This is going on the monthly slide deck."

Quinn smiles. The report took an hour to build. It will save Marcus thirty minutes every Monday for the rest of the year.

Summary

In this chapter, you turned a clean Power Query output into a reusable reporting pack that Marcus can refresh and present without rebuilding anything:

- **Clean query as a foundation**: a typed, structured Power Query output is the stable base that makes PivotTable aggregations predictable across refreshes
- **Extending an existing merge**: reopening the expand step to bring in **SessionType** from **Master_Sessions**, a small query change that unlocked both the second PivotTable and the slicer
- **Connection Only + PivotTable from connection**: loading the query as **Connection only** and inserting the PivotTable via **Use an external data source** keeps the PivotTable connected directly to the query, not to a worksheet range
- **Stable PivotTable layouts**: one PivotTable per sheet, connected to the same query connection, both controlled by a single slicer
- **Implicit measures**: Sum is correct for **Registrations** and **Attended**; Count and Distinct Count serve different purposes and the difference matters when working with row-level data (*Chapters 6–9*)
- **Stakeholder-ready formatting**: renamed value fields, tabular layout, number formatting, and a plain-cell title that describes the scope of the data
- **Safe handover**: a one-line refresh note, a **Report Connections** slicer, and a clean workbook with no scratch sheets

Deliverables created in this chapter:

- **KPI - Weekly Summary**: One sheet containing two PivotTables side by side: Registrations by Week showing the weekly registration trend, and Attended by Session Type showing total attendance by session type, both connected to the Weekly_Event_KPIs query
- **SessionType slicer**: Connected to both PivotTables, allowing one-click filtering by Workshop, Training, or Course
- **Weekly_Event_KPIs:** Query updated to include SessionType from **Master_Sessions**

In *Chapter 6*, Quinn helps Tom solve a different problem: a folder full of monthly registration exports that need to be combined into a single, clean table.. You will learn how to connect to a folder, automatically combine all the files inside **within** it, and apply consistent clean-up so the result is ready for the subsequent merges that follow.

Part 2

Cleaning, Reshaping, and Trust

In this part, you will solve the most common office data problem: folders that fill up with monthly exports. You will use Combine Files to turn a folder of registration exports into one clean, refreshable table with consistent fields and a simple, explainable de-duplication rule. You will then apply the same folder pattern to attendance logs and reshape their awkward layout (multiple session IDs crammed into single cells) into a tidy long table with one row per attendee-session. Finally, you will merge registrations and attendance into an enriched master attendee list using a safe merge workflow: choosing the right keys, picking the join type that matches the question, and preventing the row-multiplication surprises that silently corrupt merged data. Throughout, you will run a short trust loop after every combine and merge (row counts, key checks, and spot checks) so the tables you share stay reliable as new files arrive.

This section contains the following chapters:

6

Combine and Clean Multiple Files Into One Clean Table

Figure 6.1 – Tom is back with another challenge: a monthly spreadsheet marathon

Quinn is at her desk reviewing the **key performance indicator** (**KPI**) report she helped Marcus build when a message pops up from Tom.

"Hey Quinn, that sessions query you set up is still saving me every month. No more copying rows, no more broken formulas." He pauses. "Actually, could I borrow ten minutes? I've got the same problem again, in a different folder."

She finds Tom at his desk, his screen showing a familiar sight: a master spreadsheet with rows copied and pasted from four different files, each section highlighted in a slightly different shade to track which month came from where.

"Every month the booking system exports a new registration file," Tom says, gesturing at the screen. "I copy the rows in here, fix the casing, look for duplicates by eye..." He trails off. "I've already sent the wrong registration count to management twice. Once I missed a whole file."

Quinn looks at the four files sitting in the Registrations folder, `October`, `November`, `December`, `January`, and recognizes the monthly cadence immediately.

"The folder approach will work," she says. "But this is different from the sessions catalog. Every one of these rows is a booking: someone's name against a specific session. We need to build this cleanly from the start, so that when other teams ask for more, we're not going back to fix the foundations."

Tom looks up. "Meaning we can't just clean it and leave it at that?"

"We can't. The email addresses and session identifiers we standardize here are the keys that everything downstream depends on. Get those wrong, and nothing will match when we bring the tables together."

This is what makes this problem different from the one Tom brought up in *Chapter 3*. Back then, we built a reference catalog; here, we are building **transactional data**: a combined registrations table where every join key is standardized and every duplicate is handled by a deliberate business rule.

In this chapter, you'll learn to -

- Recognize when a recurring export process should be converted to a folder-based query instead of manual copy/paste
- Use the Folder or SharePoint Folder connector and **Combine Files** to build a single **Registrations_Combined** table from multiple exports
- Apply core **user interface** (**UI**) transformations: set data types, Trim/Clean text, and standardize email addresses and session identifiers; to prepare registration fields as reliable join keys for downstream
- Implement a simple, explainable de-duplication rule based on a declared key
- Run a lightweight post-refresh trust loop that catches obvious issues before reports are shared

Technical requirements

To follow along with this chapter, you will need:

- Microsoft Excel 2016 or later with Power Query, accessed via **Data** | **Get & Transform Data**

- Your `NOG-DataHub` workbook (NOG stands for Northbridge Office Group) from *Chapter 5*, which should already contain the following queries:
  - **Master_Sessions** (built in *Chapter 3*)
  - **Weekly_Event_KPIs** (built in *Chapter 4*, used in *Chapter 5*)
- The exercise files for this chapter: four monthly registration exports in the `Events/Registrations/` folder of your NOG-DataHub:
  - `Registrations_2025-10.xlsx`
  - `Registrations_2025-11.xlsx`
  - `Registrations_2025-12.xlsx`
  - `Registrations_2026-01.xlsx`

If you have not yet set up your `NOG-DataHub` folder, refer to the *Setting Up Your NOG-DataHub* section of the *Introduction* for instructions on where to find the exercise files.

Why folder-based imports beat copy-paste

Tom's approach is understandable. When a new monthly file arrives, copying the rows into a master spreadsheet feels quick. It takes fifteen minutes, and you're done.

The problem is that it compounds risk and time every month. A wrong row range leaves data out. A new column in the export shifts everything to the right. A file downloaded to the wrong folder gets missed entirely. By the time anyone notices, the numbers are already in front of management.

The better approach starts with a simple observation: a folder of files that share the same structure is already a dataset. The columns, types and meaning are the same. Power Query can treat the entire folder as a single source and combine everything automatically.

When a new monthly file arrives, there is nothing to copy. One click refreshes the query, picks up the new file, and rebuilds the combined table from scratch.

Here's how both approaches compare in this workflow:

	Manual copy/paste	**Folder-based query**
New file arrives	Copy rows, check columns, fix formatting	Click **Refresh**
Column order shifts	Manually realign	Power Query handles it

	Manual copy/paste	Folder-based query
Duplicate rows creep in	Check by eye every month	One deduplication step runs on every refresh
Time to update	15–30 minutes	Under 10 seconds

Table 6.1 – Manual copy/paste versus a folder-based Power Query approach

The `NOG-DataHub` already has the right structure for this. The four monthly registration files are in `Events/Registrations/`, ready to be connected. The same approach you used for Sessions in *Chapter 3* applies here: a different folder, the same pattern.

Now that we know why the folder approach wins, let's build it.

Combine Files: turning many exports into one table

The Combine Files experience in Power Query is designed for exactly this situation: a folder of same-structure files that need to become one table. Power Query reads the folder, shows you a list of files, lets you pick a sample to confirm the structure, and then builds the combined table automatically.

> **Important**
>
> For this exercise, continue in your `NOG-DataHub` workbook from *Chapter 5*. You will connect to the `Events/Registrations/` folder in your `NOG-DataHub`, which contains the four monthly registration export files.

Connect to the registrations folder

Follow the same folder connector pattern from *Chapters 1* through *5:* go to **Data** | **Get Data** | **From File**, choose **From SharePoint Folder** or **From Folder**, navigate to your `NOG-DataHub`, and click **Transform Data** to open the Power Query Editor.

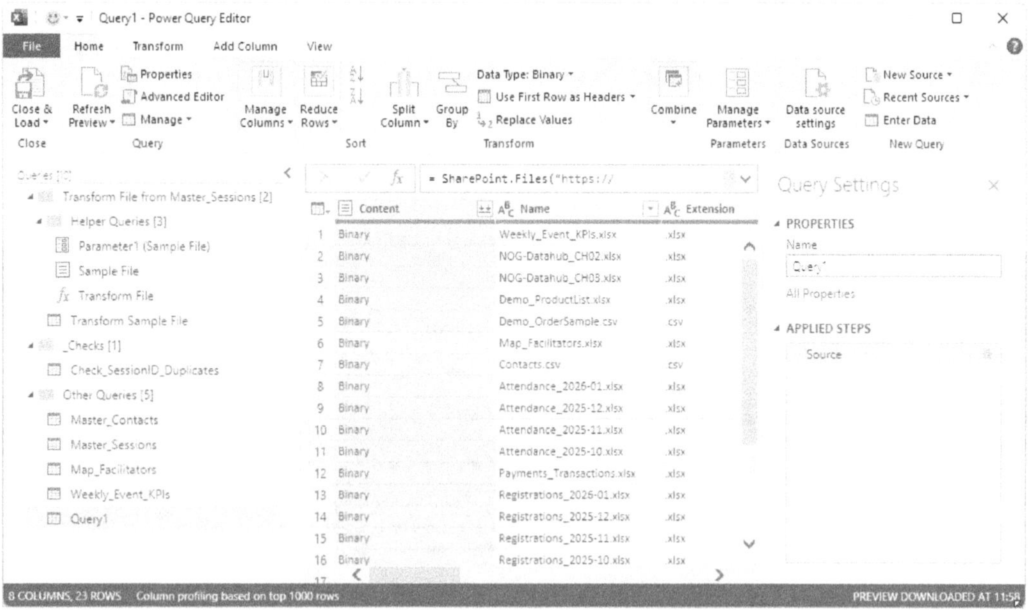

Figure 6.2 – File listing after connecting to the NOG-DataHub folder

Rename the query

Before doing anything else, rename the query so the **Queries** pane stays readable from the start:

1. In the **Query Settings** pane on the right, click on the current query name
2. Type `Registrations_Combined` and press *Enter*

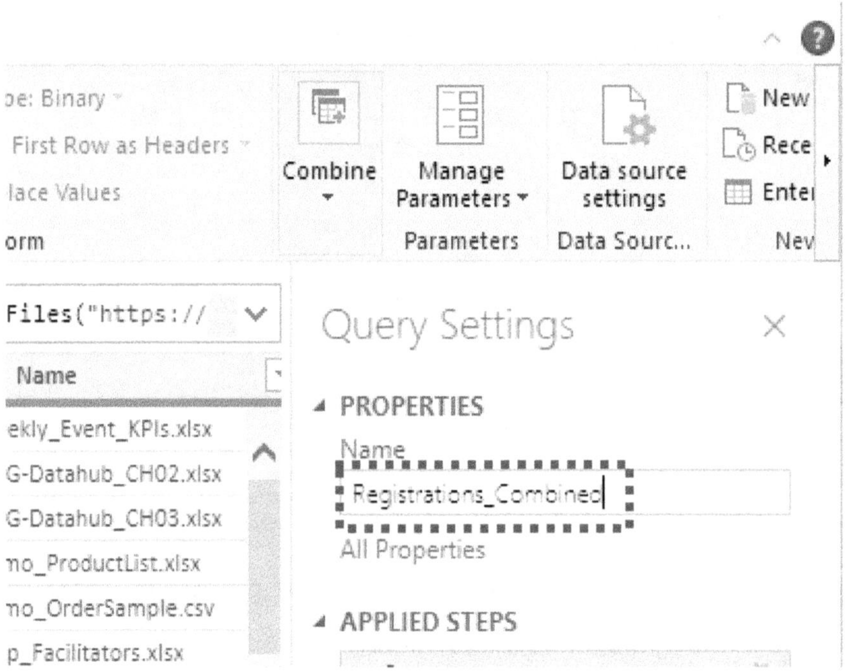

Figure 6.3 – Query Settings pane showing the query renamed to Registrations_Combined

Filter to the registration files

The **Power Query Editor** shows a table listing every file in your `NOG-DataHub`, not just the registration exports. Filter it down to the four files in the `Events/Registrations/` folder.

> **Tip**
>
> The **Folder Path** column may not be visible without scrolling right. Drag the Power Query Editor window wider or scroll the data preview to the right until the column is in view.

Start by filtering on the folder path:

1. Click the dropdown arrow on the **Folder Path** column header
2. Click **Text Filters**
3. Click **Contains**

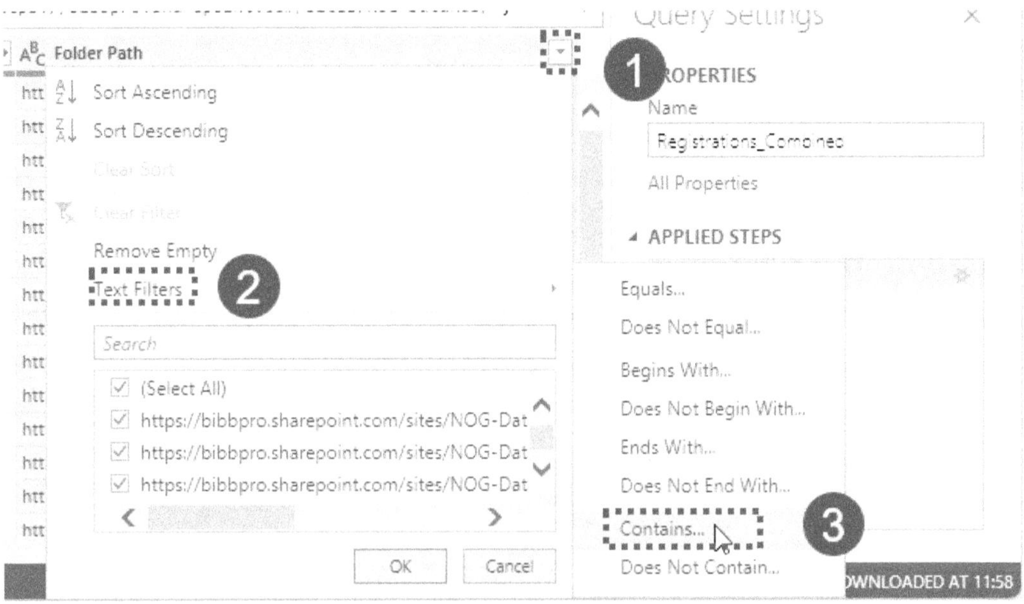

Figure 6.4 – Text Filters menu expanded to show the Contains option

4. Type `Registrations` and click **OK**

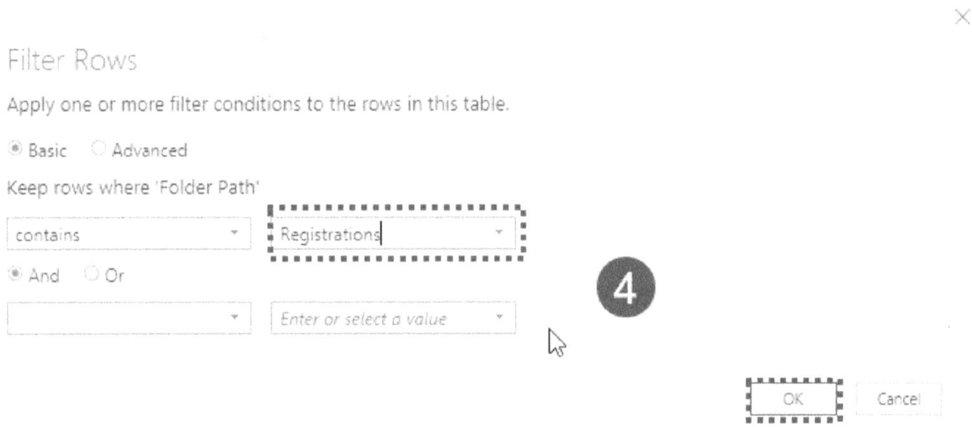

Figure 6.5 – Four Registrations files after filtering the Folder Path column

You should now see only the four `Registrations` files. If the folder contains any template or test files, filter the **Name** column in the same way, keeping only files whose name begins with `Registrations_`.

> **Tip**
>
> Always filter the file list before combining. A template or a test export sitting in the same folder will be pulled into the combined table if you do not exclude it. One stray row can break downstream reports.

Combine the files

The file list is filtered and the query is named. Now combine:

1. Click the **Combine Files** icon in the **Content** column header (the leftmost column, showing two overlapping arrows)

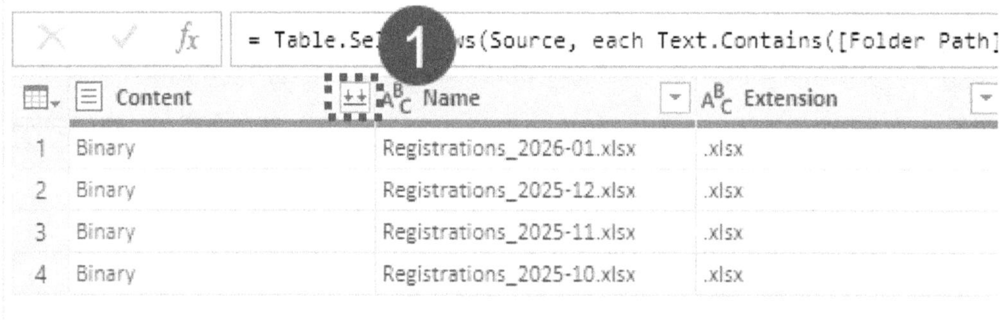

Figure 6.6 – The Combine Files icon in the Content column header

2. In the **Combine Files** dialog, when selecting **Sheet1**, Power Query shows a preview of the first file as a sample, check that the preview shows the expected columns and data
3. Click **OK**

Figure 6.7 – Combine Files dialog with sample file preview showing the registration columns

Power Query builds the combined table and returns you to the editor. The table now contains rows from all four files.

> **Note**
>
> When you click **Combine Files**, Power Query automatically creates several helper queries in a **Helper Queries** group in the **Queries** pane, including a **Transform Sample File** query. These are generated automatically and support the main query. You do not need to edit them.

Review and confirm the columns

The combined table should have nine columns: **Source.Name** (added automatically by Power Query to record which file each row came from) plus the eight data columns from the source files:

- **RegistrationID** — unique registration identifier
- **SessionID** — session the attendee registered for
- **AttendeeEmail** — attendee email address
- **AttendeeName** — attendee full name
- **RegistrationDate** — date the registration was submitted

- **RegistrationStatus** — Confirmed or Canceled
- **TicketType** — ticket category (Standard, Early Bird, VIP, Complimentary)
- **AmountPaid** — amount paid; blank for Complimentary tickets

This chapter uses all eight data columns, so we will keep them. Use **Choose Columns** to confirm the final set, unticking **Source.Name**, which confirmed the files combined correctly but is not part of the business data:

1. Click the **Home** tab
2. Click **Choose Columns**

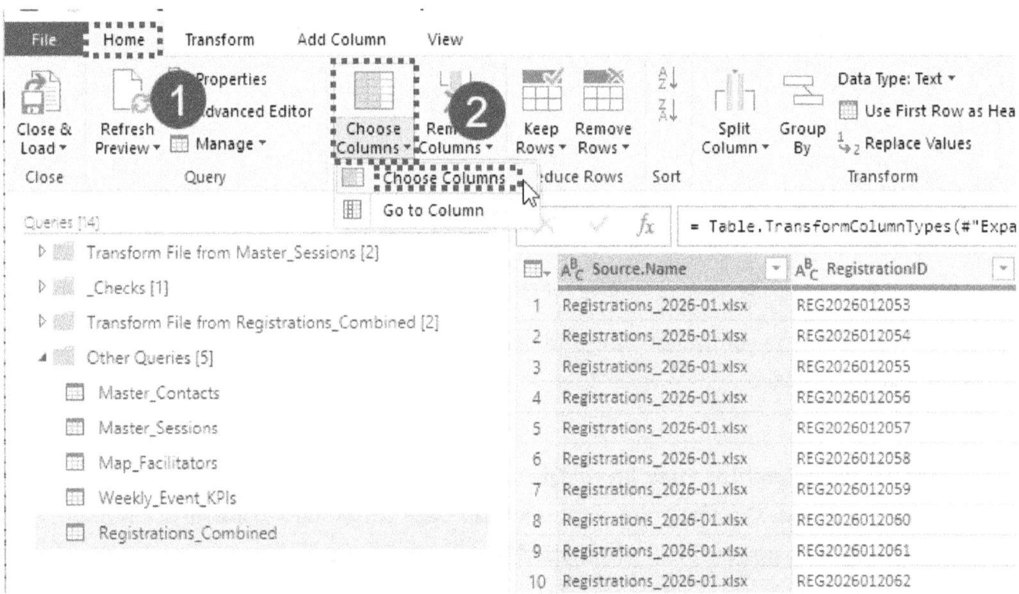

Figure 6.8 - Choose Columns dialog with all eight data columns ticked and Source.Name unticked

3. In the **Choose Columns** dialog, untick **Source.Name**
4. Click **OK**

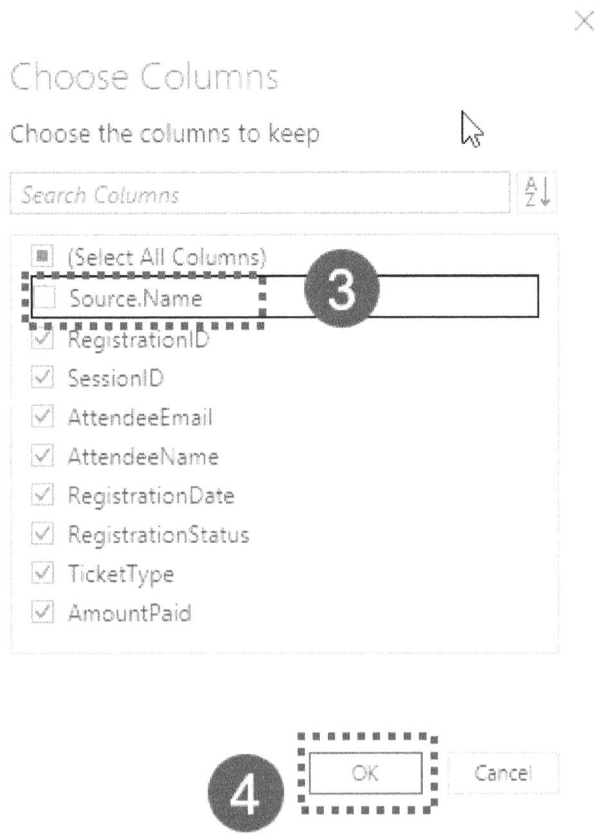

Figure 6.9 – Combined table with eight data columns and Source.Name removed

> **Tip**
>
> Prefer **Choose Columns** over removing columns. It shows every column in one list, so you can see exactly what your table contains and make deliberate decisions. It also acts as a safeguard: if the source file gains a new column in a future export, it will not silently appear in your output unless you explicitly tick it.

The combined table is in place. Now it needs cleaning.

Cleaning the type, email, and status fields

The registration exports were produced by a booking system, not a data team. That means inconsistent casing, extra spaces, and status values that vary depending on the month or the person who ran the export. None of this is unusual. Power Query has a straightforward set of tools to fix it.

Work through these transformations in order. Rename each Applied Step as you go; a descriptive step name takes two seconds and makes the query far easier to maintain.

Set data types

Power Query may not detect all data types correctly after combining files. Set them explicitly:

1. Right-click the **RegistrationDate** column header
2. Click **Change Type**
3. Click **Date**

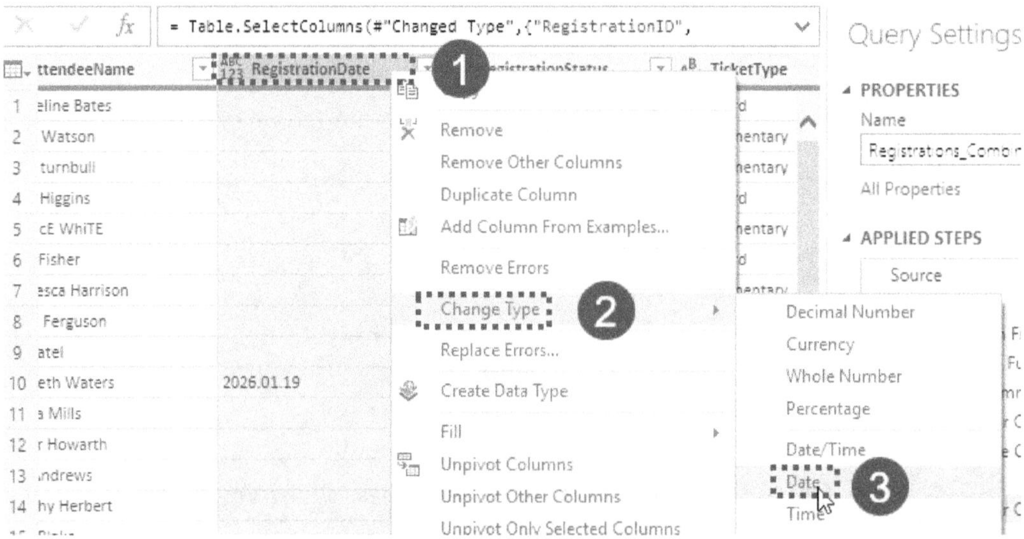

Figure 6.10 – Right-click context menu on RegistrationDate with Change Type expanded to Date

Repeat the same steps for **AmountPaid**, selecting **Decimal Number** as the type. Power Query may have already detected this correctly. If the column header already shows a decimal icon, confirm the type is set and move on. Leave the remaining six columns as **Text**.

To rename the step, right-click it in the **Applied Steps** pane, select the last step, right-click it, select **Properties**, type `Set Data Types` in the **Name** field, and click **OK**.

Power Query also has a **Rename** option on the right-click menu for a quicker single-step rename; **Properties** is shown here because it also exposes a **Description** field, which is handy when you want to document what a step does as well as naming it.

Figure 6.11 – Step Properties dialogue with the name set to Set Data Types

Trim and clean text columns

Extra spaces and non-printing characters cause silent errors: two email addresses that look identical may not match because one has a trailing space. **Trim** and **Clean** remove these automatically.

Select the columns to clean in one action:

1. Click the **AttendeeEmail** column header
2. Hold *Ctrl* and click **AttendeeName**, then **TicketType**, to add them to the selection
3. Click the **Transform** tab
4. Click **Format**
5. Click **Trim**

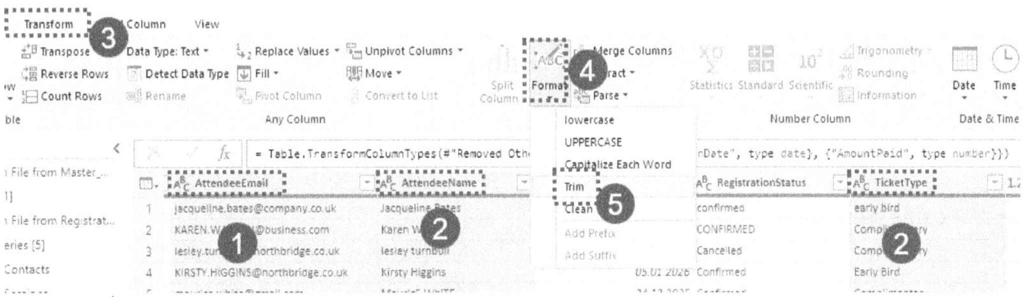

Figure 6.12 – Format menu on the Transform tab with Trim highlighted, three columns selected

6. With the same three columns still selected, click **Format** again
7. Click **Clean**

Normalize email addresses to lowercase

Email addresses in the source files are a mix of cases: `Amira.Hassan@NOG.co.uk` in one file, `amira.hassan@nog.co.uk` in another. These will not match when you merge tables in later chapters. Convert all emails to lowercase now:

1. Right-click the **AttendeeEmail** column header
2. Click **Transform**
3. Click **lowercase**

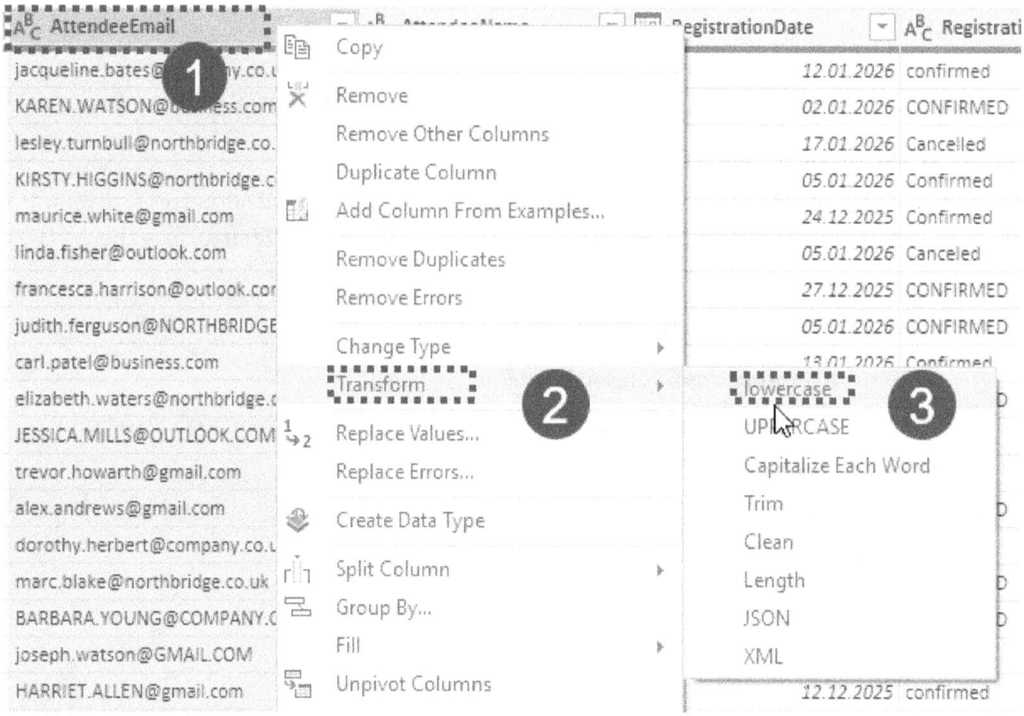

Figure 6.13 – Right-click context menu on AttendeeEmail with Transform expanded to lowercase

Rename this step `Lowercased Emails`.

Note

The M function behind this step is **Text.Lower**. You can see it in the formula bar; Power Query wrote it automatically when you used the **Format** menu. You do not need to write or edit it.

Normalize casing across text fields

Three columns share the same casing problem: mixed capitalization from different exports. Fix all three in one step:

1. Click the **AttendeeName** column header
2. Hold *Ctrl* and click **RegistrationStatus**, then **TicketType** and right-click any of the selected column headers
3. Click **Transform**
4. Click **Capitalize Each Word**

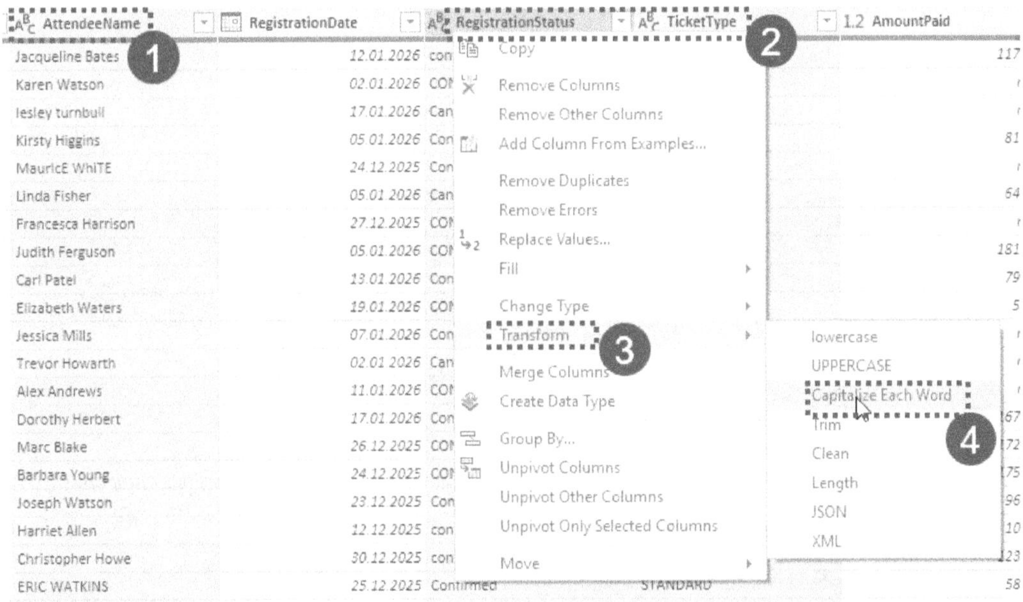

Figure 6.14 – Right-click context menu with Transform expanded to Capitalize Each Word, three columns selected

Rename this step `Proper Cased Fields`.

This handles most variants in one go: `john smith` becomes `John Smith`, `confirmed` becomes `Confirmed`, `early bird` becomes `Early Bird`. Two values still need a targeted fix.

Fix remaining value variations

RegistrationStatus has one spelling variant that casing alone cannot fix:

1. Right-click the **RegistrationStatus** column header
2. Click **Replace Values**

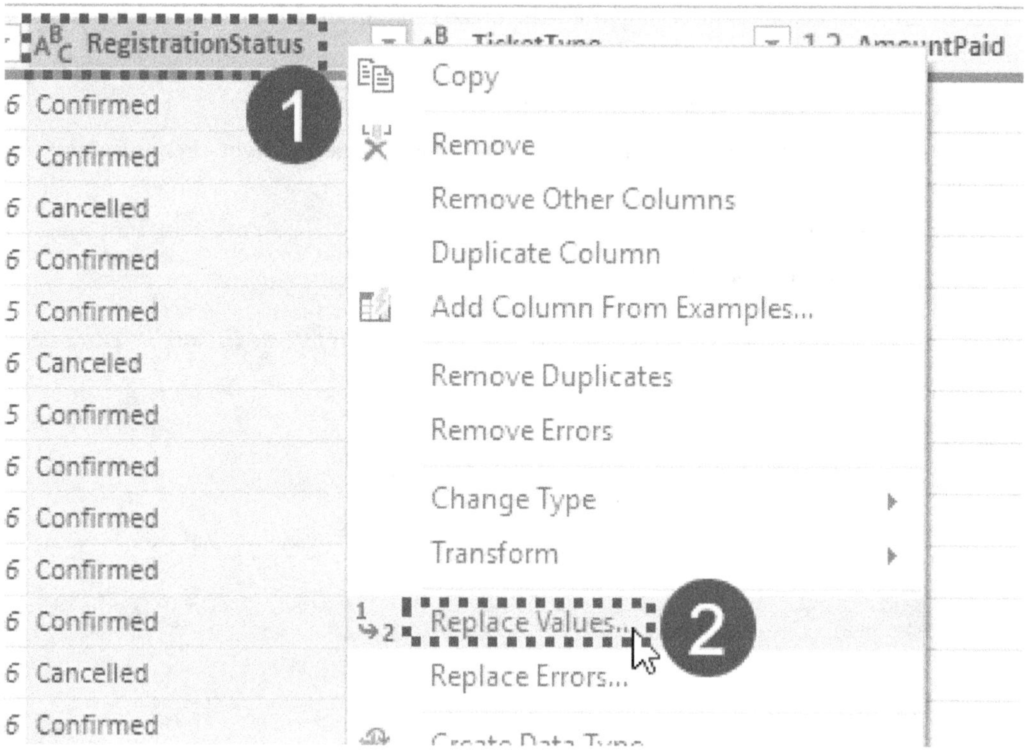

Figure 6.15 – Right-click context menu on RegistrationStatus with Replace Values highlighted

3. In the **Value To Find** field, type `Cancelled`
4. In the **Replace With** field, type `Canceled`
5. Click **OK**

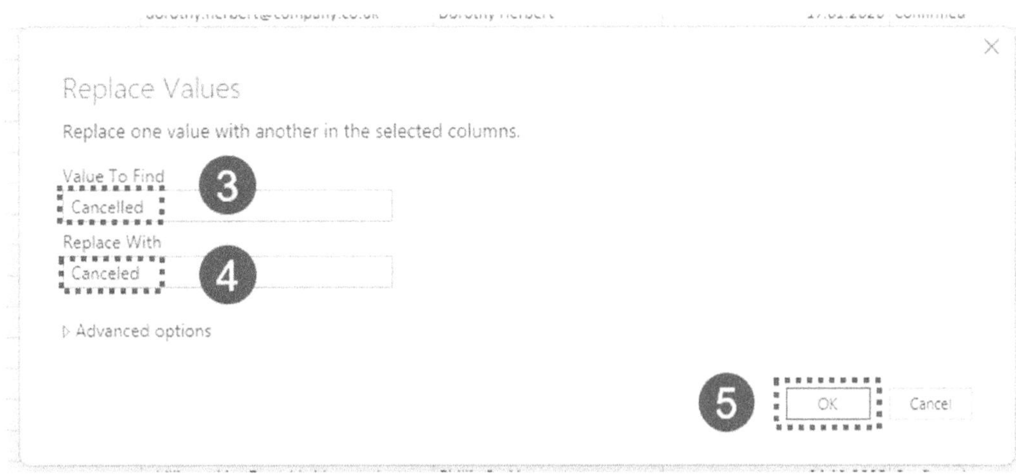

Figure 6.16 – Replace Values dialog replacing "Cancelled" with "Canceled"

Rename this step `Standardized Status (spelling)`.

TicketType has one value that **Capitalize Each Word** gets wrong: `vip` becomes `Vip` instead of `VIP`:

Right-click the **TicketType** column header, click **Replace Values**, type `Vip` in the **Value To Find** field and `VIP` in the **Replace With** field, then click **OK**.

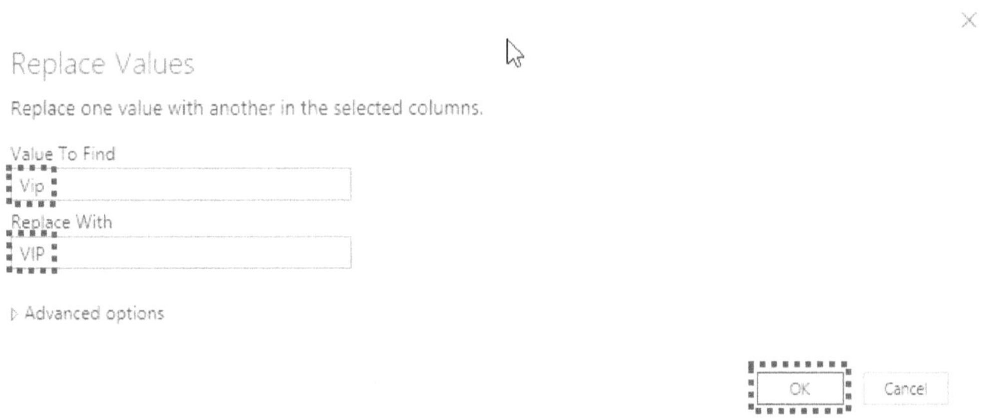

Figure 6.17 – Replace Values dialog replacing "Vip" with "VIP"

Rename this step `Standardized Ticket Type (VIP)`.

> **Tip**
>
> If you want to group registrations by organization (for example, to see how many attendees came from the same company), you can extract the email domain using **Column from Examples**, covered in *Chapter 2*. Select the **AttendeeEmail** column, click the **Add Column** tab, click **Column from Examples**, and type `company.co.uk` in the first row. Power Query will infer the pattern and extract the domain for every row.

> **AI Helper**
>
> Before running **Replace Values**, ask an AI assistant such as ChatGPT: `Here are the distinct values in my RegistrationStatus column: Confirmed, confirmed, Cancelled, Canceled. What Replace Values steps should I add in Power Query to standardize them to Confirmed and Canceled?`. The assistant will suggest the right pairs quickly. Always verify the suggestions against your actual distinct values first; open the filter dropdown on the column to see every unique value before trusting any mapping.

With all these steps in place, the **Applied Steps** pane should look something like this:

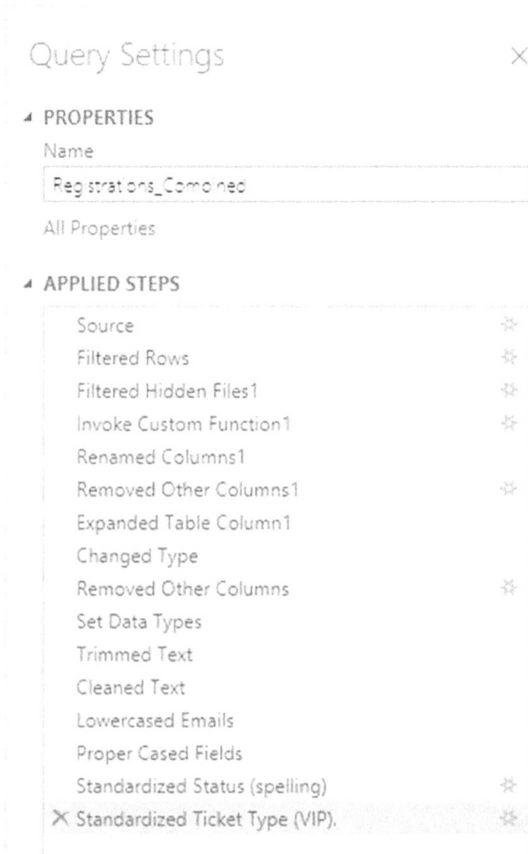

Figure 6.18 – Applied Steps pane showing meaningfully named transformation steps

The data is clean. Now let's handle duplicates.

Simple duplicate rules that don't surprise you

Duplicates in a registration table are common. An attendee cancels and re-registers. A system export runs twice. An admin corrects an entry without deleting the original. None of these are errors; they are normal events in a busy bookings system.

So, when duplicates exist, which row do you keep?

De-duplication (**dedup** for short) is the process of identifying rows that represent the same real-world event and keeping only one. To do that, Power Query needs to know what makes two rows "the same". That is the **dedup key**: the column or combination of columns whose values, taken together, uniquely identify one logical record.

In this table, a registration is uniquely identified by who registered (**AttendeeEmail**) and which session they registered for (**SessionID**). If the same email appears more than once for the same session, those rows are duplicates, regardless of what the other columns say.

Declare your dedup key

A de-duplication rule is only trustworthy if it can be stated in one sentence.

Ideally, dedup rules should be documented (a one-line description in the query's **Properties** is enough) or at minimum, this rule should be clear in your head before you apply it, clear enough that you could state it to a colleague in one sentence. If you can't, that's a signal to think it through a little more or to consider whether a different approach fits the data better.

Here is the rule for this table:

```
For each attendee registered multiple times for the same session, keep only
their most recent registration.
```

That means: if the same email address appears more than once for the same session, keep the most recent registration and discard the rest.

> **Tip**
>
> **Decision log**: Dedup key = AttendeeEmail + SessionID. Rule = keep the latest RegistrationDate. Reason: the most recent record reflects the current state: a correction, a status update, or a re-registration after a cancelation. Write this one line in a comment in the query, or in a shared document. Anyone who maintains the query later will know exactly why the rule exists.

Sort and remove duplicates

Apply the rule in two steps:

1. Click the dropdown arrow on the **RegistrationDate** column header
2. Click **Sort Descending**

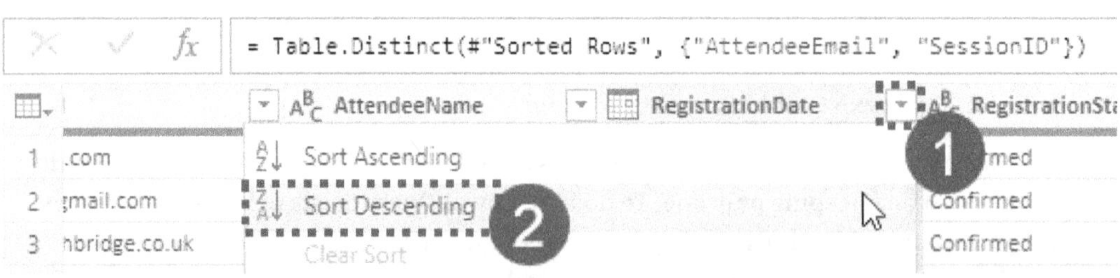

Figure 6.19 – RegistrationDate column header dropdown with Sort Descending highlighted

With the rows sorted by date (latest first), remove duplicates based on the combination of email and session in the following steps.

3. Click the **AttendeeEmail** column header
4. Hold *Ctrl* and click the **SessionID** column header and right-click either selected column header
5. Click **Remove Duplicates**

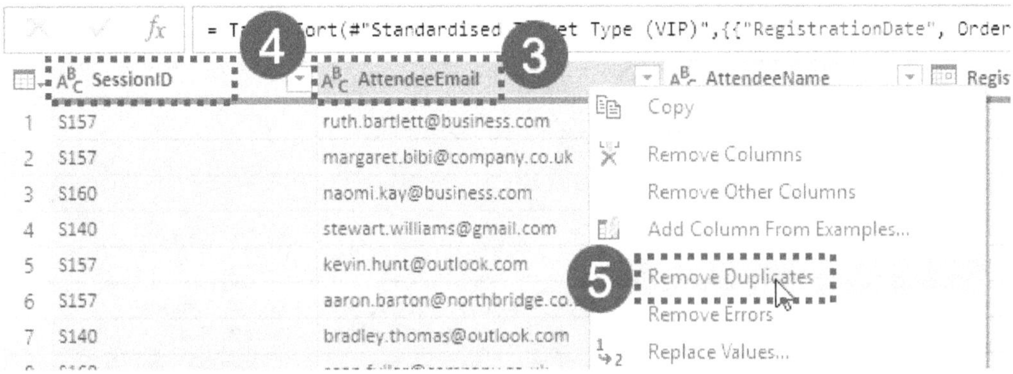

Figure 6.20 – Right-click context menu with Remove Duplicates highlighted and two columns selected

Power Query keeps the first occurrence of each AttendeeEmail + SessionID combination, which, because you sorted by date descending, is the latest registration.

> **Caution**
>
> **Remove Duplicates** keeps the first row in the current sort order. If you skip the sort step, Power Query keeps an arbitrary row, not necessarily the latest registration. Always sort before removing duplicates when the order matters.

The query is clean and deduplicated. You will verify the row count after loading it to the sheet; that is the first check in the trust loop coming up next.

The 30-Second trust loop after every refresh

Power Query queries refresh automatically when you ask them to. That is the whole point. But "refresh" means running all the same steps against potentially different input, and occasionally the input changes in ways that break assumptions. A new status value appears in the export. A column is renamed. A file with the wrong schema lands in the folder.

The trust loop is a short set of checks you run immediately after refreshing, before sharing any numbers. It does not require a testing framework or automated alerts. It takes 30 seconds and catches the most common failures.

Load the query to a sheet

Before running the checks, load the query into a worksheet:

1. Click the **Home** tab in the **Power Query Editor**
2. Click the dropdown arrow next to **Close & Load**
3. Click **Close & Load To**

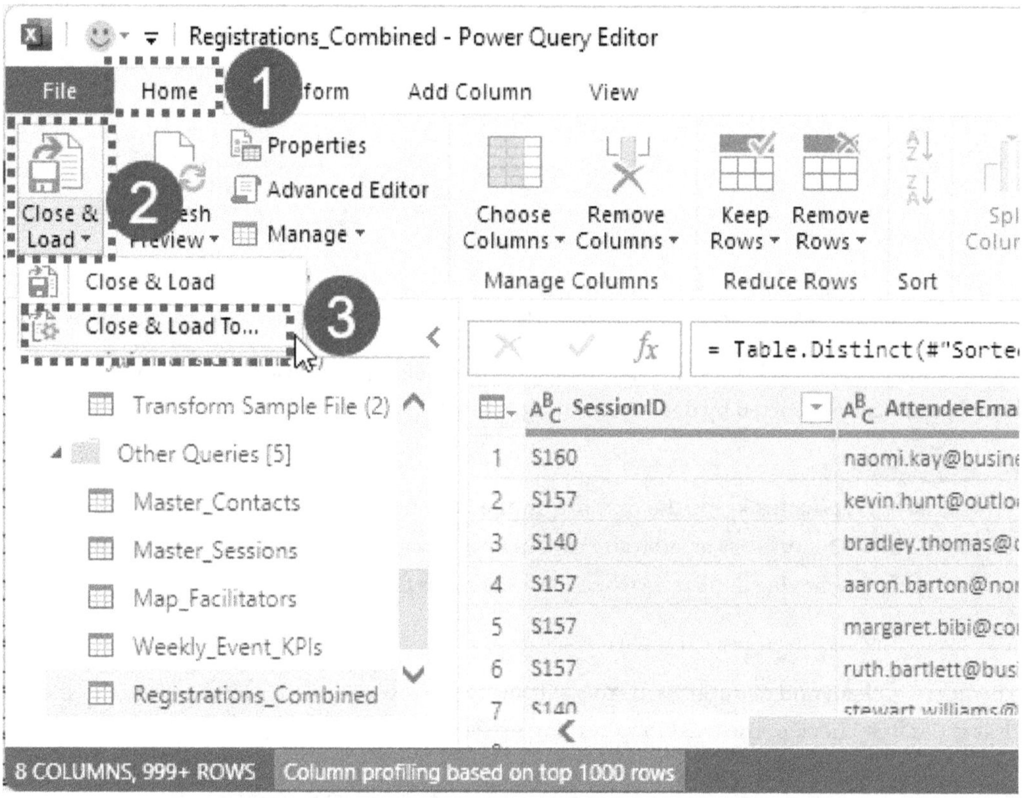

Figure 6.21 – Close and Load dropdown with Close and Load To highlighted

4. In the **Import Data** dialog, select **Table**
5. Select **New worksheet**
6. Click **OK**

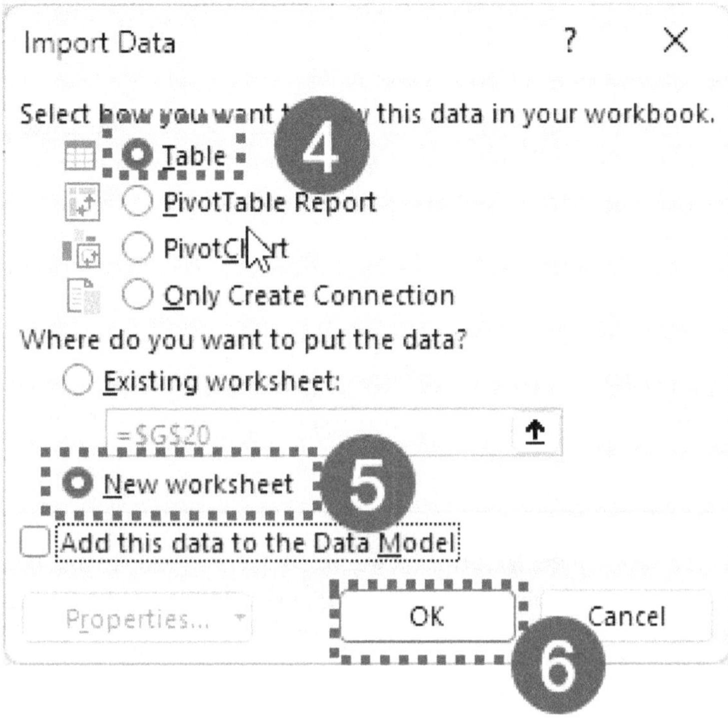

Figure 6.22 – Import Data dialog with Table and New worksheet selected

The combined, cleaned, and deduplicated registrations table appears as a Excel table on the new sheet.

The five checks

With the table loaded, run through these five checks:

1. **Row count looks plausible**: The four files should produce around 2,600 rows in total before deduplication, with a modest reduction after. A count far below that range is worth investigating before sharing.
2. **SessionID and AttendeeEmail have no blanks**: These are your dedup keys and your merge keys for later chapters. Click the filter dropdown on each column and confirm that `(Blanks)` does not appear, or has zero rows if it does.
3. **RegistrationStatus contains only two values**: Click the filter dropdown on **RegistrationStatus**. You should see exactly `Confirmed` and `Canceled`. Any other value means a **Replace Values** step was missed or a new variant has appeared in the source.

4. **RegistrationDate range is Oct 2025 – Jan 2026**: Filter on **RegistrationDate**, expand the year nodes in the filter dropdown to confirm the months, or check the earliest and latest values directly in the column.
5. **AmountPaid is blank only for Complimentary tickets**: Filter **TicketType** to **Complimentary** and confirm that **AmountPaid** is blank for those rows. Then clear the filter and spot-check a handful of Standard and VIP rows to confirm they have amounts.

> Note
>
> The trust loop is a habit, not a test suite. There are no macros to run and no automated alerts to configure. The value is in the act of looking: spending 30 seconds on deliberate checks before forwarding a number to a colleague. You will use this same loop pattern in every chapter from here on.

If all five checks pass, the **Registrations_Combined** query is ready to use. If even one fails, return to the Power Query Editor, find the step that should have caught the issue, and fix it there, not in the sheet.

With the query built, cleaned, and verified, let's recap what Tom now has and what comes next.

Summary

Tom now has a single query (**Registrations_Combined**) that pulls four months of registration exports into one clean, deduplicated table, and refreshes with one click.

Three patterns from this chapter are worth carrying forward:

- **Folder as refreshable feed**: connect to the folder, filter the file list, combine. When a new monthly file lands in the folder, a refresh picks it up automatically.
- **Standardize merge keys before you need them**: lowercase emails, consistent status values, trimmed text. Every step skipped here becomes a mismatch problem when you join tables in *Chapters 8* and *9*.
- **Trust loop after every refresh**: 30 seconds of deliberate checks before sharing numbers. A habit that catches problems early, when they are easy to fix.

In *Chapter 7*, Tom is back with another challenge: attendance data arrives with multiple sessions per row and needs reshaping before it can be used. You'll use the same folder pattern to combine attendance logs, but this time the challenge isn't cleaning the data but changing its shape.

7

Combine and Reshape Multiple Files Into a Tidy Long Table

Figure 7.1 – This time, Tom needs help retrieving attendance records

It is mid-morning when Tom appears at Quinn's desk again, this time with a different kind of question on his face.

"The registrations query is still running perfectly," he says. "Management was happy with the numbers last month." He sits down and pulls up a folder on his laptop. "There's one more thing, though. I need to know who actually *attended*; not who registered, but who showed up."

Quinn looks up from her screen. She knows the registrations table she built in *Chapter 6* records everyone who booked a place. Whether they walked through the door is a different question, and a different file.

"Let me see what you've got," she says.

Tom opens the `Events/Attendance/` folder on SharePoint. Four files sit inside: one for each month from `October 2025` to `January 2026`, matching the same monthly export pattern as the registrations.

"Same folder pattern," Tom says. "Should be the same trick, right?"

Quinn opens the October file. The first few columns look familiar (email, name, date), but then she spots the fourth column: **SessionIDs**. One of the cells reads `S001;S002;S045`. Three session identifiers, separated by semicolons, all packed into a single cell.

She nods slowly. "Almost the same trick. But look at that cell, three session IDs packed into one. If we leave it like that, we can never ask a useful question about who attended what."

"So, we split it out?" Tom asks.

"We split it. One row for every session a person attended. That shape, one row, one attendee, one session, is what this is about. You already know the folder combine; the reshaping is what's new."

That distinction is the heart of this chapter. We will combine the attendance files the same way we combined the registrations, but the real work comes after that: reshaping the data so that every row represents exactly one attendee at exactly one session.

In this chapter, you'll learn to -

- Explain what the attendance table is for and what one row represents
- Work through the folder-combine pattern as a review exercise, the same approach as *Chapter 6*, applied to attendance files
- Use **Split Column by Delimiter → To Rows** to normalize multi-session cells into a tidy long table
- Standardize join keys: email address and session identifier, so that attendance data merges cleanly with registrations in *Chapter 8*
- Validate the grain of the final table with simple row counts so that downstream reporting and modeling remain trustworthy

Technical requirements

The chapters in this book build on each other. Make sure you have completed all exercises in the previous chapter before starting this one.

To follow along with this chapter, you will need:

- Microsoft Excel 2016 or later with Power Query, accessed via **Data Get & Transform Data**
- Your `NOG-DataHub` workbook (NOG stands for Northbridge Office Group) from *Chapter 6*, which should already contain the following queries:
  - **Master_Sessions** (built in *Chapter 3*)
  - **Weekly_Event_KPIs** (built in *Chapter 4*)
  - **Registrations_Combined** (built in *Chapter 6*)
- The exercise files for this chapter: four monthly attendance logs in the `Events/Attendance/` folder of your `NOG-DataHub`:
  - `Attendance_2025-10.xlsx`
  - `Attendance_2025-11.xlsx`
  - `Attendance_2025-12.xlsx`
  - `Attendance_2026-01.xlsx`

Why attendance needs its own table

A registration and an attendance record look similar on the surface; both have an email address, a session identifier, and a date. But they answer different questions.

The registration table tells you who signed up. Someone registers when they book a place: they fill in a form, receive a confirmation, and appear in the booking system. That registration exists whether they attend or not.

The attendance table tells you who showed up. Someone appears in the attendance log only when they are actually present at a session: marked on a sign-in sheet, scanned through a door system, or checked in by a coordinator like Tom. A person can be registered for six sessions and attend only two. Or they can attend a session as a late addition without prior registration.

Think of it like a conference: the guest list (registrations) is what you prepared in advance; the sign-in sheet (attendance) is what actually happened on the day:

	Registration	**Attendance**
Question it answers	Who signed up?	Who showed up?
Created when	A booking is submitted	A person enters the session

	Registration	**Attendance**
One row represents	One booking	One person at one session
Useful for	Forecasting, revenue, confirmations	Completion tracking, certificates, follow-ups

Table 7.1 – Registrations versus attendance: what each record represents

This distinction drives everything in this chapter. The shape of the final table, one row per attendee per session, is not arbitrary. It is the only shape that can cleanly answer Tom's questions: "Which sessions had the highest attendance?" or "How many sessions did each person complete?"

That shape is called the **grain** of the table. In this chapter, the grain is one row = one attendee at one session. Every step we take is in service of that rule.

Now that we have established what the attendance table is for and why its grain matters, let's build it.

Combine attendance files from a folder

The attendance files follow exactly the same monthly export pattern as the registrations in *Chapter 6*. Four files, one folder, same structure across all four months. The folder connector approach applies here without modification; the only differences are the folder path and the file names.

> **Important**
>
> For this exercise, continue in your `NOG-DataHub` workbook from *Chapter 6*. You will connect to the `Events/Attendance/` folder in your `NOG-DataHub`, which contains the four monthly attendance log files.
>
> You've covered this pattern in *Chapter 6*. Work through these steps as a review before we move into the new material. Pay attention to the column names as you go, they differ slightly from the registrations files.

Connect to the attendance folder

Follow the same folder connector pattern from *Chapters 1* through *5:* go to **Data** | **Get Data** | **From File**, choose **From SharePoint Folder** or **From Folder**, navigate to your `NOG-DataHub`, and click **Transform Data** to open the Power Query Editor.

Power Query opens the editor and displays a table listing every file in your `NOG-DataHub`.

Rename the query

Before doing anything else, rename the query. This keeps the **Queries** pane readable and distinguishes the raw combined data from the final reshaped table you will create later in this chapter:

1. In the **Query Settings** pane on the right, click on the current query name
2. Type `Attendance_Raw` and press *Enter*

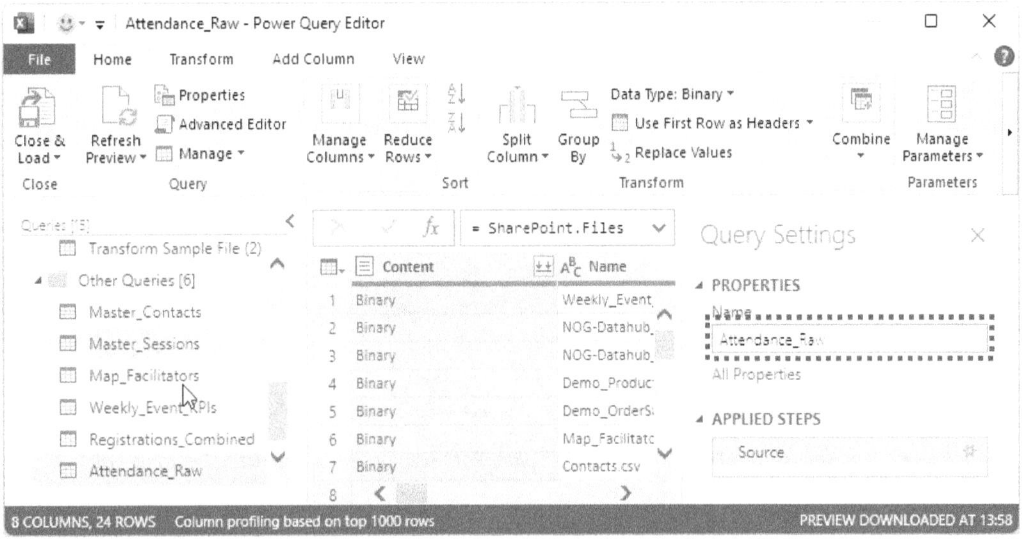

Figure 7.2 – Query Settings pane with the query renamed to Attendance_Raw

Filter to the attendance files

The file listing shows every file across the `NOG-DataHub`, not just the attendance exports. Filter it down to the four files in `Events/Attendance/`:

1. Click the dropdown arrow on the **Folder Path** column header
2. Click **Text Filters**
3. Click **Contains**

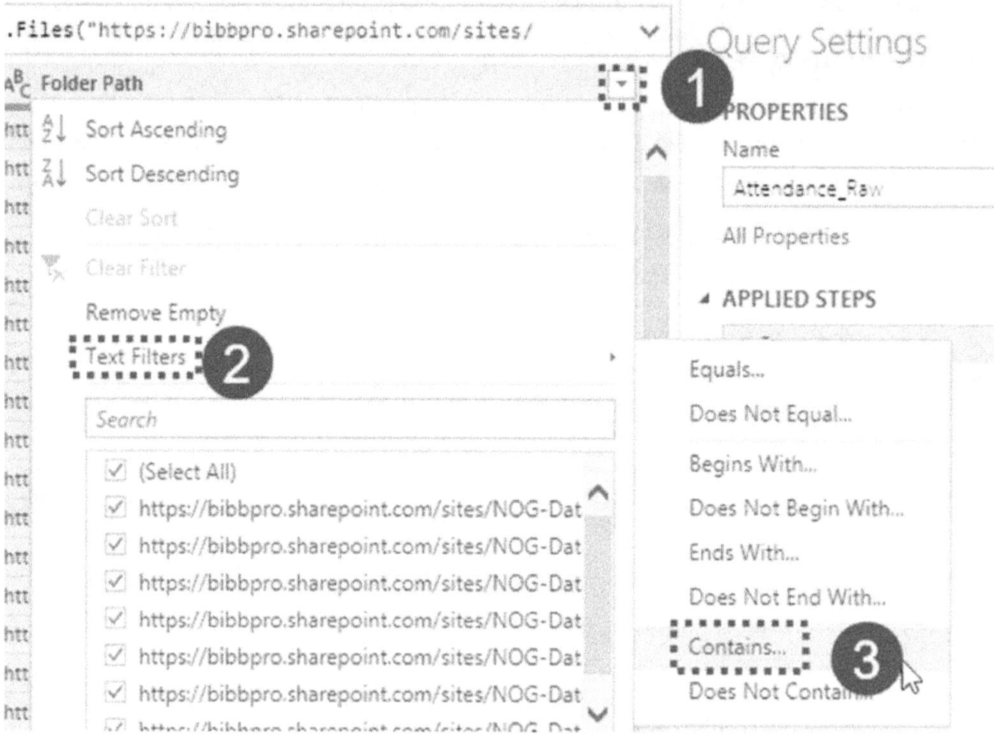

Figure 7.3 – Text Filters menu on the Folder Path column expanded to the Contains option

4. Type `Attendance` and click **OK**
5. Now filter the file names to ensure only the monthly export files are included. Click the dropdown arrow on the **Name** | **Text Filters** | **Begins With** | type `Attendance_` and click **OK**

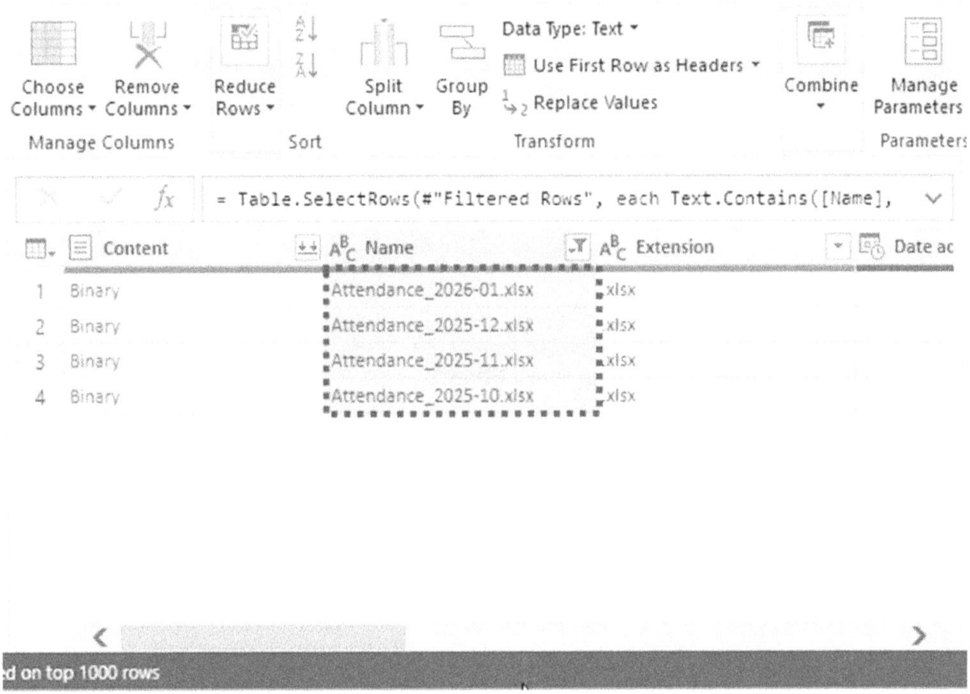

Figure 7.4 – File list filtered to the four monthly Attendance files

You should see exactly four rows: one for each monthly attendance file. If any template or test files appeared before the name filter, they will now be excluded.

> **Tip**
>
> Filter both the **Folder Path** and the **Name** columns whenever the folder might contain files that are not part of the intended dataset: templates, in-progress drafts, or archived copies. One stray file will be pulled into the combined table without any error message to alert you.

Combine the files

The file list is filtered and the query is named. Now combine the files into a single table:

1. Click the **Combine Files** icon in the **Content** column header, which shows two parallel arrows pointing down and sits in the leftmost column

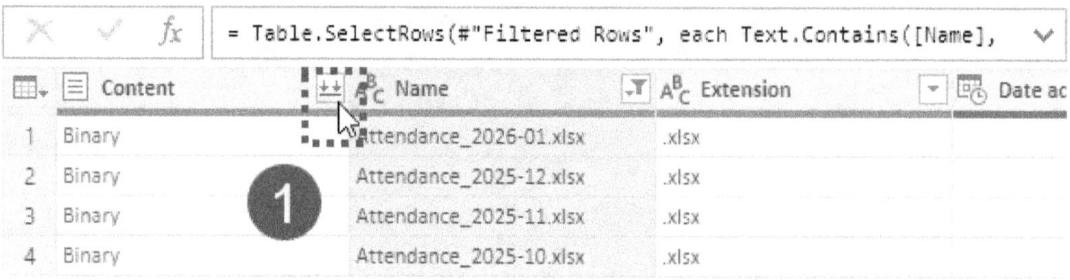

Figure 7.5 – The Combine Files icon in the Content column header

2. In the **Combine Files** dialog, select **Sheet1**
3. Confirm that the preview shows the expected columns: **AttendeeEmail**, **AttendeeName**, **SessionIDs**, **AttendanceDate**, **AttendanceStatus**, and **CheckInTime**
4. Click **OK**

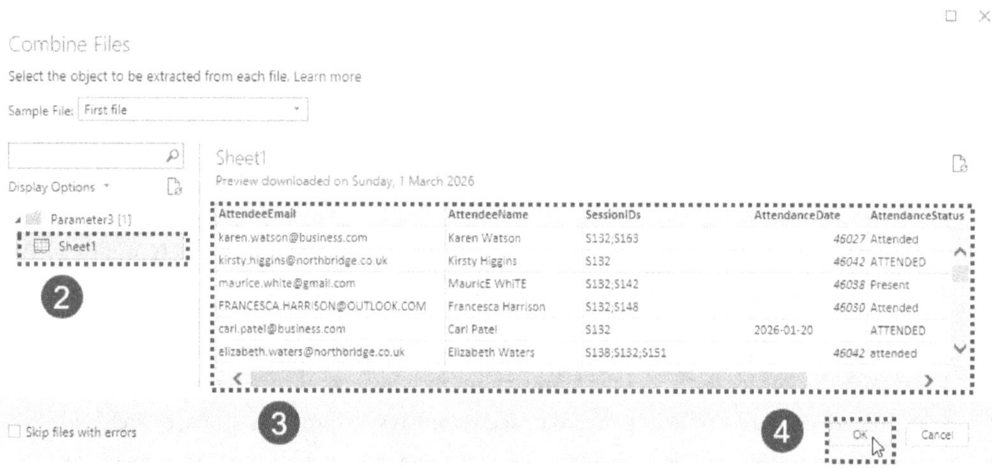

Figure 7.6 – Combine Files dialogue with the sample file preview showing the attendance columns

Power Query builds the combined table and returns you to the editor. The table now contains rows from all four monthly files.

> **Note**
>
> When you click **Combine Files**, Power Query automatically creates several helper queries in a **Helper Queries** group in the **Queries** pane (including a **Transform Sample File** query). These are generated automatically to support the main query. You do not need to edit them.

Keep only the columns you need

The combined table includes a **Source.Name** column that Power Query added automatically to record which file each row came from. That column served its purpose during the combine step, but it is not needed in the final table. Use **Choose Columns** to set the final column selection:

1. Click the **Home** tab
2. Click **Choose Columns**

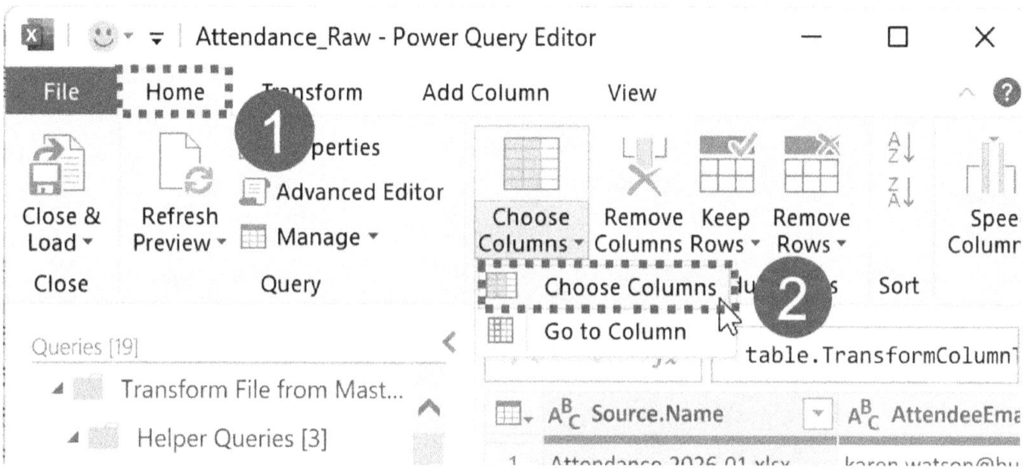

Figure 7.7 – Home tab with Choose Columns highlighted

3. In the **Choose Columns** dialog, untick **Source.Name**
4. Click **OK**

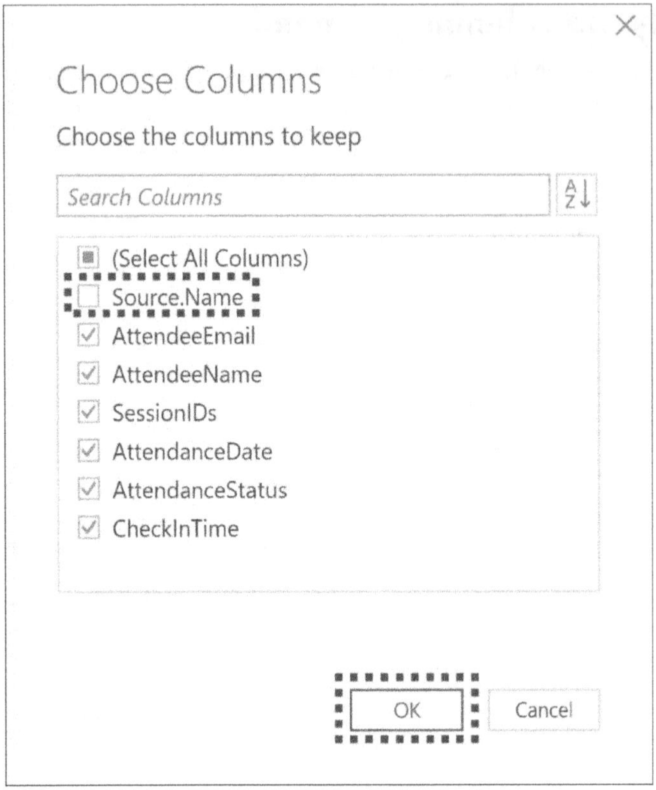

Figure 7.8 - Choose Columns dialogue with the six data columns ticked and Source.Name unticked

These are the six columns that remain:

- **AttendeeEmail** — the key that links to registrations
- **AttendeeName** — attendee full name
- **SessionIDs** — one or more session identifiers (this column needs reshaping in the next section)
- **AttendanceDate** — the date of attendance
- **AttendanceStatus** — whether the attendee was present or absent
- **CheckInTime** — the time of check-in; blank for no-shows

Now set data types on the columns that are ready. Leave **SessionIDs** as **Text** for the moment: it still contains semicolons and multiple values, and changing the type before the split step could corrupt those values:

1. Right-click the **AttendanceDate** column header

2. Click **Change Type**
3. Click **Date**

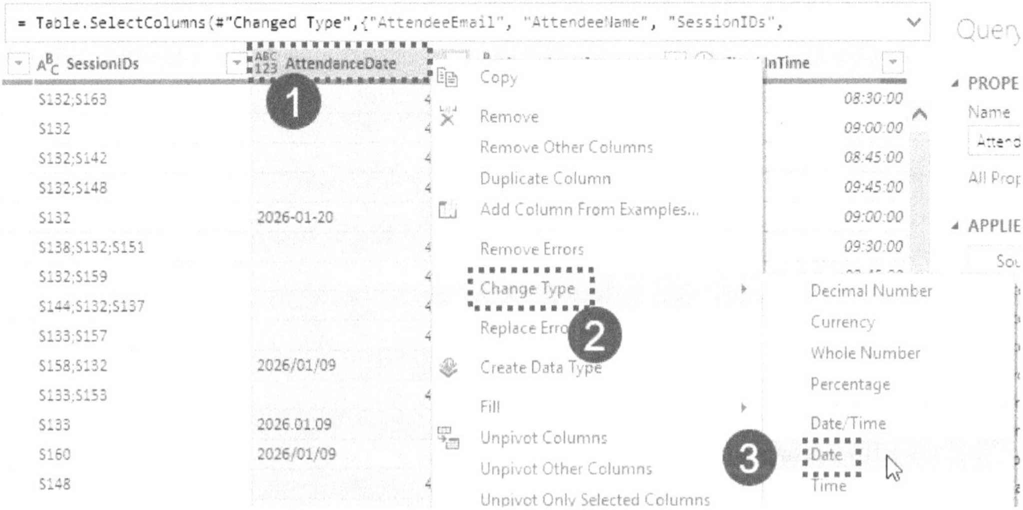

Figure 7.9 – Right-click context menu on AttendanceDate with Change Type expanded to Date

Repeat the same steps for **CheckInTime**, selecting **Time** as the type. If Power Query has already detected the column as Time, the step will confirm rather than change it; that is fine. Setting types explicitly is always preferable to relying on auto-detection. Leave all remaining columns as **Text**.

> **Tip**
>
> Set data types explicitly rather than using **Detect Data Type**. Auto-detection can misread a column containing values like `S001;S002` as text that looks numeric and produce unexpected errors. When in doubt, set **Text** first and convert specific columns individually.

The combined table is in place. Before reshaping the data, let's clean the columns that can be standardized now (email and attendance status) so the split step can focus purely on structure.

Cleaning keys for reliable matching

Two columns in this table will become join keys in *Chapter 8*: **AttendeeEmail** and **SessionID**. Cleaning them before the split means the transformations run on fewer rows, and it keeps the reshape step focused on structure rather than data quality.

> **Note**
>
> You applied the same email standardization steps in *Chapter 6* to clean **AttendeeEmail** in the registrations table. The logic here is identical. Consistent cleaning across both tables is what makes the eventual join safe.

Standardize AttendeeEmail

Remove extra spaces and non-printing characters. Then, convert all email addresses to lowercase. Apply these three steps in order:

Step 1 – trim

Follow these steps:

1. Right-click the **AttendeeEmail** column header
2. Click the **Transform** section
3. Click **Trim**

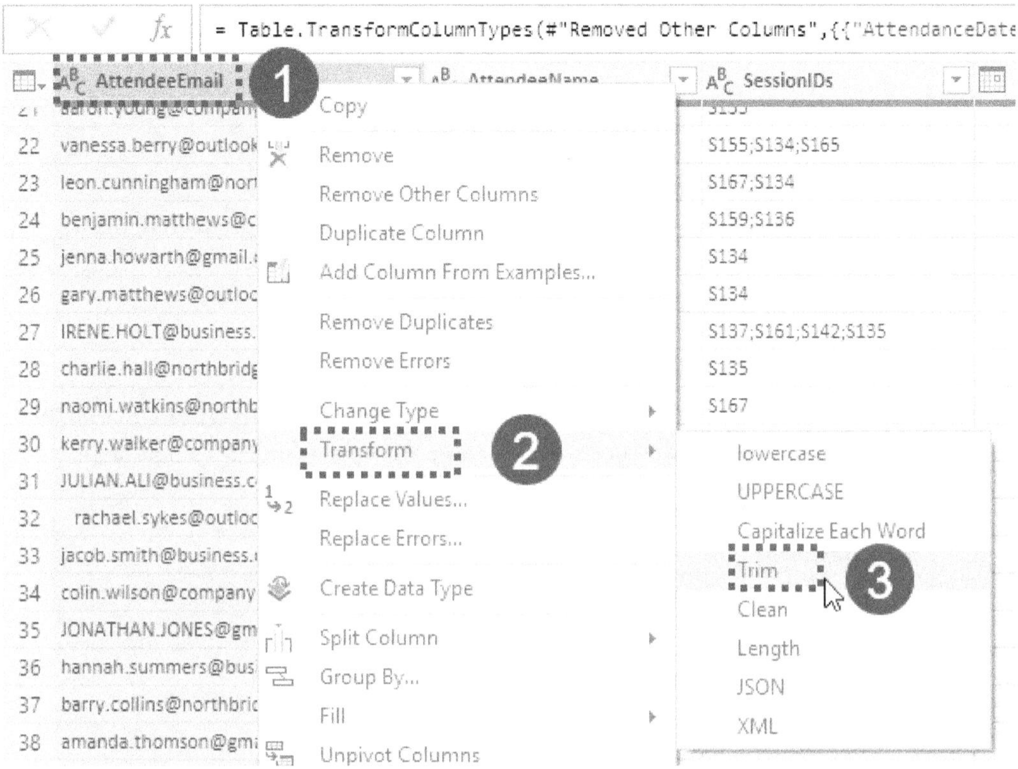

Figure 7.10 – Format menu on the Transform tab with Trim highlighted and AttendeeEmail selected

Rename the Applied Step to `Trimmed Email`.

Step 2 – clean

Follow these steps:

1. Right-click the **AttendeeEmail** header
2. Click **Transform** again
3. Click **Clean**
4. Rename the Applied Step to `Cleaned Email`

Step 3 – lowercase

Follow these steps:

1. Right-click the **AttendeeEmail** column header
2. Click **Transform**

3. Click **lowercase**
4. Rename the Applied Step to `Lowercased Email`

After these three steps, every email address in the column is trimmed, cleaned, and in lowercase, ready to match against **Registrations_Combined**.

Standardize AttendanceStatus

The **AttendanceStatus** column contains variants that represent the same two outcomes: present or absent. Different exports use different terminology:

- `Attended`, `Present`, and `attended` all mean the same thing
- `No-show` and `NoShow` both mean the same thing

Normalize to two values: `attended` and `no-show`. Start by lowercasing the entire column, this resolves all the casing variants (`ATTENDED`, `Attended`, `Present`, `present`) in a single step:

1. Right-click the **AttendanceStatus** column header
2. Click **Transform**
3. Click **lowercase**

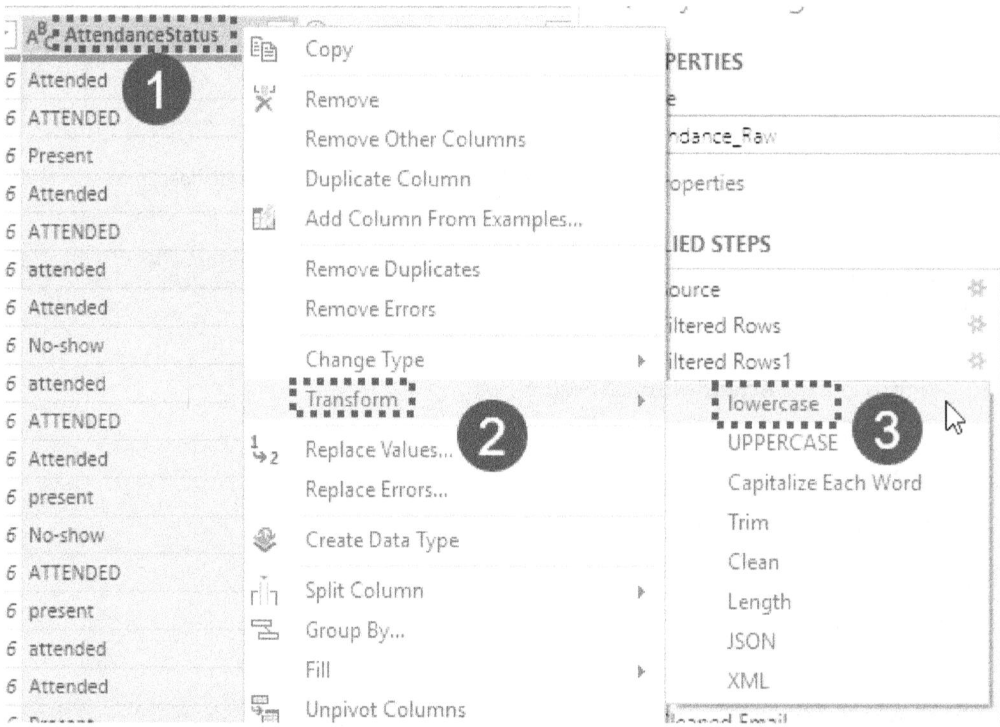

Figure 7.11 – Right-click context menu on AttendanceStatus with Transform expanded to lowercase

Rename this Applied Step to `Lowercased Status`.

> **Tip**
>
> Power Query sometimes merges consecutive transformations on different columns into a single step. If no new step appears and the previous step is updated instead, rename it to `Lowercased Email and Status` to reflect that both columns were lowercased together.

After lowercasing, two values still need a targeted fix: `noshow` (the hyphen was lost) and `present` (a different word for the same outcome). Replace each one:

1. Right-click the **AttendanceStatus** column header
2. Click **Replace Values**
3. In the **Value To Find** field, type `noshow`
4. In the **Replace With** field, type `no-show`
5. Click **OK**

Repeat the same steps to replace present with attended: find the word `present` and replace it with `attended`.

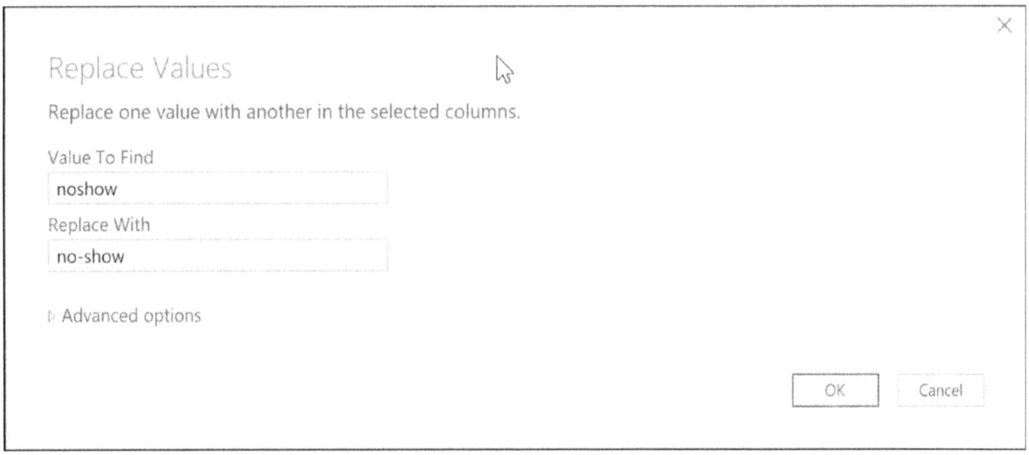

Figure 7.12 – Replace Values dialog replacing "noshow" with "no-show"

Rename the two **Replace Values** steps in the **Applied Steps** pane to `Standardized Status - noshow` and `Standardized Status - present`.

> **Tip**
>
> **Decision log**: AttendanceStatus is normalized to `attended` and `no-show` (lowercase).
>
> **Rule**: lowercase first to collapse all casing variants, then fix the two remaining spelling differences. Write this rule in a shared document or as a comment in the query so that future maintainers know why the mapping exists and can extend it if new variants appear in later exports.

After these replacements, verify the result: click the filter dropdown on **AttendanceStatus** and confirm that only attended and no-show appear.

Capitalize AttendeeName

The **AttendeeName** column arrives with inconsistent casing across the monthly exports. Capitalize each word to produce a consistent display format:

1. Right-click the **AttendeeName** column header
2. Click **Transform**
3. Click **Capitalize Each Word**

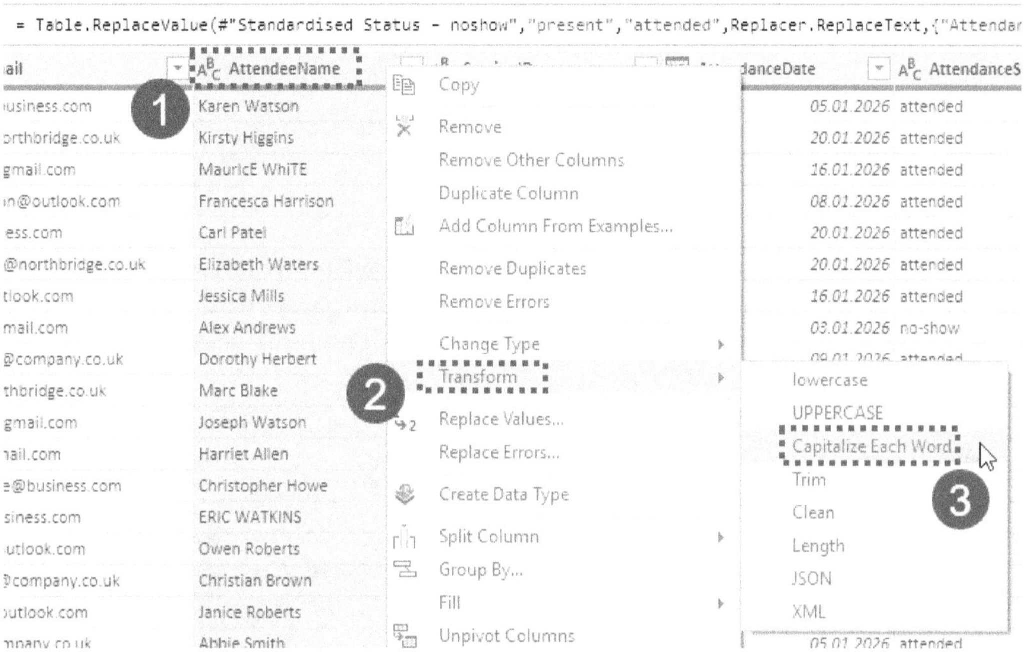

Figure 7.13 – Right-click context menu on AttendeeName with Transform expanded to Capitalize Each Word

Rename this Applied Step to `Proper Cased Name`.

With the text fields standardized, the table is ready for the reshape. The **SessionIDs** column is handled after the split, once every row holds exactly one value.

Split-to-Rows: turning Multi-Session cells into rows

The combined table has one awkward column: **SessionIDs**. Looking at the preview, you will find cells containing values like `S001;S002;S045`; three separate session identifiers packed into a single cell, separated by semicolons.

This format made sense for the system that produced the export: recording all of a person's sessions in one row keeps the file compact. But for analysis, it is a problem. If you tried to count how many people attended session `S002` right now, Power Query would not find any row containing just `S002`; it would only find rows containing the full string `S001;S002;S045`. The session-level counts would be wrong.

The fix is **Split Column by Delimiter → To Rows**. This is one of Power Query's most useful reshaping tools for business data. It takes a delimited value in a single cell and turns each delimited item into its own row, repeating the other columns (email, name, date, status) for each. One person who attended three sessions becomes three rows, each with a single SessionID.

This is what creates the grain defined at the start of the chapter: one row per attendee per session.

Spot the multi-value column

Before running the split, take a moment to inspect the **SessionIDs** column and understand the data you are working with. Identify cells that contain more than one value; they will have one or more semicolons between session identifiers, for example `S001;S002` or `S014;S027;S041`.

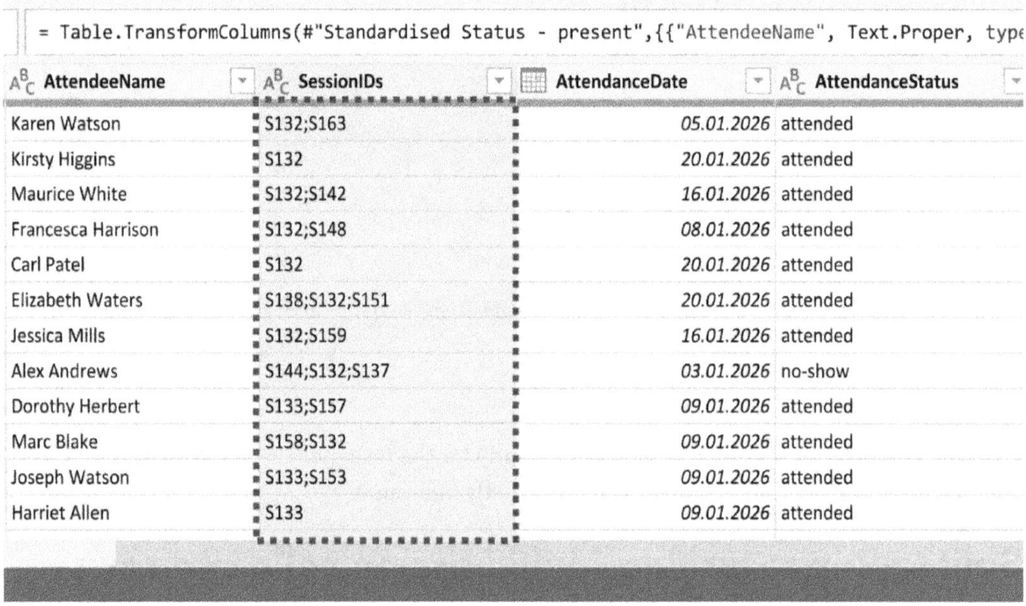

Figure 7.14 – SessionIDs column in the preview, showing cells with multiple semicolon-delimited session identifiers

Not every row will have multiple sessions: many attendees attended only one session, and those rows will pass through the split unchanged. The split only adds rows where a delimiter is present.

Note the row count shown at the bottom of the Power Query Editor window. You will compare this to the count after the split to confirm the reshape worked correctly:

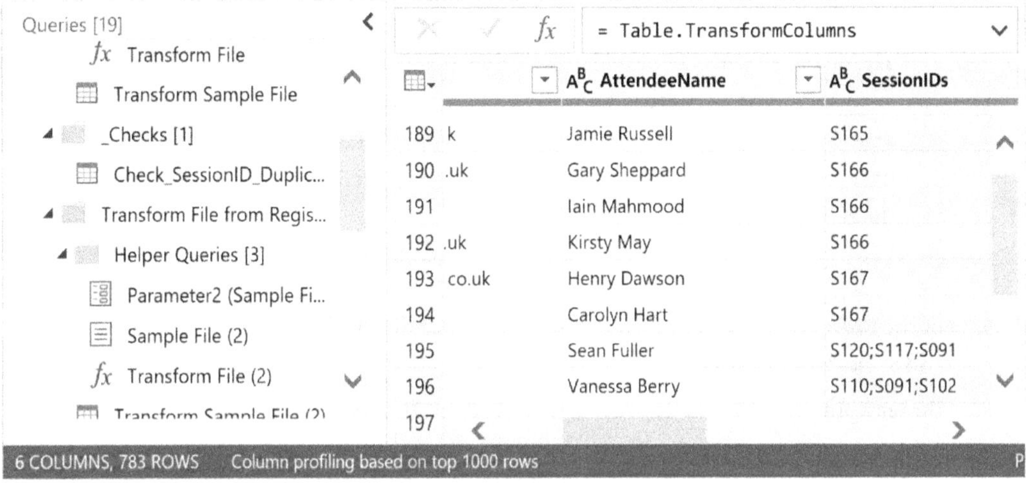

Figure 7.15 – Row count displayed at the bottom of the Power Query Editor before the split

Split SessionIDs into rows

With the **SessionIDs** column selected, apply the split:

1. Click the **SessionIDs** column header to select it
2. Click the **Transform** tab
3. Click **Split Column**
4. Click **By Delimiter**

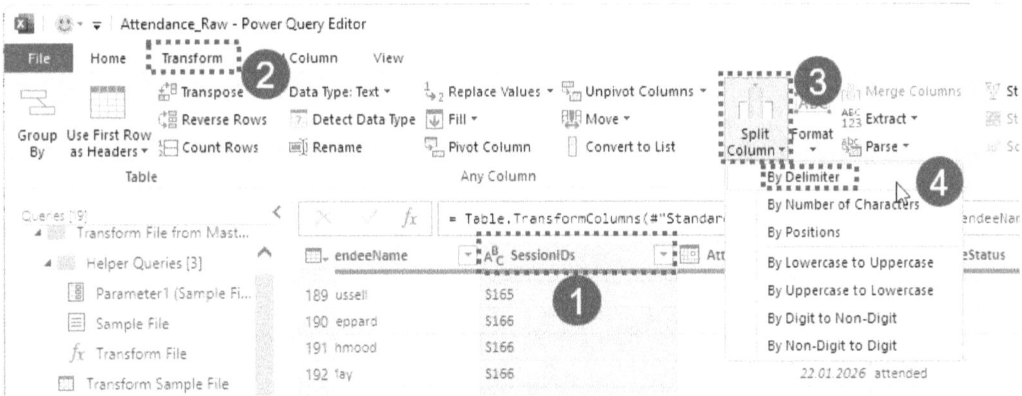

Figure 7.16 – Transform tab with Split Column expanded to show the By Delimiter option

> **Note**
>
> The delimiter you choose will usually depend on the source system and how it exports records. In this example, the values are separated with semicolons, but other systems may use commas, tabs, pipes, or another character. If the export uses a non-standard separator, choose the custom delimiter option and enter the required character.

5. In the **Split Column by Delimiter** dialog, click the **Select** or enter delimiter dropdown and select **Semicolon**
6. Under **Split at**, select **Each occurrence of the delimiter**
7. Click **Advanced options** to expand the section
8. Under **Split into**, select **Rows** (you may also see a **Quote Character** field in the **Advanced options** section — leave it at its default setting. It is not needed here)
9. Click **OK**

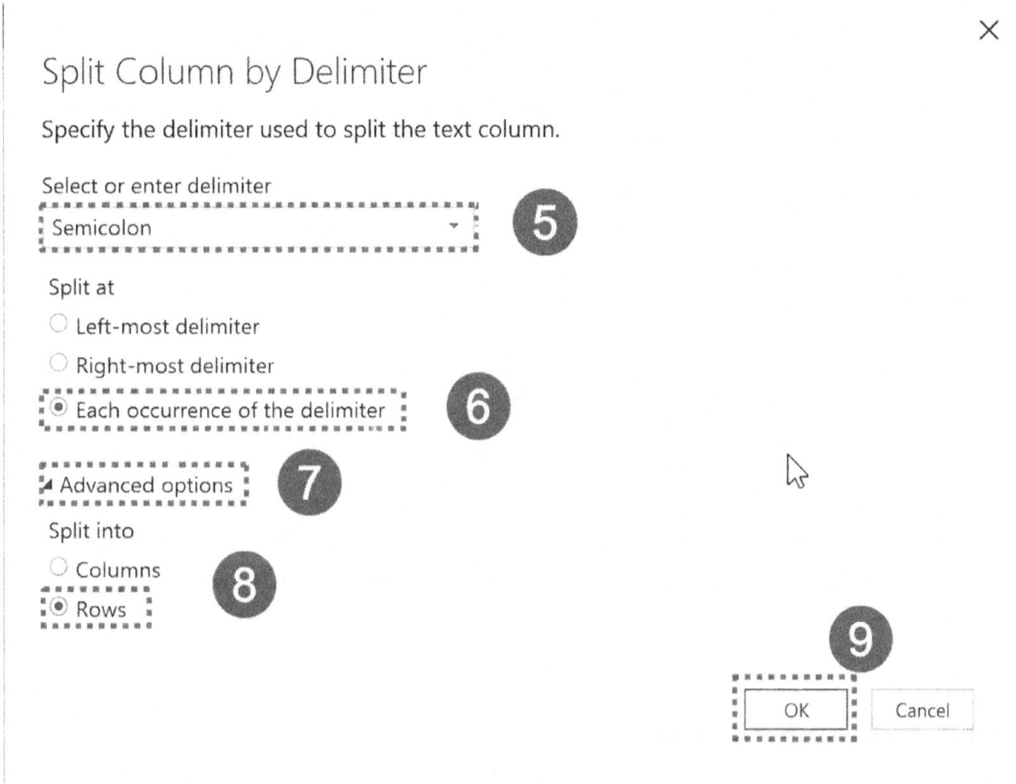

Figure 7.17 – Split Column by Delimiter dialog with Semicolon selected and Rows chosen under Split into

Power Query expands the table. Every row that contained multiple **SessionIDs** now appears as multiple rows (one per session) with the **AttendeeEmail**, **AttendeeName**, **AttendanceDate**, **AttendanceStatus**, and **CheckInTime** columns repeated across each.

Rename this step in the **Applied Steps** pane to `Split SessionIDs to Rows` so that the purpose is clear to anyone who reads the query later.

> **Caution**
>
> In the **Split Column by Delimiter** dialog, the default option under **Split into** is **Columns**, not **Rows**. Splitting into columns creates a set of new columns (**SessionIDs.1**, **SessionIDs.2**, **SessionIDs.3**), which is the opposite of what we want. If you accidentally split into columns, click the step in the **Applied Steps** pane and press *Delete* to remove it, then repeat the split, selecting **Rows** this time.

Verify the new grain

Check the row count at the bottom of the Power Query Editor. It should be higher than the count you noted before the split; the exact increase depends on how many multi-session rows existed across the four monthly files.

The new row count represents the total number of attendee-session combinations. Every row now has exactly one value in the **SessionIDs** column. You can confirm this by scrolling through the column; no semicolons should remain.

> **AI Helper**
>
> If you want to build intuition for when to use this pattern on other datasets, ask an AI assistant such as ChatGPT: `In Power Query, what does Split Column by Delimiter → To Rows do to a table? Give me a simple example showing the table before and after.`
>
> Always verify the explanation against your actual row counts in the **Power Query Editor**; the before and after row counts are the definitive check that the split worked correctly.

Keep SessionID as text

Now that every row holds exactly one value, two housekeeping steps are needed before the **SessionIDs** column is ready to use as a join key.

First, rename the column to reflect its new grain; the plural name is now misleading:

1. Double-click the **SessionIDs** column header
2. Type `SessionID` and press *Enter*

Second, confirm the data type is **Text**. After a split, Power Query may attempt to auto-detect the type. If all SessionID values look purely numeric, Power Query might convert them to whole numbers, which would silently break the join with **Master_Sessions**, where SessionID is stored as text.

> **Caution**
>
> A SessionID stored as a number will not match a SessionID stored as text, even if the underlying values look identical; 1 and "1" are different types in Power Query. The merge in *Chapter 8* will not warn you; it will simply return no matches for those rows. Protect join keys with an explicit type step every time.

The table is now reshaped, cleaned, and consistently typed. The next step is to give it its final name and load it into a sheet.

Landing on Sessions_Attendance and checking the grain

The query has the right shape, the right grain, and clean keys. Two things remain: rename it to reflect what it now contains and load it to a worksheet, so the data is available to Excel and to the queries in later chapters.

After loading, run three quick checks to confirm the reshape did what we intended. These checks take under a minute and establish a baseline you can return to after every refresh.

Rename and load the query

Follow these steps to rename and load the query:

1. In the **Query Settings** pane replace **Attendance_Raw** with `Sessions_Attendance` and press *Enter*.

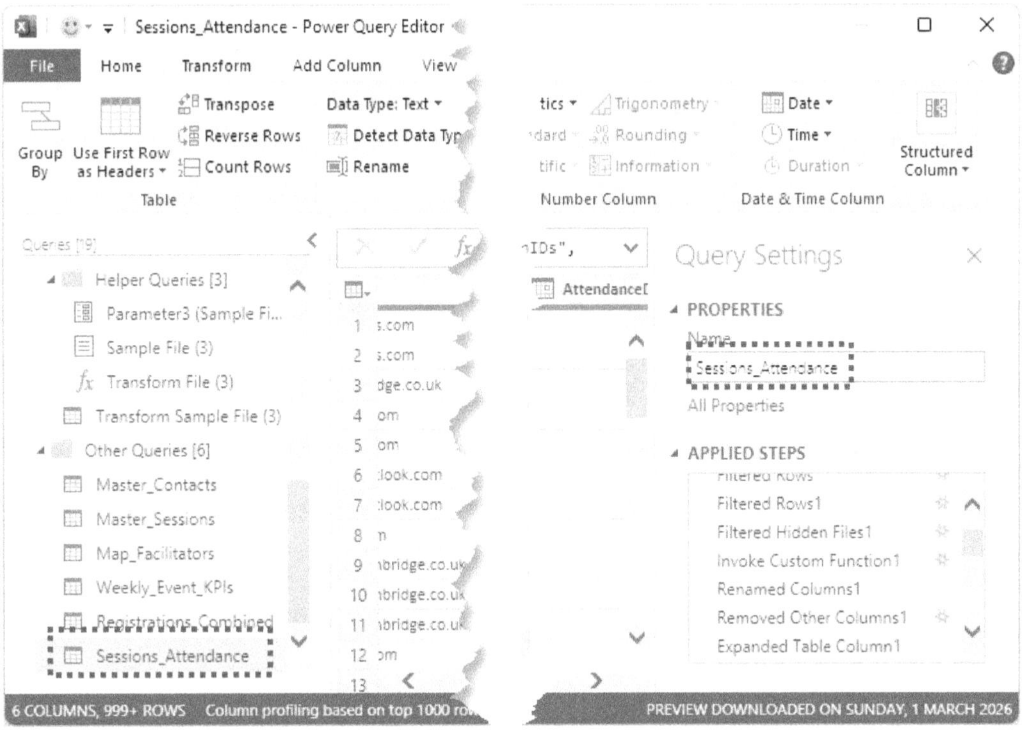

Figure 7.18 – Query Settings pane with the query renamed to Sessions_Attendance

The new name signals the change in shape: this is no longer the raw combined export; it is the reshaped long table with one row per attendee-session.

Now load the query to a worksheet.

2. Click the **Home** tab
3. Click the dropdown arrow next to **Close & Load**
4. Click **Close & Load To...**

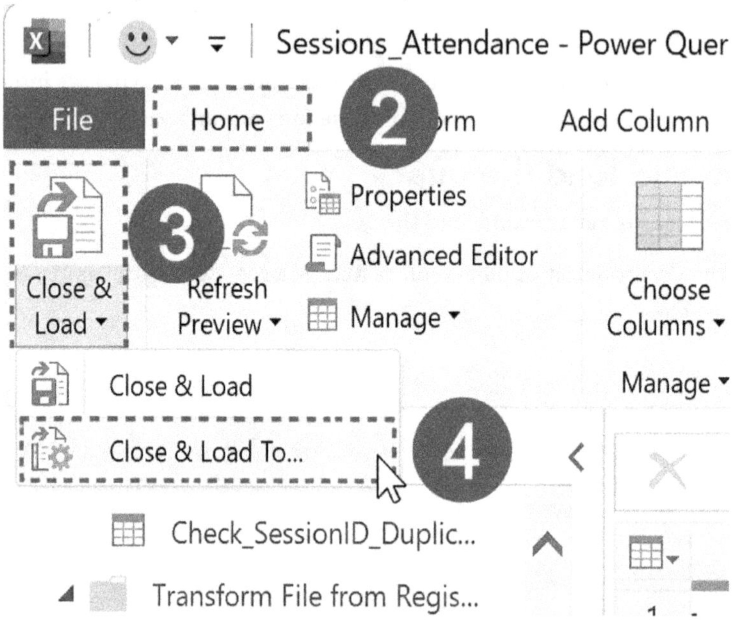

Figure 7.19 – Close & Load dropdown with Close & Load To... button highlighted

5. In the **Import Data** dialog, select **Table**
6. Select **New worksheet**
7. Click **OK**

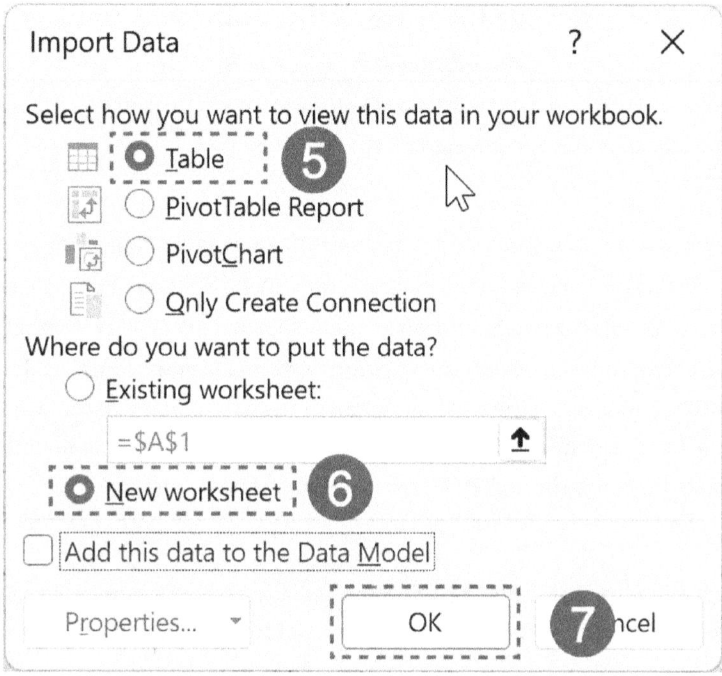

Figure 7.20 – Import Data dialogue with Table and New worksheet selected

The reshaped attendance table appears as an Excel table on the new sheet: one row per attendee per session, with clean keys and consistent status values.

Validate with row count

With the table loaded, run three checks before treating the data as ready to use:

Check 1: row count is higher than the raw file total

The combined raw table had one row per person per monthly file. After the split, the row count must be higher; every person who attended more than one session now occupies multiple rows. If the row count is the same as or lower than the raw combined count, the split step did not apply correctly. Return to the **Power Query Editor** and review the **Applied Steps** pane.

Check 2: no blanks in AttendeeEmail or SessionID

These two columns will be used as join keys in *Chapter 8*. A blank in either column means that row cannot be matched. Click the filter dropdown on each column and confirm that `(Blank)` either does not appear or has zero rows.

Check 3: AttendanceStatus contains only two values

Click the filter dropdown on **AttendanceStatus**. You should see exactly `Attended` and `No-show`. Any other value means a **Replace Values** step was missed or a new variant appeared in the source files that was not covered by the normalization steps.

> **AI Helper**
>
> To quickly count distinct values in a column, ask an AI assistant such as ChatGPT: `What Excel formula counts the number of distinct values in a column, ignoring blanks?` A common answer is a `SUMPRODUCT/COUNTIF` combination. Once you have the formula, verify the distinct **AttendeeEmail** count and the distinct **SessionID** count against the total row count. If the row total is close to what you would expect given the number of attendees and sessions, the split worked correctly. If the total looks unexpectedly high or low, investigate before using the table in a merge.

If all three checks pass, **Sessions_Attendance** is ready. If one fails, return to the Power Query Editor, find the step responsible, and fix it there, not in the sheet.

With the attendance table validated, Quinn closes her laptop and turns to Tom. "You've got the same setup as registrations now. One click refreshes everything, a new monthly file lands in the folder, and it gets picked up automatically."

Tom is already looking at the row counts on screen. "And every row is one person at one session? Even if they attended five sessions?"

"Five rows," Quinn confirms. "That's the whole point. Now you can count, filter, and merge it properly."

Summary

In this chapter, you built **Sessions_Attendance**: a clean, reshaped attendance table with one row per attendee-session. The work followed a three-part pattern:

- **Combine**: used the Folder connector to pull four monthly attendance exports into a single table, following the same approach established in Chapter 3 and reused in *Chapter 6*

- **Reshape**: used **Split Column by Delimiter → To Rows** to normalize the multi-value **SessionIDs** column, turning one row per person into one row per person per session
- **Clean**: standardized the two join keys, lowercased and trimmed AttendeeEmail, normalized AttendanceStatus to two consistent values, and explicitly set SessionID to Text to protect the merge

These three steps, combine, reshape, and clean, are a repeatable pattern. Any time you receive data where one cell holds a delimited list, **Split Column by Delimiter** | **Split to Rows** is the tool to reach for first.

In *Chapter 8*, Amira picks up where Tom and Quinn left off. She needs one master attendee list that brings together registrations and attendance, who signed up and whether they actually came. With both tables clean and consistently keyed, that merge is finally ready to run.

8

Merge Tables to Build an Enriched Master List

Figure 8.1 – Amira arrives with a familiar problem: registrations

In one table, attendance in another

It is a Tuesday morning when Amira appears at Quinn's desk, a familiar expression on her face: the look of someone who has spent the last hour doing something that should take five minutes.

"I need to send follow-up emails to everyone who attended last month's sessions," she says, setting her laptop down on the desk. "And certificates to the ones who completed the full program. But I've got registrations in one spreadsheet and attendance in another, and they don't match up the way I need."

Quinn glances at the screen. Amira has both tables open, one exported from the booking system, one from the session coordinator, and a third spreadsheet where she has been manually copying names across, checking each one by eye.

"I've been doing this for six months," Amira says. "Sometimes I miss someone. Last quarter, I sent a certificate to someone who didn't actually attend."

Quinn thinks of the two tables she built over the past two chapters: **Registrations_Combined** from *Chapter 6*, clean and deduplicated; **Sessions_Attendance** from *Chapter 7*, reshaped and consistently keyed. Both are already in the `NOG-DataHub` workbook. The matching is done; Amira just doesn't know it yet.

"You won't need to do it manually anymore," Quinn says. "Let me show you."

In this chapter, you'll learn to -

- Describe what one row in **Master_Attendees** represents and how the table will be used downstream
- Choose merge keys (**AttendeeEmail** and **SessionID**) and explain why the cleaning steps in earlier chapters are relevant now
- Build a safe left join from registrations to attendance and expand only the columns you need
- Detect and prevent row multiplication by checking the lookup side for duplicates before merging

Technical requirements

The chapters in this book build on each other. Make sure you have completed all exercises in the previous chapter before starting this one.

To follow along with this chapter, you will need:

- Microsoft Excel 2016 or later with Power Query, accessed via **Data** | **Get & Transform Data**
- Your `NOG-DataHub` workbook (NOG stands for Northbridge Office Group) from *Chapter 7*, which should already contain the following queries:
    - **Master_Sessions** (built in *Chapter 3*)
    - **Weekly_Event_KPIs** (built in *Chapter 4*)

- **Registrations_Combined** (built in *Chapter 6*)
- **Sessions_Attendance** (built in *Chapter 7*)

No new exercise files are introduced in this chapter. The merge draws entirely on the two queries already in your workbook.

What Master_Attendees is (and isn't)

Before building the merge, it helps to be precise about what the output table will contain and what it will not.

Master_Attendees is a registration-level table enriched with attendance information. One row represents one registration, with additional columns showing whether the person attended. A person who registered for three sessions will appear as three rows (one per registration), each carrying its own attendance outcome.

Column	Source	What it tells you
AttendeeEmail	Registrations_Combined	Who registered
SessionID	Registrations_Combined	Which session they registered for
RegistrationStatus	Registrations_Combined	Confirmed or Canceled
TicketType	Registrations_Combined	Standard, Early Bird, VIP, Complimentary
AttendanceStatus	Sessions_Attendance	Whether they attended or were a no-show
Attended	Derived	Yes or No flag for easy filtering

Table 8.1 – Key columns in Master_Attendees and their source

Master_Attendees is not a unique-person list. If you want to know how many distinct individuals registered across all sessions, that is a different query. A simple **Group By** on **AttendeeEmail**. **Master_Attendees** is also not a payments table; payments are added in *Chapter 9*.

The distinction matters because the grain, the rule that defines what one row represents, drives every decision in this chapter. The grain is: one row = one registration, enriched with its attendance outcome.

The left table in the merge (the table whose rows define what must appear in the output) is **Registrations_Combined**. Every registration must survive the merge, whether or not a matching attendance record was found. That requirement determines the join type.

Now that the grain is defined, let's look at how to choose the columns that link the two tables together.

Choosing merge keys that work

A **merge key** is the column or combination of columns that Power Query uses to decide which row in one table matches a row in the other. If the values in those columns are equal, the rows are joined. If they are not, there is no match.

Choosing the right key is the most important decision in a merge. A key that is too broad produces unexpected duplicate rows. A key that is too narrow leaves rows that should match unjoined.

Why a single column is not enough

For this merge, two candidates might come to mind:

- **AttendeeEmail alone**: The same person can register for multiple sessions, so the same email address appears on many rows in **Registrations_Combined**. One email in the registrations table would match every attendance row for that email, multiplying rows unexpectedly.
- **SessionID alone**: Many people registered for the same session, so the same SessionID appears on dozens of rows. The same problem occurs in reverse.

Neither column alone identifies one registration. Together, they do.

The composite key: AttendeeEmail + SessionID

The combination of **AttendeeEmail** and **SessionID** identifies one specific registration: this person, for this session. It is the same pair used as the deduplication key in *Chapter 6*; for the same reason, they define one logical record.

Tip

Decision log: Merge key = AttendeeEmail + SessionID. Both columns are already clean in the source queries, emails lowercased, and trimmed in **Chapters 6** and **7**, and SessionID set to **Text** in **Chapter 7**. No additional preparation is needed before this merge.

Why the earlier cleaning steps are useful now

The cleaning work in *Chapters 6* and *7* was preparation for this moment. Power Query matches merge keys by exact value. Two values that look identical but differ in casing or spacing will not match. Consider what happens without the earlier cleaning:

- `amira@nog.co.uk` in one table and `Amira@NOG.co.uk` in the other → no match
- `S001` stored as **Text** in one table and `1` stored as a **Whole Number** in the other → no match

Neither case produces an error. Power Query simply finds no match and leaves those rows unjoined. The attendance columns come back blank (as if the person never attended), and the **Attended** flag shows `No` for rows that should show `Yes`.

The lowercase transformation on **AttendeeEmail** and the explicit **Text** type on **SessionID**, both applied in earlier chapters, prevent exactly this.

AI Helper

If you are merging tables you did not build yourself, ask an AI assistant such as ChatGPT: `I have two tables with an email column. One has values like 'Amira@NOG.co.uk' and the other has 'amira@nog.co.uk'. What Power Query steps should I add to standardize both columns before merging?`

The assistant will suggest lowercase and trim steps. Always verify the suggestions against the actual distinct values in both columns before applying them: open the filter dropdown for each key column to see what is actually there.

The keys are chosen, and the preparation is confirmed. Now let's build the merge.

Building the master list with safe left joins

The core of this chapter is a single Power Query operation: merge queries. It takes two tables, matches rows on a shared key, and produces one wider table. The join type controls which rows survive the match.

Understanding the join types

Power Query offers several join types. For **Master_Attendees**, the choice is straightforward:

Join type	What it keeps
Left Outer	All rows from the left table; matching rows from the right. Unmatched left-table rows are kept with null values in the right-table columns.
Inner	Only rows with a match in both tables. Unmatched rows from either side are discarded.
Full Outer	All rows from both tables matched where possible, and null-filled where not.
Right Outer	All rows from the right table; matching rows from the left.

Table 8.2 – Power Query join types and what each one keeps

For Amira's use case, the right choice is **Left Outer**. **Registrations_Combined** is the left table; every registration must appear in the output, even if no attendance record was found. An **Inner join** would silently drop any registration with no attendance match, which is not what we want.

Opening Registrations_Combined in the Power Query editor

> **Important**
>
> For this exercise, continue in your `NOG-DataHub` workbook from *Chapter 7*. You will build a new query by merging the **Registrations_Combined** and **Sessions_Attendance** queries that are already in the workbook. No new data connections are needed.

Start by opening the Power Query Editor with **Registrations_Combined** active:

1. Click the **Data** tab
2. Click **Queries & Connections**
3. In the **Queries & Connections** pane on the right, double-click **Registrations_Combined**

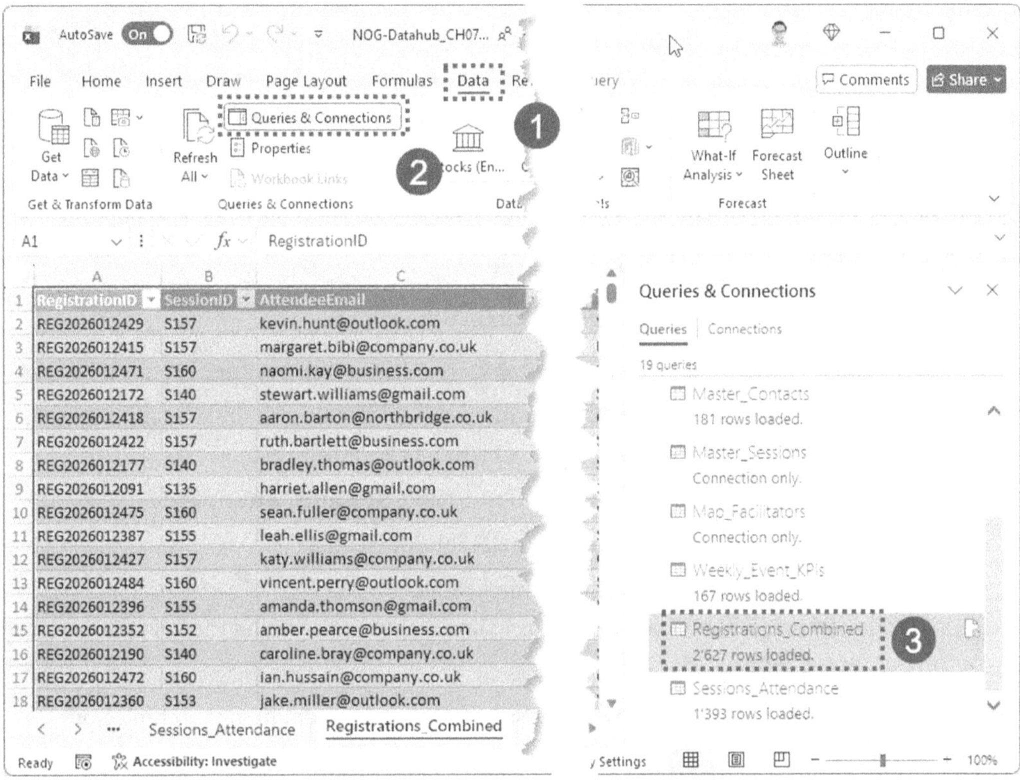

Figure 8.2 – Queries & Connections pane with Registrations_Combined listed, ready to open in the Power Query Editor

The Power Query Editor opens with **Registrations_Combined** displayed in the preview.

Creating a new merged query

With **Registrations_Combined** open in the editor, create a new query that merges it with **Sessions_Attendance**:

1. Click the **Home** tab in the Power Query Editor
2. Click the dropdown arrow next to **Merge Queries**
3. Click **Merge Queries as New**

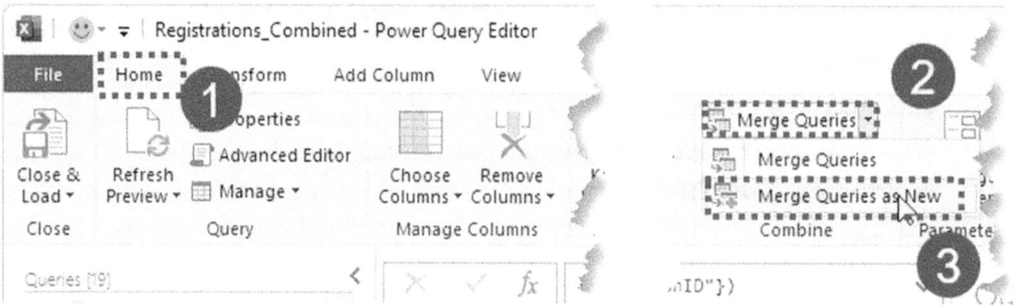

Figure 8.3 – Home tab with the Merge Queries dropdown expanded to show Merge Queries as New

The **Merge** dialog opens. The top section already shows **Registrations_Combined**; this is the left table.

Selecting the merge keys

In the **Merge** dialog, select the matching columns in both tables:

1. In the top table (**Registrations_Combined**), click the **AttendeeEmail** column header
2. Hold *Ctrl* and click the **SessionID** column header, both columns are now highlighted, with small labels showing the order in which they were selected
3. Click the dropdown in the lower section and select **Sessions_Attendance**
4. In the lower table, click the **AttendeeEmail** column header
5. Hold *Ctrl* and click the **SessionID** column header
   The column pair labels (1 and 2) appear in both tables, confirming the keys are matched in the correct order.
6. Confirm the **Join Kind** dropdown shows **Left Outer** (all from first, matching from second)
7. Click **OK**

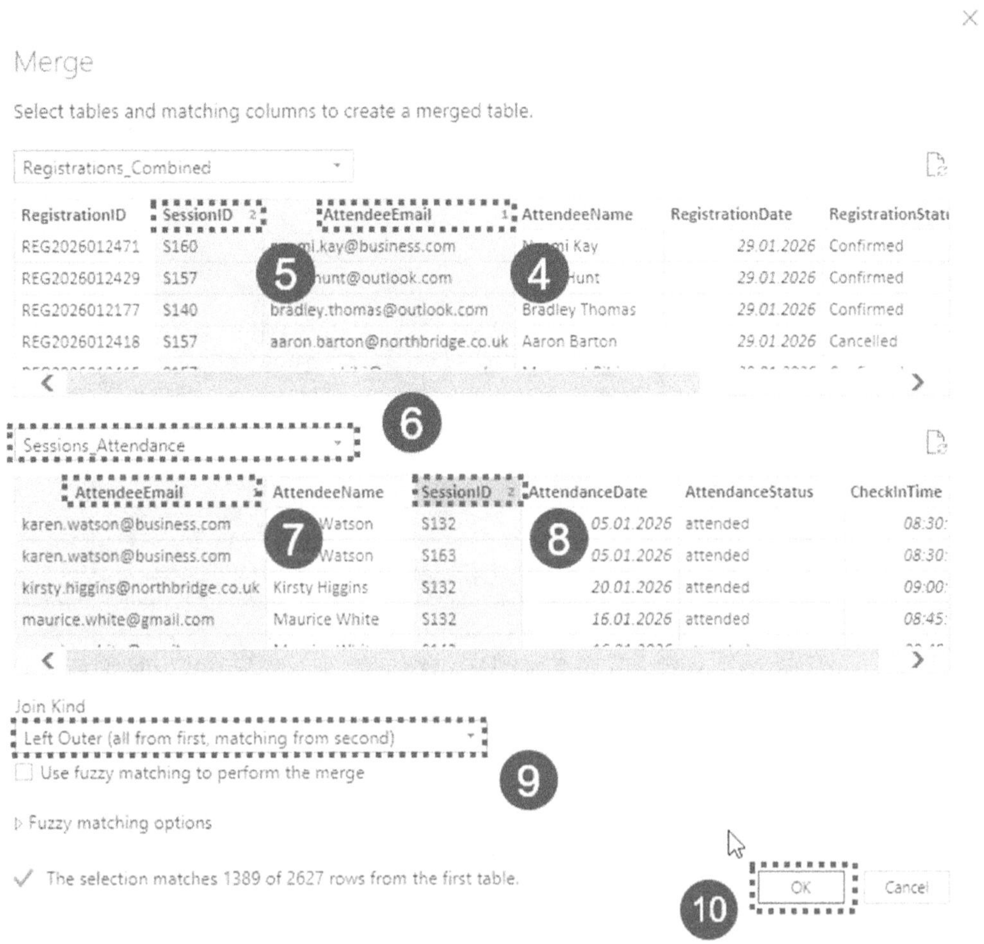

Figure 8.4 – Merge dialogue with key column pairs highlighted, and Left Outer join confirmed

Power Query creates the new query and returns you to the editor. All columns from **Registrations_Combined** are present, plus a new column named **Sessions_Attendance**. Every cell in that column shows the word `Table`; this is expected. The column is a nested table holding the matching attendance rows for each registration; the next step expands it into the individual columns you need.

Renaming the new query

With the dialog closed and the new query active, rename it before doing anything else:

1. In the **Query Settings** pane on the right, click on the current query name and type Master_Attendees and press *Enter*

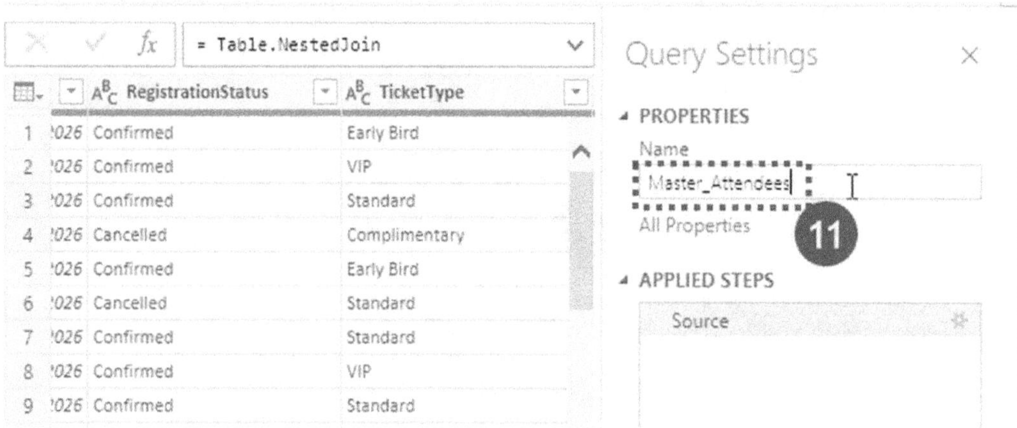

Figure 8.5 – Query Settings pane with the new query renamed to Master_Attendees

Expanding only the columns you need

The **Sessions_Attendance** column contains a nested table for each row. Expand it to bring across only the two columns Amira needs:

1. Click the *Expand* icon in the **Sessions_Attendance** column header; it shows two small outward-pointing arrows
2. In the **Expand** panel, untick **Select All Columns** to clear the selection
3. Tick **AttendanceStatus** and **AttendanceDate**
4. Untick **Use original column name as prefix**
5. Click **OK**

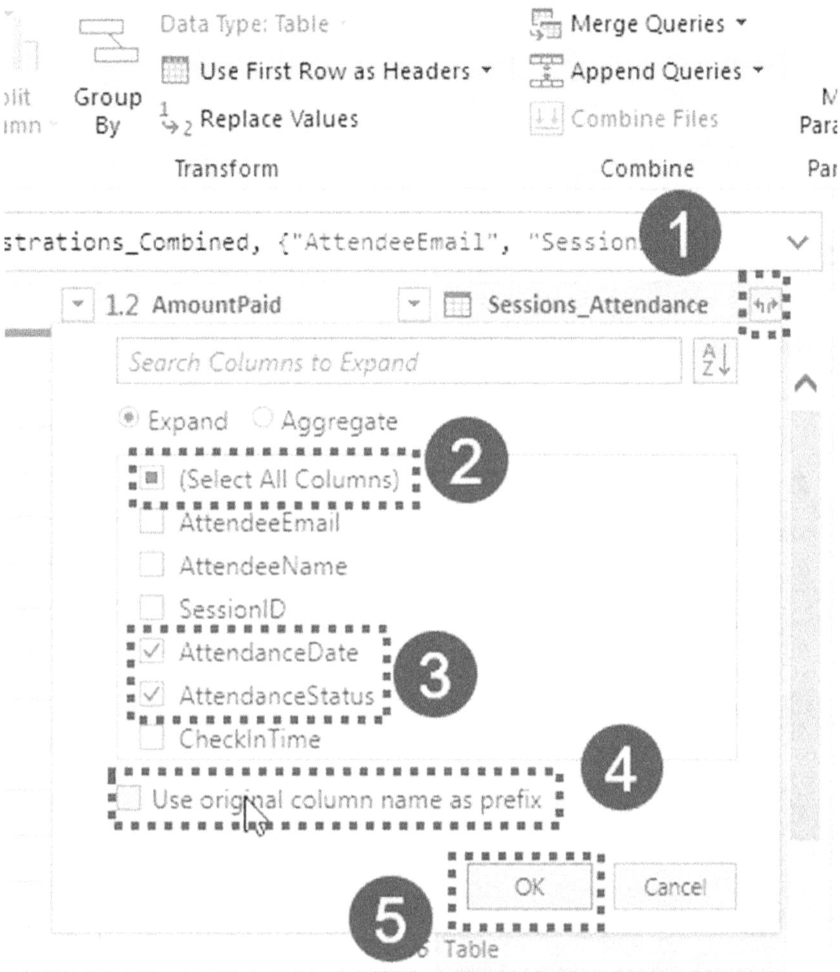

Figure 8.6 – Expand panel with only AttendanceStatus and AttendanceDate ticked and the prefix option unticked

The two attendance columns now appear in the table. Rows where no attendance match was found show **null** in both columns; these are registrations with no corresponding attendance record.

Expanding deliberately, clearing all columns first, then ticking only the ones you need, is a habit worth forming. If **Sessions_Attendance** gains new columns in a future refresh, they will not silently appear in **Master_Attendees** unless you explicitly tick them. This keeps the output stable and predictable.

> **Note**
>
> The M function behind the merge step is `Table.NestedJoin`. You can see it in the formula bar; Power Query wrote it automatically when you used the **Merge Queries** dialog. You do not need to write or edit it.

Add an "Attended?" flag

The attendance status values (`attended`, `no-show`, and `null`) are useful for filtering, but Amira also needs a simple *Yes* or *No* for certificates and follow-ups. Add a conditional column:

1. Click the **Add Column** tab
2. Click **Conditional Column**
3. In the **New column name** field, type `Attended`
4. Set the condition row: **If** `AttendanceStatus equals attended` **Then** `Yes`
5. Set the **Otherwise** field to `No`
6. Click **OK**

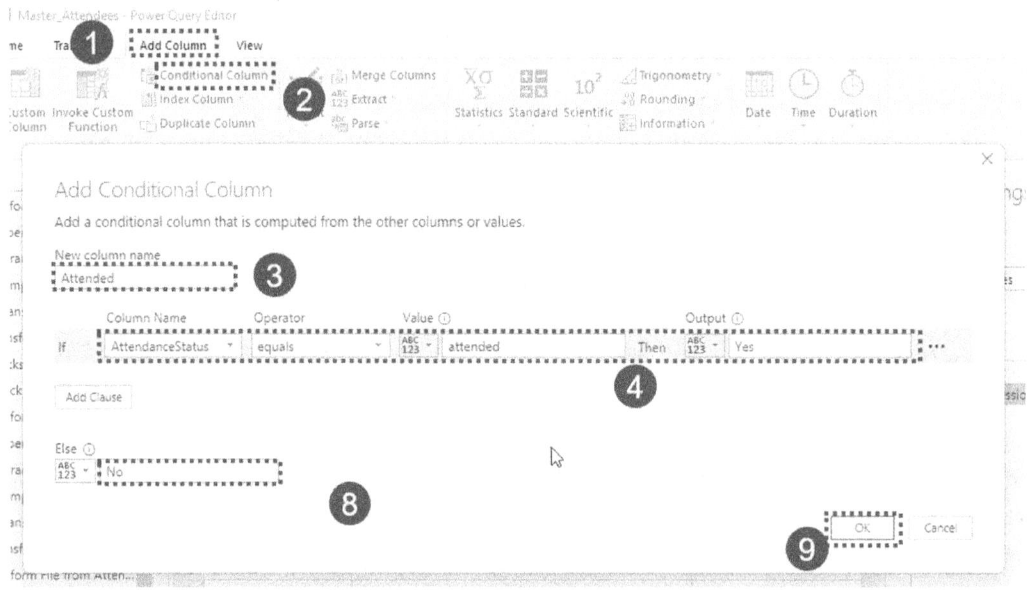

Figure 8.7 – Conditional Column dialog with the AttendanceStatus condition set to produce a Yes/No Attended flag

Note

The **Else** value of No covers two cases: rows where **AttendanceStatus** is no-show (an explicit record of absence) and rows where **AttendanceStatus** is null (no attendance record was found for that registration at all). For Amira's certificate run, both outcomes mean the same thing: the person did not attend. If you ever need to distinguish between the two, add a second condition that checks for null before the **Otherwise** clause.

The core of the query is built. Before loading it, let's look at a risk that every merge carries and confirm that this one is free of it.

Avoiding row explosion (duplicates and lookups)

The merge is built, but before loading it, it is worth checking whether the output is actually clean. Row explosion is silent, and this kind of check catches it.

What row explosion looks like

Row explosion happens when the lookup table (the right-hand side of the merge) contains more than one row for the same merge key. If **Sessions_Attendance** has two rows for the combination `amira@nog.co.uk + S001`, the merge produces two output rows for Amira's `S001` registration: one matched to the first attendance record, one to the second.

The output row count would be higher than the registration count. The table would contain duplicate registrations without any error or warning from Power Query.

Check for duplicates with Group By

The fastest way to spot row explosion is to check the merged output directly. With **Master_Attendees** open in the **Power Query Editor**, run a **Group By** on the two key columns to count how many rows exist per **AttendeeEmail** + **SessionID** combination. We group by **AttendeeEmail** and **SessionID** because these columns define the grain we declared at the start of this chapter: one row per registration, meaning each participant should appear exactly once per session. A count greater than 1 on this combination is a direct violation of that rule.

Follow these steps to run the Group By:

1. Click the **AttendeeEmail** column header and hold *Ctrl* and click the **SessionID** column header
2. Click the **Home** tab
3. Click **Group By**

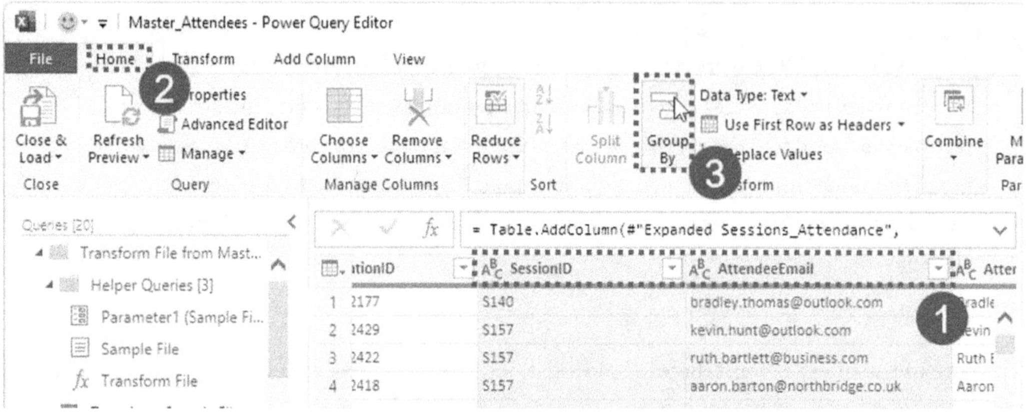

Figure 8.8 – Transform tab with Group By highlighted and AttendeeEmail and SessionID selected

4. In the **Group By** dialog, confirm both **AttendeeEmail** and **SessionID** are listed as grouping columns
5. Set the new column name to **Count** and the operation to **Count Rows**
6. Click **OK**

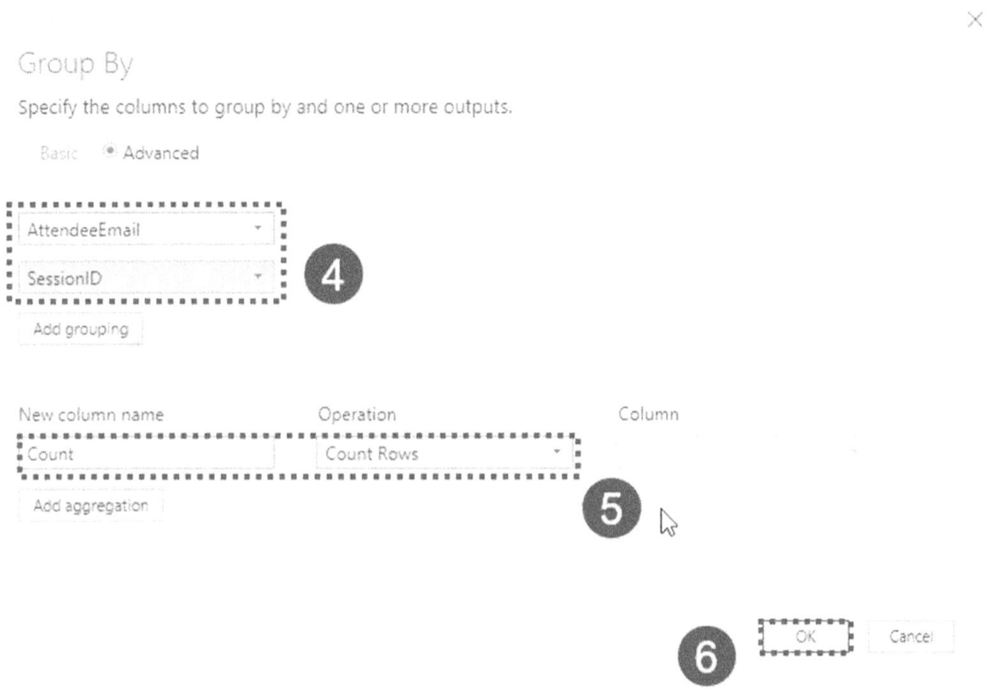

Figure 8.9 – Group By dialogue with AttendeeEmail and SessionID as group columns and Count Rows as the operation

The result is a table with one row per **AttendeeEmail** + **SessionID** combination and a **Count** column showing how many rows exist for each pair. Sort the **Count** column descending to bring the highest values to the top:

1. Click the dropdown arrow on the **Count** column header
2. Click **Sort Descending**

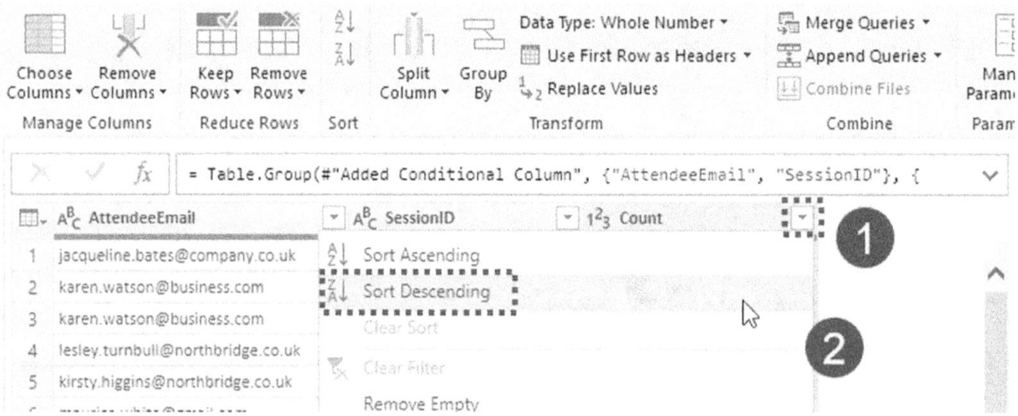

Figure 8.10 – Count column sorted descending after the Group By step

The sorted result makes the problem immediately visible. In our case, some **AttendeeEmail** + **SessionID** combinations show a **Count** of 2, confirming that **Sessions_Attendance** contains duplicate attendance records for those pairs.

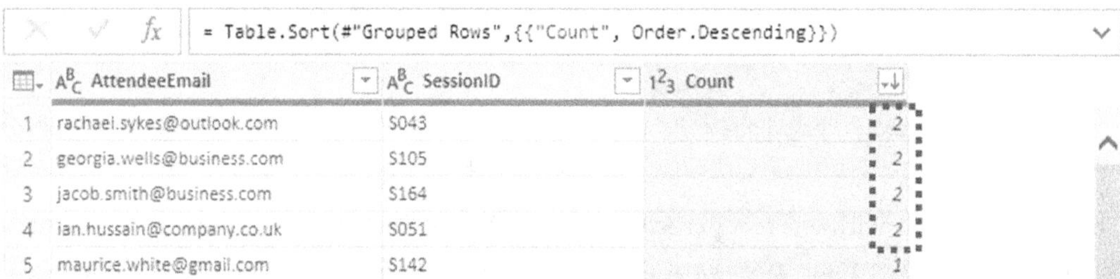

Figure 8.11 – Group By result showing duplicate AttendeeEmail + SessionID combinations with Count = 2 at the top

Any combination with a **Count** greater than 1 means row explosion has occurred; those pairs have more than one attendance record in **Sessions_Attendance** and are producing duplicate registrations in the merged output.

> **Caution**
>
> Power Query will not warn you when row explosion occurs. It silently produces extra rows. The Group By check is the deliberate step that makes the problem visible before the table reaches anyone else.

Leave the **Group By** steps in place for now; you will use them to verify the fix. Now go to the source.

Fix the duplicates in Sessions_Attendance

There are duplicates in the lookup table. In practice, this happens when a session coordinator submits the attendance log and later resubmits a corrected version; perhaps they marked someone as absent who was actually present. Both exports end up in the source files, producing two rows for the same email + session combination. The fix is the same sort-and-dedup pattern from *Chapter 6*: sort by **AttendanceDate** as descending so the most recent record comes first, then remove duplicates on the key columns. Keeping the latest record preserves the correction rather than the original mistake.

Declare the rule before applying it: Dedup key for Sessions_Attendance = AttendeeEmail + SessionID.

Rule = keep the latest AttendanceDate. Reason: the most recent attendance record reflects the current state, a correction or a re-check by the coordinator.

> Note
>
> We will edit **Sessions_Attendance,** , a query built in a previous chapter. That is intentional. The duplicates are a problem in the source query itself, so the fix belongs there. Any worksheet that loads from **Sessions_Attendance** will automatically reflect the corrected, deduplicated data on the next refresh.

Apply the fix:

1. In the **Queries** pane, click **Sessions_Attendance** to make it the active query
2. Click the dropdown arrow on the **AttendanceDate** column header
3. Click **Sort Descending**

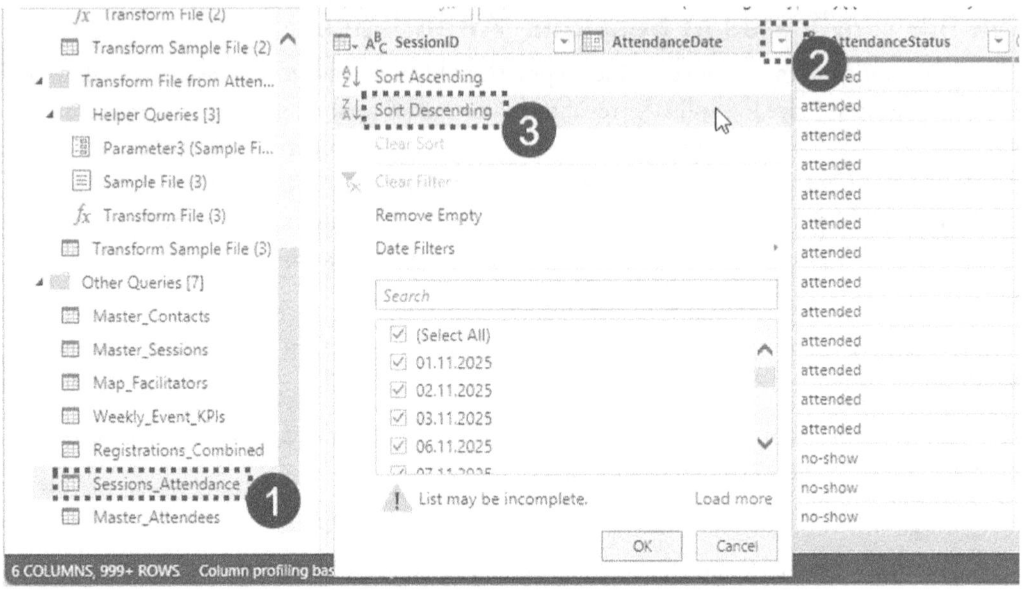

Figure 8.12 – Sessions_Attendance with Sort Descending

4. Click the **AttendeeEmail** column header
5. Hold *Ctrl* and click the **SessionID** column header
6. Right-click either selected column header
7. Click **Remove Duplicates**

Figure 8.13 – Right-click context menu on the selected AttendeeEmail and SessionID columns with Remove Duplicates

Now return to **Master_Attendees** in the **Queries** pane. Because it references **Sessions_Attendance**, it will automatically reflect the fix. The **Group By** result now shows only 1s in the **Count** column; every AttendeeEmail + SessionID combination appears exactly once.

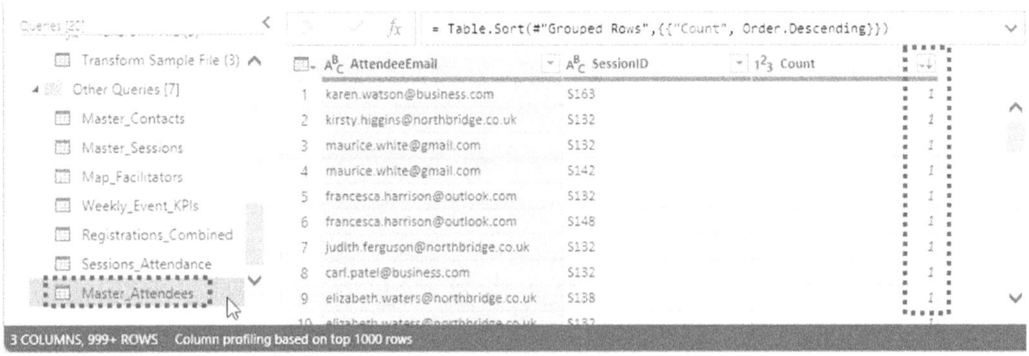

Figure 8.14 – Group By result after the fix, showing Count = 1 for all AttendeeEmail + SessionID combinations

With the fix confirmed, remove the **Group By** steps; they were only needed for the check:

1. In the **Applied Steps** pane, right-click the first **Group By**-related step
2. Click **Delete Until End**

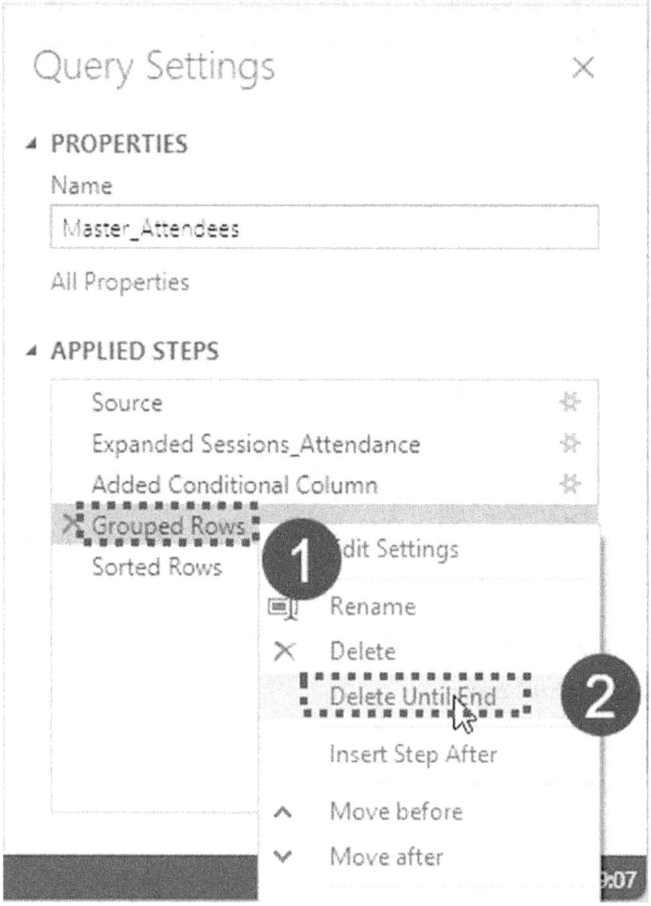

Figure 8.15 – Applied Steps pane context menu with Delete Until End highlighted on the first Group By step

> **Caution**
>
> **Delete Until End** removes the selected step and every step that follows it in one action. It is the quickest way to clean up temporary check steps, but it is irreversible; Power Query has no undo. Before using it, confirm that the step you right-click is the first one you want to remove and that nothing below it needs to be kept.

With row multiplication resolved, load the query and run the trust loop.

The trust loop for merges (counts + spot checks)

A merge produces a new table. Before that table reaches Amira (or any colleague) run a short set of deliberate checks. The version here is the same habit from *Chapters 6* and *7*, adapted for merges.

Load Master_Attendees to a sheet

Load the query to a new worksheet so the checks can be run against the final output:

1. Click the **Home** tab in the **Power Query Editor**
2. Click the dropdown arrow next to **Close & Load**
3. Click **Close & Load To...**
4. In the **Import Data** dialog, select **Table**
5. Select **New worksheet**
6. Click **OK**

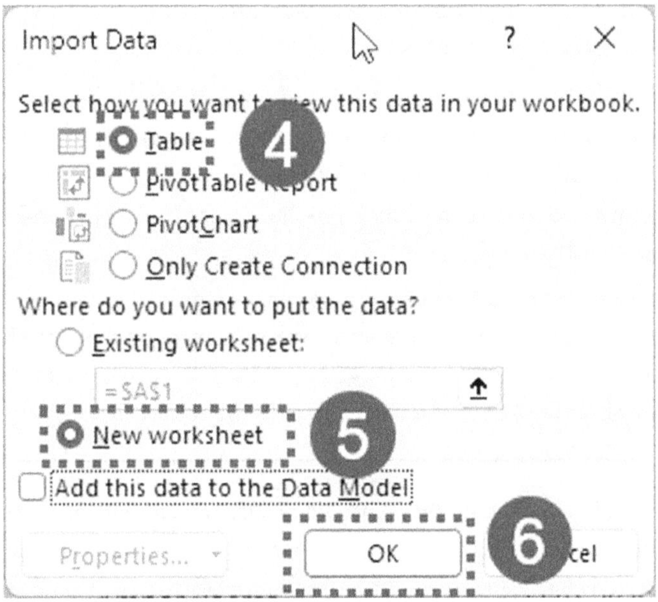

Figure 8.16 – Import Data dialog with Table and New worksheet selected

Master_Attendees appears as an Excel table on the new sheet.

The four checks

Run through these four checks before sharing the table with Amira:

1. **Row count matches Registrations_Combined**: A left join never drops rows from the left table, so the count should never be lower than **Registrations_Combined**. It can be higher if duplicates remain on the right side. In our case, having fixed the duplicates in **Sessions_Attendance**, the counts should be equal. If the count is still higher, return to the **Power Query Editor** and re-run the **Group By** check to find any remaining duplicates. If it is lower, confirm the **Join Kind** was set to *Left Outer*.
2. **No blanks in AttendeeEmail or SessionID**: AttendeeEmail and SessionID are the join keys and will be used again in *Chapter 9*. Click the filter dropdown on each column and confirm that **(Blank)** either does not appear or has zero rows. A blank in either key column means that row cannot be matched in downstream queries.
3. **Attended contains only "Yes" and "No"**: Click the filter dropdown on **Attended**. You should see exactly two values. Any other value means the Conditional Column rule was not applied correctly, return to the **Power Query Editor** and review the **Added Attended Flag** step.
4. **Spot-check three rows**: Pick one row where **Attended** is `Yes` and cross-check it against the **Sessions_Attendance** table on its own worksheet, confirm the email address, session identifier, and attendance date match. Then pick one row where **Attended** is `No` and confirm either that an explicit no-show record exists in **Sessions_Attendance**, or that no record exists at all.
5. **Blank AttendanceStatus**: This is a normal outcome. It means the person registered, but no attendance record was ever submitted for them: they may have canceled, not shown up, or simply not been logged by the session coordinator. Confirm it reflects a genuine absence of data, not a data error in the source files.

> **Note**
>
> The trust loop is a habit, not a test suite. Four checks and a spot check take under two minutes and catch the failures that matter most: an unexpected row count, a missing key, and a wrong flag value. You will use this loop every time you build or refresh a merged query.

If all four checks pass, **Master_Attendees** is ready. If one fails, return to the Power Query Editor, find the step responsible, and fix it there, not in the sheet.

Quinn turns her laptop toward Amira and scrolls through the **Master_Attendees** table. Amira leans in and filters the **SessionID** column to a session she ran last month.

"There they are," Amira says quietly. Every person who registered with a Yes or No next to their name. She clicks the filter on **Attended**, selects Yes, and the list shortens to the people who need certificates. "I've been doing this by hand for six months."

"Now it's one refresh," Quinn says.

Summary

In this chapter, you built **Master_Attendees**, a single merged table that brings every registration together with its attendance outcome. Three patterns from this chapter are worth carrying forward:

- **Left join from the "must include" table**: registrations drive the output; attendance enriches it. A left join ensures every registration survives the merge, whether or not an attendance record was found.
- **Check the lookup side before merging**: confirm that the right-hand table has one row per merge key. One step prevents silent row multiplication, a failure that Power Query will not warn you about.
- **Trust loop after every merge**: row count equal to the left table, no blank keys, expected flag values, and a handful of spot checks. The habit takes two minutes and catches the most common merge failures before they reach anyone else.

In *Chapter 9*, Priya from Finance brings a different problem: payment records that need to be reconciled against registrations. That means a different kind of join, a different set of keys, and a new challenge: matching records across two systems that were never designed to talk to each other.

Part 3

Combining and Automation

In this part, you will deepen your join skills and make your workbook easier to maintain and hand over. You will reconcile payments against registrations using left, inner, and anti joins, build exception queries that keep mismatches visible instead of silently dropping them, and derive a clear payment status to complete the **Master_Payments** table. You will then turn the workbook built across the previous chapters into something a colleague could open, understand, and adapt: organizing queries into named groups, creating parameters for values that change (such as session type and folder path), building scoped views without touching the master queries, and replacing a hard-coded source path with a parameter so that one change updates every query.

This section contains the following chapters:

9

Join and Lookup Data Safely Without a Data Model

Figure 9.1 – Priya from Finance appears at Quinn's desk with sheets that don't match

It is half past four on a Thursday, the last Thursday before month-end close, when Priya from Finance appears at Quinn's desk with a laptop under one arm and a look that Quinn is starting to recognize: the look of someone who has been staring at a VLOOKUP for three hours.

"I've got a reconciliation problem," Priya says, setting the laptop down. The screen shows a large Excel workbook: a sheet of payment records from their payment provider on the left, a sheet of event registrations on the right, and a third sheet in the middle that is clearly the product of several hours of manual matching.

"I'm trying to reconcile payments against registrations before the accounts close on Friday." She scrolls through the middle sheet. "But it never lines up cleanly. Some registrations have no payment. Some payments don't match any registration I can find. And then there are the complimentary attendees, the ones management let in for free, who aren't in either file, but I still need to account for them." She pauses. "And the amounts in the registration sheet? I've stopped trusting them entirely. Someone always edits something after the fact—a late discount, a manual correction—and half the time it never gets updated properly. The only figures I trust are the ones that come straight from the payment provider."

Quinn glances at the workbook, then at the **Queries & Connections** pane open on her own screen. **Registrations_Combined** is right there: clean, deduplicated, built in *Chapter 6*. The missing ingredient is the payment export Priya has been wrestling with manually.

"How long does this take you each month?" Quinn asks.

"Two hours, sometimes three. And I always find something wrong at the last minute."

Quinn closes Priya's laptop gently. "Leave this with me. We'll build the list once, and next month you just click Refresh."

In this chapter, you'll learn to -

- Explain what **Master_Payments** represents as a wide, pre-model table and how registrations and payments combine to form it
- Choose the right join keys and merge direction for combining registrations and payments
- Predict how left, inner, and anti joins change which rows appear in the output
- Build a left-joined **Master_Payments** table and use anti joins to create exception queries for chasing missing payments and unmatched records
- Derive a **PaymentStatus** column from joined data and validate the result with row-count and spot checks

Technical requirements

The chapters in this book build on each other. Make sure you have completed all exercises in the previous chapter before starting this one.

To follow along with this chapter, you will need:

- Microsoft Excel 2016 or later with Power Query, accessed via **Data** | **Get & Transform Data**

- Your `NOG-DataHub` workbook (NOG stands for Northbridge Office Group) from *Chapter 8*, which should already contain the following queries:
    - **Master_Sessions** (built in *Chapter 3*)
    - **Weekly_Event_KPIs** (built in *Chapter 4*)
    - **Registrations_Combined** (built in *Chapter 6)*
    - **Sessions_Attendance** (built in *Chapter 7*)
    - **Master_Attendees** (built in *Chapter 8*)
- The exercise file for this chapter, in the `Events/Payments/` folder of your `NOG-DataHub`:
    - `Payments_Transactions.xlsx`

What Master_Payments is (and isn't)

Before building any merges, it pays to be precise about what the output table will contain and what it will not.

Master_Payments is a registration-level table enriched with payment details. One row represents one registration, with additional columns showing whether a payment was received. A person who registered for three sessions and paid for all three will appear in three rows, one per registration.

The table is built from two sources:

- **Registrations_Combined**: It is already in your workbook from *Chapter 6*. This is the left, or driving, table: every registration must appear in the output, whether or not a payment was found. It already carries **TicketType**, which tells you whether a registration is Standard, Early Bird, VIP, or Complimentary.
- **Payments_Transactions**: It is a new export from the payment provider, loaded from the `Events/Payments/` folder. This is the lookup, and the authoritative source for payment amounts.

Registrations_Combined carries an **AmountPaid** column, but the payment provider's figure is the authoritative source; the registration system's amount is dropped in **Master_Payments** and replaced by the bank-confirmed value from **Payments_Transactions**.

The key columns in the final output are:

Column	Source	What it tells you
AttendeeEmail	Registrations_Combined	Who registered

Column	Source	What it tells you
SessionID	Registrations_Combined	Which session they registered for
RegistrationStatus	Registrations_Combined	Confirmed or Canceled
TicketType	Registrations_Combined	Standard, Early Bird, VIP, or Complimentary
AmountPaid	Payments_Transactions	Amount paid (null if no payment is found)
PaymentDate	Payments_Transactions	Date payment was received (null if no match)
PaymentReference	Payments_Transactions	Provider reference number
PaymentStatus	Derived	Paid, Complimentary, Pending, or Canceled

Table 9.1 – Key columns in Master_Payments and their source

Master_Payments is not a unique-person list. If you want a count of distinct individuals, that is a Group By on **AttendeeEmail**, in a separate query. It is also not a replacement for the payment provider's system. It is a reconciliation view that brings registration context and payment details together in one place for reporting and exception tracking.

> **Note**
>
> The grain (the rule that defines what one row represents) is: one row = one registration, enriched with its payment outcome and complimentary status. That grain drives every join decision in this chapter.

Now, let's look at how to connect the tables.

Choosing keys and merge directions for payments

The most important decision in any merge is choosing the join key: the column or columns that Power Query uses to determine which row in one table matches a row in the other.

Why the composite key matters

For this merge, two candidate keys might come to mind:

- **AttendeeEmail alone**: The same person can register for multiple sessions, so the same email address appears on many rows in **Registrations_Combined**. Matching on email alone would link every payment row for that person to every registration row, multiplying rows unexpectedly.
- **SessionID alone**: Many people register for the same session, so the same SessionID appears on dozens of registration rows. The same problem occurs in reverse.

Neither column alone identifies one registration. Together, they do. The combination of **AttendeeEmail** + **SessionID** identifies one specific registration: this person, for this session. It is the same composite key used for deduplication in *Chapter 6*, for the same reason.

The payment provider export may also include a **PaymentReference**, a unique identifier assigned to each transaction. PaymentReference is useful for tracing individual transactions, but it cannot serve as the sole join key here: complimentary registrations have no payment at all, so PaymentReference will be absent for those rows.

Merge direction

In every merge, one table is the left table: its rows define what must appear in the output. The other is the right table: a source of additional information.

For **Master_Payments**, the left table is **Registrations_Combined**. Every registration must appear in the output, whether or not a payment was found. A registration with no payment is not an error to be discarded; it is a gap Priya needs to track and chase. That requirement determines the join type: a **left outer join** from registrations to payments.

Source grain

Registrations_Combined was deduplicated in *Chapter 6*: one row per **AttendeeEmail** + **SessionID**. The **Payments_Transactions** file used here also contains one row per registration; NOG's payment provider sends only the final transaction status. If your own provider sends multiple rows per registration (for example, a failed attempt followed by a successful retry), apply the same Group By deduplication used for **Registrations_Combined** in *Chapter 6* before merging.

Join types at a glance

The three join types you will use in this chapter are:

Join type	What it keeps
Left Outer	All rows from the left table; matching rows from the right. Unmatched left-table rows are kept with null values in the right-table columns. (Introduced in *Chapter 8*.)
Inner	Only rows that match in both tables. Unmatched rows from either side are discarded.
Left Anti	Only rows from the left table that have no match in the right table; the registrations or payments the inner join would have missed.

Table 9.2 – Join types used in this chapter and what each one keeps

Tip

Decision log of key choices for this chapter

- **Left table**: **Registrations_Combined** — every registration must appear in the output, whether or not a payment was found.
- **Merge key**: **AttendeeEmail** + **SessionID** —the same composite key used for deduplication in *Chapter 6*.
- **Join type** (**Master_Payments**): **Left Outer** — keeps all registrations; unmatched rows get nulls in the payment columns.
- **Key columns already clean**: **Registrations_Combined** emails are lowercased and trimmed, **SessionID** is set to Text (*Chapter 6*).
- **Payments_Transactions** needs cleaning first — see the *Clean and standardize Payments_Transactions* section before merging.

With the key and direction decided, let's build the merges.

Using left, inner, and anti joins to find matches and gaps

This section builds four queries: the payment data source, a working version of **Master_Payments**, and two exception queries that expose the gaps. Start by loading the payment data into the workbook.

Load Payments_Transactions

> **Important**
>
> You will connect to the `Events/Payments/` folder in your `NOG-DataHub`, which contains the payments export file.

Follow the same folder connector pattern from earlier chapters: Continue in your `NOG-DataHub` workbook from *Chapter 8,* go to **Data** | **Get Data** | **From File**, choose **From SharePoint Folder** or **From Folder**, navigate to your `NOG-DataHub`, and click **Transform Data** to open the **Power Query Editor**.

Rename the query and filter to the payments file

Before filtering, rename the query so the **Queries** pane stays readable from the start:

1. In the **Query Settings** pane on the right, click on the current query name
2. Type `Payments_Transactions` and press *Enter*

Now filter down to the payments file:

1. Click the dropdown arrow on the **Folder Path** column header
2. Click **Text Filters**
3. Click **Contains**

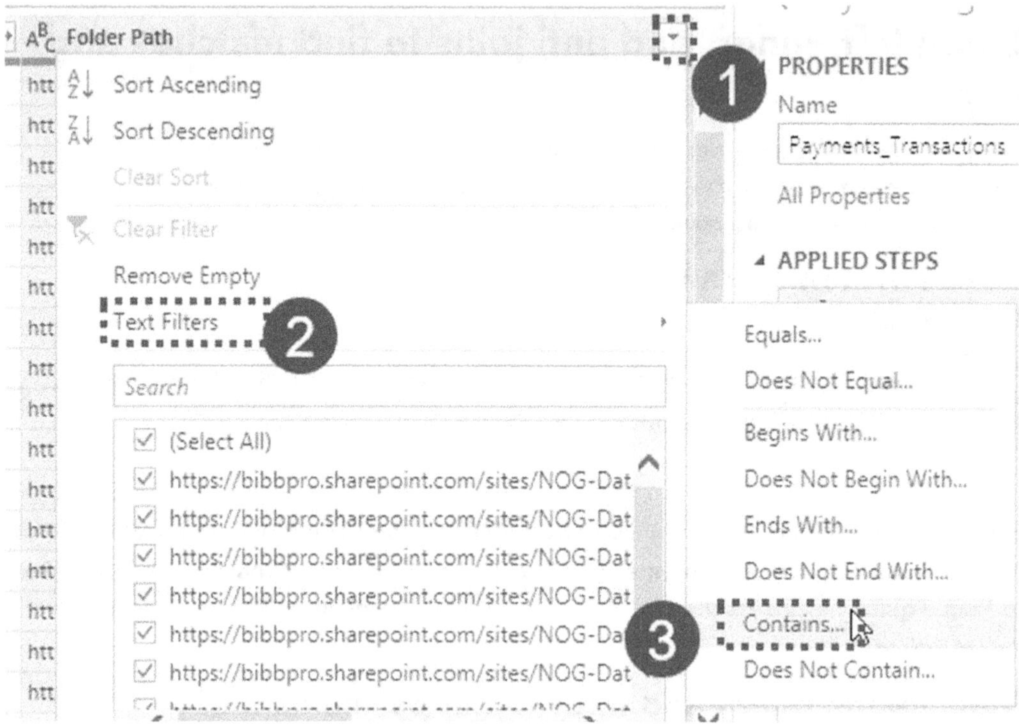

Figure 9.2 – Text Filters menu expanded to show the Contains option

4. Type `Payments` and click **OK**

You should now see only the files in the `Events/Payments/` folder. If the folder contains more than one file, also filter the **Name** column to contain **Payments_Transactions** so only the correct file remains.

Open the file

Follow these steps:

1. In the **Content** column, click the **Binary** link on the **Payments_Transactions** row

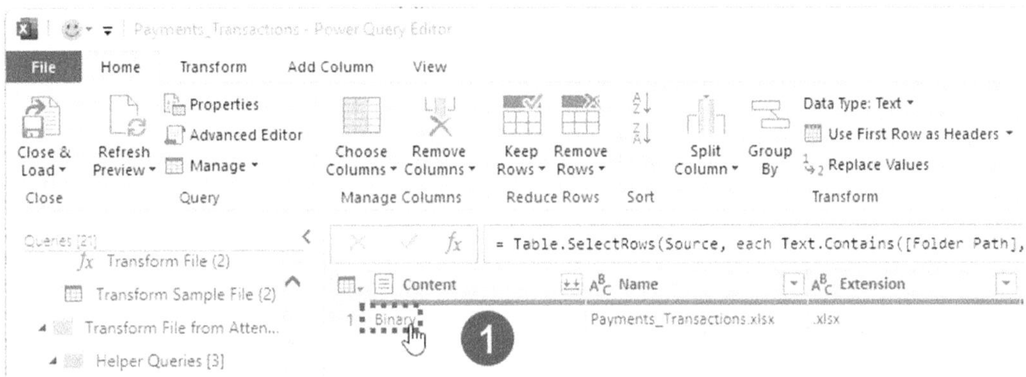

Figure 9.3 – Clicking the Binary link to open the single Payments_Transactions file

> **Note**
>
> Because there is only one payments file, clicking the Binary link is the simplest approach. If NOG's payment provider ever delivers one file per month with the same structure, switch to the **Combine Files** button on the **Content** column header; the same technique used for the multi-file session and registration folders in *Chapters 3*, *6*, and *7*.

Power Query opens the editor and shows a navigator table listing every object inside the Excel file.

2. Navigate into the data: In the **Data** column, click **Table** on the row that shows your sheet name (in this file, **Sheet1**)

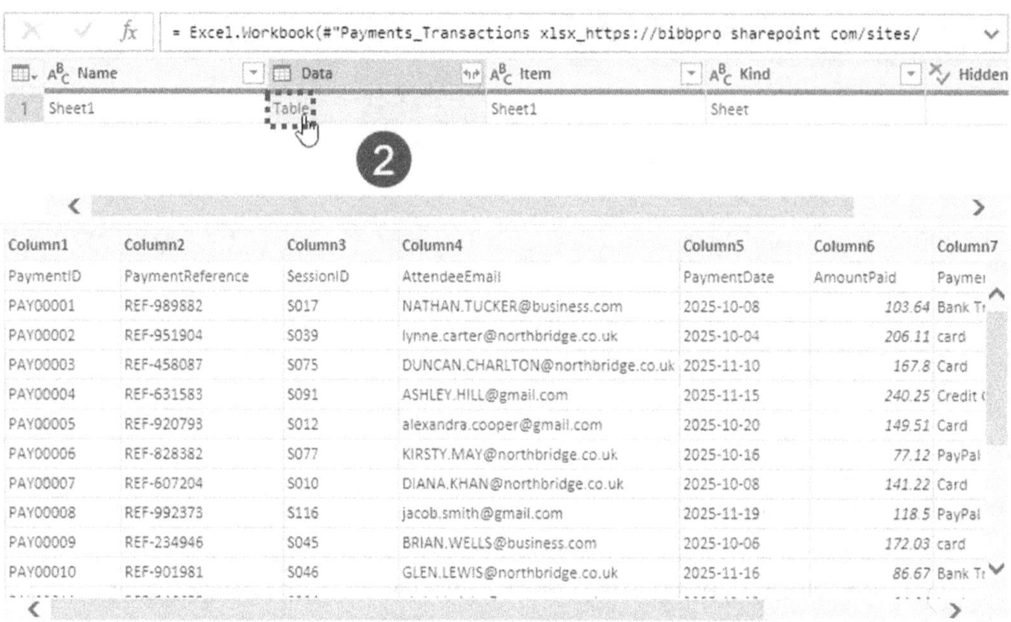

Figure 9.4 – Navigator table showing the Excel objects inside Payments_Transactions.xlsx; click Table in the Data column to drill into the sheet

> **Note**
>
> The navigator table may contain more than one row: sheets, columns, and named ranges all appear as separate entries. To navigate to any of them, click the **Table** hyperlink in the Data column for that row.

Power Query loads the payment records and applies a default type-detection step. If the column headers show as **Column1**, **Column2**, and so on instead of the actual field names, the first row has not been promoted automatically:

1. Click the **Home** tab
2. Click **Use First Row as Headers**

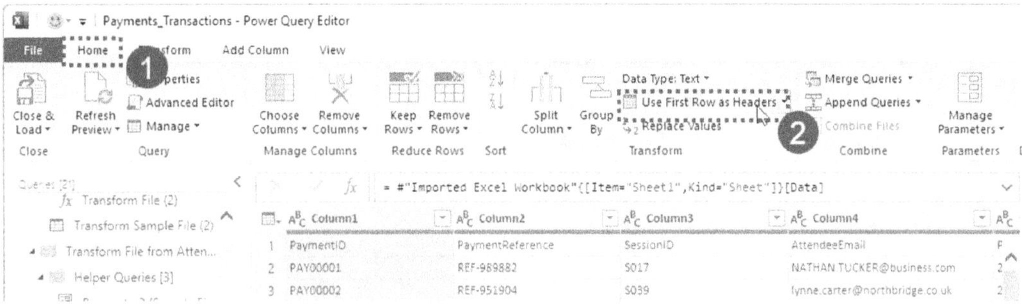

Figure 9.5 – Use First Row as Headers button on the Home tab

Check that the key columns are present and typed correctly:

- **PaymentID** — Text
- **PaymentReference** — Text
- **SessionID** — Text
- **AttendeeEmail** — Text
- **PaymentDate** — Date
- **AmountPaid** — Decimal Number
- **PaymentMethod** — Text
- **PaymentStatus** — Text

If any type is wrong, click the type icon to the left of the column header and select the correct type.

> **Note**
>
> In Power Query, Decimal Number is best for general numeric data such as percentages, averages, weights, and exchange rates, but it can sometimes produce very small rounding differences. Currency, also called Fixed Decimal Number, supports up to four decimal places and is better for prices, revenue, costs, budgets, and other financial values where consistent precision is important.

Clean and standardize Payments_Transactions

Payments_Transactions contains all payment attempts: completed, pending, failed, and refunded. Before loading it, standardize the text columns and filter to confirmed receipts only. This turns the query into a record of money that actually moved, which is the only signal that matters for this reconciliation.

Trim and lowercase the text columns:

1. Hold *Ctrl* and click the **PaymentStatus**, **PaymentMethod**, and **AttendeeEmail** column headers to select all three
2. Click **Format,** located in the **Transform** tab
3. Click **Trim**
4. Click **Format** again, then click **lowercase**

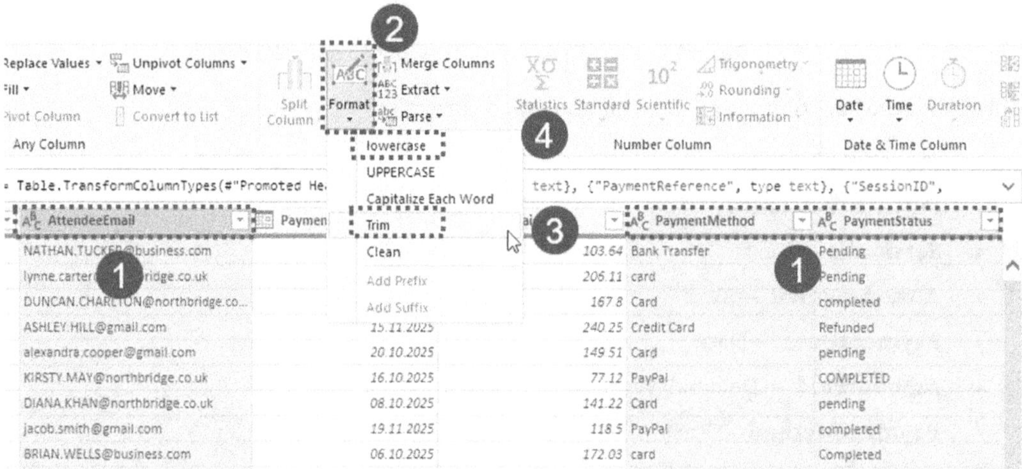

Figure 9.6 – Format menu on the Transform tab; use Trim first, then lowercase to standardize the selected columns

Standardize the **PaymentMethod** abbreviation:

1. Click the **PaymentMethod** column header to select it
2. Click **Replace Values** on the **Transform** tab
3. In **Value To Find**, type `card`
4. In **Replace With**, type `credit card`
5. Click **Advanced** options and tick **Match entire cell contents**
6. Click **OK**

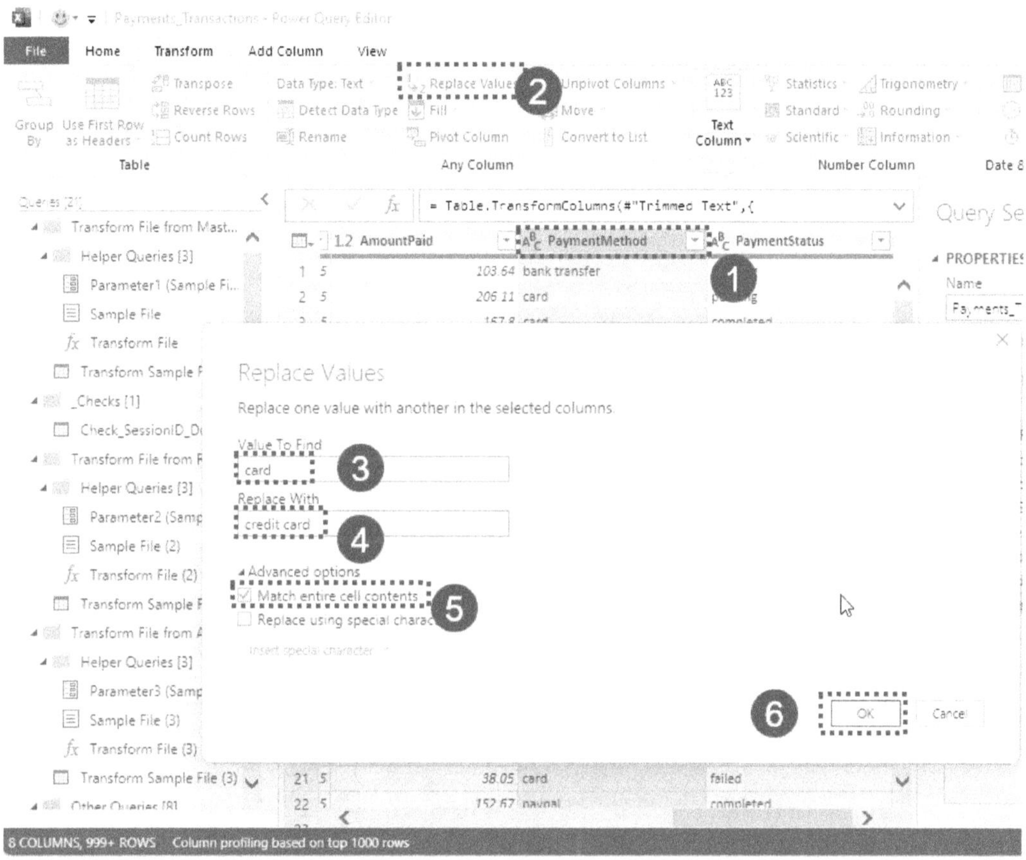

Figure 9.7 – Replace Values dialog with Advanced options expanded; Match entire cell contents prevents partial matches

> **Note**
>
> **Match entire cell contents** ensures only cells that contain exactly card are replaced. Cells already containing credit card are left unchanged.

Filter to completed transactions only:

1. Click the dropdown arrow on the **PaymentStatus** column header
2. Untick **Select All**
3. Tick **completed** only
4. Click **OK**

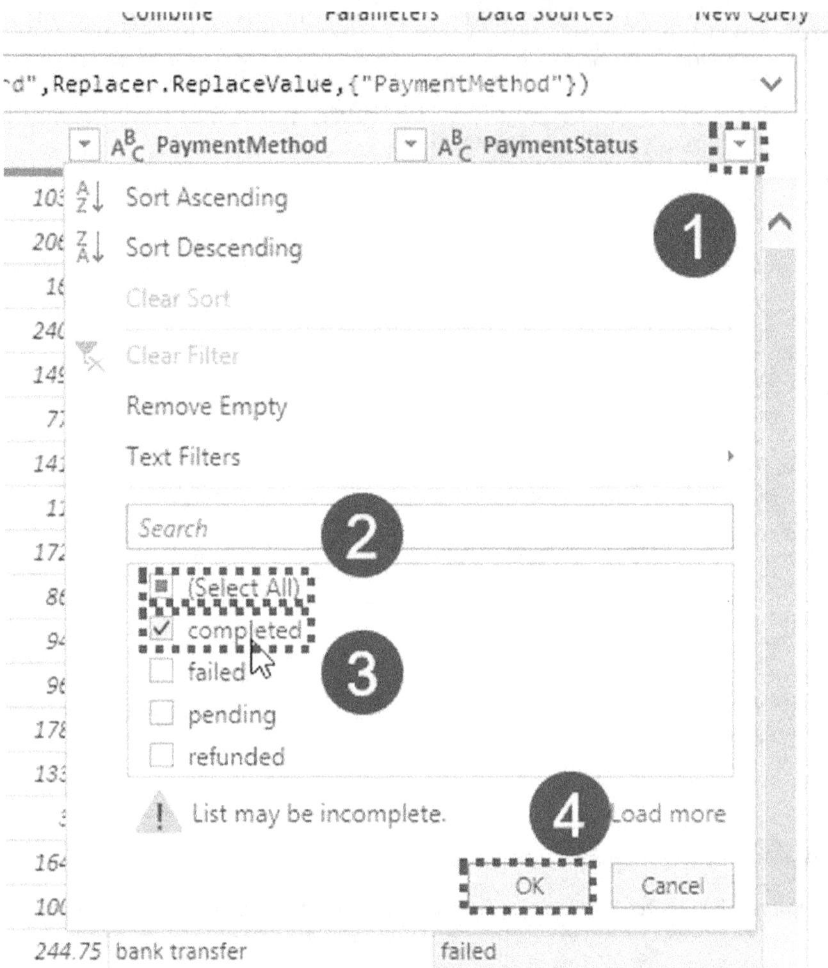

Figure 9.8 – PaymentStatus filter dropdown with only completed selected

5. Right-click the **PaymentStatus** column header and click **Remove**

After filtering to **completed** transactions only, every row in this column contains the same value; it carries no further information. Every remaining row is a confirmed receipt. Pending, failed, and refunded attempts are excluded; any registration without a matching row here will correctly appear in **Registrations_NoPayment**.

Load the query as a connection:

1. In **Home**, click the **Close & Load** dropdown arrow
2. Click **Close & Load To...**
3. Select **Only Create Connection** and click **OK**

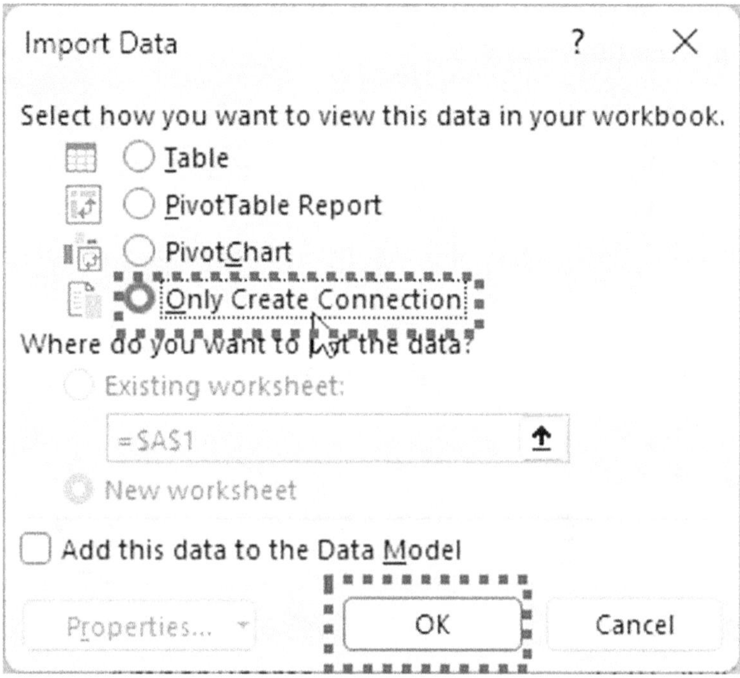

Figure 9.9 – Import Data dialog with Only Create Connection selected

Payments_Transactions is now in the workbook as a connection, ready to be used as the right-side lookup in the merges that follow.

Exercise A: left outer join – all registrations with payment details

Build the core table: all registrations, with payment columns added where a match exists. Open **Registrations_Combined** in the **Power Query Editor**.

If you are not in Power Query:

1. Click the **Data** tab
2. Click **Queries & Connections**
3. In the pane, double-click **Registrations_Combined**

Once in the Power Query editor, let's set up a new merge:

1. In the **Queries** pane, confirm **Registrations_Combined** is selected
2. Click the **Home** tab in the Power Query Editor

3. Click the dropdown arrow next to **Merge Queries**
4. Click **Merge Queries as New**

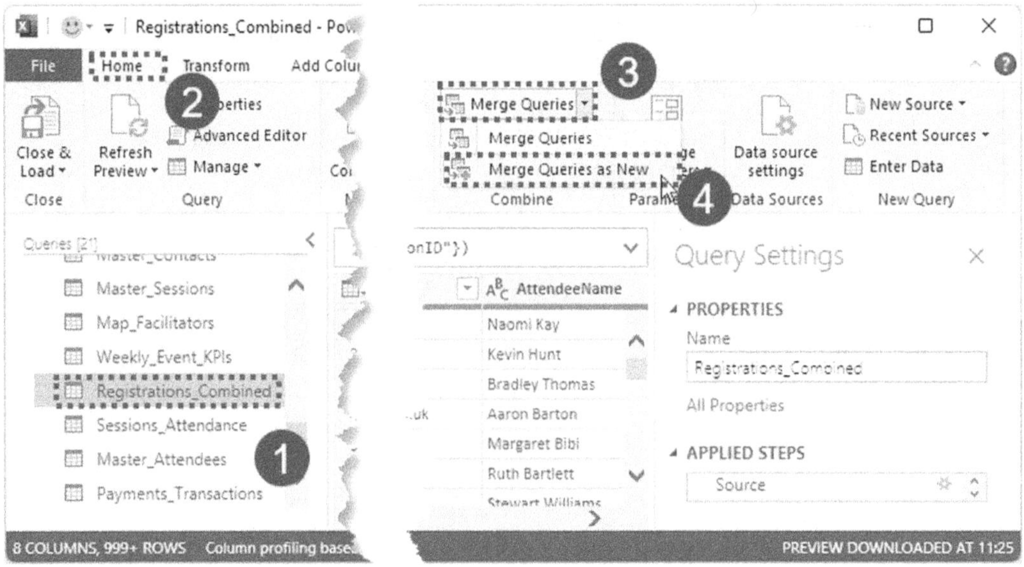

Figure 9.10 – Merge Queries as New option in the Home tab dropdown

In the **Merge** dialog:

1. Confirm the top table is **Registrations_Combined**
2. Click **SessionID**, then hold *Ctrl* and click **AttendeeEmail** in the top table
3. In the second table dropdown, select **Payments_Transactions**
4. Click **SessionID**, then hold *Ctrl* and click **AttendeeEmail** in the bottom table
5. In the **Join Kind** dropdown, select **Left Outer** (all from first, matching from second)
6. Click **OK**

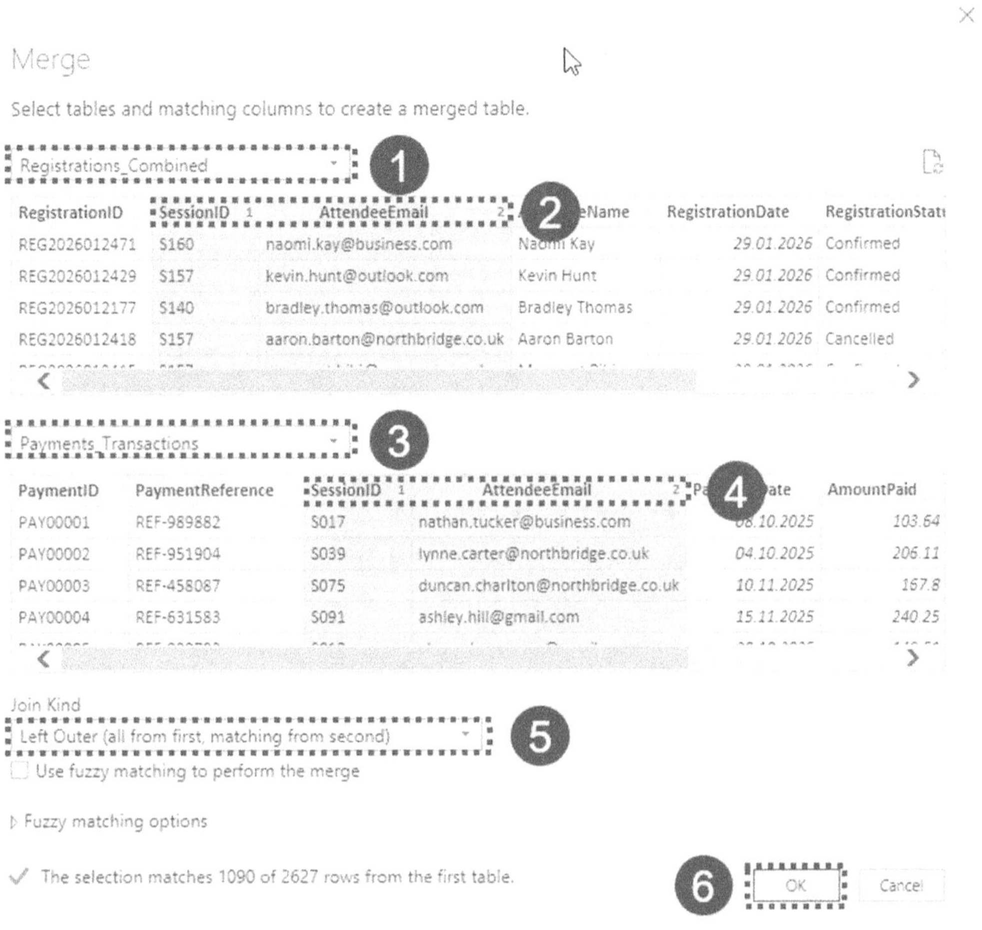

Figure 9.11 – Merge dialog configured for a left outer join on SessionID and AttendeeEmail

Rename the query and remove the registration system's AmountPaid:

1. In the **Query Settings** pane, rename the new query to `Master_Payments`
2. Right-click the **AmountPaid** column header and click **Remove**, the payment provider's figure will replace it

Expand the payment columns from **Payments_Transactions**:

1. Click the expand icon (the double-headed arrow) at the top of the **Payments_Transactions** column
2. Untick **Select All** to clear all columns
3. Tick **AmountPaid**, **PaymentDate**, and **PaymentReference**
4. Untick **Use original column name as prefix**
5. Click **OK**

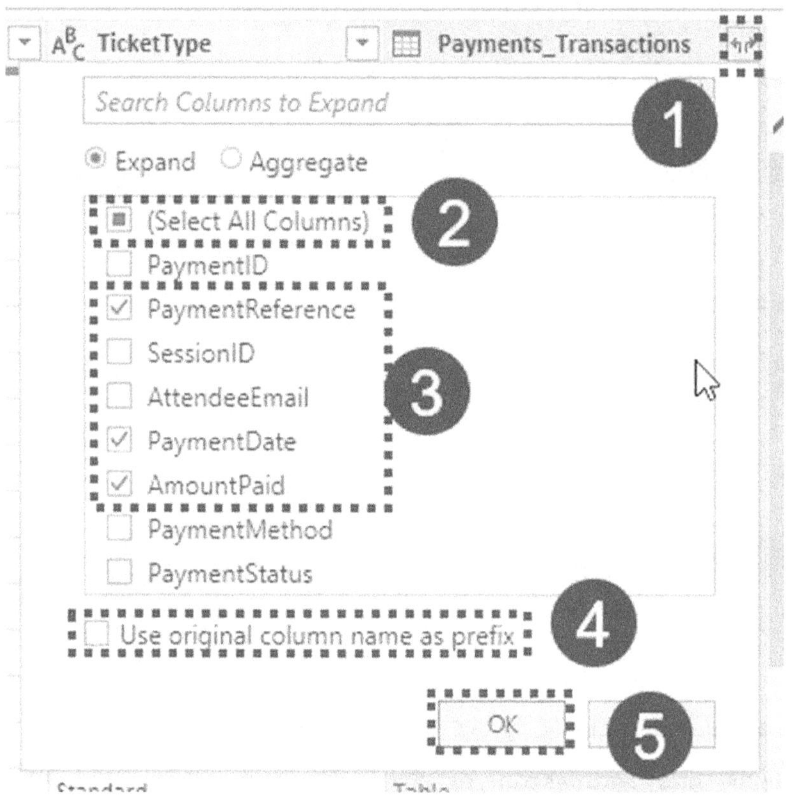

Figure 9.12 – Expand columns dialog with AmountPaid, PaymentDate, and PaymentReference selected

Rows where no payment was found will show **null** in the three payment columns; that is correct and expected. Those are the registrations Priya needs to chase.

Exercise B: Anti-joins – finding the gaps

Anti joins find rows in one table that have no match in the other. They are the most direct way to build exception reports.

Registrations_NoPayment

Switch to **Registrations_Combined** and start a new merge:

1. In the **Queries** pane, click **Registrations_Combined** to switch to that query
2. Click the **Home** tab
3. Click the dropdown arrow next to **Merge Queries**
4. Click **Merge Queries as New**

Configure the left anti join:

1. Confirm the top table is **Registrations_Combined**
2. Click **SessionID**, then hold *Ctrl* and click **AttendeeEmail** in the top table
3. In the second table dropdown, select **Payments_Transactions**
4. Click **SessionID**, then hold *Ctrl* and click **AttendeeEmail** in the bottom table
5. In the Join Kind dropdown, select Left Anti (rows only in first)
6. Click **OK**

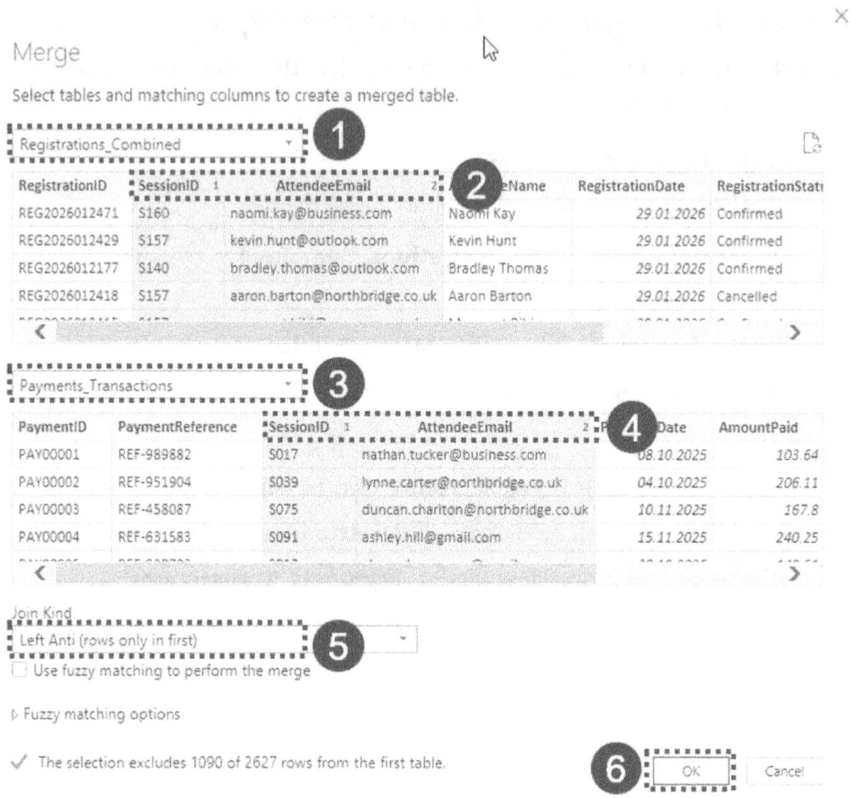

Figure 9.13 – Merge dialog configured for a left anti join to find registrations with no matching payment

7. In the **Query Settings** pane, rename the query to `Registrations_NoPayment`

Keep only the columns needed for chasing:

1. Click **Choose Columns** on the **Home** tab
2. Untick **Select All** to clear all columns
3. Tick **AttendeeEmail**, **SessionID**, **RegistrationStatus**, and **TicketType**
4. Click **OK**

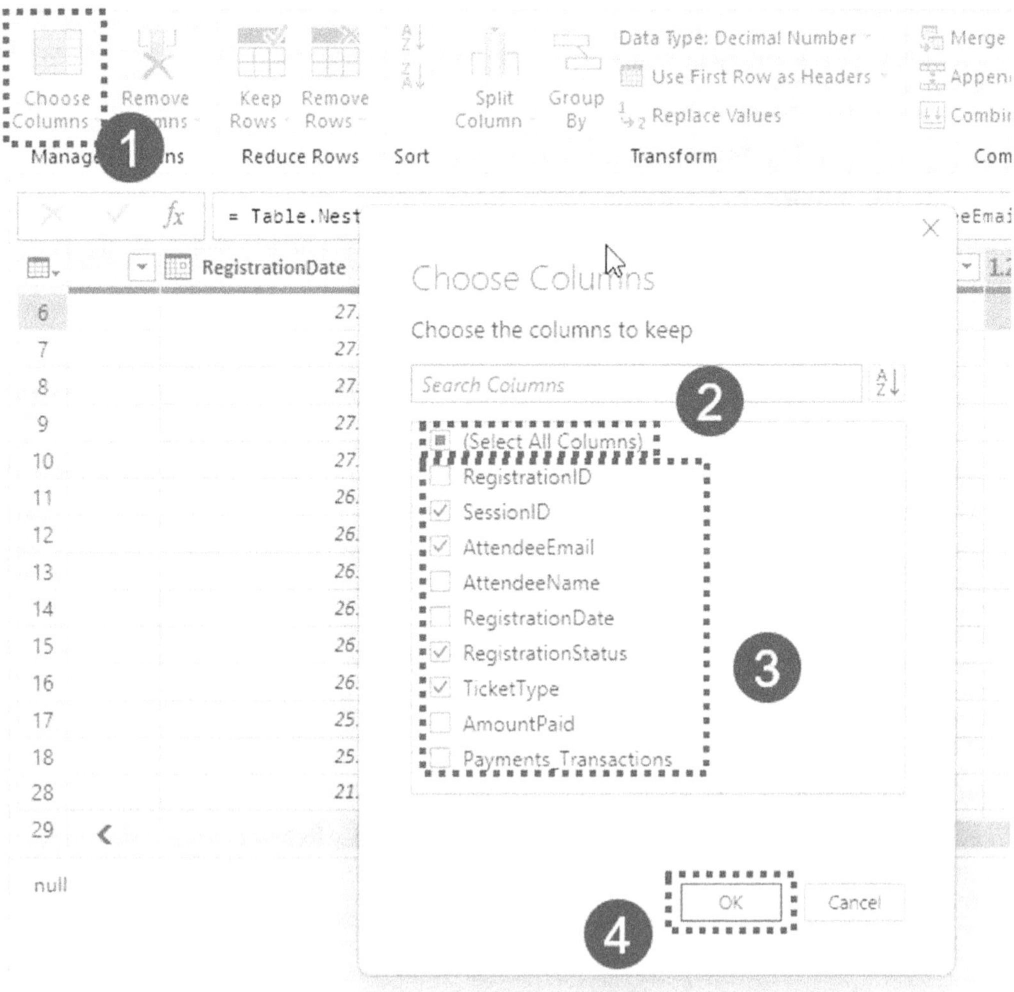

Figure 9.14 – Choose Columns dialog with the four chase list columns selected

Not every registration without a payment needs chasing. Canceled registrations have no payment obligation, and Complimentary registrations are intentionally free. Leaving them in the list would send Priya after records that are correctly unmatched, wasting time and undermining trust in the report. Filter to actionable rows only:

1. Click the dropdown arrow on the **RegistrationStatus** column header, untick **Cancelled**, and click **OK**
2. Click the dropdown arrow on the **TicketType** column header, untick **Complimentary**, and click **OK**

Load the query:

1. Click the **Close & Load** dropdown arrow
2. Click **Close & Load To...**
3. Select **Only Create Connection** and click **OK**

Payments_NoRegistration

This time, the payment table drives the anti join; you are looking for payments that have no registration to attach to.

Open **Payments_Transactions** and start a new merge:

1. In the **Queries & Connections** pane, double-click **Payments_Transactions;** make sure the **Payments_Transactions** query is selected
2. Click the **Home** tab in the Power Query Editor
3. Click the dropdown arrow next to **Merge Queries**
4. Click **Merge Queries** as **New**

Configure the left anti join:

1. Confirm the top table is **Payments_Transactions**
2. Click **SessionID**, then hold *Ctrl* and click **AttendeeEmail** in the top table
3. In the second table dropdown, select **Registrations_Combined**
4. Click **SessionID**, then hold *Ctrl* and click **AttendeeEmail** in the bottom table
5. In the **Join Kind** dropdown, select **Left Anti (rows only in first)**
6. Click **OK**

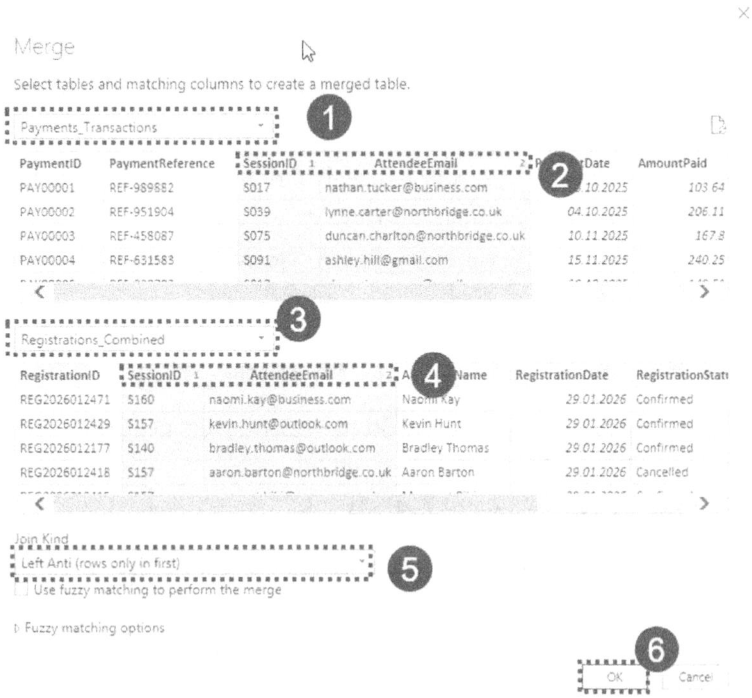

Figure 9.15 – Merge dialog for the reversed anti join, with Payments_Transactions as the driving table

Rename and load:

1. Rename the query to `Payments_NoRegistration`
2. Click the **Close & Load** dropdown arrow
3. Click **Close & Load To...**
4. Select **Only Create Connection** and click **OK**

AI Helper

Ask an AI assistant such as ChatGPT: `Explain what a left anti join does in one sentence, in plain language for a finance analyst.` Compare the explanation to what you see in your row counts; **Registrations_NoPayment** shows registrations with no matching payment; **Payments_NoRegistration** shows payments with no matching registration. If either count looks wrong, verify that **SessionID** and **AttendeeEmail** have the same data types and casing in both source tables before investigating further.

The two exception queries give Priya what she needs to act before month-end:

- **Registrations_NoPayment**: Confirmed registrations with no payment received. Priya can share this with the events team to chase.
- **Payments_NoRegistration**: Payments that do not match any known registration. These may be data-entry errors, late registrations not yet in the system, or test transactions from the payment provider.

With the exception queries in place, let's return to **Master_Payments** and add the derived status column.

Adding PaymentStatus to Master_Payments

Master_Payments currently holds all registrations with payment details, where available. One step remains: deriving the **PaymentStatus** column.

Add the PaymentStatus column

Open **Master_Payments** in the **Power Query Editor**. In the **Queries & Connections** pane, double-click **Master_Payments.**

With all source columns in place, derive the **PaymentStatus** conditional column. Unlike the status field removed from **Payments_Transactions** (which only ever contained "completed"), this column classifies each registration using business logic across both tables. The order of conditions is important: Power Query evaluates them top to bottom and stops at the first match.

Follow these steps:

1. Make sure you have the **Master_Payments** query selected in the **Query** pane
2. Click the **Add Column** tab
3. Click **Conditional Column**
4. Set **New column name** to `PaymentStatus` and configure the four conditions in this order:

	Column Name	**Operator**	**Value**	**Output**
If	Registration Status	equals	Canceled	Cancelled
Else If	TicketType	equals	Complimentary	Complimentary

	Column Name	Operator	Value	Output
Else If	AmountPaid	does not equal	null	Paid
Else				Pending

Table 9.3 – PaymentStatus conditions in evaluation order

5. Click **OK**

> **Caution**
>
> The order of conditions in a Conditional Column is significant. Power Query stops at the first matching condition. A cancelled registration with TicketType = "Complimentary" should resolve as "Cancelled"; which is why Cancelled appears first. If you reorder conditions, test edge cases before sharing the output.

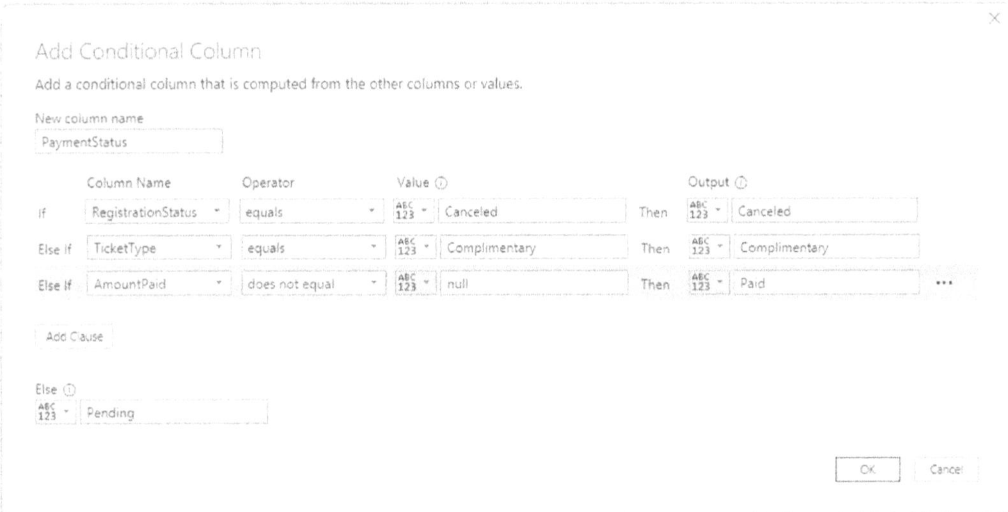

Figure 9.16 – Conditional Column dialog for PaymentStatus showing the four conditions in order

> **Caution**
>
> Ask an AI assistant such as ChatGPT: `I have a registrations table left-joined to a payments table. Some registrations are cancelled (RegistrationStatus), some are complimentary (TicketType), and rows with no matching payment have null in AmountPaid. I need a derived PaymentStatus column evaluated top to bottom. What is the safest condition order?`
>
> Use the suggestion as a starting point, then verify each status category against actual rows in your query, especially edge cases where a row could match more than one condition.

Load Master_Payments to a table

Because **Master_Payments** was previously saved as **Connection Only** earlier, **Close & Load To...** is greyed out in the editor; click **Close & Load | Close & Load** to return to **Excel:**

1. In the **Queries & Connections** pane, right-click **Master_Payments**
2. Click **Load To...**

Figure 9.17 – Right-click context menu on Master_Payments in the Queries and Connections pane

3. Select **Table** and **New worksheet**
4. Click **OK**

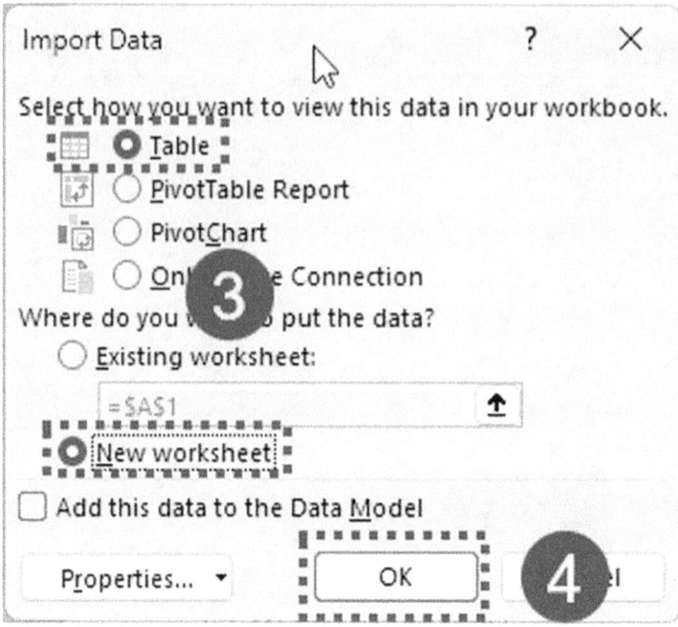

Figure 9.18 – Import Data dialog with Table selected as the load destination

Master_Payments now holds every registration, enriched with payment details and a derived status. Before handing it to Priya, confirm it is correct.

Validating the join

A wide table built from two merges carries more risk than a single clean source. Small mismatches in keys, unexpected duplicates, or a wrong condition order in PaymentStatus can silently produce wrong numbers. Four checks catch the most common problems.

Check 1: row count matches Registrations_Combined

The left outer join guarantees that **Master_Payments** has at least as many rows as **Registrations_Combined**. It should have exactly the same number: one row per registration. Compare the two row counts, either in the Power Query Editor preview or directly in the Excel tables. If **Master_Payments** is higher, the payment source contains multiple entries for some registrations; apply Group By deduplication to **Payments_Transactions** as described for **Master_Attendees** in *Chapter 8*.

Check 2: exception query row counts reviewed

Open the exception queries and sense-check their sizes:

- **Registrations_NoPayment**: A small number is expected; a large proportion of all registrations suggests a systemic problem with the payment data or the join key
- **Payments_NoRegistration**: Any rows here are worth investigating; they represent money received with no matching registration in the system

Share **Registrations_NoPayment** with Priya as her starting point for chasing outstanding payments before month end.

Check 3: Spot-check known records

Pick three to five registrations where you know the expected outcome and verify them in the **Master_Payments** table:

Scenario	Conditions to look for	Expected PaymentStatus
Confirmed, paid	RegistrationStatus = Confirmed and AmountPaid is not null	Paid
Complimentary	TicketType = Complimentary	Complimentary or Canceled
Cancelled	RegistrationStatus = Canceled	Canceled
Confirmed, no payment	RegistrationStatus = Confirmed and AmountPaid is null	Pending or Complimentary

Table 9.4 – Spot-check scenarios for validating PaymentStatus

Filter the **Master_Payments** table by **AttendeeEmail** to find each record and check the values.

> Tip
>
> **Trust loop checklist for Master_Payments:**
>
> - The row count in **Master_Payments** matches **Registrations_Combined**; one row per registration
> - **PaymentStatus** (Paid/Complimentary/Pending/Cancelled) distribution matches finance expectations.

- **Registrations_NoPayment** and **Payments_NoRegistration** reviewed and shared with the relevant teams.
- Three to five spot checks on known records pass.

Quinn saves the workbook and clicks **Refresh All**. The process that took Priya three hours now takes ten seconds.

"This is your chase list," Quinn says, pointing to the **Registrations_NoPayment** query in the **Queries & Connections** pane. "All the registrations with no payment recorded. And this one," she points to **Payments_NoRegistration**, "payments with no matching registration. Worth checking with the events team before you close the month."

Priya leans forward. "And next month?"

"New payment export in the folder, same **Refresh**. Everything updates automatically."

Priya sits back and looks at the screen for a moment. "I want one of these for every report I run."

Summary

In this chapter, you built **Master_Payments** by joining registrations, payment transactions, and complimentary registrations into a single trusted table. Along the way, you also created exception queries to identify missing matches and verified that the final output reflected the business rules correctly. Five patterns from this chapter are worth carrying forward:

- **Choose the right join for the question**: Left Outer joins enrich a complete table while preserving every row, Inner joins return only confirmed matches, and Left Anti joins surface exceptions that need investigation rather than hiding them.
- **Join on stable, business-defined keys**: Build merges on reliable keys such as **AttendeeEmail + SessionID**, validate that lookup tables contain one row per key, and resolve duplicate matches before merging to prevent double-counting.
- **Derive business status after the merge**: Create conditional columns such as **PaymentStatus** only after all relevant data has been brought together, keeping the business logic in one place where it is easy to review and maintain.

- **Keep exception queries instead of deleting problems**: Queries such as **Registrations_NoPayment** and **Payments_NoRegistration** become practical follow-up lists for the business while preserving a clean main output.
- **Validate every merge before trusting the result**: Compare row counts, review exception queries, and perform spot checks on known records to confirm that every join produced the expected outcome before moving on.

Master_Payments is ready. In *Chapter 10*, you will organize the workbook's queries into groups and introduce parameters that make the whole setup easier to maintain and hand over. Then in *Chapter 11*, **Master_Payments** joins the Excel Data Model as the payment fact table, completing the Events data model that has been taking shape since *Chapter 2*.

10

Automate Repetitive Processes

Figure 10.1 – Hannah guides Quinn on making queries and workbooks more organised for smooth handover

It is a quiet Tuesday morning when Hannah, the Senior BI Analyst, pauses behind Quinn's desk on her way to the kitchen. Quinn has the **Queries** pane open and is about to duplicate the **Master_Sessions** query. Marcus needs a workshop-only view for this week's stakeholder meeting, so Quinn plans to copy the query, manually apply a workshop filter, and load the results into a new worksheet.

"What are you doing?" Hannah asks, setting down her mug.

Quinn explains. Hannah nods slowly. "That'll work. But you'll be back here every time Marcus wants a different view." Hannah glances at the flat list of queries on Quinn's screen. "And have you ever tried running this workbook from a machine that isn't yours?"

Quinn hasn't.

"Then let's fix both things properly." Hannah pulls up a chair and continues, "I'll guide you: start with the **Queries** pane, let's make it readable first, then I'll show you how to stop hard-coding values into your steps."

In this chapter, you'll learn to -

- Organize the queries in your `NOG-DataHub` workbook into named groups so the workbook is easy to navigate and easy to hand over to a colleague
- Create Power Query parameters for values that change (such as event type and folder path) and understand when a parameter is the right tool
- Build a scoped query view by duplicating a master query and applying a parameter-based filter, without changing the master itself
- Replace a hard-coded source path with a parameter reference in the formula bar, so that one change updates every dependent query

Technical requirements

The chapters in this book build on each other. Make sure you have completed all exercises in the previous chapter before starting this one.

To follow along with this chapter, you will need:

- Microsoft Excel 2016 or later with Power Query, accessed via **Data** | **Get & Transform Data**
- Your `NOG-DataHub` workbook from *Chapter 9* (NOG stands for Northbridge Office Group), which should already contain the following queries:
    - **Master_Sessions** (built in *Chapter 3*)
    - **Weekly_Event_KPIs** (built in *Chapter 4*)
    - **Registrations_Combined** (built in *Chapter 6*)
    - **Sessions_Attendance** (built in *Chapter 7*)
    - **Master_Attendees** (built in *Chapter 8*)
    - **Master_Payments** (built in *Chapter 9*)

No additional exercise files are required for this chapter. All work builds on the queries already in your workbook.

From one-off fixes to reusable patterns

After nine chapters, your `NOG-DataHub` workbook is doing serious work. It loads files from multiple folders, combines, cleans, and reshapes them, and produces master tables that several teams rely on. That is a significant achievement.

But along the way, a problem has been building. Every source query has a folder path hard-coded in its Source step, set once when the connection was first created. If the SharePoint site moves or a colleague needs to run the workbook from a different location, every source query needs to be updated individually.

And when a stakeholder asks for a filtered view (Workshop sessions only, for example) the natural instinct is to duplicate a master query and filter it manually. That works once but becomes a maintenance burden when the scope changes or the request recurs.

This chapter introduces two tools that address this directly:

- **Query groups** — named folders in the **Queries** pane that bring order to the workbook before you add anything new, making it easy to distinguish master tables, helper queries, and configuration values
- **Parameters** — named, editable values stored once in the workbook and referenced by any query that needs them; change the parameter value, click **Refresh**, and every query that uses it updates at once

Think of a parameter like a named cell in a spreadsheet. Instead of entering the same value in ten different cells, you store it in one named cell and have every formula reference that single location. When the value changes, you update one cell. Parameters work the same way for query steps.

> Note
>
> A Power Query parameter is not a formula; it is a named value. It does not recalculate automatically. You change the value, then click **Refresh**, and Power Query picks it up.

Now that the tools are clear, let's start where Hannah suggested: with the **Queries** pane.

Organizing your queries into groups

Before adding anything new, it is worth bringing order to what you already have. The **Queries** pane currently shows a flat **Other Queries** group containing eleven queries, alongside several auto-generated groups created when you combined files from a folder. This is hard to scan and even harder to hand to a colleague. Query groups fix this without changing how any query works; they are purely organizational.

Power Query supports named groups and nested groups. A group can contain individual queries or other groups, which means you can bundle related groups under a single parent. The target structure for the `NOG-DataHub` workbook is:

- **Parameters** — empty for now; will hold the parameters you create in the next section
- **Reference** — **Map_Facilitators**
- **Helpers** — a parent group containing the three auto-generated **Transform File from...** groups and the **_Checks** group, all nested inside it
- **Outputs** — every query that produces a sheet: **Master_Contacts**, **Master_Sessions**, **Weekly_Event_KPIs**, **Registrations_Combined**, **Sessions_Attendance**, **Master_Attendees**, **Payments_Transactions**, **Master_Payments**, **Registrations_NoPayment**, and **Payments_NoRegistration**

> **Important**
>
> For this exercise, open your `NOG-DataHub` workbook from *Chapter 9*. Open the Power Query Editor by clicking the **Data** tab and then **Queries & Connections**, then double-clicking any query to enter the editor.

Creating the top-level groups

Right-click on any empty area of the **Queries** pane, below the last query, or in the gray space between groups, to get a context menu with a **New Group** option. You will repeat these four steps once for each of the four groups — `Parameters`, `Reference`, `Helpers`, and `Outputs`:

1. Right-click an empty area of the **Queries** pane
2. Click **New Group**

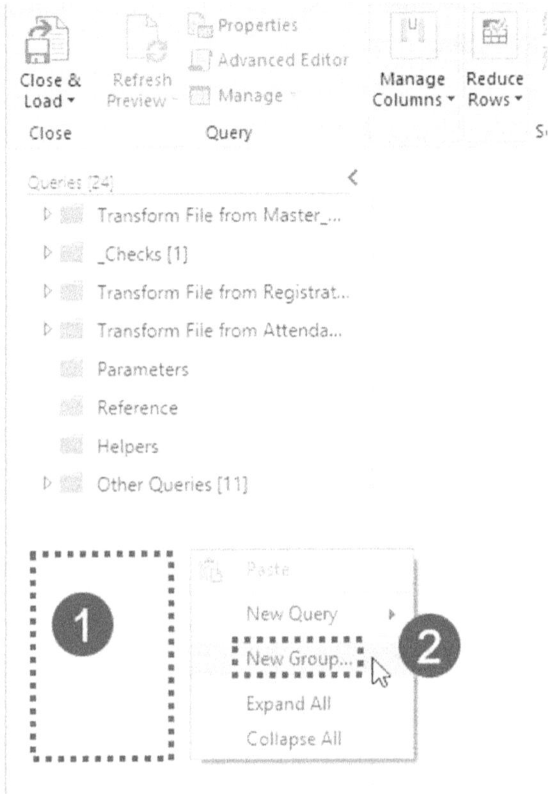

Figure 10.2 – Right-clicking empty space in the Queries pane to create a new group

3. Type the group name in the **Name** field
4. Click **OK**

Repeat to create all four groups: `Parameters`, `Reference`, `Helpers`, and `Outputs`.

Populating the groups

Still in the **Power Query Editor**, drag each query or group into its target group. The following list shows where everything goes:

- Into **Reference**: **Map_Facilitators**
- Into **Outputs**: **Master_Contacts**, **Master_Sessions**, **Weekly_Event_KPIs**, **Registrations_Combined**, **Sessions_Attendance**, **Master_Attendees**,

Payments_Transactions, **Master_Payments**, **Registrations_NoPayment**, and **Payments_NoRegistration**

- Into **Helpers**: the three **Transform File from...** groups and the **_Checks** group, drag each group as a whole; the queries nested inside move with it

Leave **Parameters** empty for now.

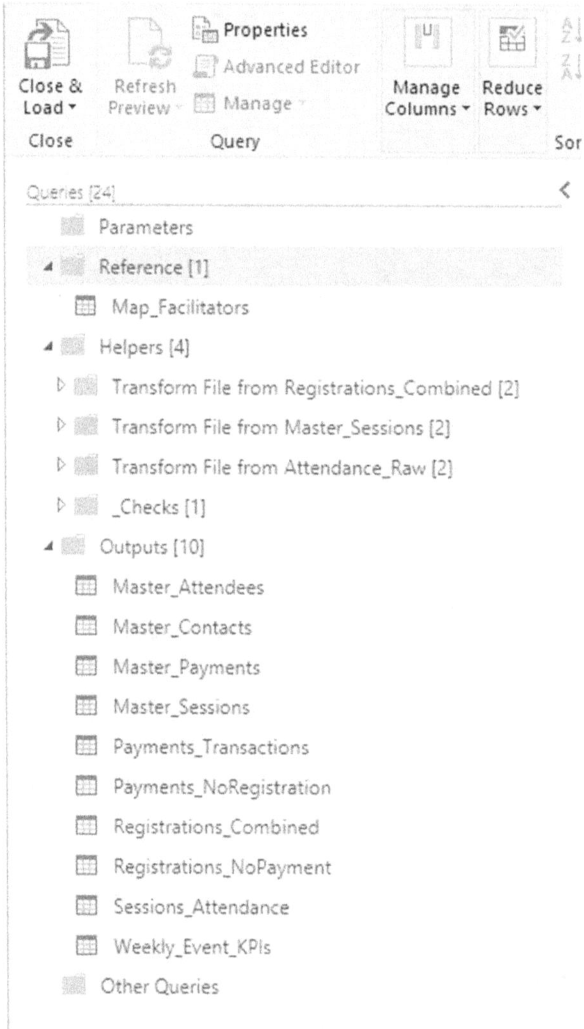

Figure 10.3 – The Queries pane after reorganization, showing the nested Helpers group and the populated Outputs group

Note

Groups can also be created and moved via the right-click menu on a query: **Move to Group** | **New Group** creates a new group and moves the query into it in one step; **Move to Group** | `[group name]` moves the query to an existing group. Dragging is faster when reorganizing many items at once.

Moving a group into another group nests it. The **Transform File from...** groups already contain their own **Helper Queries** sub-groups; those stay intact when you drag the parent group into **Helpers**.

Adding descriptions

A one-line description makes each output query self-explanatory to anyone who opens the workbook later. Add a description to each query in the **Outputs** group:

1. Right-click the query
2. Click **Properties**
3. Type a short description in the **Description** field
4. Click **OK**

You may find that some queries already have a description from an earlier chapter (for example, you added one to **Master_Sessions** in *Chapter 3*). Keep or refine what is already there; only queries without a description need a new one.

Here are examples of the kind of description that works:

- **Master_Sessions**: One row per session. Source of truth for all session-level reporting.
- **Master_Payments**: One row per registration with payment status. Built from **Registrations_Combined** and **Payments_Transactions**.
- **Registrations_NoPayment**: Exception list: registrations with no matching payment record.

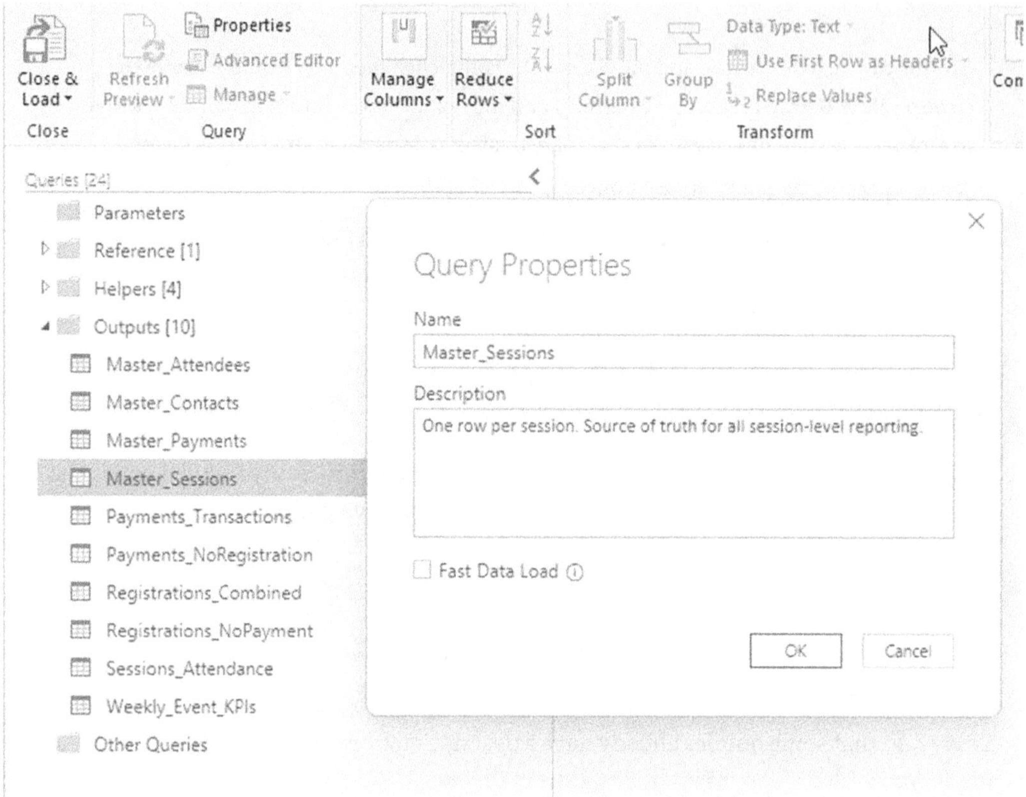

Figure 10.4 – Query Properties dialog showing a description added to Master_Sessions

Once all queries are grouped and described, click **Close & Load** and confirm that all output tables still populate correctly on their sheets. Reorganizing groups changes nothing about how queries run; if anything fails to load, the cause is unrelated to this step.

With the workbook organized, you are ready to add the first new tool: **parameters**.

Creating parameters for your workbook

A Power Query parameter is a named, typed value stored in the workbook. Instead of typing `Workshop` into a filter step, you store the value once in a parameter called **SessionType** and reference the parameter in the step. When you want to switch session type, you change **SessionType** and click **Refresh**; the step updates without you touching it.

You will now create two parameters; the rest of the chapter puts them to work:

- **SessionType** — the session type to focus on, chosen from the five standardized values in **Master_Sessions**
- **FolderPath** — the root path of your `NOG-DataHub` folder or SharePoint site

Important

For this exercise, continue in your `NOG-DataHub` workbook with the **Power Query Editor** open. The four query groups from the previous section should already exist.

Creating the SessionType parameter

Open the **Manage Parameters** dialog:

1. Click the **Home** tab in the **Power Query Editor** and click on **Parameters**
2. Click **Manage Parameters**
3. Click **New Parameter**

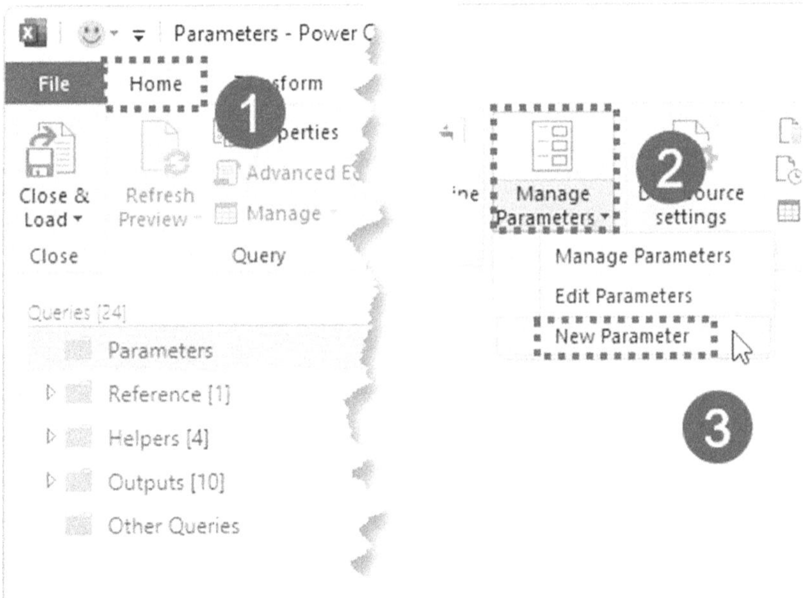

Figure 10.5 – Home tab in the Power Query Editor with Manage Parameters highlighted

Caution

The **Manage Parameters** dialog already lists three parameters: **Parameter1**, **Parameter2**, and **Parameter3** (created automatically by the Combine Files helper queries when you combined folders in earlier chapters). Do not edit or rename them; the folder-combine queries depend on them. The dialog always edits whichever parameter is highlighted in the list, so after clicking **New Parameter**, check that the new (fourth) entry is the one selected before typing the name.

Fill in the parameter details:

1. Type `SessionType` in the **Name** field
2. Set **Type** to **Text**
3. Set **Suggested Values** to **List of values**
4. Type the five session types, one per row: `Workshop`, `Seminar`, `Course`, `Training`, `Webinar`
5. Set **Default Value** to **Workshop**
6. Set **Current Value** to **Workshop**
7. Click **OK**

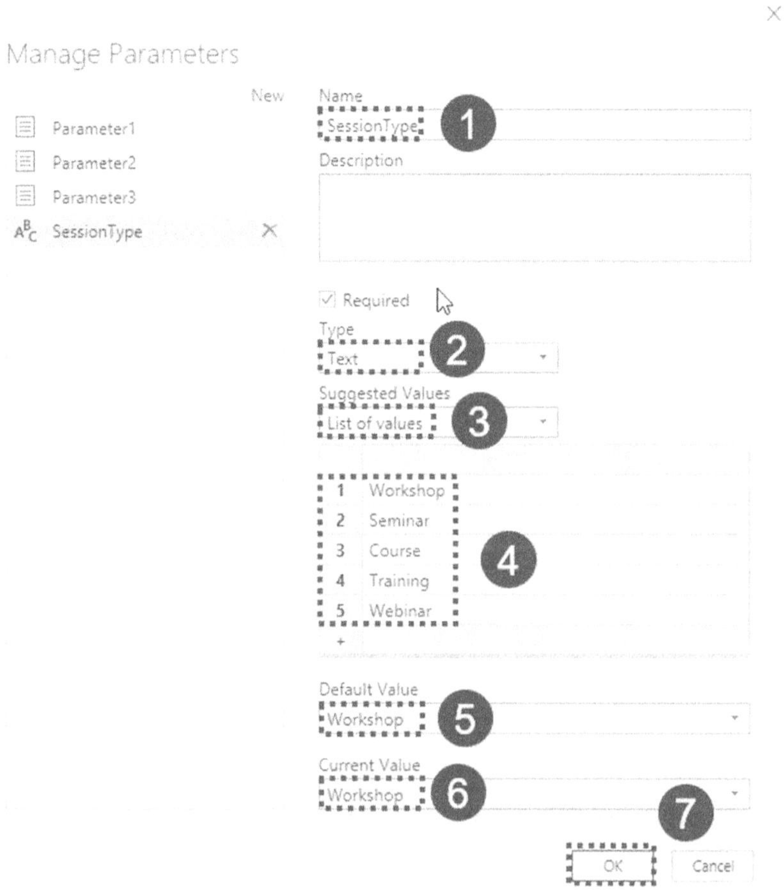

Figure 10.6 – Manage Parameters dialog with SessionType configured as a Text parameter with a list of suggested values

Creating the FolderPath parameter

Before creating this parameter, you need the exact path your source queries currently use. Find it by reading the **Source** step of one of your folder-based queries:

1. Click one of your source queries in the **Queries** pane, for example, the query that feeds **Registrations_Combined**
2. Click the **Source** step in the **Applied Steps** pane

3. Read the path from the formula bar; it will be a quoted SharePoint URL or local folder path. For example:
    - SharePoint connection: "`https://northbridge.sharepoint.com/sites/NOG-DataHub`"
    - Local folder connection: "`C:-DataHub`"
4. Copy the text inside the quotation marks only; for SharePoint, that is the full URL; for a local folder, that is the folder path

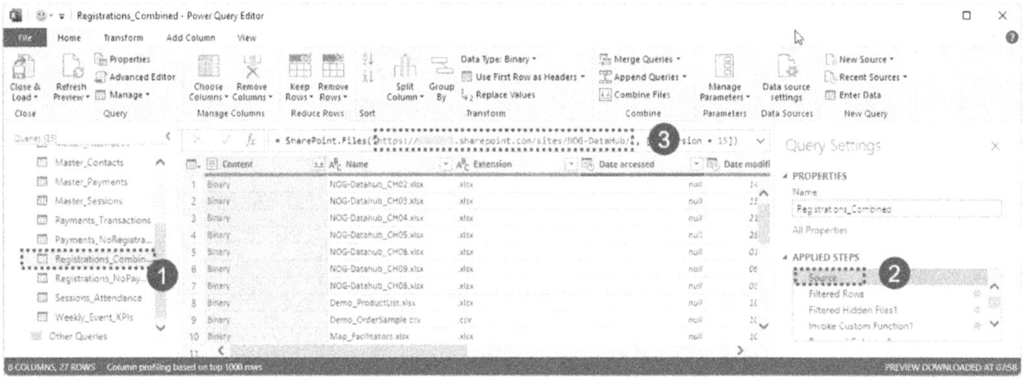

Figure 10.7 – Formula bar showing the Source step path of a folder-based source query

Keep that value to hand; you will paste it into the parameter in the next steps.

Still in the **Power Query Editor**, open the **Manage Parameters** dialog again (the same sequence as before: **Home** | **Manage Parameters** | **New Parameter)**, to add the **FolderPath** parameter:

1. Type `FolderPath` in the **Name** field
2. Set **Type** to **Text**
3. Leave **Suggested Values** as **Any value**
4. Paste your copied path into the **Current Value** field
5. Click **OK** to save both parameters and close the dialog

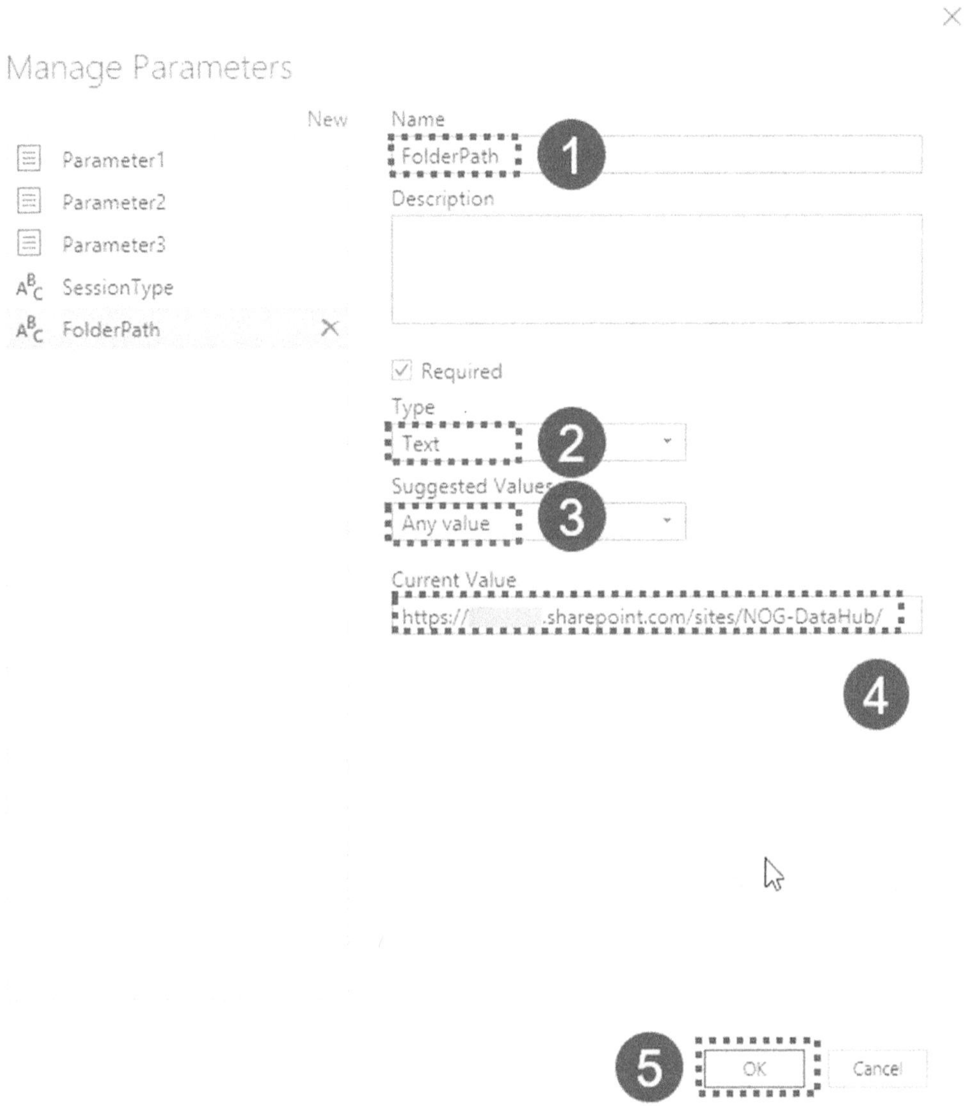

Figure 10.8 – Manage Parameters dialog with FolderPath configured as a Text parameter with the current path value

Both parameters now appear in the **Queries** pane. Power Query places new parameters in **Other Queries**, not in the group you prepared. Drag both of them into the **Parameters** group.

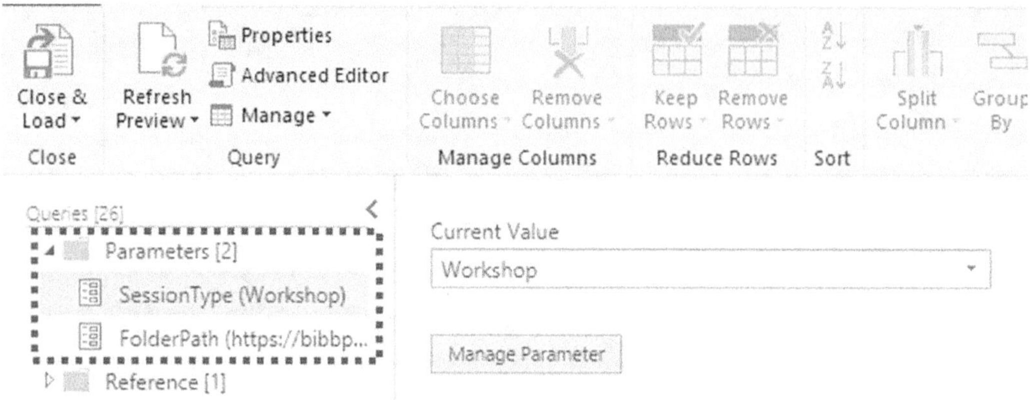

Figure 10.9 – The Parameters group in the Queries pane showing SessionType and FolderPath

> **Note**
>
> Parameters appear with a distinct icon in the **Queries** pane and cannot be loaded to a sheet. They exist only to be referenced by other queries.

At this point, neither parameter is wired into any query; creating them has not changed anything yet. The next two sections connect them.

With parameters defined, the next step is to put them to use, first in a filter, then in a source connection.

Building scoped views with parameter filters

A **scoped view** is a filtered copy of a master query. The master stays complete and unfiltered, your source of truth. The scoped view shows only the rows relevant to a specific context, such as one event type.

The correct way to create a scoped view is to duplicate the master query, not edit it. Duplicating preserves the master intact and creates an independent copy you can filter freely.

In this exercise you will create **Sessions_Workshops**: a view of **Master_Sessions** showing only Workshop sessions, filtered using the **SessionType** parameter.

Duplicating the master query

The following steps create **Sessions_Workshops** as an independent copy of **Master_Sessions**. Every step from the original is preserved, but the two queries are separate, so filtering the duplicates never affects the master:

1. Right-click **Master_Sessions** in the **Queries** pane
2. Click **Duplicate**

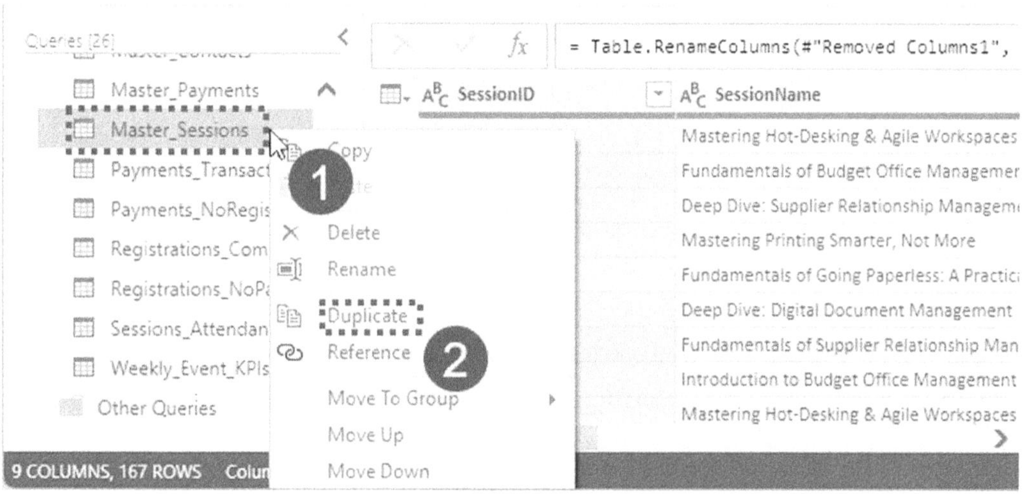

Figure 10.10 – Right-click menu on Master_Sessions showing the Duplicate option

3. In the **Query Settings** pane, clear the **Name** field and type `Sessions_Workshops`

Ensure the new **Sessions_Workshops** query is in the Outputs group.

Applying the parameter filter

With **Sessions_Workshops** open in the editor, add a filter on the **SessionType** column:

1. Click the **SessionType** column filter
2. Click **Text Filters**
3. Click **Equals**

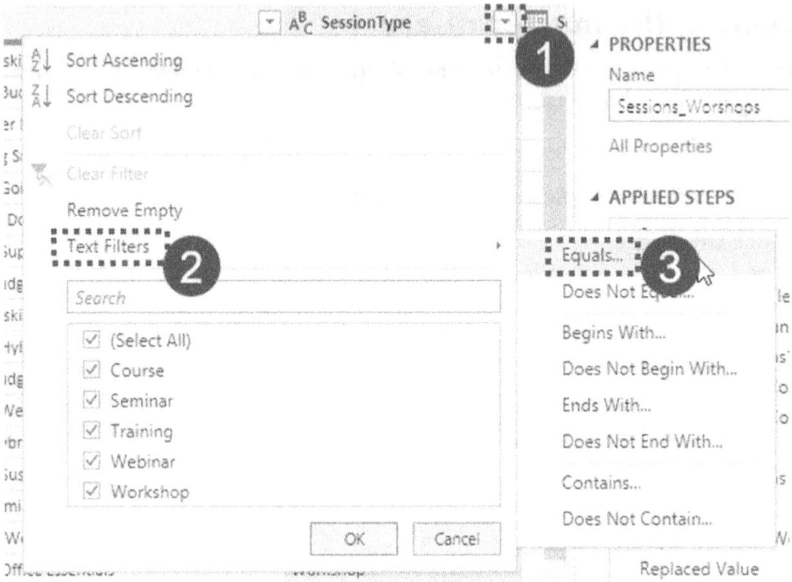

Figure 10.11 – Text Filters menu on the SessionType column header with Equals selected

In the filter dialog, replace the typed value with the parameter:

1. Click the dropdown to the right of the value field
2. Select **Parameter**
3. Select **SessionType** from the list
4. Click **OK**

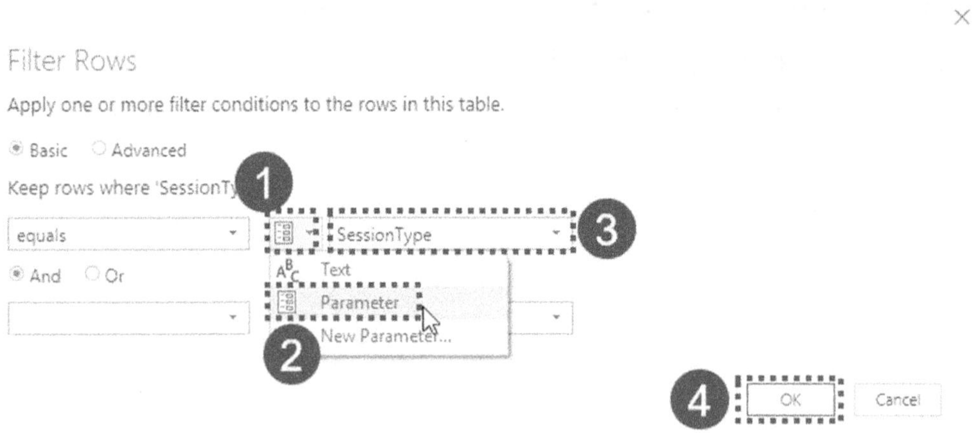

Figure 10.12 – Filter dialog showing the SessionType parameter selected as the filter value

A **Filtered Rows** step appears in the **Applied Steps** pane. The data preview updates immediately; the **SessionType** column now shows only `Workshop` rows.

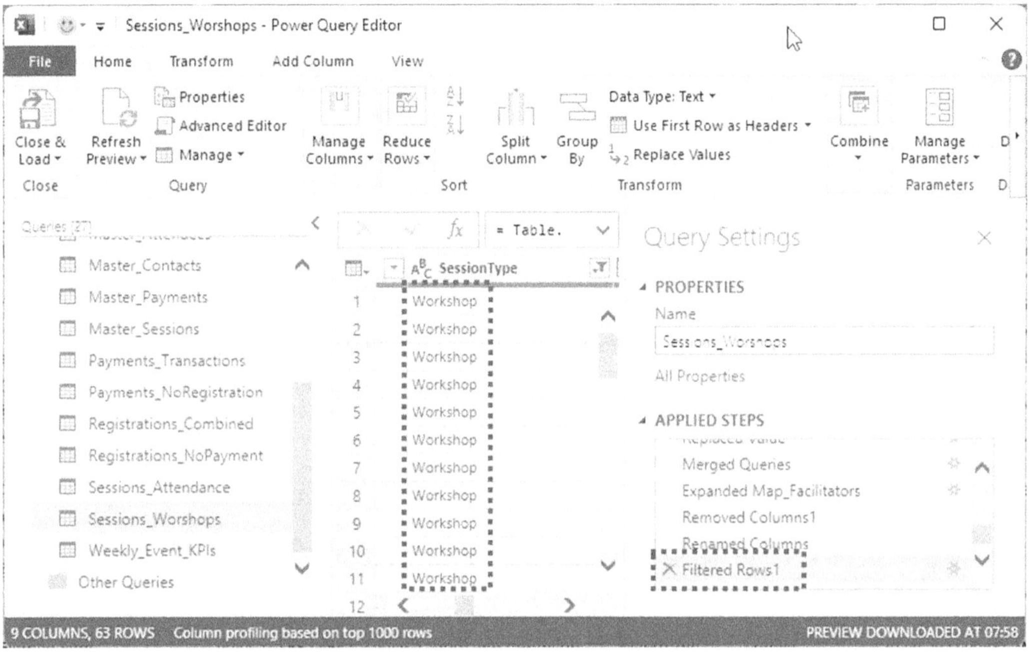

Figure 10.13 – Sessions_Workshops data preview showing only Workshop rows in the SessionType column after the parameter filter was applied

Testing the parameter connection

Before moving on, confirm that **Sessions_Workshops** is genuinely reading its filter value from the parameter, not from a fixed string buried in the step. The test takes only a few seconds inside the editor, and it proves the connection is live before you close and refresh:

Click **SessionType** in the **Parameters** group. Because you set up a list of suggested values, a dropdown appears showing all five options: `Workshop`, `Seminar`, `Course`, `Training`, and `Webinar`. Select a different value and then click **Sessions_Workshops** in the **Queries** pane, and the data preview updates to show only rows matching the new value. No need to close the editor or refresh the workbook to see the effect. **Master_Sessions** remains unchanged throughout; the master always holds the full dataset.

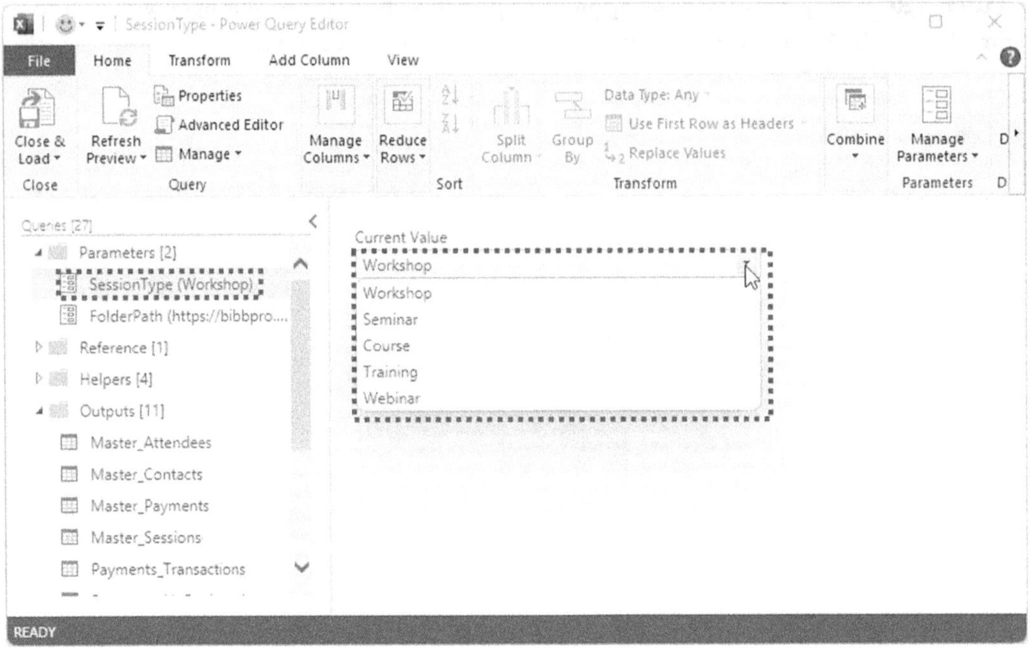

Figure 10.14 – SessionType parameter showing the suggested values dropdown with all five session type options

Set the value back to `Workshop` when you are done.

> **Tip**
>
> Always keep the master query unfiltered. Scoped views are always duplicates: the master remains your full source of truth and feeds any other query that needs the complete dataset.

Validate:

- **Sessions_Workshops** row count equals the number of `Workshop` rows in **Master_Sessions**
- Changing **SessionType** to a different value and refreshing produces the correct filtered result each time

With the parameter working as a filter, the next step is to use the same FolderPath parameter for something more fundamental: controlling where your data comes from.

Replacing a hard-coded source with a parameter

Every query that loads from a SharePoint folder or a local folder has a hard-coded path in its **Source** step. That path was set when the connection was first created. If the SharePoint site ever moves, or a colleague wants to run the workbook from a different location, every source query needs to be updated individually.

The **FolderPath parameter** fixes this. Instead of a quoted path inside the **Source** step, you refer to the parameter by name. One update to **FolderPath**, one **Refresh**, and every source query picks up the new location.

This section uses the **formula bar**, the single-line bar at the top of the Power Query Editor that shows one step at a time. This is not the Advanced Editor, which shows the entire query as a block of code. The change here is small: you replace a quoted string with a parameter name.

> **Note**
>
> The formula bar and the Advanced Editor are different tools. The formula bar shows one step at a time and is safe for targeted edits like this one. The Advanced Editor shows the full query in one block and is not used in this chapter.

Rather than editing a live source query directly, you will practice the technique on a duplicate of **Master_Contacts** first. **Master_Contacts** is a simple, single-file query built in *Chapter 2*, a safe place to prove the edit before applying it to the more complex folder-combine queries.

> **Important**
>
> For this exercise, continue in your `NOG-DataHub` workbook. The **FolderPath** parameter must already exist, and its **Current Value** must match the path used by your source queries exactly.

Duplicating Master_Contacts

First, let's create a duplicate of **Master_Contacts** and move it into the **Helpers** group, keeping it separate from the output queries while you test the technique:

1. Right-click **Master_Contacts** in the **Queries** pane
2. Click **Duplicate**
3. In the **Query Settings** pane, rename the duplicate to **Contacts_Test**

Move it into **Helpers** so it stays out of **Outputs**, you can drag it to the group or:

1. Right-click **Contacts_Test**
2. Click **Move to Group**
3. Click **Helpers**

> **Note**
>
> Duplicate a query before experimenting with its steps. The Power Query Editor has no **Undo** button; if you change or delete a step, there is no *Ctrl* + *Z* to bring it back. Your only way out is to close the editor and discard every change made since you opened it. A duplicate makes mistakes cheap.

Locating the source step

Open the **Helpers** folder and select the **Contacts_Test** query. With **Contacts_Test** open in the editor, find the **Source** step. Click the **Source** step in the **Applied Steps** pane. The formula bar shows the expression for that step. For a SharePoint connection it will look similar to:

```
= SharePoint.Files("https://northbridge.sharepoint.com/sites/NOG-DataHub",
[ApiVersion = 15])
```

For a local folder connection, it will look similar to:

```
= Folder.Files("C:\Users\Quinn\Documents\NOG-DataHub")
```

The section to be replaced is the quoted path, which is the text enclosed in double quotation marks.

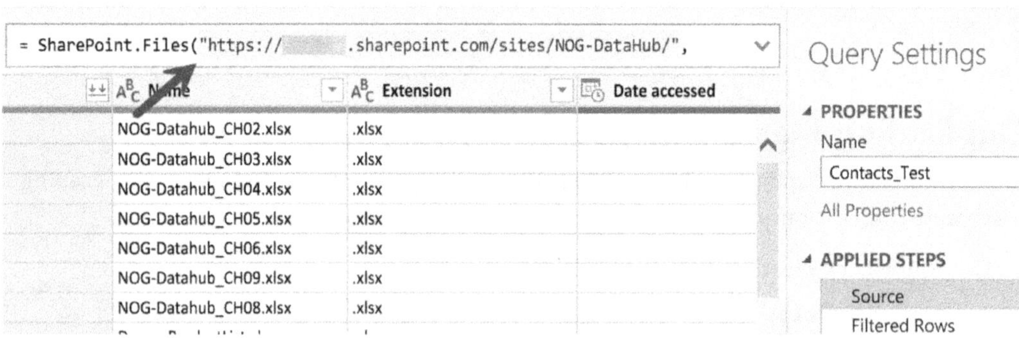

Figure 10.15 – Formula bar showing the Source step of Contacts_Test with the hard-coded path visible

Note

FolderPath only works with queries that use the same connector type. A SharePoint URL cannot be placed inside `Folder.Files()`, and a local folder path cannot be placed inside `SharePoint.Files()`; the functions expect different formats. If your workbook has both SharePoint and local folder source queries, create two separate parameters (for example `SharePointURL` and `LocalFolderPath`) and wire each one only to the queries that use that connector.

Replacing the path with the parameter

The edit is small and precise: you are replacing only the quoted path string in the formula bar with the parameter name. With the **Contacts_Test** query and the **Source** step selected, make the change:

1. Click in the formula bar to place your cursor inside the expression
2. Select the quoted path string, including both quotation marks
3. Type , no quotation marks; you are referencing the parameter, not typing a string
4. Press *Enter*

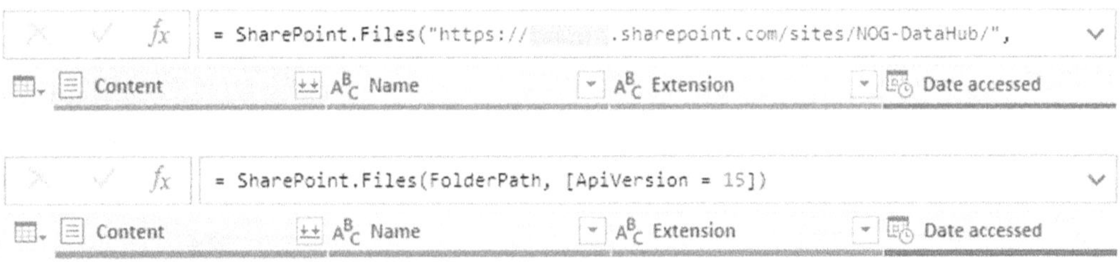

Figure 10.16 – Formula bar before the edit (quoted path) and after (FolderPath parameter name)

Power Query resolves the parameter, and the Source step continues to work exactly as before, except it now reads its path from FolderPath rather than a hard-coded string.

Caution

Only replace the quoted path string. Do not change the function name (`SharePoint.Files` or `Folder.Files`) or any other part of the expression.

AI Helper

If you are unsure what the formula bar expression means, paste it into ChatGPT and ask: `What does this Power Query Source step do, and which part is the file path?` Verify the explanation against what you see in the formula bar before making any change.

Verifying and rolling out

Check the data preview for **Contacts_Test**: it should show the same rows as **Master_Contacts**. If it does, the parameter is wired in correctly. Delete **Contacts_Test** when you are satisfied; it was only needed to prove the technique.

That is the whole technique. If you feel like it, you can now apply the same formula bar edit to the other folder-based queries in your workbook. Once every **Source** step reads its path from the parameter, a single change to **FolderPath** controls where the entire workbook loads its data from.

We will leave the workbook here for now. As a general rule, hard-coded source paths are worth avoiding whenever you have the option: a parameter costs little to create and pays for itself the first time a file moves or you share the workbook with a colleague on a different machine.

To wrap up, close the editor, and save your work. It does not matter which query is selected when you do this:

1. On the **Home** tab, click the arrow next to **Close & Load** and choose **Close & Load To...**
2. Select **Only Create Connection** and click **OK**
3. Save the workbook

Quinn leans back and looks at the **Queries** pane: four tidy groups, two parameters sitting in their own section, and **Sessions_Workshops** as a clean, scoped view below the master tables.

Hannah appears at the desk with a fresh mug of tea. "Show me."

Quinn clicks **SessionType**, selects "Webinar" from the dropdown, then clicks **Sessions_Workshops**. The preview shifts to `Webinar` rows only. She sets it back to `Workshop`. "And if the SharePoint site ever moves," Quinn says, "FolderPath is the only thing I touch."

Hannah nods. "Now it's a workbook someone else can open in six months and actually understand." She heads back to her desk. "That's the standard."

Summary

In this chapter, you added two tools to the `NOG-DataHub` workbook that make it easier to navigate, maintain, and hand over: **query groups** and **parameters**. Three patterns from this chapter are worth carrying forward:

- **Organize before you add**: named query groups bring order to the **Queries** pane without changing how any query runs. A readable workbook is easier to maintain and easier to pass to a colleague
- **Parameters over hard-coded values:** a named parameter stores a value once and lets every query that needs it point to the same place; change **FolderPath**, click **Refresh**, and every source query picks up the new location at once
- **Duplicate for scoped views, never edit the master**: **Sessions_Workshops** filters **Master_Sessions** via the **SessionType** parameter. The master stays complete and unfiltered, and the scoped view is always a derived copy

In *Chapter 11*, Hannah takes the next step. With the master tables clean, organized, and consistently keyed, she shows Quinn how to connect them into a proper data model inside Excel — the foundation for the DAX measures that follow.

Part 4

Advancing Toward Modeling and Scale

In this part, you will take the step from flat tables to a connected data model and answer the questions flat tables cannot. You will load **Master_Sessions**, **Master_Attendees**, and **Master_Payments** into the Excel Data Model, define keys and one-to-many relationships in **Diagram View**, understand cardinality and filter direction, and test the connected Events model with implicit measures. You will then write your first three DAX measures, each building on the previous (**[Total Registrations]**, **[Total Attendees]**, and **[Attendance Rate]**), and deliver an Events Performance page that answers the question every event organiser eventually asks: what percentage of registered people actually showed up? By the end of this part, you will have completed the journey from messy exports to a connected, refreshable model, with foundations that carry directly into Power BI.

This section contains the following chapters:

11

Build Your First Events Data Model in Excel

Figure 11.1 – Hannah explains the concept of the Excel data model

Marcus drops into the chair beside Quinn's desk and opens his laptop. It is the last Tuesday of the quarter, and his leadership presentation is just three days away. He has the usual slide: attendance, payments received, satisfaction. But this time, the head of events wants a breakdown.

"I need three things," Marcus says, pulling up a notes document. "Which session types are pulling in the most registrations? Which facilitators are generating the most payments? And which months were strongest for both?" He looks up. "Is that doable by Thursday?"

Quinn glances at the `NOG-DataHub` workbook. The master tables are all there — clean, refreshable, built carefully across nine chapters. "Yes," Quinn says. "Give me a bit of time to put it together."

Marcus nods and heads back to his desk.

Quinn opens **Master_Attendees** and scans the columns. **SessionType** is not there; it is in **Master_Sessions**. To answer Marcus's first question, Quinn would need to merge **Master_Attendees** back to **Master_Sessions**, bring across **SessionType**, and count by it. A new query, just for that. Quinn sketches it out mentally: merge, expand, group. Fine for one question.

But Marcus's second question is different. Payments per facilitator means joining **Master_Payments** to **Master_Sessions**. Another merge, another query. And the third question — strongest months for both registrations and payments — would need the same join twice, with two separate value columns. Three questions, three pipelines. And the moment Marcus asks a fourth, it starts again.

Quinn pushes back from the desk and walks over to Hannah's end of the office. Hannah, the Senior BI Analyst, is reviewing a dashboard report. Quinn explains the problem: clean tables, but every cross-table question needs its own merge query.

Hannah listens, then turns to her screen. "The data is all there," she says. "But your tables don't talk to each other yet. Each one answers its own question, and that's it." She opens a new window. "What you need is a model—one set of relationships defined once, so any PivotTable can use all three tables together."

What Hannah is describing is the Excel Data Model: a layer that sits beneath the workbook and holds the connections between tables. Once **Master_Sessions**, **Master_Attendees**, and **Master_Payments** are linked there, Marcus's three questions can be answered in a single PivotTable — without a single new merge query.

This chapter builds that connected model, step by step, starting with the questions Marcus needs to answer.

In this chapter, you'll learn to -

- Identify the business questions that drive the model design, and explain why flat tables cannot answer them without a connected structure
- Identify primary and foreign keys, verify their uniqueness, and load **Master_Sessions**, **Master_Attendees**, and **Master_Payments** into the Excel Data Model

- Create relationships with the correct cardinality and filter direction, and interpret the diagram view in terms of grain decisions from earlier chapters
- Test the connected model with implicit measures in PivotTables to confirm it answers Marcus's questions about registrations and payments received

Technical requirements

The chapters in this book build on each other. Make sure you have completed all exercises in the previous chapter before starting this one.

To follow along with this chapter, you will need:

- Microsoft Excel 2016 or later with Power Query, accessed via **Data** | **Get & Transform Data**
- The **Power Pivot add-in** is enabled in Excel. See the note below for setup instructions
- Your `NOG-DataHub` workbook from *Chapter 10* (NOG stands for Northbridge Office Group), which should already contain the following queries, organized into named groups:
    - **SessionType** and **FolderPath** parameters (*Chapter 10*)
    - **Master_Contacts** (*Chapter 2*)
    - **Master_Sessions** (*Chapter 3*)
    - **Weekly_Event_KPIs** (*Chapter 4*)
    - **Sessions_Workshops** (*Chapter 10*)
    - **Registrations_Combined** (*Chapter 6*)
    - **Sessions_Attendance** (*Chapter 7*)
    - **Master_Attendees** (*Chapter 8*)
    - **Master_Payments**, **Registrations_NoPayment**, and **Payments_NoRegistration** (*Chapter 9*)

No new exercise files are needed for this chapter. All work builds on queries already in your workbook.

> Note
>
> The Excel Data Model is powered by **Power Pivot**, a built-in add-in that may need to be enabled before you begin. To enable it: click the **File** tab, click **Options**, click **Add-ins**, set the **Manage** dropdown at the bottom to **COM Add-ins**, click **Go**, tick **Microsoft**

> **Office Power Pivot for Excel**, and click **OK**. Power Pivot is available on Excel for Windows (2016, 2019, Microsoft 365). It is not supported on Excel for Mac.

Start with the questions: what the flat tables can't answer

Before deciding which tables to connect or how to connect them, it is worth spending a moment on what the model has to answer.

Marcus's three questions are:

- Which session types generate the most registrations?
- Which facilitators generate the most payments?
- Which months were strongest for both?

These are not unusual questions. They are exactly the kind of cross-cutting comparisons that leadership teams ask every quarter. But look at where the data lives across the current flat tables:

Question	Column needed	Lives in	Count or sum from
Registrations by session type	SessionType	Master_Sessions	Master_Attendees
Payments by facilitator	Facilitator	Master_Sessions	Master_Payments
Strongest months	SessionDate	Master_Sessions	Both fact tables

Table 11.1 – Each of Marcus's questions spans two separate tables

Every row in that table tells the same story: the descriptive context (session type, facilitator, date) is in **Master_Sessions**, but the things to count and sum (registrations, payments) are in the other tables. To answer any one question with flat tables, Quinn would need to build a merge query. To answer all three, Quinn would need three separate merge queries — and each one would need to be rebuilt every time the question changed.

A **data model** solves this differently. Instead of merging tables for each question, you define the relationships between the tables once, and then ask any question you like by choosing fields in a PivotTable. The relationships stay in place; the question is just a matter of which fields you drag.

The structure has two types of tables:

- A **dimension table** holds descriptive, stable data or the *what* of the model. **Master_Sessions** is the dimension here. It has one row per session and carries the attributes you want to slice by: **SessionType**, **Facilitator**, **SessionDate**.
- **Fact tables** hold transactional records or the *what happened*. **Master_Attendees** and **Master_Payments** are the facts. They record events (a registration, a payment) and carry the numbers you want to count and sum.

All three tables share one key: **SessionID**. That is the column that connects a registration in **Master_Attendees** back to the session details in **Master_Sessions**, and a payment in **Master_Payments** back to the same session.

The structure is deliberately simple: one dimension, two facts, one shared key. This is exactly the arrangement you will build in **Diagram View** later in this chapter.

> **AI Helper**
>
> Data modelers use terms like *star schema* and *fact constellation* to describe arrangements like this. If you are curious about the broader vocabulary, describe your model to an LLM and ask it to explain: `I have three tables. One table has one row per session and a unique SessionID. The other two tables have one row per registration and one row per payment, and both reference SessionID. Explain what a star schema and a fact constellation are, and which pattern my model fits.`

Now that the structure is clear, let's build it.

Defining grain and keys for sessions, attendees, and payments

Before loading any table into the Excel Data Model, it helps to be precise about what each table represents and which column will carry the relationship. This is not extra theory — it is the check that prevents a broken model from returning wrong numbers in a PivotTable.

What does each row mean?

Each of the three tables has a clear grain, established across earlier chapters:

- **Master_Sessions:** one row represents one session. SessionID is unique as no two rows share the same SessionID.

- **Master_Attendees:** one row represents one registration. The same person can appear multiple times if they registered for multiple sessions. SessionID repeats.
- **Master_Payments:** one row represents one payment transaction. Like **Master_Attendees**, SessionID repeats — one session can have many payments.

This is exactly the relationship the model needs: SessionID appears once in the dimension (**Master_Sessions**) and many times in each fact (**Master_Attendees** and **Master_Payments**). In data modeling terms, **Master_Sessions** holds the **primary key**, which is the unique identifier that other tables reference. **Master_Attendees** and **Master_Payments** each hold a **foreign key**: a column that points back to the primary key in the dimension.

Verifying SessionID uniqueness in Master_Sessions

The relationship will only work correctly if SessionID is genuinely unique in **Master_Sessions**. If two rows share the same SessionID, the model cannot reliably connect registrations or payments to the right session.

You confirmed this in *Chapter 3* when you built **Master_Sessions**. If you want to verify it now before loading, here is the quickest method using Power Query:

Open **Master_Sessions** in the **Power Query Editor**:

1. Click the **Data** tab
2. Click **Queries & Connections**
3. Double-click **Master_Sessions** in the pane

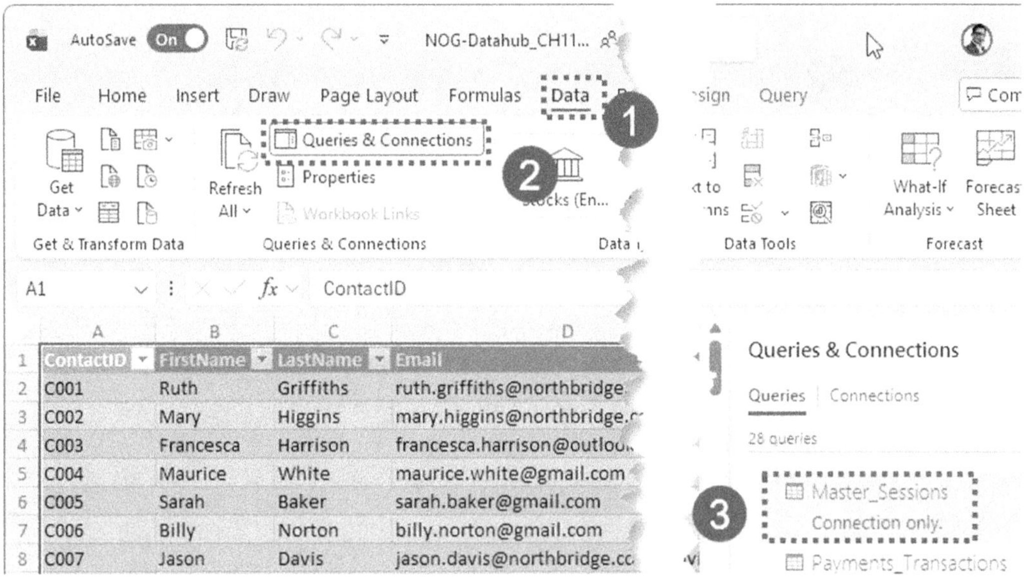

Figure 11.2 – The Power Query Editor open with Master_Sessions, ready for the Group By check

Configure the Group By:

1. Click the **SessionID** column header to select it
2. Click the **Home** tab
3. Click **Group By**
4. Confirm the new column name is `Count`, and the operation is **Count Rows**
5. Click **OK**

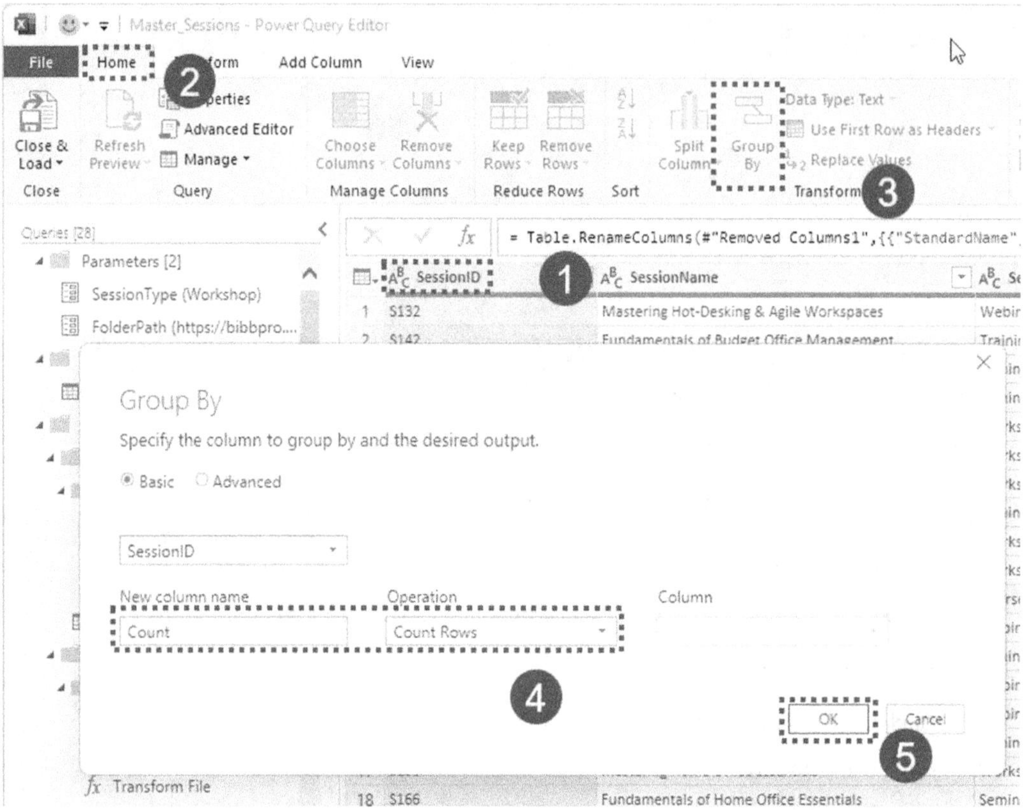

Figure 11.3 – The Group By dialog configured to count rows per SessionID value

Filter the result to surface any duplicates:

1. Click the filter arrow on the **Count** column
2. Click **Number Filters**
3. Click **Greater Than**
4. Type **1** and click **OK**

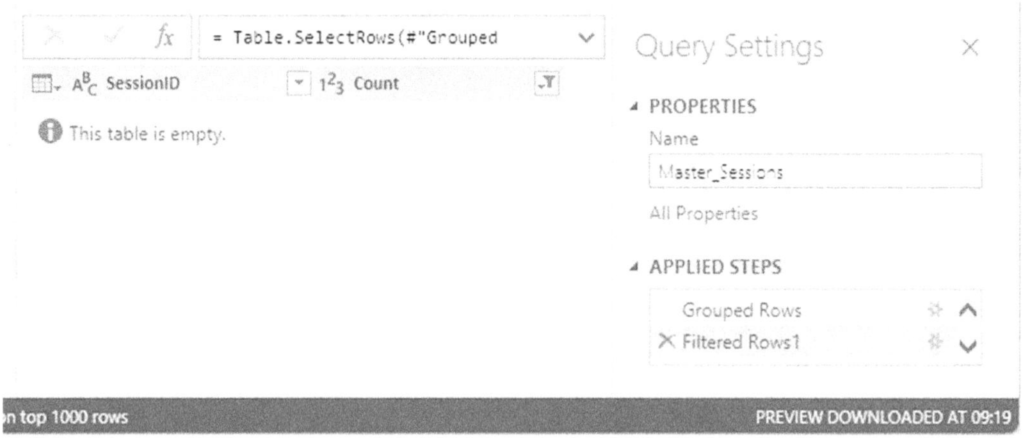

Figure 11.4 – An empty result confirms that every SessionID in Master_Sessions is unique — no duplicates exist

If the result is an empty table, SessionID is unique and the model is safe to build.

Before closing, remove the two verification steps so **Master_Sessions** is not permanently changed:

1. In the **Applied Steps** pane, click the **×** to the left of the **Filtered Rows** step (the last step) to delete it
2. Click the **×** to the left of the **Grouped Rows** step to delete it
3. Click **Close & Load**

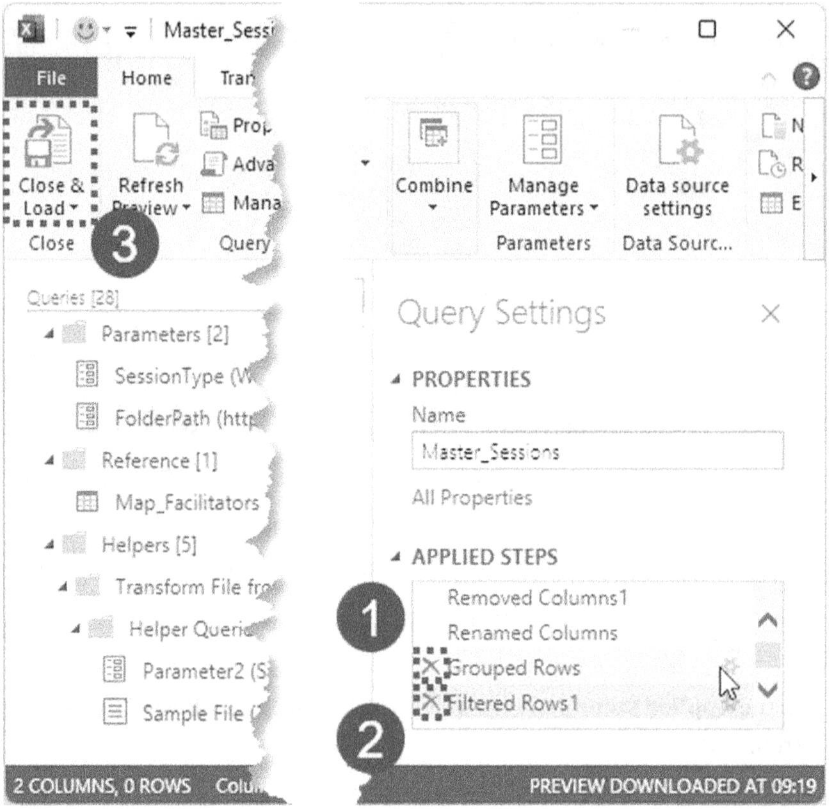

Figure 11.5 - The Applied Steps pane after removing the two verification steps, with Master_Sessions back to its original state

Master_Sessions returns to its original state. The verification was read-only in effect — the steps were added temporarily and are now gone.

Caution

If the check reveals any SessionID values with a count greater than one, do not proceed to loading. Return to your **Master_Sessions** query and investigate the duplicates. A duplicate key in the dimension table will cause the relationship to fail or produce incorrect counts in PivotTables.

Loading the three tables into the Excel data model

With uniqueness confirmed, the next step is to change the load setting for each of the three queries from a worksheet table to a Data Model connection. This removes the corresponding Excel sheets for these queries and adds the data to the Data Model instead.

Start with **Master_Sessions**. Make sure the **Power Query Editor** is closed, then change the load setting in the **Queries & Connections** pane:

1. Click the **Data** tab
2. Click **Queries & Connections**
3. Right-click **Master_Sessions** in the **Queries & Connections** pane
4. Click **Load To**

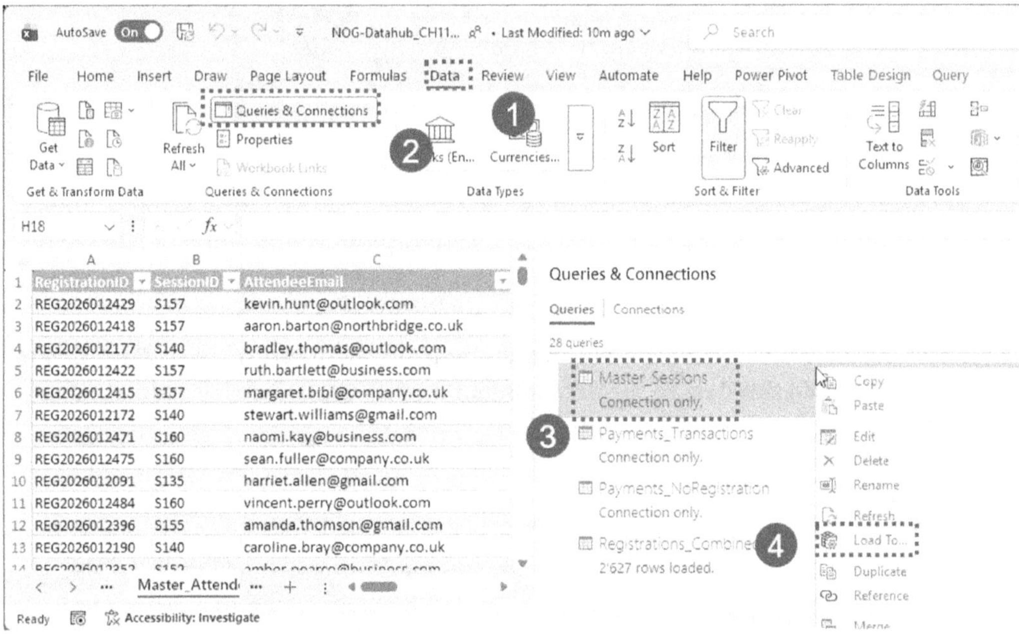

Figure 11.6 – Right-clicking a query in the Queries & Connections pane to change its load settings

In the **Import Data** dialog that opens, update the settings:

1. Select **Only Create Connection**
2. Tick **Add this data to the Data Model**
3. Click **OK**

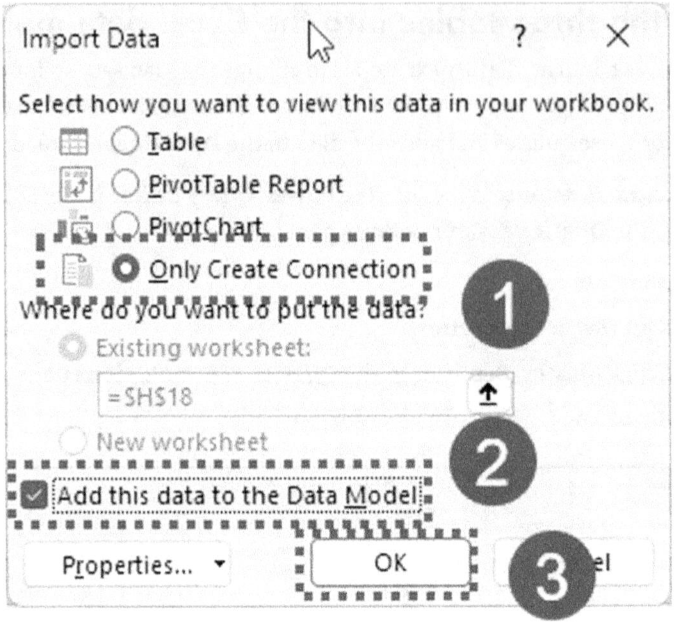

Figure 11.7 – The Import Data dialog with Only Create Connection selected and Add this data to the Data Model ticked

Repeat the same process for **Master_Attendees**, then **Master_Payments**.

Right-click each query in the **Queries & Connections** pane, click **Load To**, select **Only Create Connection**, tick **Add this data to the Data Model**, and click **OK**. The dialog and settings are identical to the steps above.

> **Caution**
>
> **Master_Attendees** and **Master_Payments** are currently loaded to worksheet tables. When you change each one to **Only Create Connection**, Excel displays a **Possible Data Loss** warning; this is expected, not an error. The data is not lost; it moves into the Data Model, but the table that holds it will disappear.

All three queries are now loaded into the Data Model. Open the Power Pivot window to confirm:

1. Click the **Data** tab
2. Click **Manage Data Model**

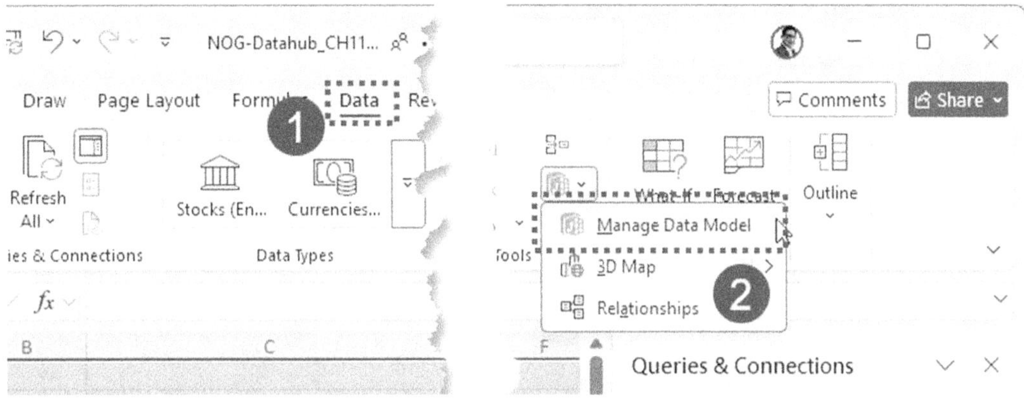

Figure 11.8 – The Manage Data Model button on the Data tab, used to open the Power Pivot window

The Power Pivot window opens, showing the three tables in **Data View**.

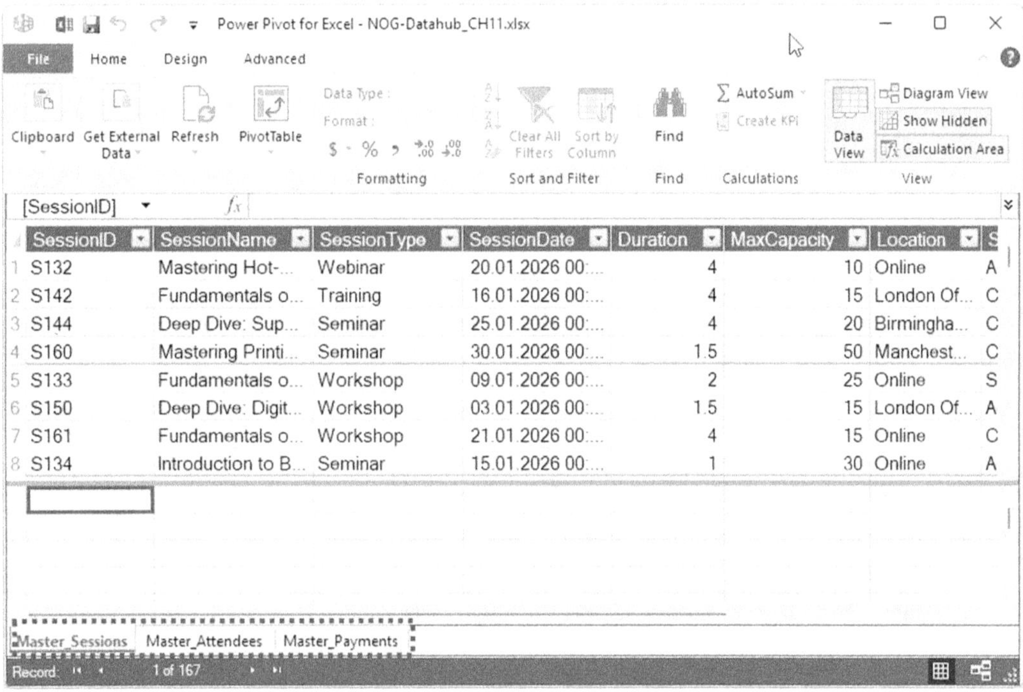

Figure 11.9 – The Power Pivot window in Data View, with Master_Sessions, Master_Attendees, and Master_Payments visible as tabs at the bottom

Switch to **Diagram View** to see the tables as boxes:

1. Click the **Home** tab in the Power Pivot window
2. Click **Diagram View**

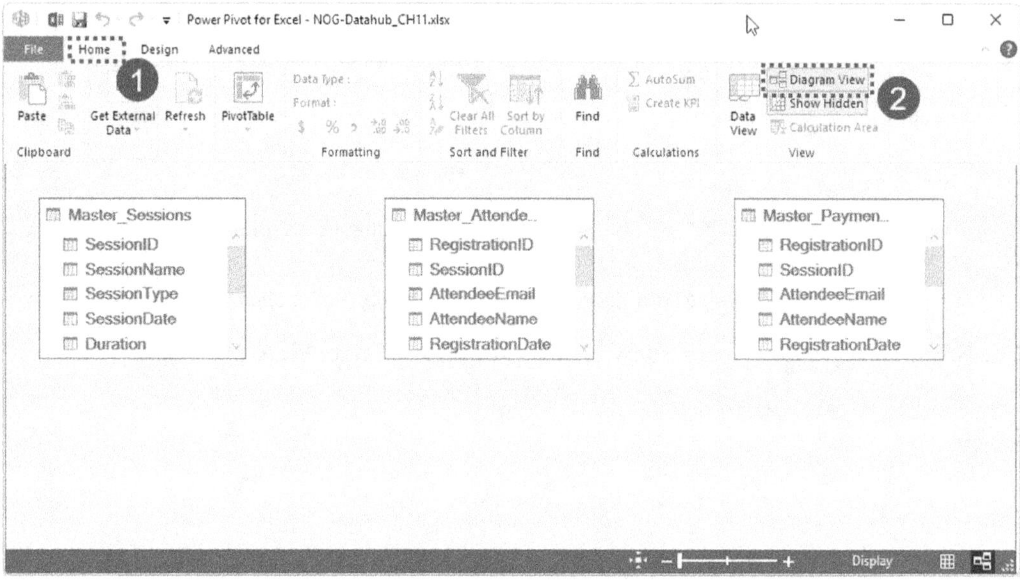

Figure 11.10 – Power Pivot's Diagram View showing the three tables as column-list boxes before any relationships are created

The three tables appear as boxes, each listing their columns. At this point, there are no connecting lines between them, and the relationships still need to be created.

> **Tip**
>
> Arrange the table boxes before creating relationships: drag **Master_Sessions** to the top center, **Master_Attendees** below and to the left, and **Master_Payments** below and to the right. This layout matches the diagram from the opening section and makes the relationship lines easier to read. Moving the boxes is purely cosmetic; it changes nothing in the data or the model, so drag them wherever you like.

With the three tables loaded and **Diagram View** open, it is time to connect them.

Creating relationships and understanding cardinality and filter direction

A relationship in the Excel Data Model is a declaration: "the SessionID in this table matches the SessionID in that table." Once declared, every PivotTable built from the Data Model can use both tables together without any manual joining.

Creating the first relationship

The first relationship connects **Master_Sessions** to **Master_Attendees**. You are connecting the primary key (SessionID in the dimension) to the foreign key (SessionID in the fact).

To create it use drag-and-drop in Diagram View:

1. In the **Master_Sessions** box, click and hold **SessionID**
2. Drag it across to the **SessionID** column in the **Master_Attendees** box and release the mouse button

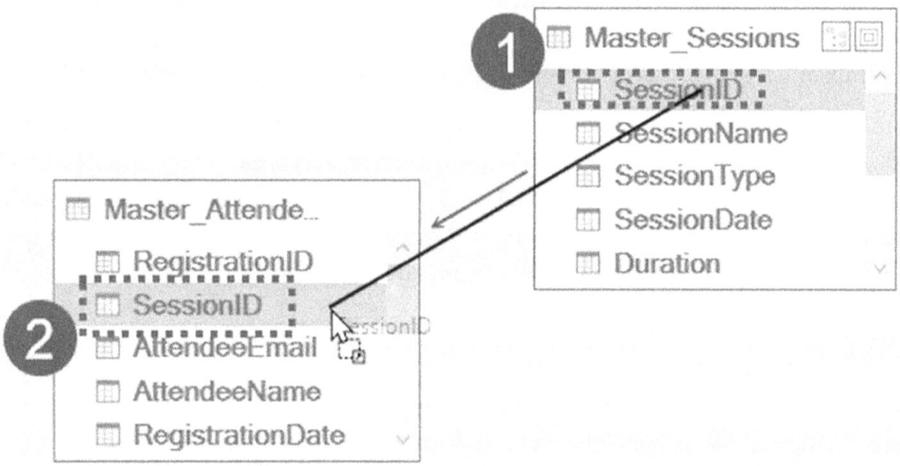

Figure 11.11 – Dragging SessionID from Master_Sessions onto SessionID in Master_Attendees to create the relationship

A line now connects the two tables. Look closely at the ends of the line:

- A **1** appears at the **Master_Sessions** end
- An asterisk (*****) appears at the **Master_Attendees** end

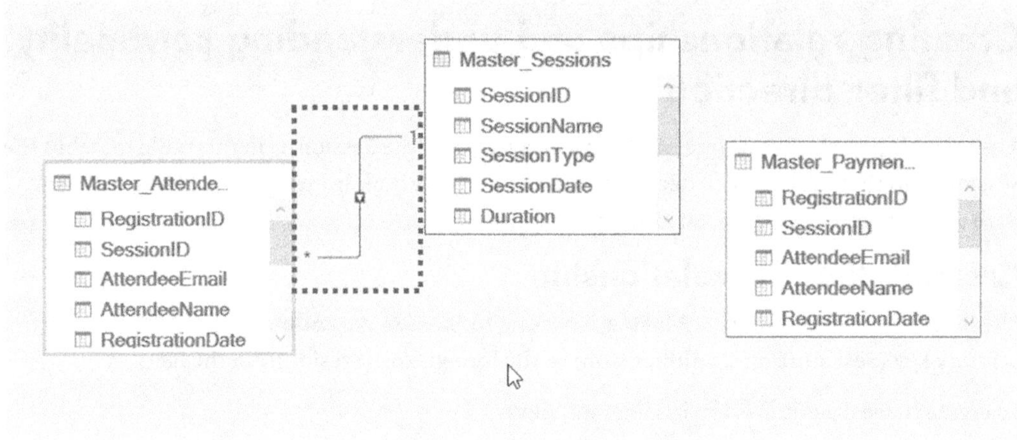

*Figure 11.12 – The first relationship in Diagram View, with the 1 at the Master_Sessions end and the * at the Master_Attendees end*

These symbols describe the relationship's **cardinality** — how many rows on each side can match. The **1** means each **SessionID** value in **Master_Sessions** appears exactly once (it is the unique primary key). The ***** means each **SessionID** value in **Master_Attendees** can appear many times (many people can register for the same session). This is a one-to-many relationship: one session, many registrations.

The line also has a small arrow pointing from the **1** side toward the ***** side. This is the **filter direction**. When a PivotTable filters by a value in **Master_Sessions** — for example, showing only Workshop sessions — that filter travels along the arrow, down into **Master_Attendees**, returning only the registrations that belong to Workshop sessions. The filter does not travel the other way: a filter on **Master_Attendees** does not automatically filter back through **Master_Sessions**.

> **Note**
>
> Single-direction filtering (from dimension to fact) is the right choice for most introductory models. It keeps filter behavior predictable and avoids a class of errors where filtering one fact table accidentally changes what is visible in another. Many-to-many and bidirectional relationships exist but are not covered here; they belong to a more advanced modeling context.

Creating the second relationship

The second relationship connects **Master_Sessions** to **Master_Payments** using the same key:

1. In the **Master_Sessions** box, click and hold **SessionID**
2. Drag it across to the **SessionID** column in the **Master_Payments** box and release the mouse button

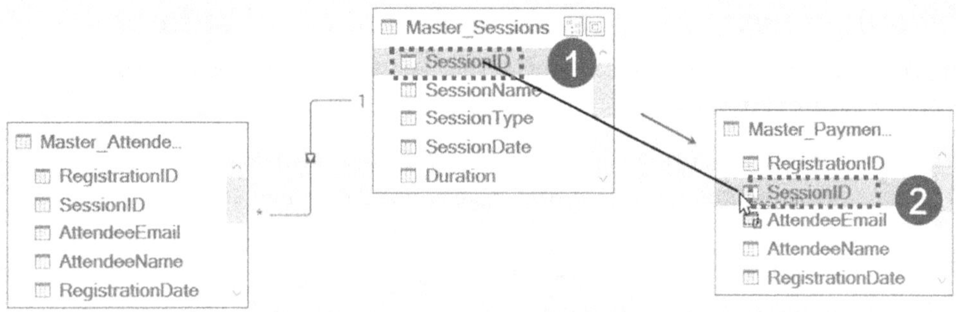

Figure 11.13 – Dragging SessionID from Master_Sessions onto SessionID in Master_Payments to create the second relationship

The completed diagram now shows two lines, both anchored at **Master_Sessions.SessionID**, with the **1** on the dimension side and the ***** on each fact. The two relationships are now in place.

You can close the Power Pivot window.

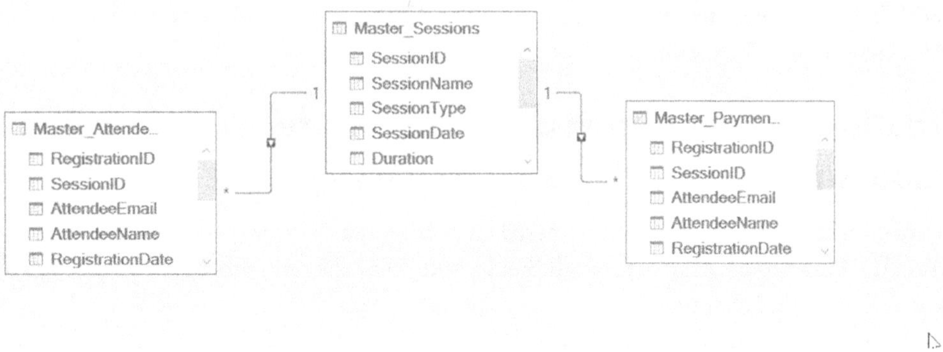

Figure 11.14 – The connected Events data model in Diagram View, with both relationships showing the 1-to-many cardinality and single-direction filter arrows

> **Tip**
>
> If you prefer a dialog to drag-and-drop, the **Manage Relationships** button on the **Design** tab in the Power Pivot window opens a list of all current relationships and lets you create new ones using dropdowns, which is useful for confirming exactly which columns are joined or for editing an existing relationship.

Why uniqueness is important and what Excel enforces

Unlike Power BI, Excel Power Pivot does not let you choose cardinality manually or set filter direction in the **user interface** (**UI**). It auto-detects both:

- **Cardinality**: Excel inspects the data and always places the 1 on the side with unique values, regardless of which end you dragged from. You cannot accidentally create the relationship "backward".
- **Filter direction**: Always flows from the unique (one) side to the many side. This is fixed — there is no option to make it bidirectional in the model UI.

What Excel cannot protect you from is a relationship where **neither side has unique values**. In that case, the relationship cannot be created at all, and Excel raises a hard error:

The relationship cannot be created because each column contains duplicate values. Select at least one column that contains only unique values.

This is precisely why the Group By check on **Master_Sessions** matters. If a duplicate SessionID had slipped through, you would not get a broken or inaccurate model — you would get no model at all. The check catches the problem before it becomes an error message mid-build.

With both relationships correctly defined, close the Power Pivot window and return to the Excel workbook. The model is ready to test.

Testing the connected events model with implicit measures

The test is straightforward: can the model answer Marcus's three questions? Build a PivotTable from the Data Model, drag in the right fields, and check the numbers against what you already know from earlier chapters.

Inserting a PivotTable from the data model

A regular PivotTable is built from a single table or range. A Data Model PivotTable draws from the connected model — all three tables at once. The field list shows every column from every table.

To insert a new PivotTable from the Data Model, click a blank cell in an empty area of the workbook and follow these steps:

1. Click the **Insert** tab
2. Click the **PivotTable** dropdown arrow
3. Click **From Data Model**

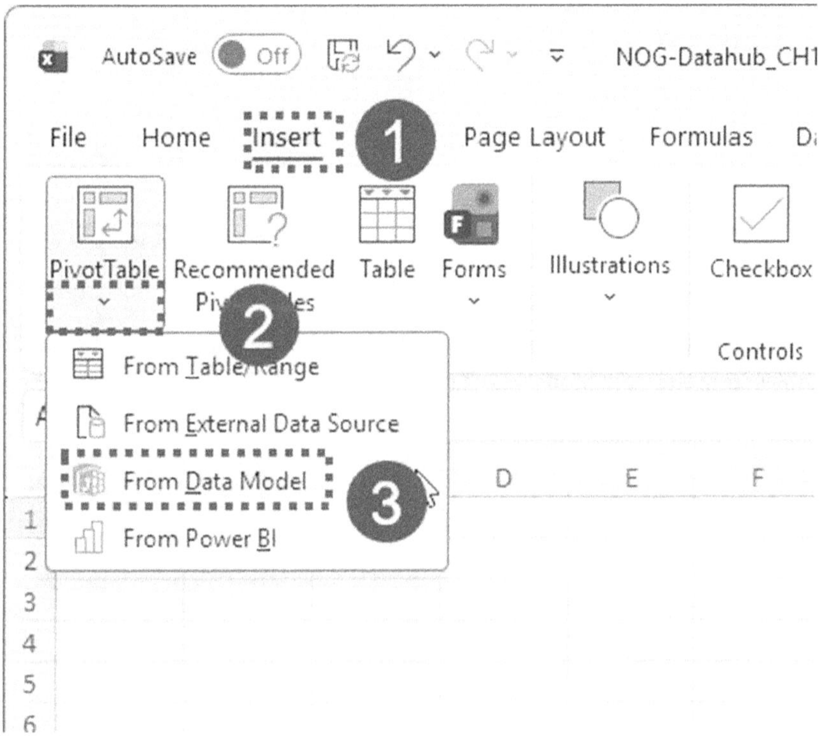

Figure 11.15 – The PivotTable dropdown on the Insert tab, with From Data Model highlighted

A dialog appears asking where to place the PivotTable:

1. Select **New Worksheet**
2. Click **OK**

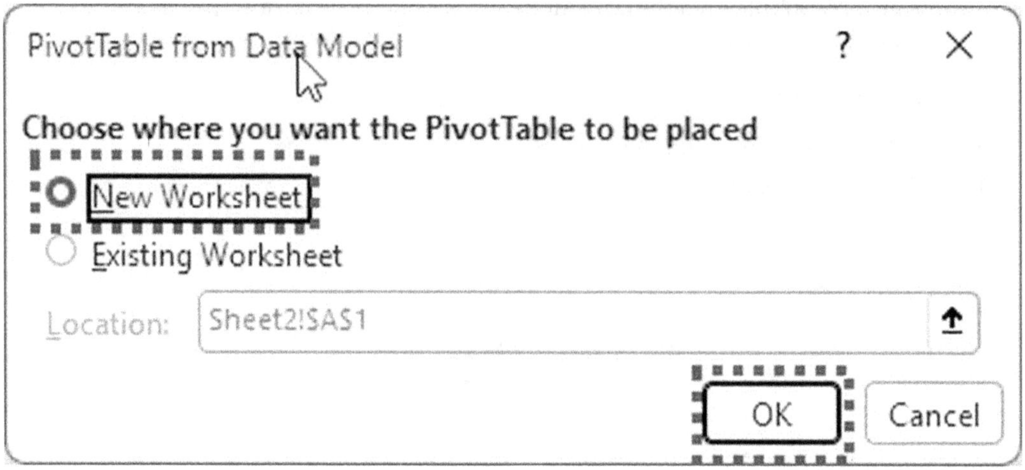

Figure 11.16 – The PivotTable placement dialog, with New Worksheet selected

Excel adds a new worksheet with an empty PivotTable, and the field list opens, showing the three tables from the Data Model. Each table is marked with a special icon that distinguishes Data Model tables from regular worksheet ranges. Expand any table to see its columns.

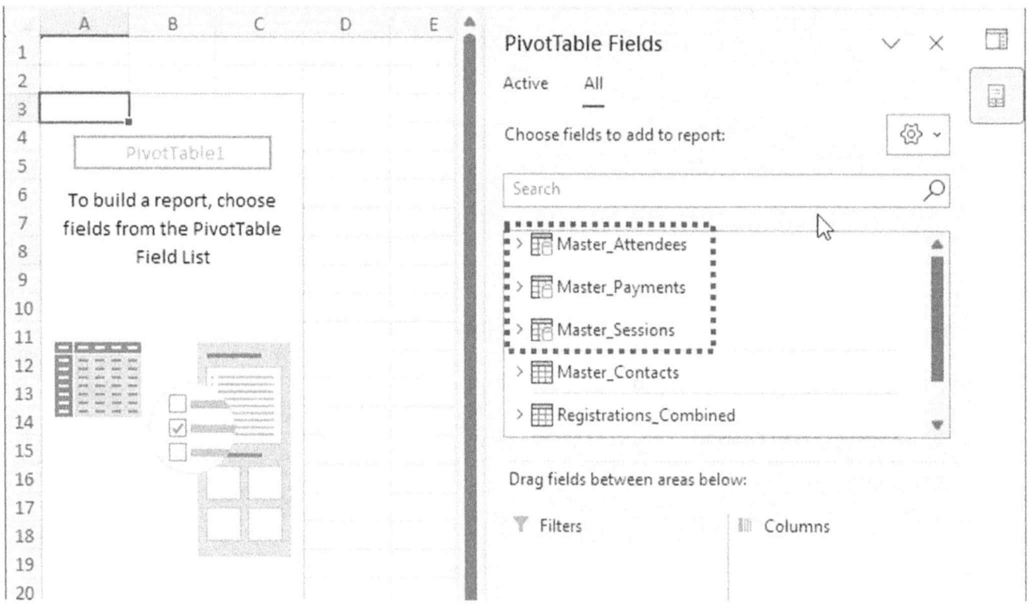

Figure 11.17 – The PivotTable field list showing Master_Sessions, Master_Attendees, and Master_Payments as Data Model tables, each marked with the Data Model table icon

Test 1: registrations by session type

Marcus's first question (which session types generate the most registrations) needs **SessionType** from **Master_Sessions** and a count of registrations from **Master_Attendees**. In a flat-table world, those live in separate queries and cannot be combined directly. In the Data Model, you drag each field from its own table.

Add the row label from the dimension:

1. In the field list, expand **Master_Sessions**
2. Drag **SessionType** to the **Rows** area

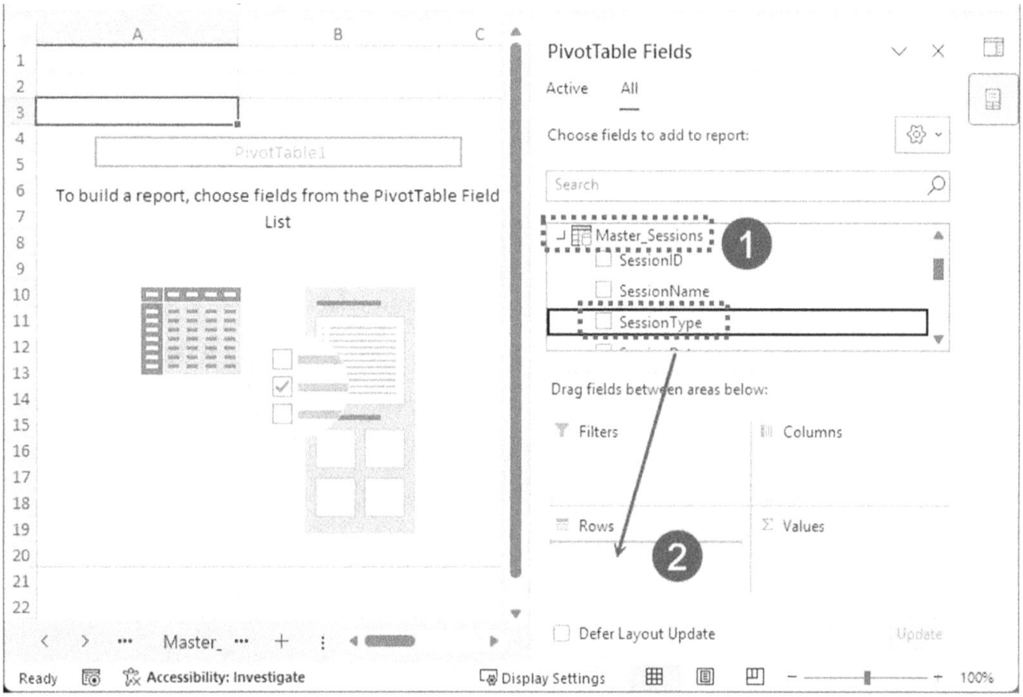

Figure 11.18 – SessionType from Master_Sessions added to the Rows area, showing session type labels in the PivotTable

Add the value to count from the fact:

1. In the field list, expand **Master_Attendees**
2. Drag **AttendeeEmail** to the **Values** area

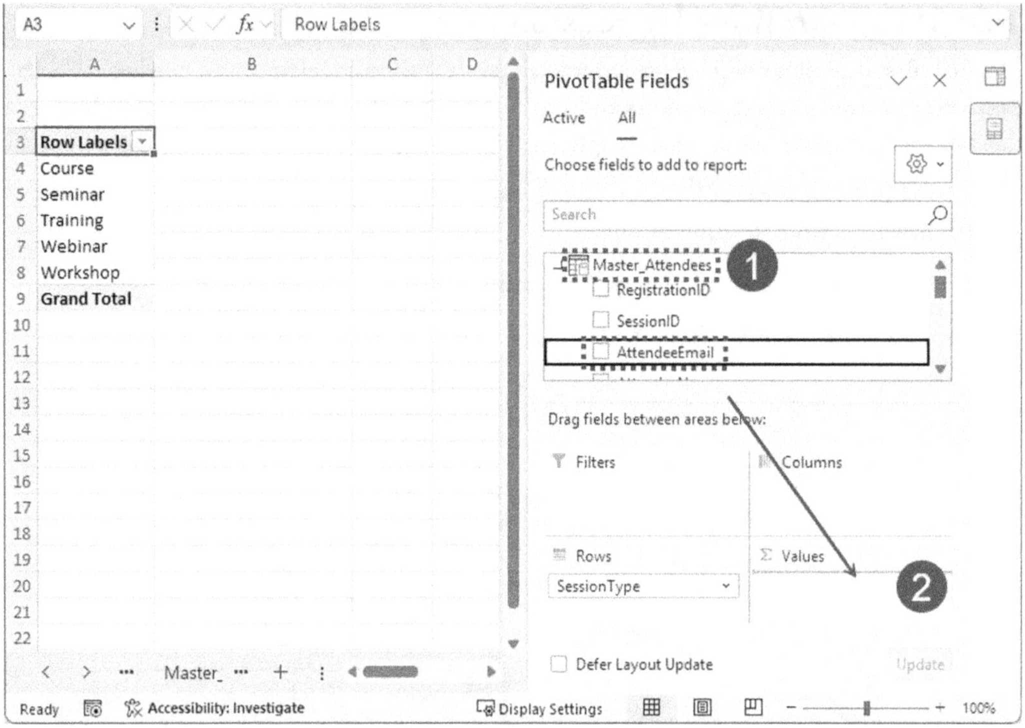

Figure 11.19 – AttendeeEmail added to the Values area, showing Count of AttendeeEmail next to each session type row

Because **AttendeeEmail** is a text column, Excel cannot sum it and sets the aggregation to **Count** automatically. Verify this is correct:

1. In the **Values** area, click the **AttendeeEmail** dropdown
2. Click **Value Field Settings**

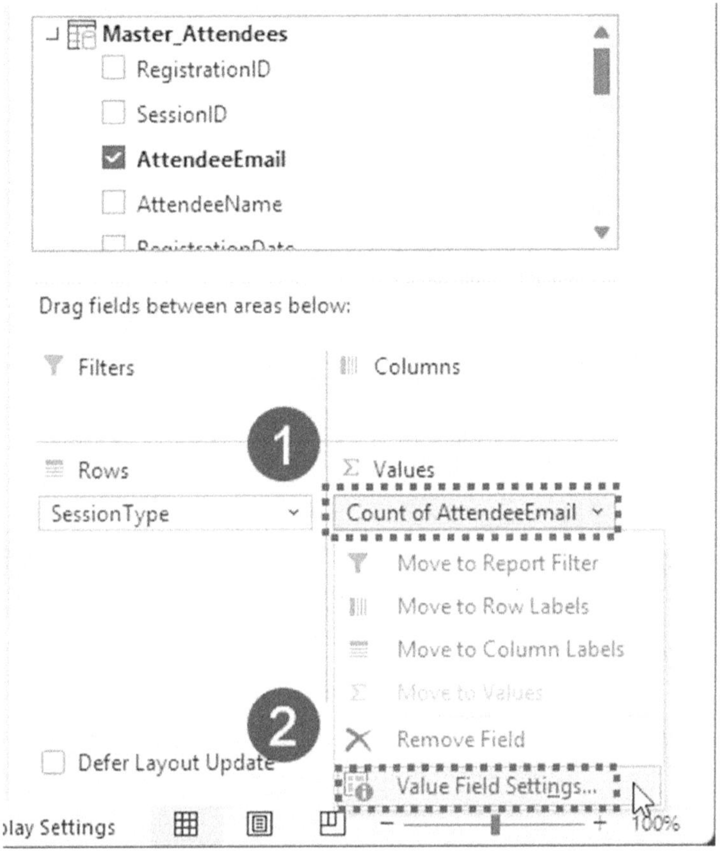

Figure 11.20 – The AttendeeEmail dropdown in the Values area, with Value Field Settings highlighted

3. Confirm **Count** is selected in the list
4. Click **OK**

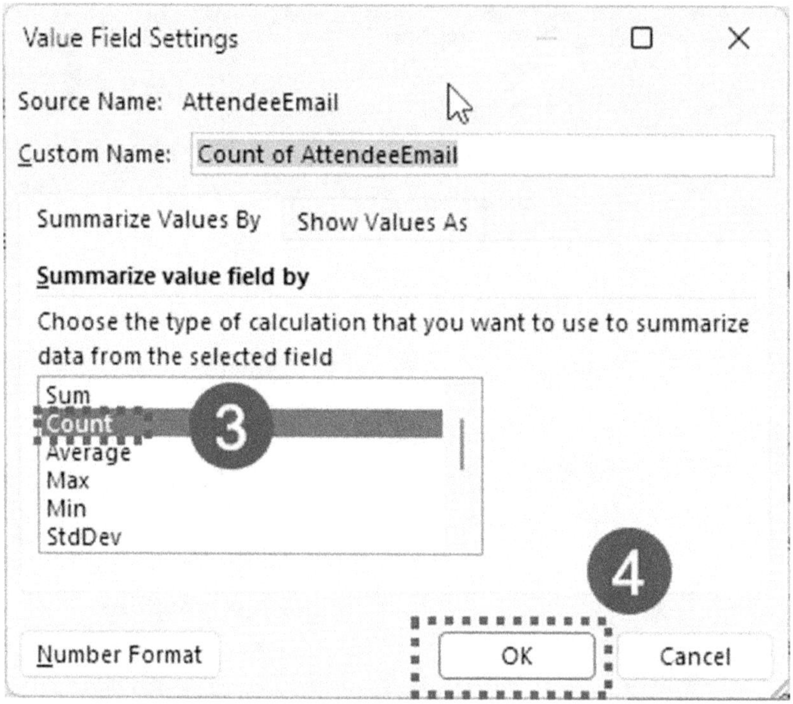

Figure 11.21 – The Value Field Settings dialog with Count selected; other operations such as Sum and Average are listed but are not meaningful for a text column

Note

For our case, only **Count** produces a meaningful result — it counts how many rows exist. Arithmetic operations (Sum, Average, Max, Min) require numeric values and will return an error for text. **Distinct Count** is also available here because this is a Data Model PivotTable — it counts unique values rather than all rows. For Marcus's question — how many registrations per session type — Count is correct.

Sort the results to put the highest registration count at the top:

1. Right-click any number in the **Count of AttendeeEmail** column
2. Click **Sort**
3. Click **Sort Largest to Smallest**

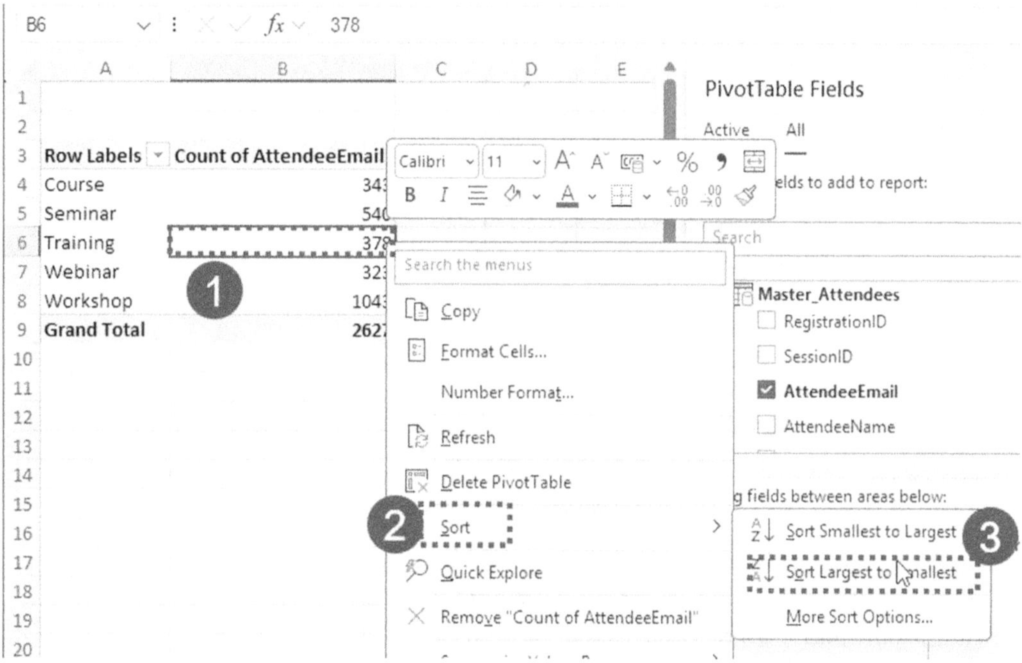

Figure 11.22 – The right-click sort menu on the Count of AttendeeEmail column, with Sort Largest to Smallest highlighted

The PivotTable reorders immediately, with the session type that has the most registrations at the top.

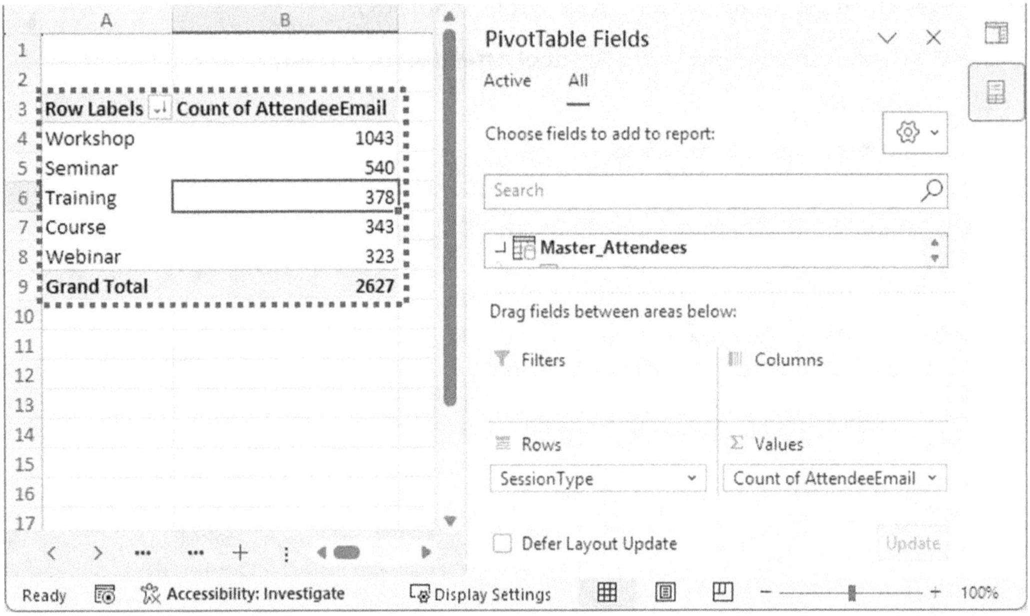

Figure 11.23 – Registrations by session type sorted descending: Workshop sessions lead, giving Marcus an immediate answer to his first question

Marcus's first question is answered. Workshop sessions generate the most registrations, sourced from two separate tables: **Master_Sessions** for the session type labels and **Master_Attendees** for the registration counts.

Test 2: payments by facilitator

The second question(which facilitators generate the most payments) needs **Facilitator** from **Master_Sessions** and **AmountPaid** from **Master_Payments**. These are from two different tables, connected through the dimension:

- Remove **SessionType** from the **Rows** area (drag it out or uncheck it in the field list)
- Remove **Count of AttendeeEmail** from the **Values** area
- From **Master_Sessions**, drag **Facilitator** to the **Rows** area
- From **Master_Payments**, drag **AmountPaid** to the **Values** area
- Confirm the value is set to **Sum of AmountPaid**

Then sort by total payments descending:

1. Right-click any number in the **Sum of AmountPaid** column
2. Click **Sort**
3. Click **Sort Largest to Smallest**

The facilitators are ranked by total payments received.

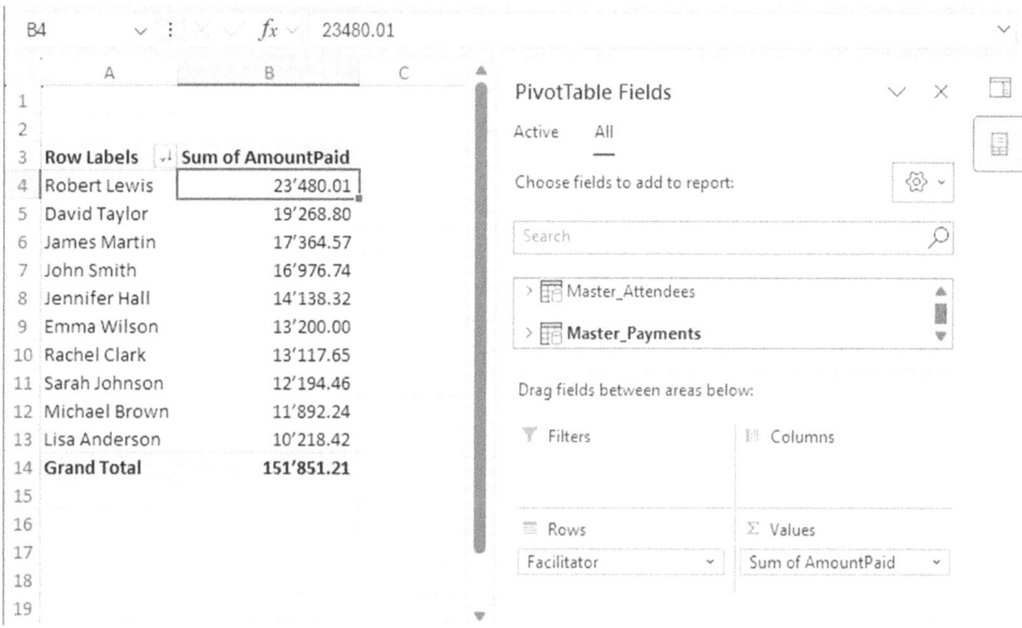

Figure 11.24 – Payments received by facilitator, sorted descending: the facilitator with the highest total payments received appears at the top, drawn from Master_Sessions and Master_Payments across the relationship

This is the cross-table moment. **AmountPaid** lives in **Master_Payments**. **Facilitator** lives in **Master_Sessions**. The relationship between them runs through **SessionID**. Without the Data Model, this PivotTable would not be possible without a manual merge.

Test 3: strongest months for both registrations and payments received

Marcus's third question asks for both metrics at once, broken down by month. Start by clearing the current PivotTable: remove **Facilitator** from the **Rows** area and **Sum of AmountPaid** from the **Values** area (drag each field out, or uncheck it in the field list).

Then add the date dimension:

1. From **Master_Sessions**, drag **SessionDate** to the **Rows** area

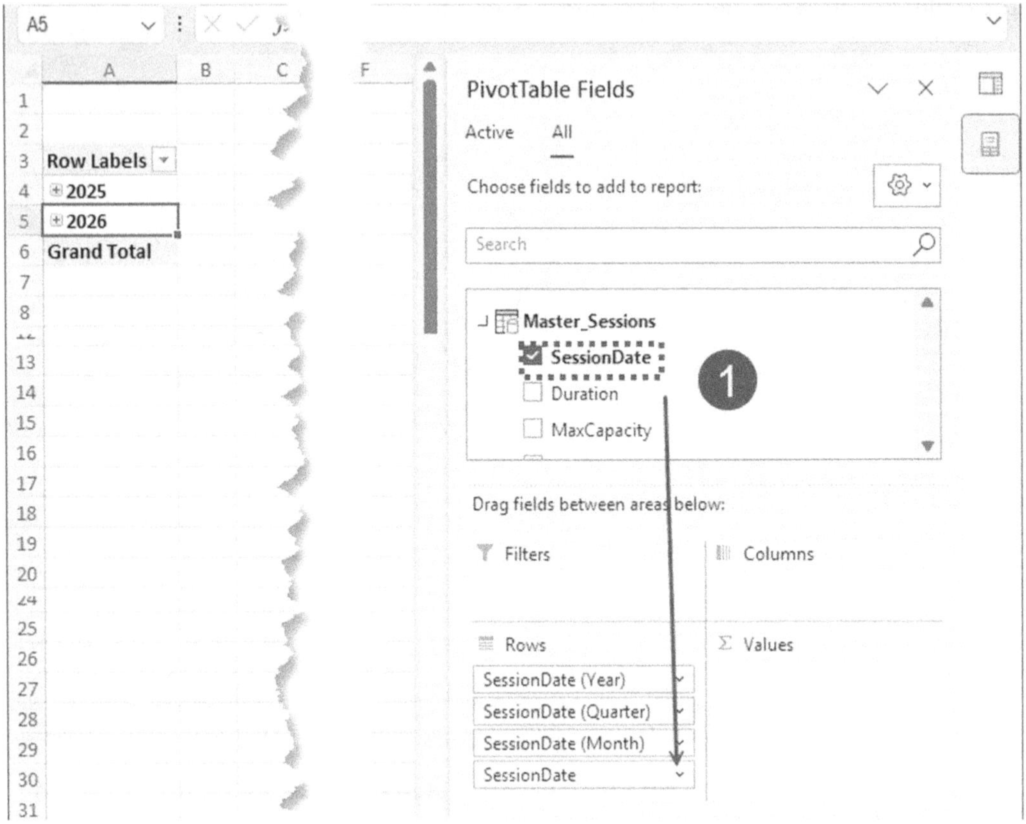

Figure 11.25 – After dragging SessionDate, Excel automatically creates a date hierarchy in the Rows area: Year, Quarter, Month, and the raw date

Excel adds four levels automatically: **SessionDate (Year)**, **SessionDate (Quarter)**, **SessionDate (Month)**, and **SessionDate** (the raw date). Keep only **Year** and **Month** by removing the other two:

2. In the **Rows** area, click the dropdown next to **SessionDate (Quarter)**
3. Click **Remove Field**
4. Click the dropdown next to **SessionDate** (the raw date level)
5. Click **Remove Field**

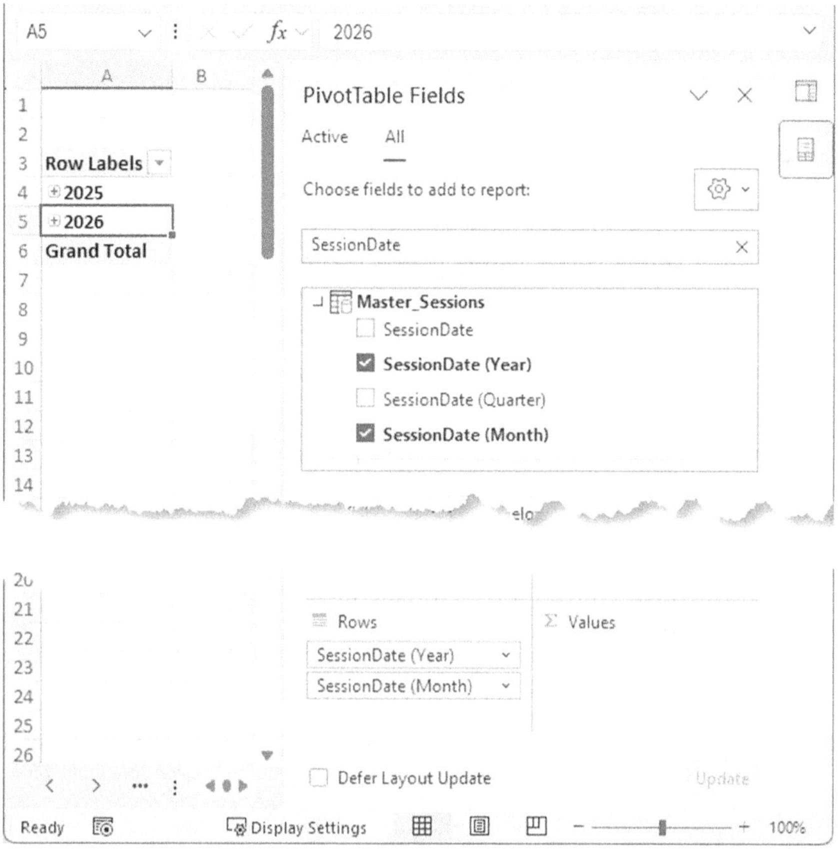

Figure 11.26 – The Rows area after removing Quarter and the raw date, leaving only Year and Month

Add both metrics to the **Values** area:

1. From **Master_Attendees**, drag **AttendeeEmail** to the **Values** area
2. Confirm the value is set to **Count of AttendeeEmail**
3. From **Master_Payments**, drag **AmountPaid** to the **Values** area
4. Confirm the value is set to **Sum of AmountPaid**
5. Click the **+** next to each year in the PivotTable to expand it and reveal the monthly breakdown

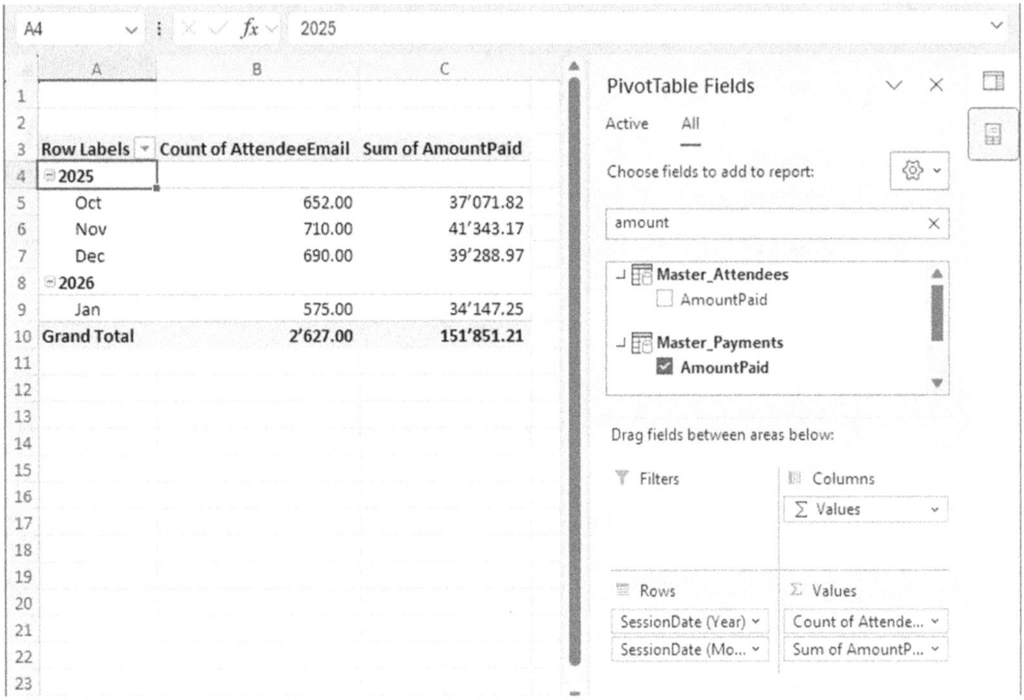

Figure 11.27 – Both metrics by month: registrations (Count of AttendeeEmail) and payments received (Sum of AmountPaid) side by side, with months derived from SessionDate in the dimension table

The PivotTable now shows both counts and sums, broken down by month, with all data sourced across three connected tables.

All three of Marcus's questions are answered in one connected model.

Running the trust loop

Before sharing any numbers, run a quick sanity check against what you already know:

- The grand total for **Count of AttendeeEmail** should match the total row count of **Master_Attendees** from *Chapter 8*
- The grand total for **Sum of AmountPaid** should match the total sum you verified in **Master_Payments** at the end of *Chapter 9*
- If either total is unexpected, check the relationship direction in Power Pivot Diagram View before looking elsewhere

> **Note**
>
> If you compare the total payments here (Sum of AmountPaid) with the **Revenue** column in **Weekly_Event_KPIs** from *Chapter 4*, the numbers will differ. This is intentional: the KPI file contains management estimates, not actual payment records. The sum of **AmountPaid** in **Master_Payments** reflects confirmed transactions from the payment provider. Which source to trust depends on the question. Marcus's "actual payments collected" question is better answered by the Payments data.

Quinn saves the file and sends Marcus a quick message: results ready.

Marcus appears at the desk three minutes later, laptop in hand. The PivotTable on screen shows the monthly view: registrations and payments side by side. Quinn swaps the fields twice, replaying the other two answers: session types ranked by registrations, then facilitators ranked by payments received. "That's the three questions," Marcus says.

"One model," Quinn says. "Add a fourth question and you drag a field. No new queries."

Marcus nods slowly. "What about attendance rate? Like, what percentage of registrations actually showed up?"

Quinn glances at the field list. The data is there — registrations and attendance status both sitting in **Master_Attendees**. But a percentage is not a drag-and-drop. "That one needs a formula. Built into the model itself."

"Can you do that?"

Summary

In this chapter, you built a connected Events data model: **Master_Sessions**, **Master_Attendees**, and **Master_Payments** linked in the Excel Data Model so that any PivotTable can draw from all three tables at once, without a merge query. Four steps made this possible:

- **Start with the questions**: Marcus's three questions showed which columns needed to come from which tables, making the model structure clear before a single relationship was created.
- **Verify the key before connecting**: The Group By check confirmed that SessionID was unique in **Master_Sessions**. A duplicate key prevents the relationship from being created entirely. The check catches the problem before it becomes an error mid-build.

- **Create the relationships**: Dragging the **SessionID** between the dimension and each fact table in Diagram View built both one-to-many relationships.
- **Test with implicit measures**: Dragging fields from different tables into a single PivotTable answered all three of Marcus's questions without a formula: registrations by session type, payments by facilitator, and both metrics side by side by month.

In *Chapter 12*, Marcus comes back with one more question: what percentage of registered attendees actually showed up? Counts and sums can be dragged into a PivotTable. A percentage cannot. The next chapter introduces DAX, explicit measures written directly into the model, starting with the three that build on the tables you connected here.

12

Answer Questions with Your First DAX Measures

Figure 12.1 – Marcus Has Follow-Up Questions

Marcus is still standing beside Quinn's desk; his laptop tucked under his arm.

"Can you get the attendance rate from the model?" he asks. "The percentage of registered people who actually showed up, as a formula that recalculates automatically?"

Quinn glances across the office. Hannah has not moved from her desk, but she is watching. "Come and see," Hannah calls.

Marcus raises an eyebrow at Quinn. They walk over together.

Hannah pulls two chairs close to her screen. "The model Quinn built is solid," she says. "Three tables, two relationships. That's all you need." She opens the Power Pivot window. "But attendance rate isn't something you can get by dragging a column. You need to tell the model what to calculate. That's what a **measure** is."

"A formula?" Marcus asks.

"A named formula," Hannah says. "One you write once and store in the model. It shows up in your field list like any other column. Drop it into a PivotTable, it calculates. Change the filter, slice by session type, it recalculates. No rebuilding."

Marcus nods slowly. "And it handles the attendance rate?"

"Once we write it, yes." Hannah looks at Quinn. "Shall we?"

Quinn opens a blank cell in the calculation area. "Let's go."

In this chapter, you'll learn to -

- Explain why some business questions require DAX measures rather than simple drag-and-drop aggregations
- Distinguish between columns and measures, and between implicit and explicit measures, so you know when to write a formula
- Create three core measures: **[Total Registrations]**, **[Total Attendees]**, and **[Attendance Rate]** using `COUNTROWS`, `FILTER`, and `DIVIDE`, each building on the previous
- Test the measures in PivotTables and confirm they answer Marcus's attendance questions accurately

Technical requirements

The chapters in this book build on each other. Make sure you have completed all exercises in the previous chapter before starting this one.

To follow along with this chapter, you will need:

- Microsoft Excel 2016 or later with Power Query, accessed via **Data** | **Get & Transform Data**
- The **Power Pivot add-in** enabled in Excel (set up in *Chapter 11*)
- Your `NOG-DataHub` workbook from *Chapter 11* (NOG stands for Northbridge Office Group), with the Events data model fully built, the following three tables loaded into the Excel Data Model and the two relationships between them defined on SessionID:
    - **Master_Sessions** (dimension, with a unique SessionID per row)

- **Master_Attendees** (fact, with one row per registration)
- **Master_Payments** (fact, with one row per payment transaction)
- Relationship: **Master_Sessions** (1) → **Master_Attendees** (*) on **SessionID**
- Relationship: **Master_Sessions** (1) → **Master_Payments** (*) on **SessionID**

> Note
>
> If you want to confirm your model matches this list, open the Power Pivot window (click the **Data** tab, then **Manage Data Model**) and switch to **Diagram View**. Both relationships should be visible there, exactly as you built them in *Chapter 11*.

No new exercise files are needed for this chapter. All work builds on the Events model already in your workbook.

Why DAX Matters

In *Chapter 11*, you answered Marcus's three questions using implicit measures, dragging **AttendeeEmail** into the **Values** area, let Excel count registrations, and dragging **AmountPaid** let it calculate the sum of payments. That approach works well for straightforward aggregations. It does not work for calculations that involve conditions or ratios.

Marcus's new question goes a step further: what percentage of registered people actually showed up? Attendance rate requires counting a specific subset of rows (only those where attendance is confirmed) and dividing by the total. That calculation cannot be expressed by dragging a single column.

That is what **Data Analysis Expressions** (**DAX**) is for. DAX is the formula language built into the Excel Data Model and Power BI. You do not need to learn the whole language; this chapter introduces three functions that cover one of the most common questions business users need to answer.

What a measure is

A measure is a named DAX formula stored in the model rather than a cell; you define it once and reuse it anywhere. Unlike a cell formula, a measure has no fixed location in a spreadsheet. Instead, it lives in the model and calculates a single result based on whatever is currently being shown in the PivotTable, the session type in the row, the month in the column, and the slicer selection. Change any filter, and the measure recalculates automatically.

Once a measure is created, it appears in the PivotTable field list alongside the table's columns. You drag it into the **Values** area exactly as you would any other field. The difference is that the result is always the calculation you defined: consistent, named, and reusable across every PivotTable in the workbook.

> **AI Helper**
>
> If a DAX formula returns an unexpected result or an error message, copy the error text and ask an LLM such as ChatGPT, but give it enough context to help: `I am writing a DAX measure in Excel Power Pivot. My model has three tables: Master_Sessions (one row per session, unique SessionID), Master_Attendees (one row per registration, SessionID foreign key), and Master_Payments (one row per payment, SessionID foreign key). I got this error: [paste error]. My formula is: [paste formula]. What does this error mean and how do I fix it?`
>
> The LLM can explain the message in plain language and suggest corrections. Always test the fix in Excel and verify the result against a number you already know. The LLM does not have access to your data.

Now that you know what a measure is, let's look at the concepts you need before writing the first one.

Columns, measures, and the difference

Before writing any DAX, it helps to be clear about two distinctions. Both are easy to mix up at first, and both affect how you think about the formulas in this chapter.

Columns versus measures

A **calculated column** is a new column added to a table inside Power Pivot, with one fixed value per row, computed once at load time and stored with the data. It is worth knowing the term exists, because you will see it mentioned in DAX documentation and tutorials. However, this book does not use calculated columns, and as a general rule they are best avoided: they consume memory for every row in the table, their values are static, and most things people reach for a calculated column to do are better handled either in Power Query (before the data reaches the model) or as a measure.

A **measure** is different. It has no rows. It returns a single aggregated result based on which rows are currently visible in the PivotTable. The same measure can return 47 in one cell and 12 in the cell below it, because each cell has a different set of rows in scope. Measures stay lean, recalculate on demand, and work correctly with every filter and slicer you add.

Every formula in this chapter is a measure.

Implicit versus explicit measures

In *Chapter 11*, you dragged **AttendeeEmail** into the **Values** area and Excel automatically created a "Count of AttendeeEmail" aggregation. That is an **implicit measure**; Excel generates it on the spot, with a generic name, and it disappears when you remove the field from the PivotTable.

An **explicit measure** is one you write yourself and name deliberately. It is stored in the model and appears in the field list permanently.

With those two distinctions clear, you are ready to write your first measure.

Building your first measure

All measures in this chapter are written in the same place: the calculation area in Power Pivot. This is the wide, gray area directly below the rows of data in Power Pivot's Data View. Clicking a blank cell there and typing a formula is the most direct way to create a measure; the formula bar at the top of the window shows exactly what you are typing, and the result appears in the cell as soon as you press Enter.

Opening the calculation area

Open Power Pivot from Excel:

1. Click the **Data** tab
2. Click **Manage Data Model**

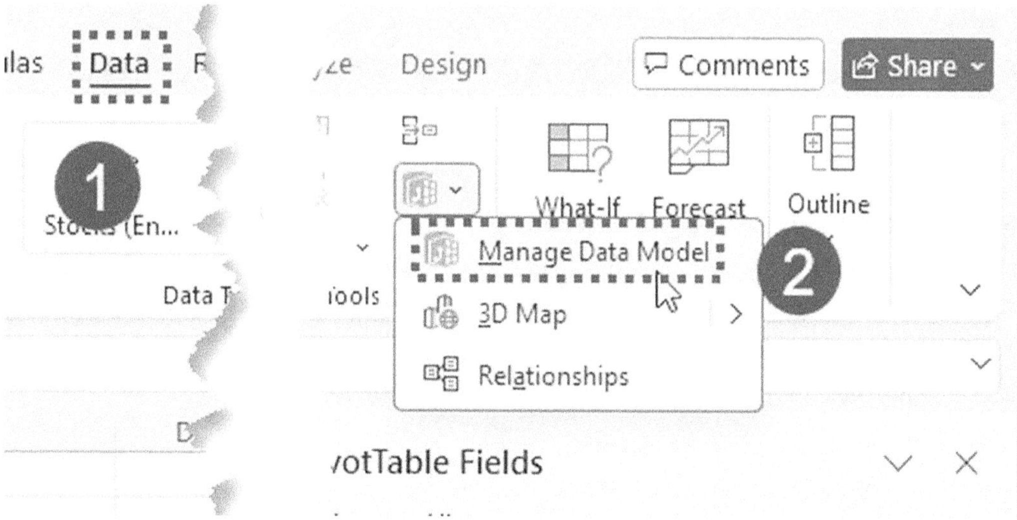

Figure 12.2 – The Manage Data Model button on the Data tab, used to open the Power Pivot window

The Power Pivot window opens in **Data View**, showing the tables as tabs along the bottom. Click the **Master_Attendees** tab to make it active.

At the bottom of the **Data View**, below the thick gray line, you will find the calculation area (see *Figure 12.3*), the empty rows where measures are stored. This is where the measures for this chapter will be.

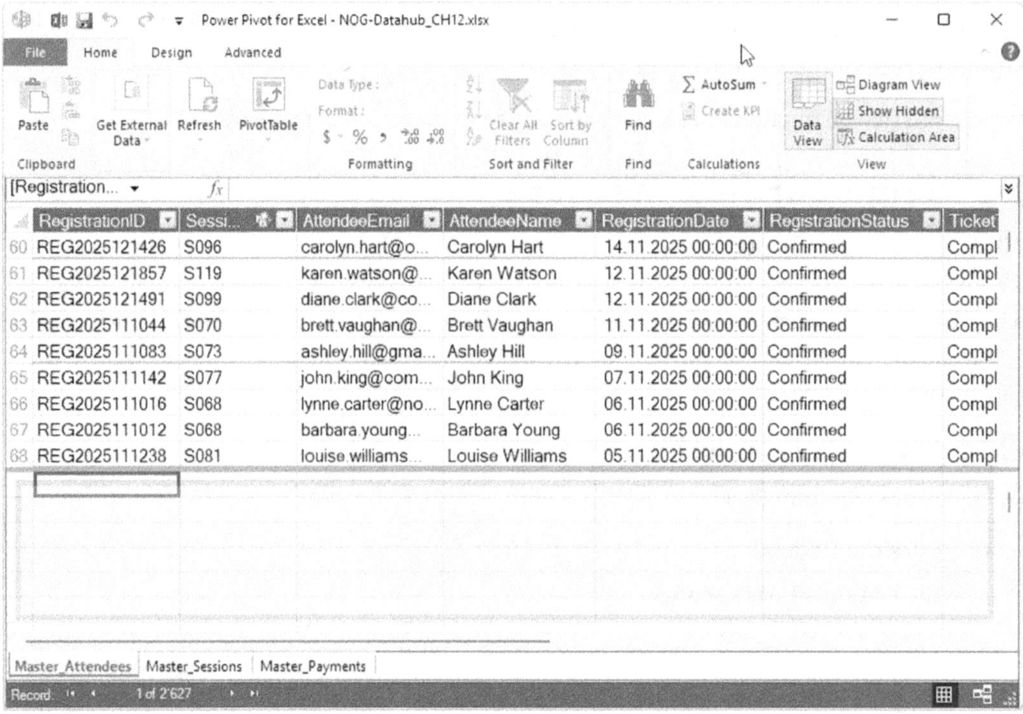

Figure 12.3 – The Power Pivot Data View with Master_Attendees active, showing the calculation area below the thick gray line

Measure 1: [Total Registrations]

The first measure answers the simplest question: how many registrations are in the model? Writing it explicitly gives it a clear name and, as you will see shortly, makes it available as a building block inside the next two measures.

Click a blank cell in the calculation area and write the measure:

1. Click any blank cell in the **calculation area**
2. In the **formula bar** at the top of the Power Pivot window, type

```
Total Registrations:=COUNTROWS(Master_Attendees)
```

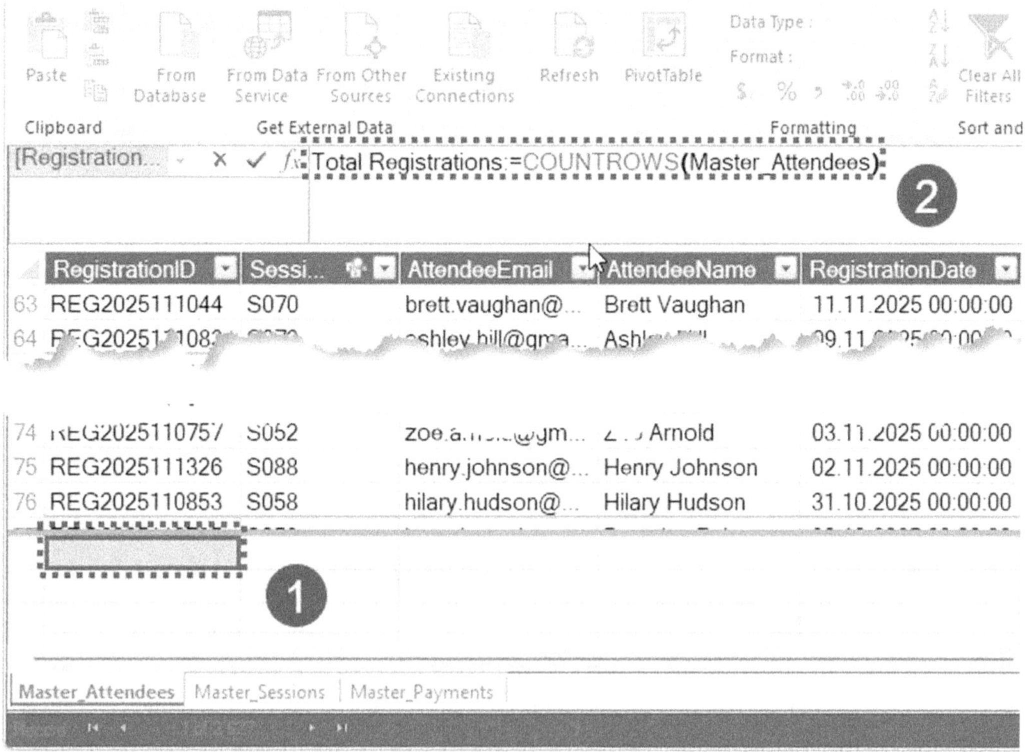

Figure 12.4 – The formula typed in the formula bar before pressing Enter

3. Press *Enter*

The cell in the calculation area now shows the total row count for the full table. The measure is saved.

If you see the measure name but no number, the column is simply too narrow; drag the column edge wider until the result is visible.

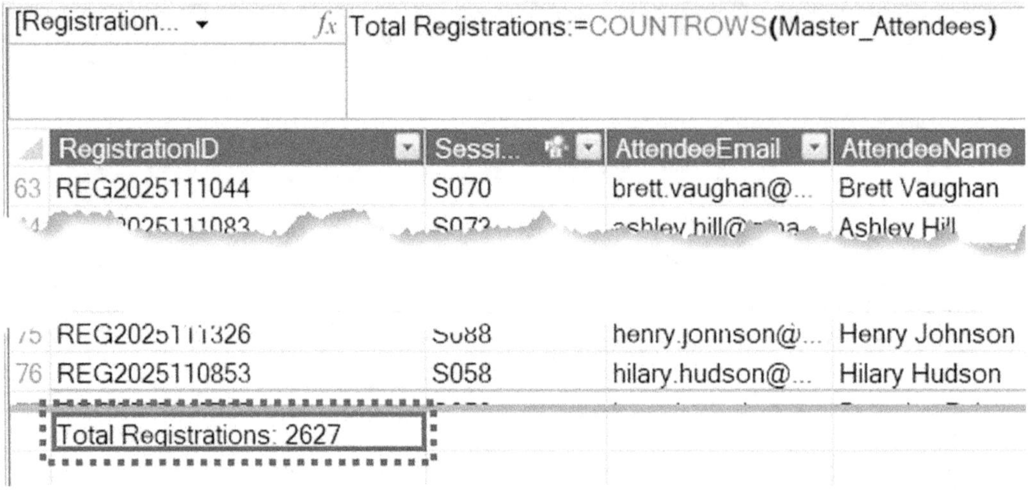

Figure 12.5 – The calculation area cell showing the row count for [Total Registrations] after pressing Enter

`COUNTROWS` counts every row in the table. In our case, it returns the total number of rows in **Master_Attendees**, one per registration.

Test the measure in a PivotTable. Close the Power Pivot window and switch back to the Excel workbook. Then, open a PivotTable from the Data Model, use the one from *Chapter 11*, or insert a new one:

1. Click a blank cell on any sheet
2. Click the **Insert** tab
3. Click the **PivotTable** dropdown arrow
4. Click **From Data Model**

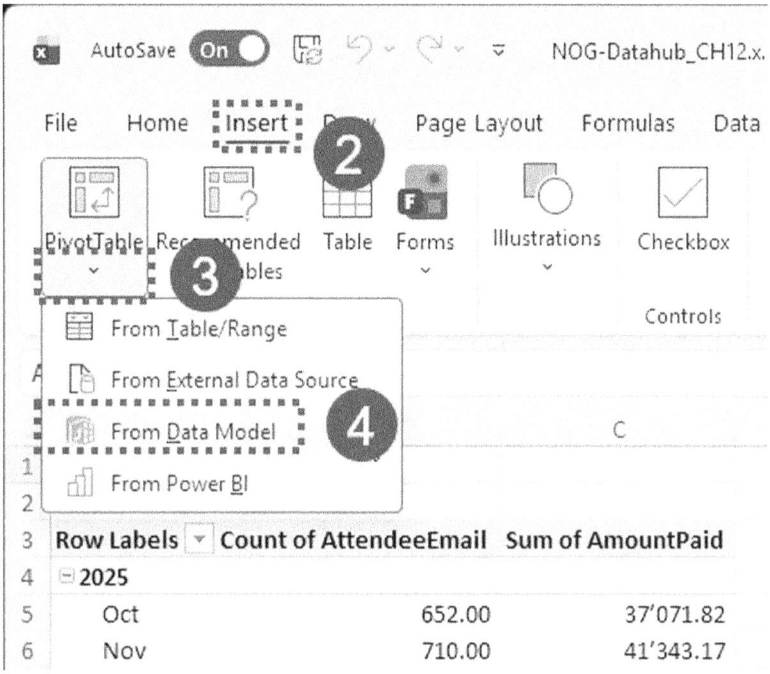

Figure 12.6 – The Insert tab PivotTable menu with From Data Model highlighted

5. Select **New Worksheet** and click **OK**
6. In the field list, expand **Master_Attendees**. The new **[Total Registrations]** measure appears there, marked with an "fx" icon.
7. Drag **[Total Registrations]** to the **Values** area
8. Drag **SessionType** from **Master_Sessions** to the **Rows** area

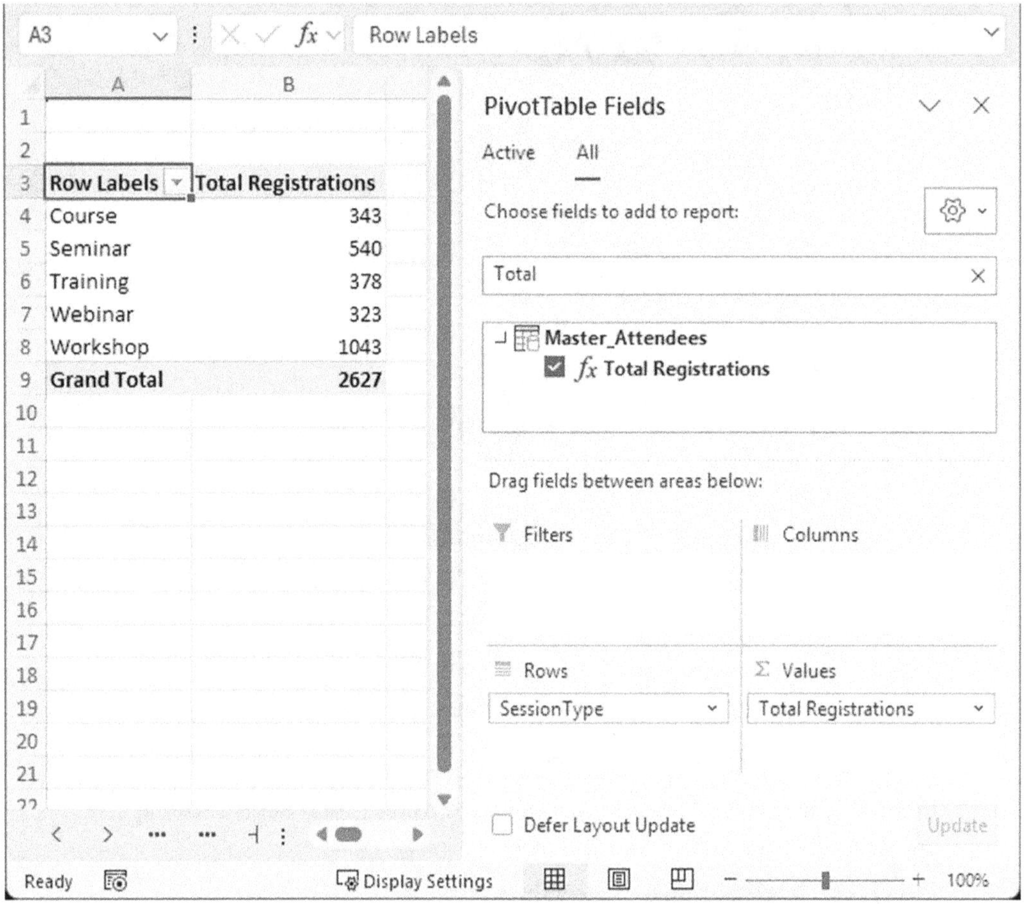

Figure 12.7 – [Total Registrations] by SessionType, confirming the measure is using the relationship between Master_Attendees and Master_Sessions correctly

The grand total should match the total row count you verified for **Master_Attendees** in *Chapter 8*. That is your trust check: if the number looks wrong, stop here and compare against the source before writing the next measure.

With the foundation measure in place, the next step is to build **[Total Attendees]**, which requires a new tool.

Using FILTER for conditional measures

[Total Registrations] counts every row in **Master_Attendees**. But to calculate the attendance rate, you need to count only a subset of those rows: the ones where the person actually attended. That means applying a condition inside the measure itself. This is what the **FILTER** function does.

How FILTER works

FILTER takes a table and a condition, and returns a smaller version of that table containing only the rows that meet the condition. This basically applies a filter in Power Query, but inside a DAX formula, evaluated fresh for every cell in the PivotTable.

The pattern is:

```
FILTER(TableName, TableName[ColumnName] = "Value")
```

The result is not a number, but a filtered table. To turn it into a number, wrap it in `COUNTROWS`, which counts the rows in whatever table it receives.

```
COUNTROWS(FILTER(TableName, TableName[ColumnName] = "Value"))
```

Measure 2: [Total Attendees]

For the attendance question, the condition is that **AttendanceStatus** equals "Attended."

> **Note**
>
> In the Power Pivot formula bar, press *Shift* + *Enter* to add a new line without confirming the formula, and *Tab* to indent. This lets you write each function on its own line and indent arguments, making the logic easier to read and debug. The formula above is shown formatted; typing it on a single line works equally well—Power Pivot does not require any specific layout.

Write the second measure:

1. Return to the **Power Pivot** window (click the **Data** tab and then **Manage Data Model** if it is closed)
2. Click a new blank cell in the **calculation area**
3. In the **formula bar**, type:

```
Total Attendees :=
COUNTROWS(
    FILTER(
        Master_Attendees,
        Master_Attendees[AttendanceStatus] = "Attended"
```

```
    )
)
```

4. Press *Enter*

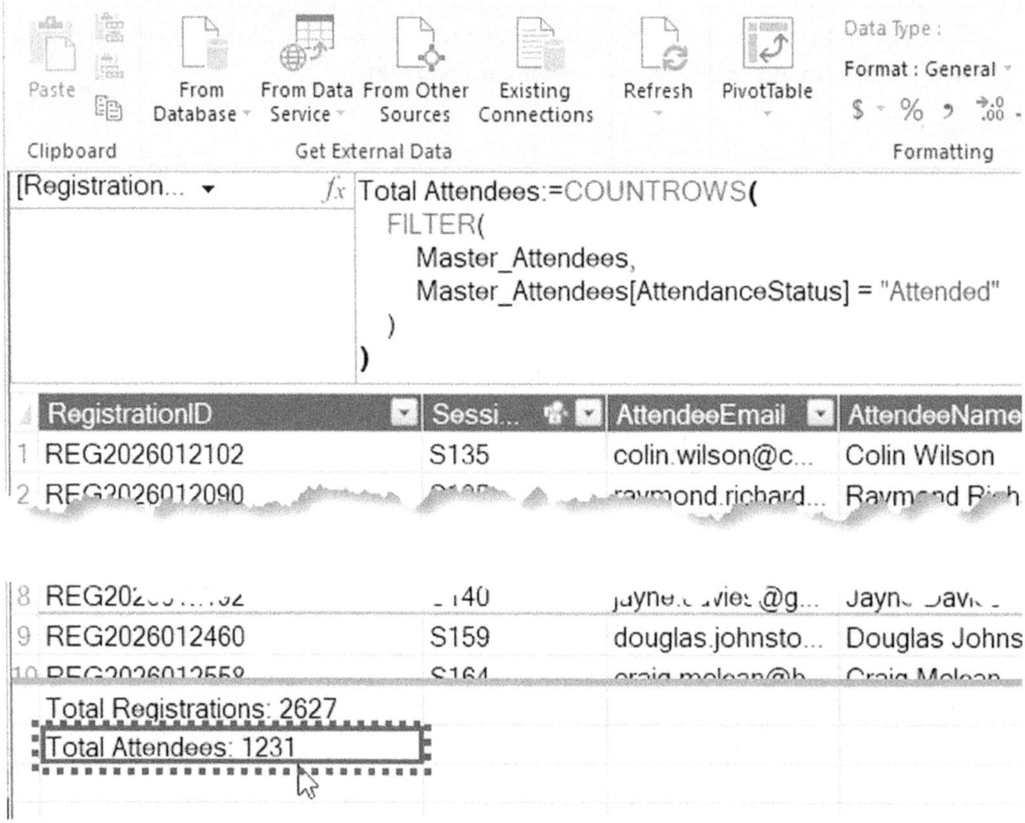

Figure 12.8 – The [Total Attendees] measure in the formula bar, showing FILTER nested inside COUNTROWS and value of calculation

Test it alongside **[Total Registrations]**: switch back to the Excel workbook and open the worksheet with the PivotTable you inserted when testing your first measure, then drag **[Total Attendees]** to the **Values** area. With **SessionType** in the rows, each cell now shows both the total registrations and the number who attended for that session category.

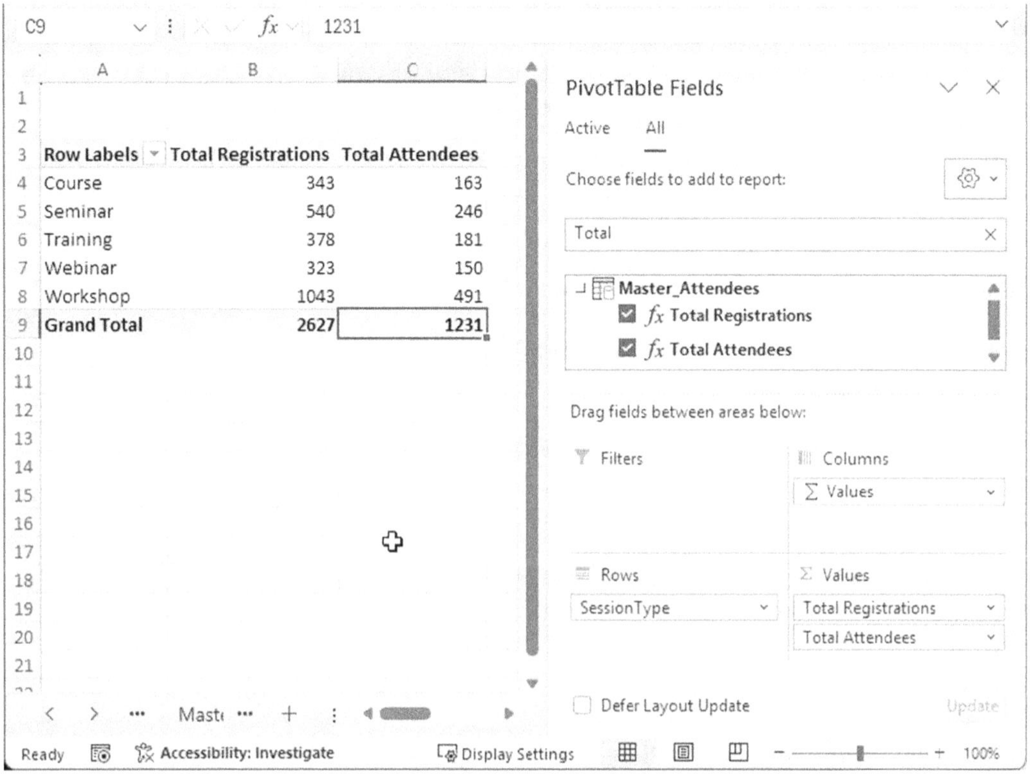

Figure 12.9 – [Total Registrations] and [Total Attendees] side by side by SessionType; [Total Attendees] is always equal to or less than [Total Registrations]

[Total Attendees] should always be equal to or less than **[Total Registrations]**. If it is higher for any row, check the **AttendanceStatus** values in **Master_Attendees**; there may be a spelling variant that is matching unexpectedly.

> **Caution**
>
> If **[Total Attendees]** returns zero for all rows, check the exact text in the **AttendanceStatus** column of **Master_Attendees**. The `FILTER` condition uses "Attended" with a capital A. If the source data uses a different capitalization or spelling (for example, "attended" or "ATTENDED") the condition will not match. Open **Master_Attendees** in Power Query, check the **AttendanceStatus** column values, and adjust the formula to match.

Measure 3: [Attendance Rate]

With **[Total Registrations]** and **[Total Attendees]** both written, the third measure simply divides one by the other. This is where the measures start working together.

The `DIVIDE` function takes two arguments (a numerator and a denominator) and returns their quotient. Unlike the plain / operator, `DIVIDE` returns blank instead of an error when the denominator is zero, which keeps the PivotTable clean when a session has no registrations.

Return to Power Pivot and write the third measure:

1. Click a new blank cell in the **calculation area**
2. In the **formula bar**, type

```
Attendance Rate:=DIVIDE([Total Attendees],[Total Registrations])
```

3. Press *Enter*

Notice that the formula references **[Total Attendees]** and **[Total Registrations]** by name, the measures you wrote in this chapter. DAX measures can call other measures, which is exactly why writing them as named building blocks is useful.

Format the measure as a percentage:

1. Click the **[Attendance Rate]** measure cell in the calculation area
2. Click the **Home** tab
3. Click the **Format** | **General** dropdown in the **Formatting** group
4. Click **Percentage**

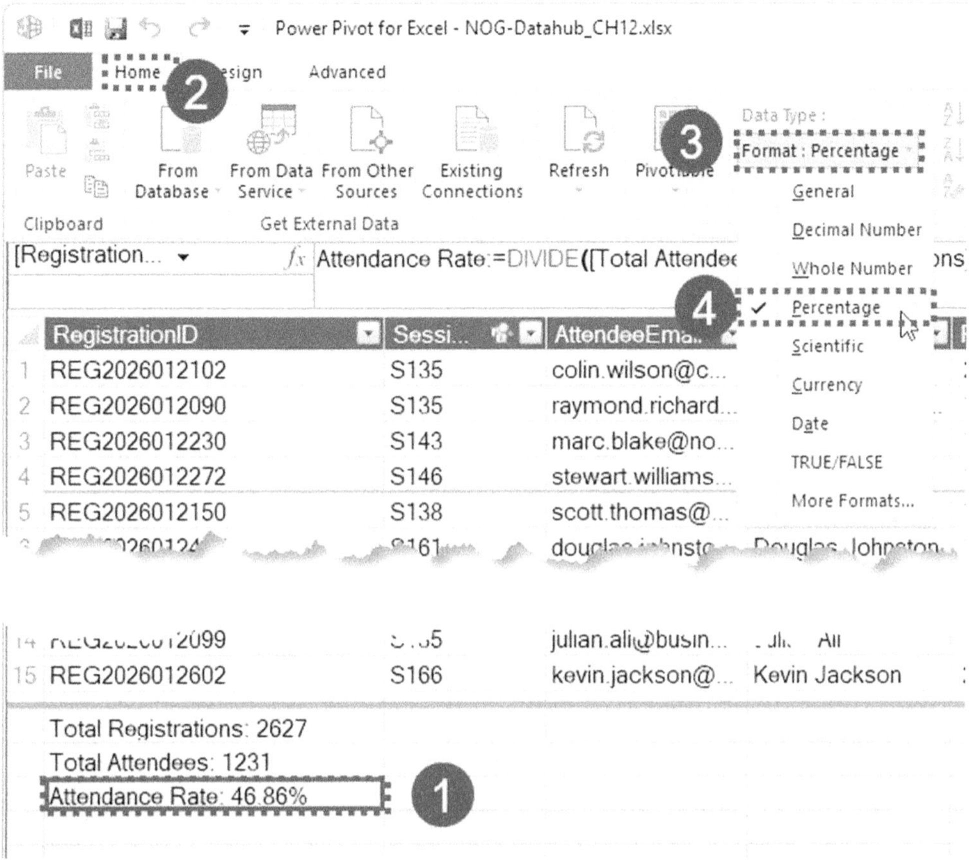

Figure 12.10 – The Format dropdown on the Home tab with Percentage selected for the [Attendance Rate] measure

5. Test in the PivotTable by dragging **[Attendance Rate]** to the **Values** area

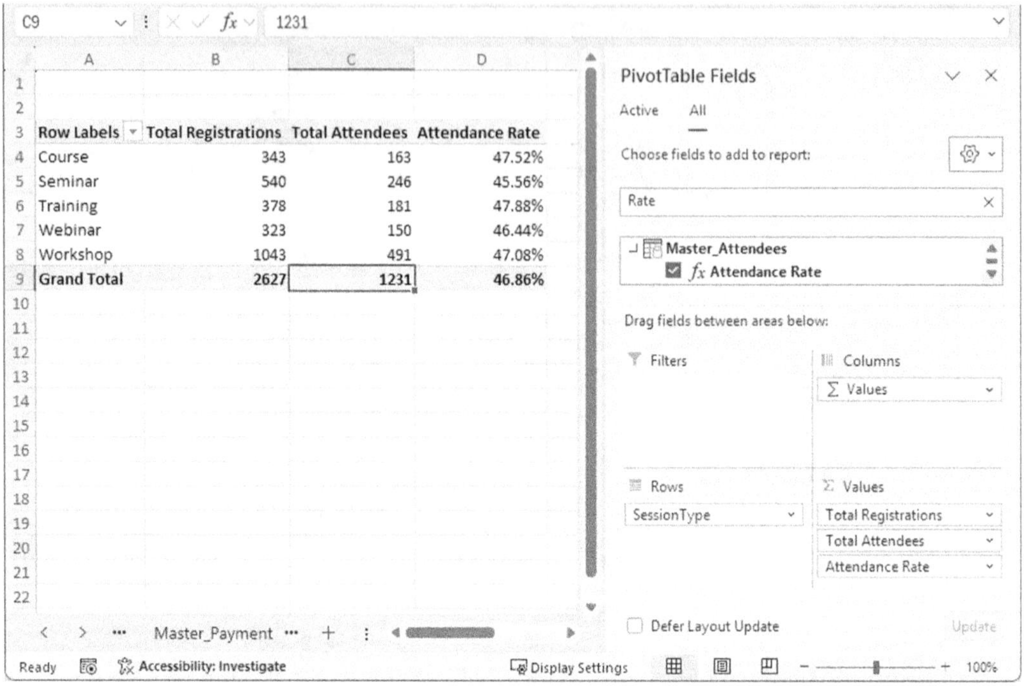

Figure 12.11 – All three measures side by side by SessionType: [Total Registrations], [Total Attendees], and [Attendance Rate] as a percentage

6. **Verify one row manually**. Pick any SessionType, note its **[Total Attendees]** and **[Total Registrations]** values, and divide them with a calculator. The result should match **[Attendance Rate]** to one decimal place. If it does, the measure is correct.

> **Note**
>
> DAX is a deep language with many more functions and patterns beyond what this chapter covers. If you want to explore further (for example, adding payment totals, calculating averages, or applying time intelligence) search for "DAX for beginners" or describe a specific question to an LLM and ask it to suggest the right formula pattern. The three measures in this chapter are enough to see how DAX thinks; the rest builds from here.

All three measures are now written and tested.

Testing and organizing metrics for stakeholders

The PivotTable with all three measures is already on the sheet from the testing steps. The final task is to give that sheet a proper name and add a slicer so Marcus can filter by facilitator.

Finishing the events performance page

Right-click the sheet tab and rename it `Events Performance`.

Add a **Month** breakdown by dragging **SessionDate** from **Master_Sessions** to the **Rows** area below **SessionType**. Excel creates a date hierarchy automatically, just as it did in *Chapter 11*. If you are reusing that chapter's PivotTable, the extra levels may already be removed; in that case, skip the next two steps. Otherwise, remove the Quarter and raw date levels to keep only Year and Month:

1. In the **Rows** area, click the dropdown next to **SessionDate (Quarter)** and click **Remove Field**
2. Click the dropdown next to **SessionDate** (the raw date) and click **Remove Field**

The rows now show SessionType with Year and Month nested inside each category.

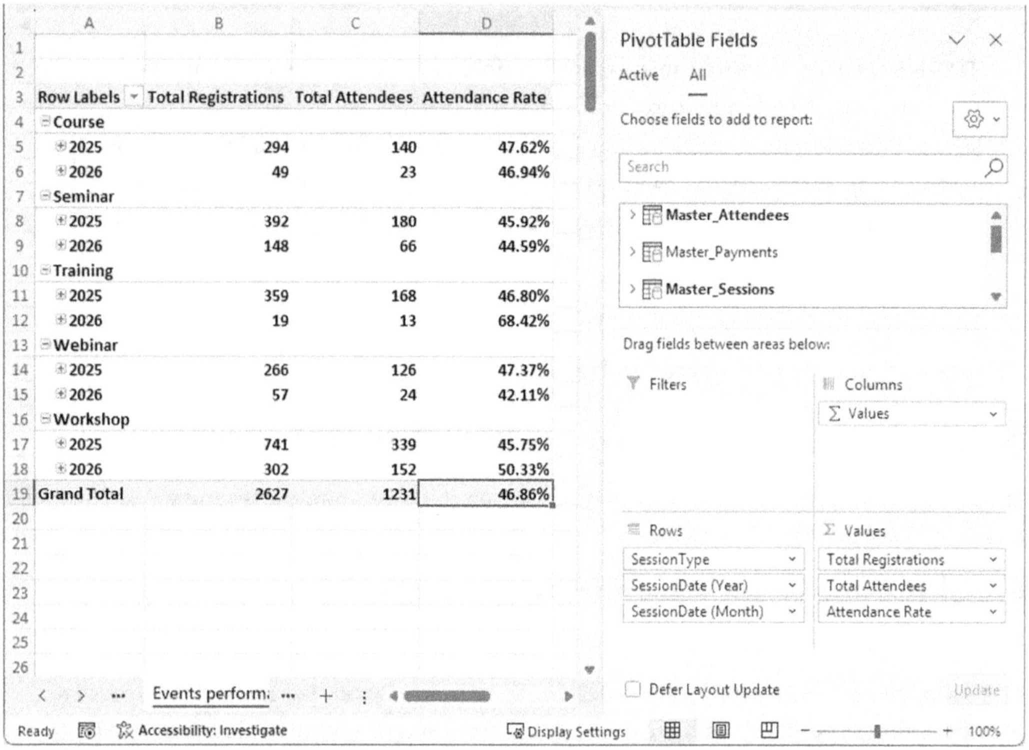

Figure 12.12 – The PivotTable with SessionType and Month nested in the Rows area

Add a **Facilitator** slicer so Marcus can filter the page to a specific facilitator:

1. Click anywhere inside the PivotTable
2. Click the **PivotTable Analyze** tab
3. Click **Insert Slicer**

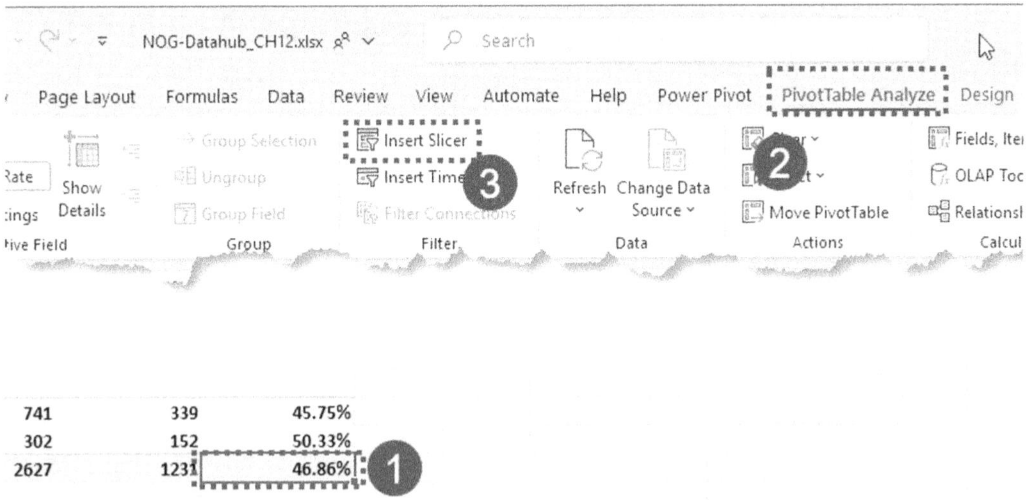

Figure 12.13 – The Insert Slicer button on the PivotTable Analyze tab

4. From **Master_Sessions**, tick **Facilitator**
5. Click **OK**

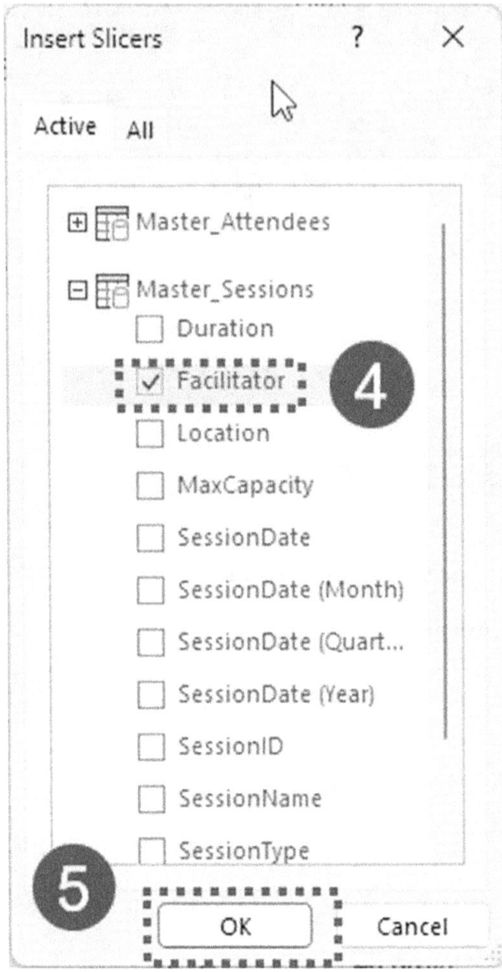

Figure 12.14 – The Insert Slicers dialog with Facilitator selected

After clicking **OK**, the **Facilitator** slicer appears on the sheet alongside the PivotTable. Your **Events Performance** page now shows all three measures by **SessionType** and **Month**, with the slicer ready for Marcus to filter the view by individual facilitator.

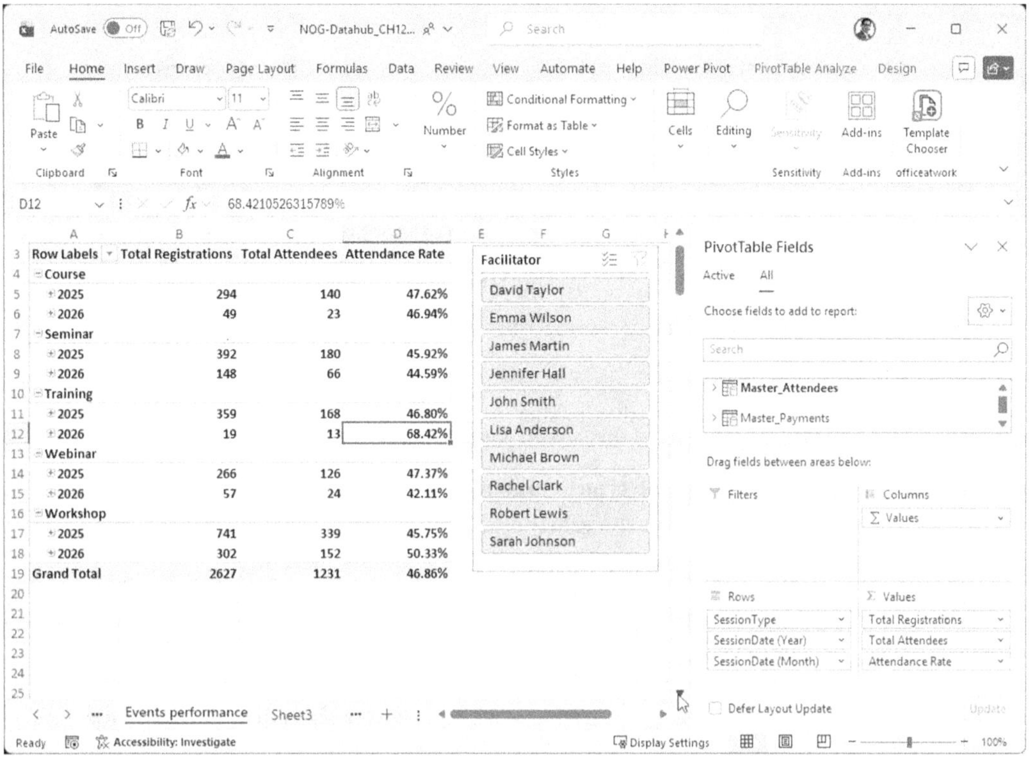

Figure 12.15 – The Events Performance sheet with the three-measure PivotTable and a Facilitator slicer, ready for Marcus's review

Running the trust loop

Before sharing the page with Marcus, verify the numbers against what you already know:

- The grand total of **[Total Registrations]** should match the total row count of **Master_Attendees** confirmed in *Chapter 8*
- **[Total Attendees]** should be equal to or less than **[Total Registrations]** for every row
- **[Attendance Rate]** at the grand total level should be a plausible percentage, not zero, not above 100%

If any number looks wrong, return to Power Pivot, open the relevant measure with **Edit Measure**, and reread the formula carefully before investigating the source data.

> **AI Helper**
>
> Once the measures are working, ask an LLM such as ChatGPT to suggest clear, business-friendly names or draft a short description of the page: `I have a PivotTable showing Total Registrations, Total Attendees, and Attendance Rate by Session Type and Month for a corporate events program. Write a two-sentence description a manager could read at the top of this page.`
>
> Check the draft against your actual numbers before adding it to the workbook.

Quinn saves the workbook and turns the screen toward Marcus.

Marcus leans in. He reads the session type breakdown: registrations, attendees, attendance rate in one row per category. He sees the yearly and monthly details. He clicks a facilitator name in the slicer, and both the rows and the grand total update instantly.

"That's it," he says. "That's the question."

"One model," Quinn says. "Refresh the queries and every number updates."

Hannah stands and stretches. "And if Marcus comes back with a sixth question next quarter?"

"Drag a field," Quinn says. "Or write one more measure."

Hannah smiles. "That's the idea."

Summary

In this chapter, you wrote three DAX measures (**[Total Registrations]**, **[Total Attendees]**, and **[Attendance Rate]**) and tested them in an Events Performance PivotTable with a Facilitator slicer. Three patterns from this chapter are worth carrying forward:

- **Build measures as named building blocks**: **[Total Registrations]** gives **[Total Attendees]** something to filter against, and both give **[Attendance Rate]** something to divide. Writing each formula as a small, reusable piece keeps the logic short, readable, and easy to extend.
- **Use FILTER for conditional counts**: `FILTER` takes a table and a condition and returns only the rows that match. Wrapping it in `COUNTROWS` turns that filtered table into a

number, which is the pattern behind every conditional aggregation you will write in DAX.

- **Prefer DIVIDE over /**: `DIVIDE` handles divide-by-zero gracefully, returning blank rather than an error. Whenever a measure involves a ratio or percentage, `DIVIDE` keeps the PivotTable clean and avoids confusing errors when a session has no registrations.

The Events model is now complete: three clean tables, two relationships, and three measures that answer real business questions.

Final thoughts

This is where the book ends, but not Quinn's journey, nor yours. At NOG, there will be new folders, new questions, a seventh request in Monday's inbox; at your desk, the next messy export, or the next report someone needs by Friday. Both journeys continue the same way this one began: one source, one query, one refresh you can trust.

Applying what you have learned

The best way to make the learning stick is to apply it as soon as possible. Pick one report you currently rebuild by hand (a weekly export cleanup, a monthly consolidation) and rebuild it as a query: connect to the folder, shape the data once, load, refresh, and run the trust loop. Start small, as Quinn did with Amira's contact list; the habits compound from there.

> **Note**
>
> If you have questions about the book, head to its GitHub Discussions page at `https://github.com/PacktPublishing/Power-Query-for-Excel-Users/discussions`. Ask about the exercises, share what you built, and get help if a step does not work as expected.

Where to go next

Along the way, perhaps without realizing it, you have also built a strong foundation for stepping into Power BI or Microsoft Fabric. Power Query lives natively in Power BI, and in Fabric, you will find it as **Dataflows**. The interface looks slightly different, but every function you have learned in this book is there waiting for you. And when you decide to take that step, you can explore the following books:

- If you want to master the M language behind every step you have built in this book, *The Definitive Guide to Power Query (M)* (`https://www.packtpub.com/en-us/product/the-definitive-guide-to-power-query-m-9781835089729`) is the deep dive to take
- If you want to learn Power BI, *Learn Power BI* (`https://www.packtpub.com/en-us/product/learn-power-bi-9781801810074`) is a good place to start

Keep learning at bibb.pro

Finally, I would like to invite you to my website, bibb (`https://bibb.pro`), where you will find tutorials, tools, and articles on Power Query, Power BI, Fabric, data visualization, and the wider Microsoft data stack, including the Power BI Theme Generator used by report builders around the world.

Wherever you take it next, whether Power BI, Microsoft Fabric, or simply a calmer Monday morning in Excel, you now have the foundation: clean, repeatable data you can trust.

13

Unlock the Code Bundle and the PDF Version

Your copy of this book includes the following exclusive benefits:

Complete Code Bundle

Download the full source code for this book's examples and projects.

DRM-Free PDF Version

Download DRM-free PDF and ePub copies of this book.

7-Day Packt Library Access

Get 7-day unlimited access to 8,000+ books and videos. No credit card required.

Available for first-time Packt+ trial users only.

Next-Gen Reader Access

Read this book on Packt Reader with progress sync, dark mode and note-taking.

Follow this guide to unlock them. The process takes only a few minutes and only needs to be completed once.

Unlock this book's free benefits in three easy steps

Step 1

Have your purchase invoice ready for *step 3*. If you have a physical copy, scan it using your phone and save it as a PDF, JPG, or PNG.

For more help on finding your invoice, visit `https://www.packtpub.com/unlock-benefits/help`.

> Note
>
> **Note**: If you bought this book directly from the Packt website, no invoice is required. After *step 2*, you can access your exclusive content right away.

Step 2

Scan the QR code or go to `packtpub.com/unlock`.

On the page that opens (similar to *Figure 13.1* on desktop), search for this book by name and select the correct edition.

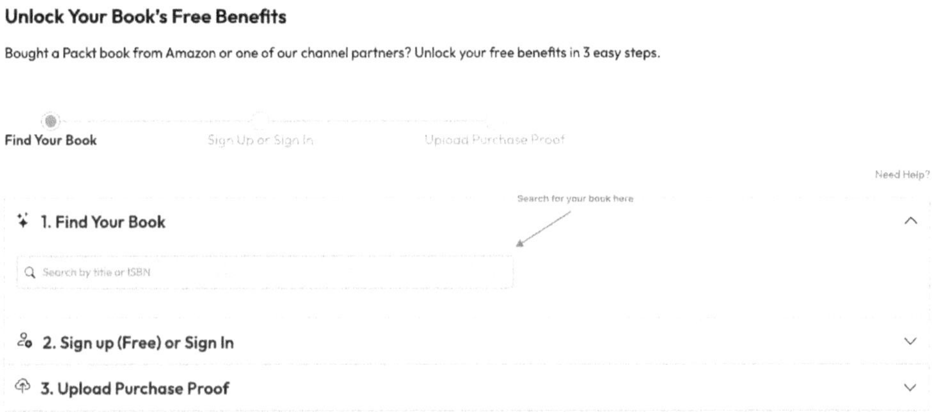

Figure 13.1: Packt unlock landing page on desktop

Step 3

After selecting the book, sign in to your Packt account or create one for free. Then, upload your invoice (PDF, PNG, or JPG, up to 10 MB). Follow the on-screen instructions to finish the process.

Need help?

If you get stuck and need help, visit `https://www.packtpub.com/unlock-benefits/help` for a detailed FAQ on how to find your invoice and more. This QR code will take you to the help page.

Note

Note: If you are still facing issues, reach out to `customercare@packt.com`.

Other Books You May Enjoy

If you enjoyed this book, you may be interested in these other books by Packt:

AI for Everyday Automation

Dipankar Sarkar

ISBN: 978-1-80808-981-7

- Automate email triage and response drafting using AI-assisted workflows
- Generate meeting summaries, action items, and follow-ups in minutes
- Conduct research and create structured briefs faster with AI tools
- Build reports, proposals, and business documents using reusable prompt chains
- Extract tasks and status updates automatically from conversations and meeting notes
- Analyze spreadsheets and messy data without advanced Excel skills
- Create professional content and communications faster while maintaining your personal voice

Power BI for Finance

Martin Kratky

ISBN: 978-1-83763-501-6

- Apply multi-currency handling and group consolidation techniques in Power BI
- Model discounted cash flow and company valuation scenarios
- Design and manage write-back workflows with Dynamics BPP and Acterys
- Integrate Excel and Power BI using live connections and cube formulas
- Utilize AI, Copilot, and LLMs to enhance automation and insight generation
- Create complete finance-focused dashboards for sales and operations planning

Packt is searching for authors like you

If you're interested in becoming an author for Packt, please visit `authors.packt.com` and apply today. We have worked with thousands of developers and tech professionals, just like you, to help them share their insight with the global tech community. You can make a general application, apply for a specific hot topic that we are recruiting an author for, or submit your own idea.

Share your thoughts

Now you've finished *Power Query for Excel Users,* we'd love to hear your thoughts! Scan the QR code below to go straight to the Amazon review page for this book and share your feedback or leave a review on the site that you purchased it from.

`https://packt.link/r/1807427730`

Your review is important to us and the tech community and will help us make sure we're delivering excellent quality content.

Index

K

www.ingramcontent.com/pod-product-compliance
Lightning Source LLC
LaVergne TN
LVHW060020210926
848481LV00013B/3751